A COUNTRY MERCHANT, 1495–1520

Around 1500 England's society and economy had reached a turning point. After a long period of slow change and even stagnation, an age of innovation and initiative was in motion, with enclosure, voyages of discovery, and new technologies. It was an age of fierce controversy, in which the government was fearful of beggars and wary of rebellions. The 'commonwealth' writers such as Thomas More were sharply critical of the greed of profit hungry landlords who dispossessed the poor. This book is about a wool merchant and large scale farmer who epitomises in many ways the spirit of the period.

John Heritage kept an account book, from which we can reconstruct a whole society in the vicinity of Moreton-in-Marsh, Gloucestershire. He took part in the removal of a village which stood in the way of agricultural 'improvement', ran a large scale sheep farm, and as a 'woolman' spent much time travelling around the countryside meeting with gentry, farmers, and peasants in order to buy their wool. He sold the fleeces he produced and those he gathered to London merchants who exported through Calais to the textile towns of Flanders. The wool growers named in the book can be studied in their native villages, and their lives can be reconstructed in the round, interacting in their communities, adapting their farming to new circumstances, and arranging the building of their local churches.

A Country Merchant has some of the characteristics of a biography, is part family history, and part local history, with some landscape history. Dyer explores themes in economic and social history without neglecting the religious and cultural background. His central concerns are to demonstrate the importance of commerce in the period, and to show the contribution of peasants to a changing economy.

A Country Merchant, 1495–1520

Trading and Farming at the End of the Middle Ages

CHRISTOPHER DYER

OXFORD
UNIVERSITY PRESS

OXFORD

UNIVERSITY PRESS

Great Clarendon Street, Oxford, OX2 6DP,
United Kingdom

Oxford University Press is a department of the University of Oxford.
It furthers the University's objective of excellence in research, scholarship,
and education by publishing worldwide. Oxford is a registered trade mark of
Oxford University Press in the UK and in certain other countries

© Christopher Dyer 2012

The moral rights of the author have been asserted

First Edition published in 2012
First published in paperback 2014

Published in the United States of America by Oxford University Press
198 Madison Avenue, New York, NY 10016, United States of America

British Library Cataloguing in Publication Data
Data available

Library of Congress Cataloging-in-Publication Data
Dyer, Christopher, 1944–
A country merchant, 1495–1520 : trading and farming at the end of the Middle Ages / Christopher Dyer.
p. cm.
Includes bibliographical references and index.
ISBN 978–0–19–921424–2 (hbk.)

1. Heritage, John, b. ca. 1470. 2. Merchants—England—History—16th century—Case
studies. 3. Farmers—England—History—16th century—Case studies. 4. England—Economic
conditions—16th century. 5. England—Social conditions—16th century. 6. Great Britain—
Commerce—History—To 1500 7. Great Britain—History—1485– I. Title.
HF3515.D94 2012
381.092—dc23
2012006115

ISBN 978–0–19–921424–2 (Hbk)
ISBN 978–0–19–871598–6 (Pbk)

Preface

John Heritage is remarkable because of the survival of the records that tell us much about a type of merchant-farmer, and also about the people around him. In 1967 I first encountered the name John Heritage as a tenant of a pasture at Upper Ditchford in the manor of Blockley (Gloucestershire) in 1507. In the 1980s the Heritage name emerged from other sources. Nat Alcock edited mid-sixteenth-century accounts, some of which were compiled by Thomas Heritage, John's son, who kept livestock at Burton Dassett in Warwickshire. John Langdon, then a research student, discovered the inventory of Roger Heritage, John's father, who died in 1495, and used it in his research into draught animals. Then the M40 motorway was planned to run through Burton Dassett, leading to important excavations of the site of Dassett Southend. Nat Alcock and I wrote papers about the history of Burton (still unpublished), in which the Heritage family figured. There then followed an article about Roger Heritage as an early form of capitalist farmer, in which I identified his son John as an enterprising and ruthless figure, but that story ended in 1497. It did not occur to me that the John Heritage who took over his father's farm in 1495–7 at Burton Dassett could be the same man as the John Heritage who held land 18 miles (29 km) away at Upper Ditchford ten years later. Until this point our knowledge of him was based on perhaps a dozen references in leases and accounts of bailiffs and receivers. Then Roger Bowers, a historian of music, while pursuing research in Westminster Abbey, discovered John's account book. Knowing of Nat Alcock's edition, he told him of his find. Nat passed the news to me. I saw the manuscript in about 1995 and transcribed it slowly over the next eight years. It showed that John held pastures at both Burton Dassett and Upper Ditchford, and traded as a wool merchant in the Gloucestershire town of Moreton in Marsh. He can still be called a country merchant because his business was conducted in the villages and fields where wool was produced. In 2001 I decided to write an interpretative book rather than edit the text, because the document gained in significance when links were made between the accounts and the dozens of other sources of the same period. John Heritage himself became a more three-dimensional figure, who built a far-flung network of contacts, through which the interactions of a whole society can be seen.

My debts to Nat Alcock, Roger Bowers, and John Langdon are apparent from the above, and also to Nick Palmer for drawing me in to the Burton Dassett project. Nat Alcock has since given further help with the family tree of the Palmer family, who intermarried with the Heritages. Archivists made documents accessible at Westminster Abbey, and at more than twenty archives and record offices where I found relevant material. I was also helped by the Historic Environment Records in the shires in which Heritage operated and a number of libraries, especially at Leicester and Birmingham. These individuals have assisted with specialist advice: Caroline Barron and John Oldland (London); David Clark (buildings); the late

Christopher Elrington (feet of fines); Richard Goddard (credit); Hugh Hanley (Aylesbury); Mairi Macdonald (Stratford fraternity); Nick Mayhew (coins); Ben Parsons (proverbial literature); Sandy Pearson and Claire Townsend (database). Access for fieldwork came from Stephen Asquith, Mr and Mrs T. Fudge, Andrew Knight, John Playfair, F. H. Reason, and Caroline Warren. David Aldred, Bryn Gethin, Ben Morton, and Jenny Dyer helped with planning of sites. The University of Leicester provided two study leaves and financial aid; All Souls College, Oxford, awarded a visiting fellowship; the British Academy helped with a grant from their Small Grants scheme; and the Aurelius Trust funded the illustrations. Andy Isham drew the figures, and Tessa Holubowicz, Neil Quinn, and Penny Upton helped in other ways. Matthew Tompkins prepared much of the index. Sue Campbell and Arthur Cunynghame of Loose Chippings Press provided photographs. Rupert Cousens, Stephanie Ireland, and Emma Barber of Oxford University Press helped the progress of the book with encouragement and efficiency. I benefited from comments when I presented my findings to seminars at Leicester University, All Souls College, Oxford, the University of Paris IV, and the Blockley Antiquarian Society (now the Blockley Heritage Society), and I was given wise advice by Richard Hoyle, an 'anonymous' reader for the publishers. Jenny Dyer gave the text a critical reading.

Christopher Dyer
September 2011

Contents

List of Maps and Figures

List of Tables

Abbreviations

AB	Westminster Abbey Muniments, 12258 (John Heritage's Account Book)
Ag. HR	*Agricultural History Review*
B & GLS	M. Faraday (ed.), *The Bristol and Gloucestershire Lay Subsidy of 1523–1527*, Gloucestershire Record Series, 23 (2009)
Dom. Inc.	I. S. Leadam (ed.), *The Domesday of Inclosures 1517–1518*, 2 vols., Royal Historical Society (London, 1897)
Ec. HR	*Economic History Review*
GA	Gloucestershire Archives
Guild Reg.	M. Macdonald (ed.), *The Register of the Guild of the Holy Cross, St Mary, and St John the Baptist, Stratford-upon-Avon*, Dugdale Society, 42 (2007)
L and P	J. S. Brewer, J. Gairdner, and R. H. Brodie (eds.), *Letters and Paper, Foreign and Domestic, of the Reign of Henry VIII* (London, 1864–1920)
MSG	R. Hoyle (ed.), *The Military Survey of Gloucestershire, 1522*, Gloucestershire Record Series, 6 (1993)
TNA: PRO	The National Archives: Public Record Office
VCH	*Victoria County History*
WAM	Westminster Abbey Muniments
WCRO	Warwickshire County Record Office
WGLS	N. W. Alcock (ed.), *Warwickshire Grazier and London Skinner 1532–1555*, British Academy Records of Social and Economic History, new series, 4 (Oxford, 1981)
WRO	Worcestershire Record Office
WT	M. Faraday (ed.), *Worcestershire Taxes in the 1520s: The Military Survey and Forced Loans of 1522–3 and the Lay Subsidy of 1524–7*, Worcestershire Historical Society, new series, 19 (2003)

Locating Places Mentioned in this Book

The usual custom in a book of this kind is to identify any place mentioned with reference to the county to which it belongs, but this would be complicated in the case of many of the villages, parishes, and townships mentioned here because they have had their county changed in the twentieth century. There would be many entries such as Blockley (Worcs., now Glos.). This list tells the reader in which shire each place lay in *c.*1500, and in which county it is now located.

Gloucestershire *c.*1500, still in Gloucestershire
Aston Subedge
Batsford
Bourton on the Hill
Broadwell
Chipping Campden
Condicote
Donnington
Ebrington
Guiting Power
Temple Guiting
Hidcote (Bartrim and Boyce)
Longborough
Maugersbury
Mickleton
Moreton in Marsh
Norton Subedge
Oddington
Saintbury
Sezincote
Snowshill
Stow on the Wold
Lower Swell
Upper Swell
Todenham
Weston Subedge
Willersey

Gloucestershire *c.*1500, now in Warwickshire
Admington
Clopton
Little Compton

Lark Stoke
Preston on Stour
Quinton
Sutton under Brailes

Gloucestershire *c*.1500, now in Worcestershire
Cow Honeybourne

Oxfordshire *c*.1500, still in Oxfordshire
Chastleton
Chipping Norton
Churchill
Kingham
Great Rollright
Little Rollright
Sarsden

Warwickshire *c*.1500, still in Warwickshire
Barcheston (including Willington)
Barton on the Heath
Burmington
Cherington
Long Compton (including Weston juxta Cherington)
Ilmington (including Compton Scorpion, Foxcote)
Stourton
Stretton on Fosse
Whitchurch
Great Wolford
Little Wolford

Worcestershire *c*.1500, still in Worcestershire
Broadway

Worcestershire *c*.1500, now in Gloucestershire
Blockley (including Aston Magna, Middle and Upper Ditchford, Dorn, Draycott, Northwick, Paxford, Upton Wold)
Cutsdean
Daylesford
Evenlode

Worcestershire *c*.1500, now in Warwickshire
Shipston on Stour
Tidmington
Tredington (including Armscote, Blackwell, Darlingscott, Longdon, Newbold, Talton)

A Note on Weights and Measures

Heritage bought wool in tods of 28 pounds and sacks of 364 pounds (13 tods to the sack).

He sold wool in London in sacks and cloves (also known as nails), which weighed 7 pounds (a quarter of a tod). A sack contained 52 cloves. Sometimes wool was measured in stones of 14 pounds. Metric equivalents: 1 tod = 12.6 kilograms; 1 sack = 163.8 kilograms.

Distances are given here primarily in miles. A mile is 1.6 kilometres.

Areas of land are given in acres, equivalent to 0.40 hectares.

Standard units of landholding in the region were called yardlands in English, and that term is used here. Other writers call these virgates, which is based on the Latin form of the term. These units varied but a median figure is about 30 acres or 12 hectares.

Grain was measured in quarters and bushels (8 bushels = 1 quarter). According to one estimate, a quarter of wheat weighed about 420 pounds (189 kilograms).

1

Introduction: Living in 1495–1520

This book is about an individual, but also about the times and places in which he lived. The central figure, John Heritage, was born in about 1470 in east Warwickshire, and he was active between 1495 and 1520 mainly in Moreton in Marsh in Gloucestershire. Described by contemporaries as a yeoman, his occupations can be listed as farmer, wool merchant, grazier, general trader, and moneylender. He was by no means unusual in following this combination of occupations, and his contemporary Edmund Dudley, surveying society in his *Tree of Commonwealth* in 1509, links together merchants, graziers, and farmers as a characteristic group of wealthy and substantial people.[1] Heritage stands out, however, as a unique individual, simply by the fortunate accident that his account book for 1501–20 has survived, so we know a good deal about him, his business, and the people linked to him.

History is not a discipline governed by strict rules, but certain understandings have greatly influenced the subject since the end of the nineteenth century. Historians, it was and is proposed, should study themes and problems, and at an early stage of any piece of historical writing they should define the issues and dilemmas that they seek to resolve, or set out the research questions that are to be answered. A subject should not be explored just because there are high-quality or abundant sources, and the discovery of evidence should not alone justify historical research. And finally, in the later part of the twentieth century it was widely held that biography should be avoided as it is a form of writing ill-suited to a problem-solving agenda, and liable to entice the scholar into the trivia of personalities.

Recently, among a number of changes to the discipline, biography has become more acceptable, but this book attempts to avoid breaching the principles of scientific history. It cannot aspire to be a biography in the conventional sense because the absence of personal sources, such as letters, diaries, or even a will make it very difficult to judge Heritage's character or motives. Truth be told, even when these sources exist the biographer can be tempted into speculations and amateur psychology that are not securely based in evidence. Nonetheless, a piece of historical writing focused on a named individual has a better chance of attracting readers and stimulating the imagination of the author, than abstract generalizations about an anonymous mass of people.

[1] D. M. Brodie (ed.), *The Tree of Commonwealth: A Treatise Written by Edmund Dudley* (Cambridge, 1948), 39–48.

Heritage deserves attention because his activities throw light on unsolved historical problems that need further investigation. The largest question must centre on the transition of an agrarian society into the modern world. Other issues are more specific to the fifteenth and sixteenth centuries, notably the role of enclosures, engrossing, and the conversion of cultivated land to pasture in changing the economy. Did rural depopulation begin the destruction of the peasantry? Did trade and a commercial mentality undermine traditional rural society? Does the period around 1500 mark a significant stage in the move from a society of communities to one based on the individual? John Heritage and the country in which he lived promise to throw light on these general questions.(Fig. 1.1) Had the accounts been kept by a staple merchant exporting wool to Calais, or a monastic official, their contents would have deserved the attention of historians, but they would not have illuminated the particular issues about land, its control and management, and the impact of commerce. The discovery of a source came at an opportune moment to address an existing agenda of historical questions.

John Heritage's interest for historians does not arise from his celebrity. He lived at the same time as famous people who have been the subject of biographical writing: John Colet, Thomas More, John Skelton, Edward Stafford (third duke of Buckingham), and Thomas Wolsey.[2] Heritage had probably not met any of these men, but a nephew of his attended Colet's school at St Paul's in London, both Stafford and Wolsey held manors within the area from which he bought wool, and his brother worked as an administrator under Wolsey, so he certainly knew of them. A play by Skelton was chosen as the theme of a set of wall paintings in the church of Oddington, which lay near to one of the roads often used by Heritage when dealing in wool, and visiting his daughter.[3] More in his *Utopia* wrote about problems that concerned everyone in the early sixteenth century: depopulation, begging, crime, family discipline, and the role of the state in the lives of individuals.

Heritage's active life coincided with momentous events in world history. In the early stages of European imperial expansion and globalization Vasco da Gama (in 1498) landed in India, and in 1520 Mexico was about to fall to Spanish conquerors. Within Europe French kings were invading Italy, Machiavelli wrote *The Prince*, and in 1517 Luther took his first public steps in demanding radical reform of the Church. In England the Tudor dynasty established its authority, and Henry VIII began to extend royal power in ways that previous rulers had scarcely imagined.

Heritage in his small Gloucestershire town was not cut off from these events, and as a regular traveller between London and Moreton in Marsh he would have served as one of those channels of communication that kept people in the provinces

---

[2] For example, J. Arnold, *Dean John Colet of St Paul's: Humanism and Reform in Early Tudor England* (London, 2007); J. A. Guy, *The Public Career of Sir Thomas More* (New Haven, CT, 1980); idem, *Thomas More* (London, 2000); M. Pollet, *John Skelton: Poet of Tudor England* (London, 1971); B. Harris, *Edward Stafford, Third Duke of Buckingham, 1478–1521* (Stanford, CA, 1986); P. Gwyn, *The King's Cardinal: The Rise and Fall of Thomas Wolsey* (London, 1990).

[3] J. Edwards, 'The Mural and the Morality Play: A Suggested Source for a Wall-Painting at Oddington', *Transactions of the Bristol and Gloucestershire Archaeological Society*, 104 (1986), 187–200; P. Neuss (ed.), *John Skelton, Magnificence* (Manchester, 1980).

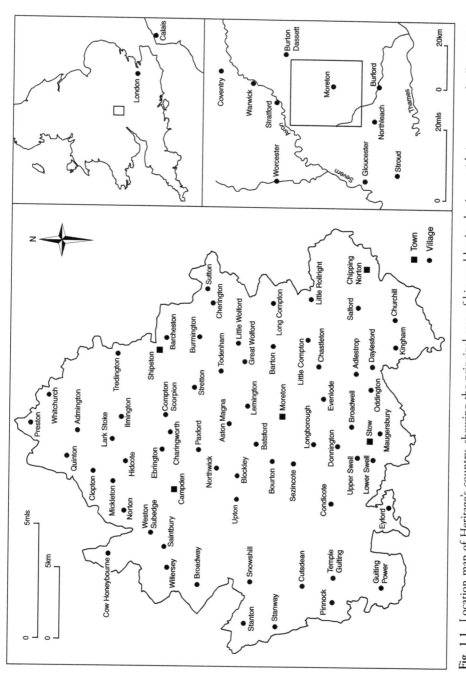

Fig. 1.1. Location map of Heritage's country, showing the principal area of his wool-buying business with its towns and villages. The regional and national settings are indicated.

aware of the latest news. Ripples spread into Heritage's neighbourhood from distant places. In 1506 Thomas Alen, a rich merchant of Stow on the Wold, in his will left to his wife 'a nut gilt with the cover of the same', by which he meant a cup made of a coconut shell, embellished with a silver gilt foot and rim, and provided with a lid. Coconuts from the Indian Ocean had been imported along with Eastern spices in small numbers in earlier centuries, but they became more readily available after the opening of direct trading voyages by the Portuguese at the end of the fifteenth century.[4] They were bought by London goldsmiths who provided them, as they did for cups of maple wood (mazers), with precious metal settings, and sold them as 'Indian nuts'. They attracted purchasers because of their exotic origin, and supposed medicinal and aphrodisiac properties. Their owner would have drunk imported wine from them, and in particular the relatively expensive sweet wines from the Mediterranean. John Heritage would have encountered Alen, and may have seen this unusual and ornate cup in his house in Stow.

A completely different repercussion of overseas contacts comes from near the western edge of Heritage's area of commercial operations, in the village of Toddington. The lord of the manor, William Tracy, died in 1531, leaving a will that revealed he had at some time in the 1520s adopted the main tenets of Lutheran belief, regarding Christ rather than the saints as his redeemer, and putting emphasis on faith rather than good works as the basis for salvation.[5] The will was printed and became a celebrated document of the English Reformation, and in Tracy's Gloucestershire, shortly after Heritage left the county, the reformed religion was attracting recruits. These included William Tyndale, the translator of the Bible, who spent much time on the continent. Anyone living in the county would have been aware of these unorthodox religious opinions in the 1520s, and before that time they would certainly have been familiar with the home-grown ideas of the Lollard heresy, adherents of which were being discovered in Gloucestershire. In 1511–12 a large group of heretics were facing a high-profile series of trials in the largest city in the west Midlands, Coventry.[6]

On a more mundane level, Heritage and his contemporaries contributed through their taxes to the expenses of Henry VIII's splendour at the Field of the Cloth of Gold in 1520, and to the costs of his military adventures in France. He also formed part of the merchant community that struggled with the embargos and interruptions to trade consequent on Henry VII's tortuous negotiations with the authorities in the Low Countries, after which stability was restored to the benefit of overseas commerce.[7] In order to become involved in overseas ventures, it was not necessary

---

[4] TNA: PRO, PROB 11/15, fo. 192r; M. Campbell, 'The Table and Feasting', in R. Marks and P. Williamson (eds.), *Gothic: Art for England 1400–1547* (London, 2003), 320.

[5] C. Litzenberger, *The English Reformation and the Laity: Gloucestershire, 1540–1580* (Cambridge, 1997), 29–31.

[6] Litzenberger, *English Reformation*, 39–40. A Newent woman in 1517–18 ate meat on Friday and refused to offer a candle at the feast of the Purification of the Blessed Virgin Mary; S. McSheffrey and N. Tanner (eds.), *Lollards of Coventry 1486–1522*, Camden Society, 5th ser., 23 (London, 2003).

[7] A. F. Sutton, *The Mercery of London: Trade, Goods and People, 1130–1578* (Aldershot, 2008), 323–35.

to sail to Newfoundland with ships from Bristol or embark on the pilgrimage to Palestine, as did some of Heritage's contemporaries, because wool dealing had considerable international importance.

Heritage was clearly not an ignorant provincial with narrow horizons, but his main interest for historians lies in his role of connecting the local rural world with international markets. An innovator in his management of his first farm at Burton Dassett, he settled into a more routine existence in his middle years, and did not make a great fortune or play a public role like other merchants from the Midlands such as Hugh Clopton or Robert Tate.[8] Because he was pursuing a relatively conventional way of life as a grazier and wool merchant, we can expect that he provides a useful guide to the activities of dozens of similar men: he serves as a representative rather than an exception. Historians have taken various routes to explaining and interpreting the place of the years 1495–1520 in a longer time perspective, and these alternative visions of the period will now be outlined. This survey will begin with the view that the relationship between population and resources determined the character of this period; next, the idea that changes in property and agricultural methods gave rise to the birth of capitalism will be considered; the third section will be devoted to the part played by institutions and state policy; in the fourth, commercialization, including the importance of towns and the money supply, will be assessed; and the final explanatory theme will be the idea that there was a reordering of the social structure.

POPULATION AND RESOURCES

In the late twentieth century, prominence was given to fluctuations in numbers of people as an explanation of economic and social change.[9] Demographic movements were in part driven by biological factors, in particular by mortality caused by disease, and this explanation was advocated by those studying the period before 1536 when the main evidence consists of records of deaths.[10] Disease was prevalent at all levels of society, and relatively affluent groups such as Benedictine monks were afflicted, so that mortality cannot be assigned an economic cause. Deaths from hunger must have been very rare, as basic foodstuffs were relatively cheap and plentiful. Those scholars working on the sixteenth century had the advantage of parish registers, which recorded marriages and baptisms as well as burials, and they were able to see a pattern of the economy influencing marriage and fertility. In good

[8] *Guild Reg.*, 25–6; Sutton, *Mercery of London*, 233, 288, 338; A. Sutton, *A Merchant Family of Coventry, London and Calais: The Tates, c.1450–1575* (London, 1998), 71–3.

[9] M. Postan, *The Medieval Economy and Society: An Economic History of Britain 1100–1500* (London, 1972).

[10] J. Hatcher, 'Mortality in the Fifteenth Century: Some New Evidence', *Ec. HR*, 2nd ser., 39 (1986), 19–38; B. Harvey, *Living and Dying in England, 1100–1540: The Monastic Experience* (Oxford, 1993), 112–45; P. Nightingale, 'Some New Evidence of Crises and Trends of Mortality in Late Medieval England', *Past and Present*, 187 (2005), 33–68; J. Hatcher, A. Piper, and D. Stone, 'Monastic Mortality: Durham Priory, 1395–1529', *Ec. HR*, 59 (2006), 667–87.

times marriage occurred at an earlier age (early to mid-twenties) and more children were conceived; hard times led to delayed marriage and a smaller number of births.[11]

The period 1495–1525 poses many difficulties for understanding population and its connection to economic and social change. The English population was probably in the region of 2.2 to 2.3 million, which is based on the lists of taxpayers in the early 1520s, together with local counts of people and later more comprehensive lists from which back projections can be made.[12] This is an extraordinarily low figure, which represents a dramatic reduction from the 5 or 6 million of *c.*1300. It is similar to the population of England in the eleventh century calculated from Domesday Book (1086), which means that Henry VIII's England was no more populous than that of William the Conqueror, though more people lived in towns in the early sixteenth century, and pursued, both in town and country, a greater variety of specialist occupations than were available in 1086.[13] The local consequences of this thinly spread population can be seen in many villages that contained no more than a dozen houses, having had twice that number in *c.*1300, and a proportion of settlements were either deserted or had shrunk down to a handful of inhabitants. This meagre population was not the inevitable consequence of plagues, for in continental Europe, particularly in Italy, millions of people had been carried off in successive epidemics but population levels were climbing back by the 1490s.[14] The English population had experienced high levels of mortality towards the end of the fifteenth century, but after an epidemic in 1499–1500 severe outbreaks were less frequent, and the plague of 1512–13 was the only noteworthy episode of disease in the first twenty years of the new century.[15] The whole period from the late fourteenth century until the early sixteenth would in theory have been a favourable one for marriage, with opportunities to acquire land and employment. There may well have been some modest population growth, but the sustained increase in numbers came after 1520.[16] It is worth noting that the upwards surge of the mid-sixteenth century was not caused by a relaxation in epidemics, as severe outbreaks are recorded in the 1540s, 1550s, and 1560s.[17]

The output of agriculture did not change greatly in the early sixteenth century. The tithe grain collected in Durham, serving as a sample of the total crop, suggests that production was at quite a low level between 1500 and 1520, followed by a

---

[11] E. A. Wrigley and R. S. Schofield, *The Population History of England, 1541–1871: A Reconstruction*, 2nd edn. (Cambridge, 1989), 402–53; for an application of this model to the later Middle Ages, L. R. Poos, *A Rural Society after the Black Death, Essex 1350–1525* (Cambridge, 1991), 111–29.

[12] Wrigley and Schofield, *Population History*, 563–8.

[13] C. Dyer, *Making a Living in the Middle Ages: The People of Britain, 850–1520* (New Haven, CT, 2002), 94–5.

[14] S. R. Epstein, *An Island for Itself: Economic Development and Social Change in Late Medieval Sicily* (Cambridge, 1992), 60–74.

[15] C. Creighton, *A History of Epidemics in Britain*, 2nd edn. (London, 1965), 243–50, 287–92.

[16] R. Smith, 'Plagues and Peoples: The Long Demographic Cycle, 1250–1670', in P. Slack and R. Ward (eds.), *The Peopling of Britain: The Shaping of a Human Landscape* (Oxford, 2002), 177–210, especially 181–4.

[17] Smith, 'Plagues and Peoples', 198–9; Wrigley and Schofield, *Population History*, 650–5.

decline after those decades. In Norfolk the productivity of land per acre was unchanged between the fifteenth and seventeenth centuries.[18] The movements in prices, wages, and rents were all connected with the ups and downs of population, but not in a simple way. The price of grain, an important element in agricultural profits and in the cost of living, had been generally low since 1375. Wheat, the main bread grain, was being bought and sold in 1495–1520 in most years for 5*s* and 6*s* per quarter, with variations depending on region, and with fluctuations from year to year. A daily loaf of bread for an individual for a year cost about 8*s*, which was very affordable for most consumers, and if the price increased, cheaper rye or barley could be substituted. The prevalent low prices left the producer with slender profits, as cultivation carried high costs in the wages of agricultural workers, and barns, ploughs, and carts required expenditure on high wages and dear materials. Wheat prices rose because of a bad harvest in 1512, barley and oats became more expensive from 1517, and wheat prices increased again in 1519.[19] The year 1520 marks the watershed between an age of cheap corn and an era of rising prices, which means that the high cost of grain in individual years can be blamed on bad harvests, but by the 1520s larger underlying movements, such as the influx of silver from the New World, and the beginnings of population growth, were pushing prices upwards.

The years between 1495 and 1520 represent the last phase of an era of high wages. Wage rates varied between regions, but did not move rapidly over time, as there was an element of custom which decided in much of the south of England that 6*d* per day was an appropriate rate of pay for a skilled worker, such as a carpenter, and labourers received 4*d* per day.[20] Earnings could be quite substantial because labour was in high demand and short supply, so workers who were paid by the day had the chance of working for many days, and family earnings could also reach considerable levels through the opportunities for women and children to obtain employment. Real wages, measured by the spending power of earnings, attained peaks in 1486, 1495, and 1509, but in the teens of the sixteenth century were beginning a long-term decline that became confirmed when the price of food began its decisive upward movement around 1520.[21] Wages broadly reflected the low levels of population, but the labour shortage should have been corrected by the encouragement that wage rates gave to early marriage and the consequent rise in births, but evidently this mechanism did not operate, as many young people apparently chose not to take advantage of the opportunities for forming new households.

[18] B. Dodds, *Peasants and Production in the Medieval North-East: The Evidence of Tithes, 1270–1536* (Woodbridge, 2007), 113–21; B. M. S. Campbell and M. Overton, 'A New Perspective on Medieval and Early Modern Agriculture: Six Centuries of Norfolk Farming, c.1250–c.1850', *Past and Present*, 141 (1993), 38–105.

[19] P. Bowden, 'Agricultural Prices, Farm Profits, and Rents', in J. Thirsk (ed.), *The Agrarian History of England and Wales*, IV, *1500–1640* (Cambridge, 1967), 593–616, 814–70; W. G. Hoskins, 'Harvest Fluctuations and English Economic History 1480–1619', *Ag. HR*, 12 (1964), 28–46; C. J. Harrison, 'Grain Price Analysis and Harvest Qualities, 1465–1634', *Ag. HR*, 19 (1971), 135–55.

[20] D. Woodward, *Men at Work: Labourers and Building Craftsmen in the Towns of Northern England, 1450–1750* (Cambridge, 1995), 169–72.

[21] E. H. Phelps Brown and S. V. Hopkins, *A Perspective of Wages* (London, 1981), 13–59.

Rents for land reflect levels of demand that would tend to increase if the population was rising, and if greater profits could be made from agriculture. Many local studies confirm the expectation that rent levels attained rather low levels, if compared with those prevailing before 1350 or those that were to be charged in the late sixteenth century. Many rents were of course fixed by law or custom, so we focus on leasehold land, which was subject to periodic renegotiation, and the entry fines that could be levied from land held by the custom of the manor when a new tenant took over a holding. In general rents did not change dramatically, though pasture land was more likely to show increases than arable. Leasehold rents both for arable and pasture rose on the Duchy of Lancaster estates in north Derbyshire, but on other estates much land was held on lease for long terms of years and so could not be readily adjusted.[22] Entry fines might be fixed too – at places in West Berkshire they were levied at a rate of 13s 4d per yardland (below 6d per acre) in the late fifteenth and early sixteenth centuries – but elsewhere in the country they were not embedded in some customary agreement and tended to increase in the period 1470–1530, depending on the local circumstances.[23] In the early sixteenth century the estates of the earls of Northumberland saw a rising trend, and in Norfolk we find manors where fines rose between the mid-fifteenth century and 1515–32, for example from 17.5d per acre to 23.6d per acre.[24] This was a modest but still definite rise, and although in the Midlands fines rarely reached 12d per acre, increases such as a doubling between the 1490s and 1500–20 are recorded at Hanbury in Worcestershire.[25] Entry fines were a product of complex forces: population growth could be a factor, and so could the productivity and profitability of the land. Often a consideration was the quasi-political relationship between the tenants and a lord, as a move to increase fines might provoke an uncomfortable reaction from tenants.

To sum up this discussion, no one can ignore the level of population as a major contributor to the world in which John Heritage and his contemporaries operated. In pursuing his career we need to know about the thinly peopled countryside, the high wages, the cheap food, and the narrow profits, especially from arable farming. In the background lay the long-term fall in population that followed the crisis of the fourteenth century, and which continued as a powerful influence 150 years later. In the short term, the main dynamic element was the beginning of movement (from about 1517, and especially after 1520) in the direction of increased population, high prices, and rising demand for land. The decades 1500–20 have been described as pivotal, which separated two distinct long-term phases.[26]

[22] I. S. W. Blanchard (ed.), *The Duchy of Lancaster's Estates in Derbyshire 1485–1540*, Derbyshire Archaeological Society Record Series, 3 (1971), 1–22.

[23] M. Yates, *Town and Countryside in Western Berkshire, c.1327–c.1600* (Woodbridge, 2007), 145.

[24] J. M. W. Bean, *The Estates of the Percy Family 1416–1537* (Oxford, 1958), 51–67, 138–40; J. Whittle, *The Development of Agrarian Capitalism: Land and Labour in Norfolk, 1440–1580* (Oxford, 2000), 79–82.

[25] A. C. Jones, 'Bedfordshire: Fifteenth Century', in P. D. A. Harvey (ed.), *The Peasant Land Market in Medieval England* (Oxford, 1984), 244–5; C. Dyer, *Lords and Peasants in a Changing Society: The Estates of the Bishopric of Worcester, 680–1540* (Cambridge, 1980), 287–90.

[26] H. R. French and R. W. Hoyle, *The Character of an English Rural Society: Earls Colne, 1550–1750* (Manchester, 2007), 25. An earlier influential view of the period is in I. S. W. Blanchard, 'Population Change, Enclosure and the Early Tudor Economy', *Ec. HR*, 2nd ser., 23 (1970), 427–45.

The causes of that turn of events cannot be determined with any certainty. Population growth after a long period of stagnation may have been the prime mover, but that might have been connected to price rises. Changing levels of population had different consequences depending on the nature of the society affected, and they could not in themselves lead to the innovations in technology or social organization of the kind that we observe in the early sixteenth century, which leads us to turn to other explanations.

THE TRANSITION TO CAPITALISM

In the years around 1500, elements survived of a traditional feudal society, which could trace its origins in the centuries before 1000 AD, in which the aristocracy lived on rents paid by peasant tenants coordinated in manorial lordships. Tenants occupied standard holdings, yardlands, half-yardlands, or oxgangs, burdened with well-defined obligations, including the cash equivalent of the labour services that had once been owed by their predecessors. Lords still held demesnes, large pieces of land that occasionally were cultivated for the benefit of the lord's household or to produce for the market, but since c.1400 most were wholly leased out for a fixed annual rent in cash. Not only were the elements of the 'bipartite' structure of the manor, tenant land and demesne, identifiable, but the institutions of lordship still functioned. A manorial court met regularly, often twice or four times a year, at which the customary tenants transferred their holdings under the supervision of the lord or his representative, the steward. New tenants did homage, and swore an oath of fealty, as they had done for centuries. When a new lord took over the manor, either because a new abbot had been elected or because the manor had come in to the hands of a new lay lord through inheritance or purchase, the tenants formally recognized their new lord. Lords (not all of them) might also exercise delegated royal jurisdiction at the View of Frankpledge, at which offences such as neglect of roads or ditches, or the breaking of the assize of ale by selling drink at an excessive price, could be presented and offenders amerced (fined). The whole system ran on a well-established routine, in which inevitable antagonisms were blunted by cooperation, for example in agreement on the routine running of the fields in which both tenant land and demesne had a share.

Around 1500 the arrival of a more ruthless type of landowner can be observed, who disrupted time-honoured compromises and arrangements. These entrepreneurs wished to manage the demesnes at maximum efficiency and profitability, which meant enclosing the land and converting it to pasture. This could be extended to the common pasture shared with the villagers. The tenants whose rents had often fossilized at a rather low level, often got in the way of modernization, and were forced to leave by measures designed to make their lives impossible, such as putting very large numbers of the lord's or his farmer's animals on the common pasture and fallow field, and also by direct eviction. The enclosers, engrossers, and depopulators could be the old landlords converted to a more commercial outlook, including abbots, but the promoters of radical change are usually identified as gentry landlords, farmers (who held demesnes on lease), and graziers. Some of them might have a direct involvement in the commercial world, because wool merchants, clothiers, and tuckers (fullers) acquired leases and sometimes became lords of the manor. The commission set up by Wolsey to investigate enclosure and depopulation in 1517 produced a great quantity of documents that were published and analysed around the year 1900 by Leadam, who became embroiled in a controversy with Gay about the scale and character of the enclosure movement.[27] In an important book published in 1912, Tawney broadened the inquiry to deal with a range of disruptions of established rural society, not just by farmers enclosing commons, but also by engrossers taking over large numbers of holdings, conversion of tenancies into leasehold, and the raising of rents. The amount of eviction of tenants varied, because some landholders, such as those who had occupied land on the waste without proper title, could be removed, but tenants by customary tenure, the copyholders, were sometimes protected.[28]

Tawney doubted whether the policies that he documented led to the destruction of many villages, but Beresford, who sympathized with the general drift of his ideas, discovered hundreds of 'lost villages' that he believed had been removed to make way for sheep pastures in the late fifteenth and sixteenth centuries. His book was published in 1954, and led to a slow-burning debate.[29] Everyone agreed that villages were deserted, especially in vulnerable regions such as the east Midlands, but some researchers found that the villages decayed from within before their fields were converted to pastures, and others noted that the last villagers sometimes left in the seventeenth century, long after the heyday of depopulating enclosure.[30]

The subject developed a broader academic appeal when Brenner published in 1976 an hypothesis about the origins of capitalism.[31] He criticized the demographic approach because it offered no specific explanation of the outcomes of the change in the relationship between population and land. He based his arguments on international comparisons. In one country the peasantry were weakened, and in another strengthened, depending on property relations and social structure. In England he argued that the peasants lacked security of tenure, which gave the lords (he emphasized the role of the gentry) the opportunity to expropriate the peasants' land and convert it into large leasehold farms.

Brenner's thesis attracted a range of criticisms, and its great value was to revive interest in the subject and to encourage other historians to think carefully about

---

[27] E.g. E. F. Gay and I. S. Leadam, 'The Inquisitions of Depopulation in 1517 and the "Domesday of Inclosures"', *Transactions of the Royal Historical Society*, new ser., 14 (1900), 231–303.

[28] R. H. Tawney, *The Agrarian Problem in the Sixteenth Century* (London, 1912).

[29] M. W. Beresford, *The Lost Villages of England* (London, 1954).

[30] These alternative views, with references to the earlier literature, can be found in C. Dyer and R. Jones (eds.), *Deserted Villages Revisited* (Hatfield, 2010).

[31] R. Brenner, 'Agrarian Class Structure and Economic Development in Pre-Industrial Europe', *Past and Present*, 70 (1976), 30–75; R. W. Hoyle, 'Tenure and the Land Market in Early Modern England: Or a Late Contribution to the Brenner Debate', *Ec. HR*, 2nd ser., 43 (1990), 1–20; M. E. Mate, 'The East Sussex Land Market and Agrarian Class Structure in the Late Middle Ages', *Past and Present*, 139 (1993), 46–65.

their assumptions.[32] One of the most fruitful conclusions of the debate was to show that the peasants, far from being victims and 'losers', had been robust defenders of their own interests. One study of peasant landholding concluded that instead of being expropriated by their lords, the more acquisitive and enterprising peasants were the chief engrossers of their neighbours' holdings, and therefore peasants expropriated each other.[33]

Brenner's thesis contributed a valuable generalization about the limits of the population model as a means of explaining historical trends, and he was right to give prominence to property and social power. If demography determined landholding, we would expect in England a new fragmentation of holdings and a proliferation of smallholding after the 1520s, returning to the situation before 1349. Instead, although new cottages spread over wastes and commons, the accumulations of agricultural land that had been created in the fifteenth century persisted.[34] In the same way, the land that had been converted from arable to pasture did not revert back to cultivation, but remained as permanent grassland.[35]

Brenner was right to highlight the shift in the control of resources from the traditional lords to the farmers, who could be gentry but often came from non-aristocratic sections of society, including the peasants. They could break the 'bipartite' structure of the manor because they leased the demesne only and could ignore the peasant tenants or seek to undermine them. The severing of the connection that had existed for centuries left the lessee with a farm isolated from the village and the peasants. The farmer might employ labourers from the village, but often the farm was staffed with living-in servants who came from a distance.[36] The farmers could also build up new groupings of land that had no connection with the old estates. They collected leased demesnes on the basis of their potential for profit, to create new estates that were more homogeneous than those held by the great monasteries. It suited the monks in the tenth and eleventh centuries to combine land on hills, in valleys, and in woodlands, because they were intending a degree of self sufficiency and non-market exchange of resources. The new capitalist graziers concentrated on a limited range of pastoral products for the market, so they created a grouping of enclosed pastures, preferably in close proximity. We see such novel leasehold estates in the hands of the Spencers of Hodnell and later Althorp (a family well known to Heritage).[37] Another strategy pursued in the vicinity of London

---

[32] Responses were conveniently gathered together in T. H. Aston and C. H. E. Philpin (eds), *The Brenner Debate: Agrarian Class Structure and Economic Development in Pre-Industrial Europe* (Cambridge, 1985); a continental perspective is P. Hoppenbrouwers and J. Luiten van Zanden (eds), *Peasants into Farmers? The Transformation of Rural Economy and Society in the Low Countries (Middle Ages–19th Century) in Light of the Brenner Debate* (Turnhout, 2001).

[33] Whittle, *Agrarian Capitalism*, 305–15.

[34] K. Wrightson, *Earthly Necessities: Economic Lives in Early Modern Britain* (New Haven, CT, 2000), 137–41; K. B. Stride, 'Engrossing in Sheep-Corn-Chalk Areas: Evidence in Norfolk, 1530/1–1633', *Norfolk Archaeology*, 40 (1989), 308–18.

[35] French and Hoyle, *English Rural Society*, 25.

[36] Farmers are characterized in C. Dyer, *An Age of Transition? Economy and Society in England in the Later Middle Ages* (Oxford, 2005), 194–210.

[37] H. Thorpe, 'The Lord and the Landscape, Illustrated through the Changing Fortunes of a Warwickshire Parish, Wormleighton', *Transactions of the Birmingham Archaeological Society*, 80 (1962), 38–77.

by such newcomers as Henry Coote at Cheshunt in Hertfordshire, was to buy up land and rent it out for a good return, in his case for more than £30 per annum. This has been described as a new manor, but an alternative term would be a property portfolio.[38]

The birth of capitalism is a legitimate theme to pursue in this period, but capitalism developed over centuries, and it would be difficult to argue that this was the dominant feature of the twenty-five years that are being considered here. The countryside inhabited by landlords, farmers working large leaseholds, and landless agricultural labourers was still a distant prospect in 1520, but it is still worth noting that steps were being taken in that direction.[39]

INSTITUTIONS

The English countryside provided a safe environment for production and exchange, but stability was threatened between 1455 and 1497 by civil war. Fortunately for the great majority of the population the armies of that period were relatively small, the campaigns infrequent and brief, and they did not destroy towns or swathes of countryside. It was nonetheless a benefit for security and confidence that the reign of Henry VII saw an end to the fighting, and that the first Tudors, with exceptions in 1512–14 and 1523, did not repeat the large-scale and long-term military adventures on the continent of their Lancastrian and Plantagenet predecessors.

Neither internal warfare nor violent crime disturbed internal trade to a major degree. The Scottish border was sufficiently threatening to require the bishop of Carlisle to travel with an armed escort, but in lowland England bags of money, letters, and packages were regularly carried by riders and carts in reasonable confidence that they would reach their destinations.[40] This was not of course because the state employed a police force, but it provided a framework within which society policed itself. Every village and town was expected to set a watch, and choose a constable. The local gentry served the Crown in offices as sheriffs and justices of the peace with a duty of maintaining order. The public peace depended on a partnership between the state and those with local influence.

In the same way the government supervised, without detailed intervention, systems of exchange, having designated the places (as a result of local initiatives) where markets and fairs would be held. These ensured, even after many of the markets had fallen into disuse by 1500, that most of the population could in a single day attend a market and return home after transactions had been completed.[41] Regulations, often made and enforced at the local level, sought to protect

---

[38] P. Glennie, 'In Search of Agrarian Capitalism: Manorial Land Markets and the Acquisition of Land in the Lea Valley *c.*1450–*c.*1560', *Continuity and Change*, 3 (1988), 11–40.

[39] These issues are debated in R. H. Hilton (ed.), *The Transition from Feudalism to Capitalism* (London, 1976); R. J. Holton, *The Transition from Feudalism to Capitalism* (London, 1985).

[40] Cumbria County Record Office, DRC/2/29 (account of 1485–6).

[41] A. Everitt, 'The Marketing of Agricultural Produce', in J. Thirsk (ed.), *Agrarian History*, 4, 467–88.

the purchaser from cheating and excessively high prices.[42] The Crown controlled the mints, and apart from an occasional lurch into debasement, maintained a high quality and reliable coinage. In 1495–1520 high-value transactions were based on a gold coin, the angel, which was worth 6s 8d, and the most commonly used coins, silver groats, half-groats, pennies, halfpence, and farthings. A testoon worth 12d was introduced in 1504. The king's subjects could trust the coins, but were inconvenienced by the shortage of small change when many everyday purchases cost a halfpenny or a farthing.[43]

The tax burden was low by the standards of earlier and later centuries in England, and by the demands of continental states, but the taxpayers showed no gratitude, and disturbances in 1489 and 1497 warned rulers against experimenting with new methods of assessment that were regarded as lacking legitimacy.[44] Henry VII maximized royal revenues, from land for example, through the efficient and even unscrupulous administration of Richard Empson and Edmund Dudley (Empson being a landowner in north Gloucestershire who was probably known to Heritage). Both were executed by Henry VIII to appease opinion among those who resented their financial methods. In this relatively peaceful environment property prices were quite stable. Interest rates also were not liable to alarming surges, and remained at a relatively low level, around 5 per cent. Kings maintained their distance from their subjects, but Henry VII and his son were both aware of the need to cultivate opinion, which resulted in the use of public proclamations to advertise their policies, often relating to economic and social matters such as the currency and vagrancy.[45]

If there was a state policy on the economy, it was closely associated with the need to protect and expand the Crown's revenues, hence the various treaties designed to encourage overseas commerce. In the reign of Henry VII trade was a diplomatic lever to protect the insecure English king from conspiracies hatched overseas. Privileges in overseas trade were extended to merchants belonging to associations, such as the Merchant Adventurers, but internal trade was relatively free and unregulated, without many monopolies.[46]

An important strand running through state policy from the 1480s to the 1540s and beyond was the need to exercise some restraint on enclosures and depopulation. The statute on depopulation of 1489 was enforced patchily, and Wolsey

---

[42] J. Davis, *Medieval Market Morality: Life, Law and Ethics in the English Marketplace, 1200–1500* (Cambridge, 2012), 176–273.

[43] P. Grierson, *The Coins of Medieval Europe* (London, 1991), 200–1.

[44] W. Ormrod, 'England in the Middle Ages', in R. Bonney (ed.), *The Rise of the Fiscal State in Europe, c.1200–1815* (Oxford, 1999), 19–52; R. W. Hoyle, 'Resistance and Manipulation in Early Tudor Taxation: Some Evidence from the North', *Archives*, 20 (1993), 158–76.

[45] On interest rates, S. R. Epstein, *Freedom and Growth: The Rise of States and Markets in Europe, 1300–1750* (London, 2000), 60–3; P. L. Hughes and J. F. Larkin, *Tudor Royal Proclamations, I, The Early Tudors* (New Haven, CT, 1964). On the general point of institutional stability, G. Clark, *A Farewell to Alms: A Brief Economic History of the World* (Princeton, NJ, 2007), 145–65; J. L. van Zanden, *The Long Road to the Industrial Revolution: The European Economy in Global Perspective, 1000–1800* (Leiden, 2009), 22–5.

[46] A. F. Sutton and L. Visser-Fuchs (eds), *The Book of Privileges of the Merchant Adventurers of England 1296–1483*, British Academy Records of Social and Economic History, new ser., 42 (Oxford, 2009), 313–16.

began investigations into the subject from 1517, perhaps influenced by rising prices in that year.[47] This put the Crown in the delicate position of seeking to punish landlords who were its natural allies, and from whose ranks were recruited the local officials, members of parliament, and other functionaries of royal government. Those in power were persuaded that enclosure and the 'putting down of towns' ought to be prevented because these activities damaged the state by reducing the number of productive peasants who contributed to direct taxes, and among whom soldiers were recruited.[48] Hugh Latimer, a preacher and eventually bishop of Worcester, in a sermon that highlighted the problems of rural society, remembered that his peasant father, along with many others, had equipped himself with armour and weapons, and rode from Leicestershire to London to help to disperse rebels in 1497 – but if peasants like him were impoverished and deprived of their land, who would defend the Crown in the future?[49] It was commonly alleged that expelled villagers would swell the ranks of the vagrants and beggars, and their sense of injustice might encourage them to rebel.

The state also extended its protection over those with grievances about a wide range of matters, not just enclosure and depopulation. The courts of equity, such as Chancery and the Court of Requests, heard complaints from peasants against lords and other oppressors. Tenants by copy of court roll, who in theory could not bring cases to the common law courts, again could seek redress from Chancery.[50] Evidently the Crown, in its policy of supporting the peasantry who were such valuable contributors to the state, was bringing them within its jurisdiction.

The role of the state, then, was partly to provide an environment in the long term that was conducive to trade and production, but in the period 1495–1520 it was also intervening in economic matters on behalf of those adversely affected by changes in agriculture.

COMMERCIALIZATION

In the 1980s and 1990s the idea of commercialization was applied to the Middle Ages as an alternative to the previously prevalent emphasis on population and resources. The most marked intensification of commerce was located in the thirteenth century, when markets were founded, towns grew in size and number, rents were converted into cash, the use of money was more widely disseminated, lords and peasants both produced for sale, and a land market flourished in villages, especially in eastern England.[51]

As commercial activity was inevitably reduced in scale after 1349, because the number of transactions declined and the demand for basic foodstuffs such as grain

---

[47] Gwyn, *King's Cardinal*, 411–35.
[48] R. H. Britnell, *The Closing of the Middle Ages? England, 1471–1529* (Oxford, 1997), 203–4.
[49] G. E. Corrie (ed.), *Sermons by Hugh Latimer*, Parker Society (1844), 101.
[50] J. H. Baker, *The Oxford History of the Laws of England* (Oxford, 2003), 641–51; C. M. Gray, *Copyhold, Equity and the Common Law* (Cambridge, MA, 1963), 23–53.
[51] R. H. Britnell, *The Commercialisation of English Society 1000–1500* (Cambridge, 1993).

was bound to diminish, one might expect that commercialization either stagnated or even went into reverse by the period 1495–1520. There was no reversal, however: rents were usually paid in cash, and much agriculture was directed towards the market. There was even a growing specialization in production: in the countryside some peasants and farmers turned their land entirely to grazing livestock, and among the towns, to take two examples, Birmingham became famous for its blades and Chipping Walden for saffron.[52]

By 1495 the number of functioning markets had fallen and towns were reduced in size, but society retained its commercialized character. Most of the markets that disappeared from the record had been held in villages, and some of them may not have ever flourished. The better-established and larger-scale urban markets still survived. The towns most severely affected by urban decline, leading to a loss of more than half of their population, and a drop in the value of their market tolls and stall rents, were the east-coast ports that suffered from the fall in wool exports; larger towns like Winchester seemed more vulnerable to shrinkage; York faced competition from smaller clothmaking towns; and the market towns like those in Leicestershire were serving a corn-growing countryside at a time of low prices and reduced demand.[53] The interdependence of town and country was recognized in a proclamation of 1526, which condemned the 'pulling down of towns' (meaning villages) and made the point that the active inhabitants of 'borough towns' (towns in our sense), notably artificers, merchants, chapmen, and victuallers, who made their living from providing for the needs of the tillers and husbandmen of the countryside, would lose their livelihood as a result of rural depopulation.[54]

There is no need to talk about 'de-urbanization' and other potential catastrophes because a halving of the population was a universal experience between 1348 and 1495, which means that townspeople were just as numerous in relation to the population as a whole as in the thirteenth century. A society in which about a fifth of the population lived in towns (in a pre-modern economy) had not suffered from a disastrous urban recession or retreat of commerce.[55]

Not all towns shrank severely in size. London was successful in building on its existing position at the peak of the urban pyramid. Including its large suburbs of Southwark and Westminster, London's population in *c*.1500 exceeded sixty thousand, perhaps three-quarters of its size in 1300.[56] Its role as capital of the kingdom was secure, with all kinds of benefits from the constant stream of visitors attending the law courts or participating in other official business. Leading magnates still maintained their town houses in the suburbs such as Holborn and the Strand,

---

[52] On urban specialization, C. Dyer, 'Small Places with Large Consequences: The Importance of Small Towns in England, 1000–1540', *Historical Research*, 75 (2002), 1–24, esp. 18.

[53] A. Dyer, *Decline and Growth in English Towns, 1400–1640* (Basingstoke, 1991); idem, '"Urban Decline" in England, 1377–1525', in T. R. Slater (ed.), *Towns in Decline AD 100–1600* (Aldershot, 2000), 266–88.

[54] Hughes and Larkin (eds), *Proclamations*, 154–6.

[55] S. H. Rigby, 'Urban Population in Late Medieval England: The Evidence of the Lay Subsidies', *Ec. HR*, 63 (2010), 393–417.

[56] C. M. Barron, *London in the Later Middle Ages: Government and People 1200–1500* (Oxford, 2004), 238–42.

which was familiar to John Heritage who on more than one occasion visited the bishop of Worcester's house on the Strand. By 1495 a high proportion of the export trade in wool and cloth was concentrated in London, which made it essential for traders like Heritage to send their produce to the capital. London also handled a great volume of imported goods, which again attracted provincial merchants.[57] London was also an industrial centre, with artisans producing high-quality manufactures, such as Thomas Alen's coconut cup, and a number of the monumental brasses and bells still visible in provincial churches, including Gloucestershire.[58] The brasses and the goldsmiths' work are only two examples of the cultural standards set by the capital. It was a centre for legal education, where provincial gentry sent their sons, and its schools were also attended by boys from the Midlands, including one of Heritage's nephews who went to St Paul's (see p. 33).

Provincial towns that also avoided recession for at least part of the period following the Black Death (1348–50) included those engaged in clothmaking. Cloth was made at Colchester and Coventry, and they both expanded when other large towns were losing population. Their growth was not sustained, and Coventry in particular was suffering severe problems in the first quarter of the sixteenth century. This was not the case in some of the smaller towns that served the clothmakers in their surrounding countryside, such as a number of centres in Devon including Tiverton. This town and its hinterland prospered from the manufacture of kerseys, and brought great wealth to John Greenway, a clothier rich enough to extend the parish church with a porch and ornate chapel in 1517, and later to found an almshouse in the town.[59] In some clothmaking districts new towns might develop, when in general the 'new town movement' had come to a complete stop. Stroud in Gloucestershire is a notable example.[60]

The countryside had its own commercial life, and towns were not the venue for all sales and purchases. We know of unofficial and informal markets, and especially in the period around 1500 sales were often negotiated directly between producer and buyer, either at the farm gate or an inn.[61] In villages ale, and to a lesser extent bread, meat, and candles, were sold by retailers. As had always been the case, bargains over the sale of land, and contracts for the hire of labour, were agreed in private. Villagers around 1500, anxious for an efficient way of travelling to markets or to deliver goods to purchasers, took steps to maintain roads, using the manor court to order repairs, delegating the care of highways to small committees of villagers, and sometimes as individuals bequeathing money for work on roads and bridges. The most remarkable indication of the flourishing of commerce in the

---

[57] *ibid*, 304–5.

[58] M. Norris, *Monumental Brasses: The Memorials*, I (London, 1977), 132–76; M. Bliss and F. Sharpe, *Church Bells of Gloucestershire* (Gloucester, 1986), 44–6.

[59] R. H. Britnell, *Growth and Decline in Colchester, 1300–1525* (Cambridge, 1986); C. Phythian-Adams, *Desolation of a City: Coventry and the Urban Crisis of the Late Middle Ages* (Cambridge, 1979); A. E. Welsford, *John Greenway, 1460–1529: Merchant of Tiverton and London. A Devon Worthy* (Tiverton, 1984).

[60] *VCH Glos.*, XI, 99–145.

[61] C. Dyer, 'The Hidden Trade of the Middle Ages: Evidence from the West Midlands', in *idem, Everyday Life in the Middle Ages* (London, 1994), 297–300.

countryside comes from rural clothmaking. Its spread can be traced by the building of fulling mills, and by the records of textile artisans in the military survey of 1522, or over a longer period the references to significant occupational descriptions in court records. Spinners, weavers, fullers (or tuckers), shearmen, dyers, and clothiers colonized the villages and hamlets of Devon, Somerset, and Wiltshire in the south-west, west Berkshire and south Gloucestershire further east, and in the south-east Kent, Essex, and East Anglia. In the north rural clothmaking flourished in the West Riding of Yorkshire, Lancashire, and the Lake District, and it also developed in Wales. In some English districts, such as south-west Suffolk, more than a third of the population were pursuing non-agricultural occupations. The presence of so many cloth-workers stimulated local food production, and the clothing areas show up as pockets of prosperity when tax assessments are mapped and compared. Profits flowed into the hands of clothiers, the entrepreneurs who coordinated production and who sold the cloth.[62]

Some statistics allow us to locate the years 1495–1520 in the ebbs and flows of commercial history. The export of wool, which was in continuous decline for almost two centuries, was falling gently after 1495. Having hovered around 30,000 sacks in the 1350s, by 1495–6 wool cargoes had fallen to a little more than 12,000 sacks, and were down to 9,500 in 1519–20. In between these dates the annual totals were always below 10,000 and dipped under 5,000 in 1505–6.[63] In that year Heritage, who traded in wool on a modest scale, probably sent to London about 43 sacks, which amounted to approximately 1 per cent of the total exported. Most wool was being made into cloth in England, much of it for exports that climbed from just below 60,000 cloths in 1496–7 to 70,000 in 1500–1, and almost 100,000 in 1519–20. This represented an impressive growth from very small numbers in the mid-fourteenth century and 40,000 per annum around 1400.[64] Internal consumption is not recorded, but the home market cannot have amounted to less than 160,000 cloths, bringing the overall production to near a quarter of a million cloths in the early years of the sixteenth century.

The output of tin mines in 1515–20 reached the highest level known since records began in the twelfth century, exceeding two million pounds in 1521.[65] Much of this metal was exported, with a modest proportion in the form of pewter. Pewter exports had peaked in the early and mid-fifteenth century, but were climbing back to an average annual total of 30 tons of vessels in the decade 1511–20.[66] Pewter was in high

[62] E. M. Carus-Wilson and O. Coleman, *England's Export Trade 1275–1547* (Oxford, 1963), 48–72.

[63] *ibid*, 75–115.

[64] Poos, *Rural Society*, 58–72; N. R. Amor, 'Merchant Adventurer or Jack of All Trades? The Suffolk Clothier in the 1460s', *Proceedings of the Suffolk Institute of Archaeology and History*, 40 (2004), 414–36; E. M. Carus-Wilson, 'Evidences of Industrial Growth on some Fifteenth-Century Manors', in *idem* (ed.), *Essays in Economic History*, II (London, 1962), 151–67. The best study of a rural cloth industry is M. Zell, *Industry in the Countryside: Wealden Society in the Sixteenth Century* (Cambridge, 1994). Britnell, *Closing of the Middle Ages*, 235, doubts whether the expansion in the export trade in cloth, tin, and lead added more than 18,000 full-time jobs to the economy, 1471–1529.

[65] J. Hatcher, *English Tin Production and Trade before 1550* (Oxford, 1973), 152–63.

[66] *ibid*, 176–87; J. Hatcher and T. C. Barker, *A History of British Pewter* (London, 1974), 76.

demand within England, and many peasant households owned a few plates and saucers. The coal industry was flourishing in various parts of the country, with about 40,000 tons being carried each year from Newcastle in 1508–11, much of it destined for London.[67] The wealden iron industry was very active in this period, and there were new technical developments such as the first blast furnace in Sussex in 1496.[68] The first English paper mill near Hertford, also recorded in the 1490s, contributed to an expanding London-based printing industry.[69] All of this suggests a rather healthy picture of a commercial economy in which industries were feeding demand on the continent as well as within the country, and which were adopting new technologies. The decline of the wool trade cannot be regarded as a disaster, as demand for wool was increasing thanks to domestic clothmaking so the producers did not suffer, and the move away from the export of raw materials to supplying continental Europe with manufactured goods suggests a healthy development in England's position in the global economy. High-quality English wool was replaced in the textile industry of Flanders by Merino wool imported from Spain.[70]

Commercial life was expanding mainly because of increased consumer demand. A growth in consumerism has been identified in the eighteenth century, but it had a modest precursor in the later Middle Ages. Once we assumed that most spending came from the aristocracy, on such commodities as wine, imports of which were recovering by 1500 after the disruption of the French trade at the end of the Hundred Years War.[71] Around 1500 people of different ranks were buying a broader range of goods and services, coinciding with a phase of timber-framed building for both rural aristocrats and peasants which had risen in the middle and late fifteenth century and reached a high level in the period 1500–33.[72] The earliest evidence for village houses having glass windows comes from around 1500, and at this time villagers drank from stoneware vessels imported from the Rhineland.[73] An insight into a yeoman's consumer behaviour and mentality comes from the probate inventory of John Andrew of St Neots in Huntingdonshire, compiled in 1506.[74] His 86 sheep, 13 cattle, and 2 horses do not suggest a very large farm. Nonetheless Andrew's household goods included a coverlet for his bed worth 13*s* 4*d*, a chafing dish, and eighteen pieces of pewter. He owned high-quality clothes, notably a

[67] J. Hatcher, *The History of the British Coal Industry, I, Before 1700: Towards the Age of Coal* (Oxford, 1993), 486–7.

[68] H. Cleere and D. Crossley, *The Iron Industry of the Weald*, 2nd edn. (Cardiff, 1995), 111–17.

[69] D. C. Coleman, *The British Paper Industry 1495–1860* (Oxford, 1958), 40–1; Sutton, *Merchant Family*, 22–5. The paper of which John Heritage's account book was made can be shown from its watermark to have been manufactured in southern France or north Italy: A. Stevenson (ed.), *C. M. Briquet, Les Filigranes. Dictionnaire Historique des Marques du Papier* (Amsterdam, 1968), 2, 567; 4, nos. 11136, 11137, 11139, 11140.

[70] J. Munro, 'Spanish Merino Wool and the Nouvelles Draperies: An Industrial Transformation in the Late Medieval Low Countries', *Ec. HR*, 58 (2005), 431–84.

[71] M. K. James, *Studies in the Medieval Wine Trade* (Oxford, 1971), 38–59.

[72] S. Pearson, 'The Chronological Distribution of Tree-Ring Dates, 1980–2001: An Update', *Vernacular Architecture*, 32 (2001), 68–9.

[73] D. D. Andrews and G. Milne (eds), *Wharram: A Study of Settlement on the Yorkshire Wolds, I, Domestic Settlement, Areas 10 and 6*, Society for Medieval Archaeology, Monograph Ser., 8 (London, 1979), 73, 94–5, 115.

[74] TNA: PRO, PROB 2/696.

tawny gown furred with budge, which was an expensive imported lambskin, another gown of the same colour lined with satin, and a fur-lined jacket of purple camlet. He was a pretentious consumer, imitating his superiors. The chafing dish shows that food was being kept hot for meals, as it would be in an aristocratic hall, and his preference for fur and silk linings, for camlet, a fine fabric, and for the colour purple all suggest that he had his eye on the style of the landed gentry. He came quite near to breaking the limits imposed by the sumptuary laws passed in 1510 and 1514, but he (or rather his successor, as he died in 1506) would have put himself beyond the legal limit if he had worn a gown of camlet as distinct from a jacket of that material.[75]

The amount of cash in circulation declined in the fifteenth century, and it has been argued that this had a decisively depressive effect on the economy.[76] The latest estimate values the whole currency in circulation in the early fourteenth century at £2 million, and in about 1470 the total would have been below £1 million.[77] The European silver mines had ceased to be productive, and precious metals were draining to the east to pay for luxury goods such as spices and silks. There is bound to be scepticism about an explanation for complex changes based on a single economic factor, particularly when prices did not show signs of universal deflation as economics would predict. By the time we reach our period of 1495–1520 the problem had become less acute, as more silver was being mined on the continent, and the gold coinage was being supplemented by metal from west Africa, with the result that the total of coins in circulation had a value amounting to between £1.4 and £1.6 million.[78] There was still a bullion problem, however, because coinage was in such short supply that when transactions were made on credit the sums were repaid very slowly. Credit seems, however, to have been increasingly available after about 1490.

To sum up, commercialization has given us a very useful means of setting the period in a context. With the help of this approach, we can recognize the dynamic elements in the period, and correct the impression of a sluggish economy implied by the relatively static population.

SOCIAL RESTRUCTURING

Edmund Dudley in his *Tree of Commonwealth* of 1509 emphasized the organic nature of society, advocating the concord and unity that would bind the different ranks – nobles, merchants, craftsmen, husbandmen, servants, and labourers together in an harmonious whole.[79] He was to some extent continuing in the

---

[75] M. Hayward, *Rich Apparel: Clothing and the Law in Henry VIII's England* (Farnham, 2009), 17–39.

[76] J. Day, 'The Great Bullion Famine of the Fifteenth Century', in *idem, The Medieval Market Economy* (Oxford, 1987), 1–54.

[77] M. Allen, 'Silver Production and the Money Supply in England and Wales, 1086–c.1500', *Ec. HR*, 64 (2011), 114–31.

[78] P. Nightingale, 'Gold, Credit and Mortality: Distinguishing Deflationary Pressure in the Late Medieval English Economy', *Ec. HR*, 60 (2010), 1,081–1,104.

[79] Brodie (ed.), *Tree of Commonwealth*.

tradition of the medieval idea that society was divided into three orders (the clergy who prayed, nobility who fought, and commons who worked), each with its rights and responsibilities. His analysis gave more attention to sections of society who would not figure prominently in the three-orders scheme, such as farmers, yeomen, graziers, merchants, and craftsmen. A few years later Thomas More envisioned a society – which bore some resemblance to London – consisting of well-disciplined households (including some slaves) living in cities, without much reference to a nobility or even a monarchy.[80]

Modern interpretations of the period used to emphasize the setbacks experienced by the nobility after the civil wars of the fifteenth century, and the so-called 'rise of the middle class', for example allowing men of non-aristocratic urban origins like Wolsey and Thomas Cromwell to take over the reins of power. This idea has been discredited for so long that it should not form part of our collective historical consciousness, but it still lingers. It was given an afterlife by the argument that a 'middling sort' emerged during the sixteenth century, but this referred to the better-off peasants, farmers, traders, and artisans who administered the poor law in their parishes.[81]

For contemporaries a major concern was the spread of vagrancy and begging. They criticized the greed of the rich, who dispossessed villagers, or dismissed their servants when they reached old age, but they also blamed the poor for their reluctance to work. Historians explain the strength of feeling about this subject with difficulty, but they can identify a growing concern for the poor, which resulted in the foundation of almshouses, attempts to organize more effective relief schemes, and efforts to enforce social discipline, even at the level of restricting games and imposing sumptuary laws.[82]

It sometimes seems that this was a period of growing equality, as the power of lords was slipping, to be replaced by the gentry who gained in importance as JPs enforcing the law at local level. Serfdom was withering away, wage-earners were well rewarded, education was widely available, and the deserving poor received more support. On the other hand the king was still close to a circle of great lords who seemed to display their wealth and status ostentatiously. Henry VII in particular promoted more oligarchic constitutions in towns, and women, whose social standing had advanced after 1350, seemed to be held back and disadvantaged.[83]

In the division of society into three orders, which dominated thinking from the ninth to the fourteenth century, the clergy occupied a prominent place alongside the warriors and workers. There is some evidence that in the early years of the six-

---

[80] G. M. Logan and R. M. Adams (eds), *Thomas More: Utopia* (Cambridge, 1989).

[81] K. Wrightson, 'Sorts of People in Tudor and Stuart England', in J. Berry and C. Brooks (eds), *The Middling Sort of People: Culture, Society and Politics in England, 1550–1800* (Basingstoke, 1994), 28–51.

[82] P. Slack, *From Reformation to Improvement: Public Welfare in Early Modern England* (Oxford, 1999).

[83] J. Lee, 'Urban Policy and Urban Political Culture: Henry VII and his Towns', *Historical Research*, 82 (2009), 493–510; M. K. McIntosh, *Working Women in English Society 1300–1620* (Cambridge, 2005), 37–42.

teenth century, churchmen did not figure as prominently as was once the case in the consciousness of the articulate laymen. Dudley, for example, pays them little attention, and religion was not a very important feature of More's *Utopia*. In the England in which the intellectuals lived and wrote, the Church remained as prominent as ever, with large holdings of land, a very visible presence through its buildings and personnel, and with a strong influence on education and culture. Historians hold divergent views of religious devotion in the half century before the Reformation, the first part of which coincides with our focus period of 1495–1520. To some this was a period of religious enthusiasm, continuing the fifteenth-century commitment to a very Catholic religion of ritual and ornaments.[84] To others, while recognizing the piety of the later medieval period, the early sixteenth century shows signs of a cooling in enthusiasm, when it became more difficult to recruit clergy, the clergy came under more criticism, and there was a falling off in membership of some religious fraternities.[85] We can still observe a very strong lay involvement in the life of the parish, in which churchwardens organized fundraising for the church building and its fittings. Laymen and women devoted large sums of money to various types of chantry, which would deliver prayers and the celebration of masses for the salvation of their souls after death. Those who could not afford an individual chantry could be assured of prayers through their membership of a fraternity. Personal religious observance is apparent from the presence of religious books and devotional images in the home, and participation in pilgrimages.

Merchants deserve attention here because one of them is the central figure of this book. They were not a new social or occupational category, and were well established in larger towns and ports where they managed overseas or long-distance trade, both in large cargoes of relatively cheap goods or in consignments of valuable commodities.[86] Their numbers were not large, with perhaps sixty of them in 1522 in the city of Coventry with its 1,300 households.[87] They formed a self-conscious group, who occupied the more important offices in self-governing towns, and maintained a degree of solidarity. The gentry often made use of their services and interacted with them, but they were clearly separated; the merchants were also aware of the gulf of wealth and way of life that divided them from the artisans and husbandmen. Although merchants had occupied a crucial niche in society for centuries, they constantly changed their commodities, destinations, methods of trading, and outlook.

In our period they formed associations, of which that of the Merchants of the Staple was most celebrated, with a membership of 480 in 1505. This was an elite of wool exporters, which did not include the middlemen who collected wool from the growers, the woolmen, also known as woolmongers or broggers, to which

---

[84] E. Duffy, *The Stripping of the Altars: Traditional Religion in England, c.1400–c.1580* (New Haven, CT, 1992).

[85] R. Whiting, *Local Responses to the English Reformation* (Basingstoke, 1998).

[86] The best study is J. Kermode, *Medieval Merchants: York, Beverley and Hull in the Later Middle Ages* (Cambridge, 1998).

[87] Phythian-Adams, *Desolation of a City*, 306–19.

group Heritage belonged. The Cotswold woolmen were in competition with one another, but their memorial brasses have common characteristics suggesting that they shared an outlook.[88] They chose to be commemorated by brasses, that is, plates of a copper alloy which was engraved with an image of the deceased and his wife or wives, and set in a stone slab. A useful contrast is found in the church of Barcheston where William Willington is represented by a three-dimensional alabaster effigy showing him in armour. Willington was one of Heritage's rivals, but he was a Merchant of the Staple and bought the lordship of a manor, so he had joined the gentry, and earned the right to a superior memorial.[89] Cotswold woolmen were depicted as 'civilians', that is, in their everyday clothing. The brasses often represent the trade of the person remembered with a wool sack, or a sheep, or a merchant's mark, often at the feet. (Fig. 1.2) The inscriptions on the tombs express simple religious sentiments, sometimes in English: '... pray for the soul of ...'

Fig. 1.2. Part of a woolman's brass from Northleach church, Gloucestershire. Sheep and wool sack, with merchant's mark, from a memorial which may be that of William Midwinter of Northleach, *c.*1500. The sheep does not have the characteristics of the Cotswold breed, as the brass was engraved in London. The woolmen's brasses with images of their trade indicate their sense of a shared identity.

Sources: C. T. Davis, *The Monumental Brasses of Gloucestershire* (London, 1899); W. Lack, H. M. Stuchfield, and P. Whittemore, *The Monumental Brasses of Gloucestershire* (London, 2005), 320, 322.

---

[88] A. Hanham, *The Celys and their World: An English Merchant Family in the Fifteenth Century* (Cambridge, 1985), 245; N. Saul, 'The Wool Merchants and their Brasses', *Transactions of the Monumental Brass Society*, 17 (2008), 315–35.

[89] For Staple merchants living in the country, acquiring land, and joining the gentry, Yates, *Western Berkshire*, 197–200. These were really 'country merchants', whereas Heritage was based in a town, though his business was conducted in the country.

Woolmen, however, looked beyond their Cotswold environment, and their connections with the capital enabled them to commission their brasses from superior London workshops, which also supplied stone slabs cut from the Purbeck marble quarries in Dorset.

We would be right to see the period 1495–1520 as fitting into a longer period in which the social hierarchy and perceptions of society were being adjusted to new circumstances, and these clearly connect with the other trends of the period.

These five approaches to the period are rivals, and compete with one another for the attention of historians. Some of the ideas are compatible, and there are certainly elements of overlap that lead the advocates of different approaches to highlight the same tendencies. Historians can only advance the subject by testing existing hypotheses through empirical research and by devising new syntheses. No one can read and digest all of the information, which is why it is necessary to select particular people and places for investigation, preferably using high-quality sources.

SOURCES

Historians of medieval England are especially fortunate in the large quantities of surviving documents that were generated by administrative processes of accounting and the holding of courts. These sources can sometimes give a misleading impression for the period 1495–1520 because an administrative inertia ensured that documents were written in a tradition which was no longer relevant to a new age. The officials of landed estates compiled rentals and surveys that recorded the names and holdings of tenants, but did not notice the subtenants.

Bailiffs compiled financial accounts which often preserved archaic information, and include none of the details of cultivation and the marketing of produce that they contained before the demesnes were leased. The manor court rolls itemize the transfers of land held by customary tenure (again omitting subtenants, except to punish those who illicitly sublet their land), but the litigation and reports of petty offences that once took up most of the court's time had largely disappeared. Similar comments could be made about other records that confined themselves to administrative formalities, such as the bishops' registers.

John Heritage's account book can be regarded as one of the new generation of more informal documents compiled by the people who were playing an important role in the period, but whose archives have not usually survived. The names of the hundreds of people who supplied him with wool can be found in the more conventional sources, and we are fortunate that his area of operation, the vicinity of Moreton in Marsh, has a high survival rate of records. The great church estates held much of the land, and part of the archives of Evesham Abbey, Pershore Abbey, Westminster Abbey, the bishopric of Worcester, and Worcester Cathedral Priory are quite fully preserved, as well as smaller quantities of records from other monasteries and lay estates, such as that of the Fortescue family. The most relevant of the state archives that contain a mass of information about individuals are the military survey of 1522 and the subsidy lists for 1524 and 1525, but much can be gleaned from the judicial records, especially from the equity courts to which the local people took their complaints, and the inquiries of the commissions investigating enclosure and depopulation in 1517–18. Wills had been compiled for centuries before Heritage's day, but they survive in greater numbers around 1500, and provide insights into many dimensions of economy, society, religion, and culture. Readers will see that part of the research has used a prosopographical approach, which means finding out as much as possible from all available sources about the people who supplied Heritage with wool. For understanding the background to the transactions recorded in the account book, much survives of the buildings and landscapes of the period, so this evidence stands alongside that derived from documents.

2

Family and Household: John Heritage and his Contemporaries

In exploring John Heritage's place in society we will begin with an outline of his family life, and then compare him with families and households among his contemporaries, mainly in his 'country' but also more generally.

JOHN HERITAGE AND HIS FAMILY

Heritage is an unusual name, originally given by his neighbours to someone who had gained an inheritance of land. This good fortune was regarded as the defining characteristic of the individual, which then became a family name. The inheritance probably came about in the thirteenth century, when most surnames originated, but was unusual because it derived from the Norman French. People bearing the name are recorded in south Warwickshire in the later Middle Ages, going back to 1310–11, and the family has survived in that district to the present day.[1] John Heritage, the central figure of this book, was born in about 1470 at Burton Dassett in south-east Warwickshire. (Fig. 2.1) He was named after his grandfather (here called John Heritage senior), who with Margaret his wife lived at Burton and had prospered there. At the end of the fifteenth century a freeholding of 1 ¾ yardlands (or virgates to use the more latinate term, each of about 30 acres) is mentioned at Burton, which may well have been a long-term family possession.[2] John Heritage senior and Margaret first appear in the records in 1466–7, when they joined the fraternity (or guild) of the Holy Cross at Stratford upon Avon.[3] They were probably in their forties; John senior was long lived, and was still functioning in 1495.[4] John senior's son Roger also joined the fraternity in 1466–7 as a single man, which must mean that he was unmarried, as husbands and wives would normally join as a couple.[5] A year or two afterwards, probably when he was in his late twenties, he found a wife, called Elizabeth, and they appear as Roger and Elizabeth Heritage in 1476 when they enrolled (together with John senior and Margaret) in another

---

[1] F. T. S. Houghton, E. Stokes, and L. Drucker (eds.), *Warwickshire Feet of Fines, 2, 1284–1345*, Dugdale Society, 15 (1939), 66.
[2] He must have been born after 1466. On the freeholding, *WGLS*, 33.
[3] *Guild Reg.*, 259. He sponsored other recruits in the following year, 263–4.
[4] TNA: PRO, PROB 2/457, refers to debts to John Heritage the elder.
[5] *Guild Reg.*, 259.

Fig. 2.1. Burton Dassett, Warwickshire. Looking south from the hilltop stone tower that was originally built as a windmill, the distant top of the tower of the parish church can be seen immediately to the right of the mill, on the skyline among the trees. This was John Heritage's parish church for his first twenty-seven years. The Heritage house stood near to the church, and the land to the right (west) of the church in the middle distance was called Heritage Field (author's photograph).

major Warwickshire fraternity, that of Knowle.[6] Elizabeth did not join the Stratford fraternity until 1492–3, and died in the next two or three years.[7]

The records of the fraternities are invaluable in providing information about individuals who are so obscure that they have left little trace in other documents. Obscure they may have been, but they were not poor. The act of joining a fraternity is itself a good guide to status and wealth, as it cost 13s 4d for a married couple at Stratford, and the Knowle guild charged individuals 3s 4d. This fee could only be afforded by people of some substance, including better-off landholders, ranging from peasants with at least 30 acres of land to the gentry. Recruits from the towns included traders and wealthier artisans. Country people like the Heritages wanted to associate themselves with the fraternity for a variety of motives. They hoped that their souls would benefit from the prayers of the chantry priests employed by the fraternities, and they gained spiritual comfort from attending the ceremonies – processions and religious service – which the fraternities organized. They may have

[6] W. B. Bickley (ed.), *Register of the Guild of Knowle* (Walsall, 1894), 80.
[7] *Guild Reg.*, 357.

expected that membership, especially in the case of an important local urban centre like Stratford, would give them useful contacts among the traders and artisans with whom they wished to do business. The annual guild feast was both a special occasion, when non-aristocrats could eat and drink like lords, but also an opportunity to meet potential customers, and to cement existing commercial relationships. The fraternity offered a service for settling quarrels, and if two brothers were in dispute over a debt the master would organize a 'love day' when an arbiter would broker a compromise. In short their links with the fraternities show that the Heritage family were relatively wealthy, and they also had an ambition to secure for themselves a place in the religious, social, and trading networks of their county.[8]

It is easy to see the practical value that Roger found in his membership of fraternities, because he was selling on a large scale grain, wool, dairy produce, livestock such as beef cattle, and rabbits. This produce came from the demesne of Burton Dassett (amounting to 200 acres of arable, with much grazing land as well) leased originally from the joint lords of the manor, William Belknap and Sir John Norbury.[9] His inventory of 1495 reveals him to have had 2 ploughs, 860 sheep, and 40 cattle. His household contained six servants, who worked no doubt as ploughmen, shepherds, and dairymaids. He paid an annual rent of £20 to his landlords, and could have made £10 per annum for himself.

John Heritage, the central figure of this book, spent his early years in this busy, crowded farmhouse. His mother Elizabeth produced at least four sons and four daughters during the 1470s and 1480s, resulting in a household (with servants) possibly with sixteen residents (Fig. 2.2).[10] The house's contents are revealed in Roger's inventory of 1495, and they tell us something of the way of life and domestic routine. The kitchen was capable of feeding more than a dozen people, with its five brass pots, six pans, and three spits. The ale was brewed in a 'bakhouse', which had two lead vessels and various vats and containers for large quantities of liquid. Bread-making equipment is not mentioned, and loaves may have been delivered by a local baker.[11] The household was gathered together for meals served in the hall, and Roger can be imagined sitting at the head of the table in the only chair, and his wife, children, and servants, with occasional guests or visiting workers, occupying forms down the 'long table'.

The seating plan emphasized the superiority of Roger as the head of the household, who provided the good food and drink that they all enjoyed. The occasion would have been a dignified one: the table was provided with a linen tablecloth, and for special events with honoured guests pewter plates and silver spoons were available. The children and servants seated on their forms all looked up to Roger, and he

---

[8] R. H. Hilton, *The English Peasantry in the Later Middle Ages* (Oxford, 1975), 91–4; G. Rosser, 'Going to the Fraternity Feast: Commensality and Social Relations in Late Medieval England', *Journal of British Studies*, 33 (1994), 430–46.

[9] *WGLS*, 34–5; C. Dyer, 'Were There Any Capitalists in Fifteenth-Century England?', in *idem*, *Everyday Life in Medieval England* (London, 1994), 305–27.

[10] TNA: PRO, PROB 11/10, fo.231v (will).

[11] TNA: PRO, PROB 2/457 (inventory). For bread deliveries around early sixteenth-century Buckingham, E. H. Shagan (ed.), 'Rumours and Popular Politics in the Reign of Henry VIII', in T. Harris (ed.), *The Politics of the Excluded, c.1500–1850* (Basingstoke, 2001), 37–8.

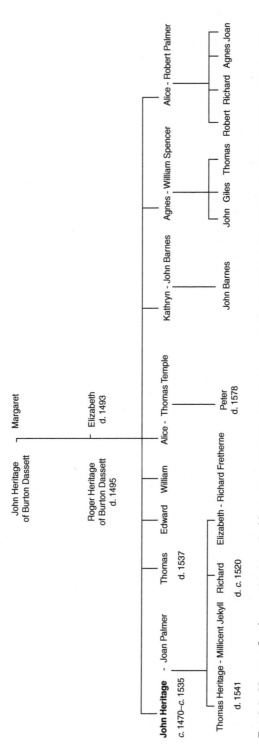

Fig. 2.2. Heritage family tree. Sources: *Guild Reg.* 259, 357, 368, 460; Bickley (ed.), *Guild of Knowle*, 80, 106; TNA: PRO, PROB 11/10, fo. 231v; PROB 11/25, fo. 73v; PROB 2/457; *WGLS*, 15–18; WAM 8365; AB, fo. 76v; Bowers, 'Schooling of the Sons of Midland Gentry'.

expected to exercise authority over them. In his will he instructed his executors not to hand over bequests to his younger sons if they were 'wasters' or of evil condition or disposition. Similarly, his daughters had to be ruled in their choice of marriage partners by 'my executors and their friends' (friends meaning relatives) or they would lose their bequest. They would suffer a similar fate if they were of 'evil will or disposition'. Roger was unusually distrustful of his children, or at least had a high regard for morality and discipline, and expected his children to observe their place in the hierarchy.[12] The naming of the children show the parents' regard for the maintenance of family memories, which helped to bind the generations together. In a very traditional way John Heritage, the eldest son, was named after his grandfather. Roger's daughters, or at least those who survived, were not named after their mother or paternal grandmother, but calling two of them 'Alice', a not unusual circumstance, results from the custom of naming children after their godmothers.

Roger Heritage, when he wrote his will in 1495, planned that his role at the head of the household should be taken by John, his eldest son, as he bequeathed to his younger sons Thomas, Edward, and William sums of money (£13 6s 8d each), and £6 13s 4d to each of his daughters: Alice, Kathryn, Agnes, and the second Alice. John was to receive the land, farm stock, and goods. The total of £66 13s 4d left to the children in money, and the sums reserved for pious bequests and other beneficiaries, were not readily available in a chest full of coins. Rather the heir, John, was obliged to find the money over a period of years as his brothers came of age or his sisters married. It was above all he who, as the new head of the family and the sole executor of Roger's will, made the judgements about their 'evil disposition', and the situation, even without Roger's moralistic instructions, was potentially a tense and contentious one. Quite apart from considering whether his siblings deserved their inheritance, John would have had difficulties in finding the money from the income of the farm.

John Heritage was brought up in the unusually large parish of Burton Dassett, with 132 tenants in 1279 grouped into five separate settlements in its 5,000 acres.[13] On the slopes of a hill stood the impressive parish church, and a nearby isolated hilltop site was occupied by a tower windmill, built in stone probably in the fourteenth century, which stood out in John's day and in altered form still serves as a landmark for the whole district (see Fig. 2.1).[14] From the end of the thirteenth century the settlement of Southend, on lower ground, was granted a market and had a wide street called Newland, a boothhall, a shop, a chapel, and a small community of traders and artisans.[15] This partly developed town survived into the late fifteenth century, though by then the rural population of the parish had dropped, and one of the villages, Temple Hardwick, was deserted. The local agricultural economy was dominated in the thirteenth century by open fields devoted to corn

---

[12] On assertive fathers, and the limitations on their authority, M. S. Hartman, *The Household and the Making of History: A Subversive View of the Western Past* (Cambridge, 2004), 34–69.

[13] T. John (ed.), *The Warwickshire Hundred Rolls of 1279–80: Stoneleigh and Kineton Hundreds*, British Academy Records of Social and Economic History, 19 (1992), 224–9.

[14] J. Langdon, *Mills in the Medieval Economy: England 1300–1540* (Oxford, 2004), 113.

[15] C. Dyer, 'The Hidden Trade of the Middle Ages', in *idem, Everyday Life*, 292–3.

growing, as was true throughout the Feldon district of east and south Warwickshire, and most of the land was cultivated in the narrow strips of which traces still
survive as ridge and furrow.[16] Much of this arable at Burton was converted to pasture by the late fifteenth century, again in line with neighbouring parishes.[17] John
would have been fully aware of the changes that had occurred because he would
have seen the grass growing on the previously ploughed land. He would have been
familiar with the field called 'Old Leys' (recorded in the 1540s), which was so
called because a whole block of land had been converted from arable to pasture.[18]
He would also have passed daily the sites of ruined and abandoned houses, some
of which had fallen down so long ago that their foundations were covered with
grass. Edward Belknap, lord of the manor in 1517, in his defence made to the
enclosure commission stated that for some time in the period before 1500 'housing fell in great ruin and decay' so he was not responsible, nor was any previous
lord because the cause of the problem was decay, not deliberate depopulation.[19]
The young John would have appreciated the advantage that his father enjoyed
from this reduction in the number of tenants, which gave him the space to practise
a type of mixed farming in which sheep and cattle keeping played an important
part alongside corn-growing. Roger had carried out a limited programme of enclosure according to Belknap's defence. John at some point formed the view that even
more advantage could be had from pushing these processes even further.

In 1495 after the death of Roger Heritage, the young John found himself taking
over the large agricultural enterprise that his father had developed on the demesne
leased from Belknap and Norbury. Roger had interests and connections beyond
Burton, which are hinted in his will. He knew well nine parishes adjoining Burton,
as he made bequests to their churches, and the overseer of his will came from
nearby Farnborough.[20] Further afield he had links with Aylesbury in Buckingham-
shire, as in 1495 he was owed money by Richard Gibbons who held the Swan Inn
in the street called Kingsbury, and Roger may well have stayed there on his way to
London.[21] We know of his membership of the Stratford fraternity, and his gifts of
corn in his will to the friars of Coventry and Warwick suggest that he was familiar
with those towns. In 1486–7 he acted as joint farmer of the demesne of the manor
of Quinton (Gloucestershire) and so was temporarily a tenant of the lords there,
the fellows of Magdalen College, Oxford.[22] This tenancy came to him because he

---

[16] The ridge-and-furrow has been systematically mapped from aerial photographs in a programme
of Warwickshire Museums and the then Royal Commission on Historical Monuments (England),
which can be seen through the Heritage and Environment Record maintained by Warwickshire
County Council.

[17] C. Dyer, *Warwickshire Farming 1349–c.1520: Preparations for Agricultural Revolution*, Dugdale
Society Occasional Paper, 27 (1981), 9–12, 16–21, 28–30.

[18] *WGLS*, 35.

[19] N. W. Alcock, 'Enclosure and Depopulation in Burton Dassett: A Sixteenth-Century View',
Warwickshire History, 3 (1977), 180–4.

[20] TNA: PRO, PROB 11/10, fo.231v. They were not simply the nine nearest churches, so he presumably selected them for his own reasons.

[21] On the Swan Inn, Birmingham Archives and Heritage, Hampton MSS. 1821 (I am grateful to
Mr Hugh Hanley for this reference).

[22] Magdalen College, Oxford, 35/12 (Quinton manorial account).

was acting as executor for Edward Empson, who may have been related to the Northamptonshire family that produced Richard Empson, Henry VII's notorious official.

John Heritage inherited some of his father's range of contacts, and like him looked to horizons far beyond Burton Dassett. A matter of concern after Roger's death must have been organizing marriages for John's four sisters, as in 1495 they were probably in their teens or early twenties. At the time that Roger's will was written, in August 1495, their marriages still lay in the future, though negotiations had probably begun for one or two of them, hence his insistence that they should follow advice. The choice of their husbands therefore partly resulted from Roger's agreements, brought to fruition by John, but some may have been negotiated from the beginning by John. We do not know a great deal about John Barnes, who married Kathryn, except that he came from Northamptonshire. On the other hand William Spencer of Badby, also in Northamptonshire, who married Agnes, belonged to the celebrated family of graziers, one branch of which became lords of the manor of Althorp. The older Alice became the wife of Thomas Temple, a merchant of Witney in Oxfordshire some time after 1501, so that arrangement was certainly made by John Heritage.[23] These marriages forged alliances between families of similar status, as farmers, graziers, and small-town merchants all moved in the same circles and occupied a rank just below the gentry. No doubt they aspired to acquire the sizeable quantity of freehold land and above all the manorial lordship that would enable them to be judged as gentlemen by their contemporaries. The choice of marriage partners could cause friction between parents and children, as we know from the Paston letters and warnings in wills about taking advice from the older generation. The family's concern for making advantageous matches had to be reconciled with the personal preferences of the young people.[24] John Heritage, in his mid-twenties, inherited the difficult diplomatic role that involved making agreements with families at some distance (between 11 and 30 miles from Burton), while encouraging and cajoling his sisters into accepting the eligible young men selected by his father or himself.

John Heritage's own marriage had presumably been set in motion by Roger and Elizabeth a few years earlier, shortly before 1493.[25] His wife was Joan Palmer, the daughter of Richard Palmer of Moreton in Marsh (Gloucestershire), and she therefore came from the same farming and trading background as did the husbands of John's sisters. We can only guess how this alliance was formed between two similar but geographically quite distant families – Moreton and Burton lay 18 miles (29 km) apart. Roger owed money in 1495 to a Robert Palmer, who might have been Joan's brother, and earlier business connections between the families probably paved the way for the marriage.

[23] On the Spencers, H. Thorpe, 'The Lord and the Landscape Illustrated through the Changing Fortunes of a Warwickshire Parish, Wormleighton', *Transactions of the Birmingham Archaeological Society*, 80 (1962), 38–77; on the Temples, *WGLS*, 21–4.

[24] E.g. K. Dockray, 'Why did Fifteenth-Century English Gentry Marry?: The Pastons, Plumptons and Stonors Reconsidered', in M. Jones (ed.), *Gentry and Lesser Nobility in Late Medieval Europe* (Gloucester, 1986), 61–80.

[25] Bickley (ed.), *Guild of Knowle*, 106 records John and Joan joining in 1493.

John had been prepared for the considerable demands of adult life by a period at school, as was his brother Thomas, who became a clergyman, and presumably his other two brothers. The school favoured by Roger for his sons is unknown. The nearest endowed grammar school was at Warwick, or they might have attended Stratford-upon-Avon school at a distance of 14 miles (which was attached to a fraternity of which Roger was a member), but as the boys would have had to live away from home they were not tied to the immediate locality.[26] John wrote his account book in English, with a few Latin words, so he had probably attended a grammar school long enough to pick up an acquaintance with Latin. After schooling, like so many of his contemporaries, John may have been sent to serve in a household, where he would gain useful experience in preparation for adult life. It would be almost pure speculation to suggest that a suitable placement for the son of a farmer, with ambitions for his children, would have been with the Palmers at Moreton in Marsh. This supposition is strengthened by the upbringing of John's sister Alice, who by 1501 was a servant in the household of Emote Fermor who belonged to a wealthy wool-dealing family at Witney in Oxfordshire.[27] While there she met Thomas Temple, a merchant of the same town, who became her husband. If Roger thought that his children would benefit from spending a few years familiarizing themselves with a woolman's business, he may well have selected the Palmers as suitable mentors for John.

Having dealt with the marriage of Agnes, Kathryn, and the elder Alice Heritage, and that of John himself, we are left with that of the second Alice, who was the youngest of the daughters. She was married to Robert Palmer, the son of Richard who died in 1496, and the brother of Joan Heritage. This appears to have been a match negotiated by John Heritage after his move to Moreton. 'My aunt Alice Palmer' was mentioned by John Heritage's son Thomas in 1534, and she died soon after. Thomas Heritage the elder, her brother, acted as her executor.[28]

Before pursuing John's life further, his brothers' careers need to be sketched. Two of them seem to have remained in the Burton area. William Heritage was living at Radway in 1514, and 'Heritage of Radway' is a figure in Warwickshire sheep-keeping in the mid- sixteenth century.[29] Edward Heritage is known to have bought in 1499 a holding of land at Broad Marston and Pebworth (on the Warwickshire/Worcestershire border) in partnership with another east Warwickshire landowner, John Makernes.[30] A Roger Heritage, who must have been a relative, was living at Kineton in Warwickshire, not far from Burton Dassett, in 1524, and the Kineton Heritages took in sheep from the Burton pasture in the 1540s.[31]

Thomas had the most remarkable upward ascent through the Church and State, incidentally revealing the importance of patronage that helped other members of

---

[26] N. Orme, *English Schools in the Middle Ages* (London, 1973), 205, 317–18.

[27] J. R. H. Weaver and A. Beardwood (eds), *Some Oxfordshire Wills*, Oxfordshire Record Society, 39 (1958), 70–1.

[28] *WGLS*, 118; TNA: PRO, REQ2 3/329.

[29] Bickley (ed.), *Guild of Knowle*, 222; *WGLS*, 93.

[30] C. R. Elrington (ed.), *Gloucestershire Feet of Fines*, Gloucestershire Record Series, forthcoming, 190.

[31] TNA: PRO, E179 192/122 m.13 (lay subsidy for Warwickshire); *WGLS*, 90, 125.

the family in more modest ways. He was presumably born around 1470, went to an unknown school, and then attended Oriel College, Oxford, where he remained as a fellow between 1500 and 1512. The patronage of the Belknaps, lords of the manor of Burton, may have helped his career at Oxford, but he did not remain there because after five years of poisonous quarrelling in his college, he was expelled from his fellowship. In a grovelling letter to the provost he referred to the assistance he would receive from his 'good lord', who may have been a member of the Spencer family, into which his sister had married. He certainly became rector of Great Brington in Northamptonshire, of which the patron was Sir John Spencer of Althorp. He accumulated many other benefices, and was promoted by Wolsey and Cromwell. His most important post was as Surveyor of the King's Works, in which position he administered the building of the royal palace of Whitehall. In the last year of his life, 1536–7, he was rector of Hackney and lived in the very large rectory.[32] He will be called Thomas the elder here to distinguish him from his nephew Thomas, John's son.

Thomas the elder and his nephew remained in contact with the Belknaps, and in 1532 on a visit to the Midlands they called on Alice, the widow of Edward Belknap (the son of William Belknap, lord of Burton in Roger Heritage's time) at her house at Weston under Wetherley. Through Gerard Dannett, Belknap's son-in-law and holder of part of the Belknap estate, a Leicestershire gentleman who was esquire of the body to both Henry VII and Henry VIII, Thomas Heritage the elder was put in touch with John Colet, the founder of St Paul's school. This presumably enabled Thomas the elder to arrange for Peter Temple, the son of Alice, his sister, who had married Thomas Temple, to gain a place at this progressive and prestigious establishment. He looked after the boy while he was living in London, paying for his lodgings, clothing, books, and other needs, and performed a similar service for four other nephews, the three sons of Agnes Spencer and John Barnes, Kathryn's son, who were attending either Eton or Westminster.[33]

We left John Heritage in Burton Dassett, taking over the farm, sorting out his father's affairs as executor of his will, and arranging the marriages of his sisters. In his mid-twenties, he was having to act on his own, as his mother had died shortly before his father, and he was the only executor of the will. His brother Thomas was away at university in Oxford, but could have been consulted on occasional visits, and the vicar of Burton, Master Thomas Knyght, may have been a source of advice. If John's wife Joan resembled some of her contemporaries, she knew about practical matters of estate management, and having experienced life in a wool trader's

[32] G. C. Richards and C. L. Shadwell, *The Provosts and Fellows of Oriel College, Oxford* (Oxford, 1922), 44; G. C. Richards and H. E. Salter (eds), *The Dean's Register of Oriel, 1445–1661*, Oxford Historical Society, 84 (1926), 8–35; *L and P*, 4, pt. 2, p. 1,940; pt. 4, p. 2,403; 5, pp. 116, 324, 449, 617, 747; H. M. Colvin (ed.), *The History of the King's Works*, 3 (London, 1975), 15, 20–1; A. B. Emden, *A Biographical Register of the University of Oxford to 1500*, 2 (Oxford, 1958), 917; Northamptonshire Record Office, Temple of Stowe, 40/6 (inventory of Hackney rectory). Thomas Heritage's possessions are listed in fifteen rooms.

[33] R. Bowers, 'Schooling and the Sons of Midlands Gentry in the Early Sixteenth Century', unpublished paper, citing mostly WAM 12257. The visit to Alice Belknap in 1532–3 is in fo.24r.

house she could make commercial decisions.[34] The years 1495–7 presented John with challenges and opportunities, which were to change his life in drastic ways. A number of simultaneous events were transforming his circumstances at the same time that he was recovering from the upheaval following his father's death. His father's landlord, William Belknap, had died in 1488 leaving a seventeen-year-old son Edward, who took over the management of the estate in the 1490s. In 1496 he became sole lord of the manor with the agreement of Sir John Norbury. He had ideas for improving the manor, which must have been agreed with John Heritage; it is even possible that the new thinking began with John. We can envisage two ambitious young men, who had grown impatient with the old-fashioned ways of their fathers, and could see radical changes that would improve the profitability of Burton, for the benefit of both the landlord and the farmer. In May 1497 Edward leased 'all the closes of the township of Burton' 'with a field adjoining' to John for forty-one years for an annual rent of £21, and in the following summer of 1497, according to the report made to the enclosure commissions twenty years later, he forced the inhabitants to leave twelve messuages (houses). A total of 360 acres (30 acres per holding) was enclosed with 'fences and ditches' and converted from cultivation to pasture 'of brute beasts'.

Apparently the former open fields, which were surrounded by hedges already as they had to be closed off temporarily each year to protect the growing crops, became the new closes as the hedges were turned into permanent barriers, preventing access by the villagers. The sixty people who had worked the land and lived in the houses had to leave and wander, according to the highly coloured account of the enclosure commission, in a state of idleness.[35] Two days before the lease, John sold a messuage and 1 ¾ yardlands (50 acres) of freehold land to Belknap.[36] This was necessary as the strips of land in this holding were mingled in the open fields that were to be turned into closes. Heritage was showing his disregard for tradition by selling the family's holding, including presumably the house in which the Heritages had lived. He was said to be formerly of Burton, so the house had been vacated. The enclosed pasture was a valuable asset that would bring in high returns from the sale of wool and livestock, at a reasonable rent. Evidence from a generation later shows that Burton had been divided up into a number of farms, one of which was known as 'Heritage Field', with others known by such names as Town Field and Old Leys (see Fig. 2.1).[37]

After this coup John and Joan might have settled in a new house in Burton and lived long and well from the proceeds of their productive farm. Their circumstances changed, however, because Richard Palmer of Moreton in Marsh had died in the autumn of 1496. Joan and John were summoned to the bedside of the dying man, at which John witnessed the will. Richard Palmer left Joan a burgage in

---

[34] There are many examples of capable women managers among the gentry, and hints of it at a lower social level: M. E. Mate, *Daughters, Wives and Widows after the Black Death: Women in Sussex, 1350–1535* (Woodbridge, 1998), 140–3, 158–60, 182–3.
[35] *WGLS*, 31–8; *Dom. Inc.*, 2, 424–5.   [36] *WGLS*, 33.   [37] *ibid*, 37–8.

Moreton, that is, a house with business premises facing onto the town's main street.[38] It would have been a matter of routine property management to find a tenant for the house and make arrangements to collect the rent, but instead John and Joan soon moved to Moreton, and by 1500, when an outline of his first accounts survives, he was well-established as a trader in wool. In reversal of the normal pattern of a wife leaving her family home to live with her husband, as Joan had done in about 1492, John uprooted himself to move to his wife's home town. In doing so he changed his whole way of life, moving from country to town, and from farming to trade (or rather, to a combination of trading and farming). The farm at Burton had to be delegated to a shepherd, and Heritage would have to supervise from a distance the management of the seven hundred to a thousand sheep that he kept there. There may have been personal considerations: perhaps Joan was especially anxious to return to her family, or perhaps the depopulation of Burton promised a legacy of problems. In the vicinity of Moreton he soon acquired a pasture on lease at Upper Ditchford in Blockley, shared with other tenants, and was keeping sheep at many places within a few miles of Moreton.

While John Heritage was dealing with the affairs of his father, his will, and his brothers and sisters, he was also creating a family of his own, though it seems to have been relatively small. His daughter Elizabeth was alive in 1520; and she married Richard Fretherne of Adlestrop, who was called his 'brother' by Thomas Heritage the younger in 1533.[39] Two sons are recorded, Richard who stayed at home and died young, and Thomas who had a very successful career in London. Richard had been born by 1496, and makes an appearance in court in 1514 for involvement in an affray in Moreton. A Richard Heritage makes an appearance in the account book, but it may be a Warwickshire relative of that name.[40] Richard was apparently dead by about 1520, when an unknown hand, possibly that of Thomas the younger, wrote a sentence in John's account book asking for God's mercy on his soul.[41] Thomas was born in about 1500. In 1507 John Heritage paid 15*s* 6*d* for 'boarding of my children', which might imply that some of them were at school, perhaps at Chipping Campden or Chipping Norton, both of which grammar schools had been founded in the mid-fifteenth century.[42]

The boarding charge may have been paid for Thomas who had reached the age of seven when schooling began. One of the benefits that he gained was a clearer and neater handwriting than his father's, though he may have acquired that from his mother before embarking on formal education. He went on in his teens to be apprenticed to a London skinner, probably in 1516 or soon after, and he became a

---

[38] TNA: PRO, PROB 11/10, fo.41r. The property was called Irenmonger House, and attached to it was a *quartron* (quarter yardland) of land.

[39] Elizabeth was mentioned in Joan Heritage's draft will, which may have been made *c.*1520: AB, fo.87v; *WGLS*, 120.

[40] In Richard Palmer's will the Moreton property was bequeathed to Joan and her son Richard (1496); he appears in Moreton court in WAM 8365, and 'Richard Heritage' appears in the account books AB, fo.25r and 75r.

[41] AB, fo.76v.

[42] AB, fo.92v; Orme, *English Schools*, 203, 205, 206, 217, 299.

fully fledged member of the Skinners' Company in 1524–5.[43] The chief concern of skinners had originally been the import of furs and skin and making of fur garments.[44] Like many London companies, however, their members diversified into varied activities, and Thomas Heritage is revealed from his own account book in the 1530s buying wool in the Midlands and Hertfordshire, sending into the Midlands miscellaneous goods from London such as tar, cloth, spices, fish, and even a hat. He dealt in large quantities of Spanish iron. The base of his Midland operations was still Burton Dassett, where he kept in 1533–6 more than six hundred sheep and one hundred cattle, all in the charge of local agents. He bought wool around Burton, but also across Warwickshire from Coughton in the west to Ryton on Dunsmore in the east. He still retained important contacts with his father's former country, as he bought wool fells in Broad Campden and refers to purchases from 'my cousin Mab Palmer', and he supplied tar to his brother-in-law Richard Fretherne. His agent for the payment of money in 1534 to a Campden trader was 'my aunt Alice Palmer'.[45] Thomas held property in Moreton in Marsh in 1538, perhaps his father's former house.[46] He married a London widow after 1532, and died in 1541 when he appears to have been well-off, having a house with seven rooms, but he was not very rich as his inventory reached a total of £131.[47]

The later stages of John Heritage's life are a complete mystery. The last entries in his account book are dated to 1520, and he must have left the Moreton area as he does not appear in the Gloucestershire military survey of 1522 or the lay subsidies of 1524–5, or any other local records.[48] Joan Heritage left a draft of a will of which only part survives interpolated into the account book, which might suggest that she died by 1520, but people often made wills many years before they died.[49] A statement in Thomas junior's commercial account book beginning in 1532 refers to a payment to Robert Raymand that was made 'at my father's house without Cripplegate', 'my father and my mother and my wife being by', which contradicts the supposition that she had died much earlier.[50] Thomas's more personal account book of 1531–3, which focused on his dealings with his uncle Thomas, makes no reference to either John or Joan, but if money was not involved, he had no need to mention them.[51]

---

[43] On mothers as teachers of reading, N. Orme, *Medieval Children* (New Haven, CT, 2001), 243–5; *WGLS*, 18.

[44] E. M. Veale, *The English Fur Trade in the Later Middle Ages* (Oxford, 1966). A point of contact between skinners and the wool trade was the trade in wool fells, that is, sheepskins: J. J. Lambert, *Records of the Skinners of London, Edward I to James I* (London, 1933), 25.

[45] *WGLS*, 117, 118, 120, 121, for the references to the Campden and Moreton districts. He had a servant called John Palmer in 1531–2, WAM, 12257*.

[46] GA, CMS 64 (Moreton court roll).

[47] *WGLS*, 18.

[48] The John Heritage who appears in the military survey of 1522 at Chadshunt (Warwickshire) near Burton Dassett was probably a nephew, TNA: PRO, SC12/16/10.

[49] AB, 87v.

[50] *WGLS*, 120.

[51] WAM 12257*. A considerable number of documents that might throw light on John Heritage's residence, focused on Cripplegate, have not yielded any trace of his presence. The search was guided by D. Keene and V. Harding, *A Survey of Documentary Sources for Property Holding in London before the Great Fire*, London Record Society, 22 (1985).

Not even a brief account of John Heritage is complete without more attention being given to the Palmer family, with whom his life was so closely intertwined (Fig. 2.3). (Readers should be warned that the family had many branches and used a limited range of first names, so they are difficult to disentangle, and they might wish to move to the next page.) A Richard Palmer of Moreton in Marsh was active in that town in 1461–2, and in the latter year he bought a burgage to add to his existing properties. A man of the same name, who could have been the same man, died in 1496, and the division of his inheritance between his children Robert, Agnes, and Joan precipitated (as we have seen) John Heritage's move to Moreton to occupy the burgage that his wife had inherited.[52] Robert took over as the leading member of the family in Moreton, and had a woolhouse from which he conducted a business similar to John Heritage's, and also kept sheep on rented pastures. He was married to Alice, John Heritage's youngest sister, as we have noticed.

More Palmers lived at Lower Lemington to the east of Moreton, and they enjoyed superior wealth and status. John Palmer, who could have been Joan Heritage's nephew, is described in John Heritage's time as a gentleman, and his wife Mary was the sister of William Greville of Arle, who held among other properties the manor of Upper Lemington.[53] The family legend recorded in about 1540 was

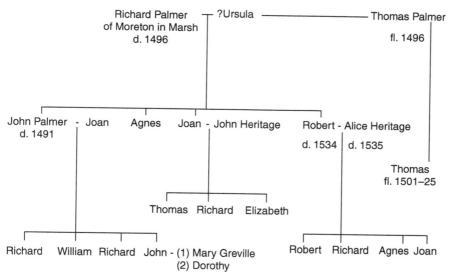

Fig. 2.3. Palmer family tree.

Sources: TNA: PRO, PROB 11/9, fos. 39v–40r; PROB 11/10, fo.41r; PROB 11/25, fo.73v; Bickley (ed.), *Guild of Knowle*, 175; information from N. W. Alcock.

---

[52] WAM 8360: in a court held 27 April 1462 Richard Palmer was a juror and affeeror; will: TNA: PRO PROB 11/10, fo.41r.

[53] *MSG*, 171; Bickley (ed.), *Guild of Knowle*, 175.

that 'Palmer of Lemington' 'began with a very small portion of land, and being a gallant fellow, and clothed in mighty colours, got a rich widow in Lemington to wife'.[54] This might refer to the John Palmer that Heritage knew, who had married a rich woman from Lemington, but the legend may relate to an earlier generation, as Leland dated the marriage before 1460, 'eighty years or more hence'. John Heritage in his accounts calls both John and Mary 'cousin', which was used in a general sense for a relative.[55] We might be tempted to think that the status-conscious John Heritage was rather anxious to emphasize his close connection with the landed gentry. A third line of Palmers were based on Bourton on the Hill. A fourth branch of the family is represented by Thomas Palmer, who lived at Moreton, and could have been the son of a Thomas Palmer who was Richard's brother. He had a very close business relationship with John Heritage, which lasted from 1502 to 1515. The recorded connections between the Palmers and the Heritages may have gone back to Roger's days in the early 1490s, and in the early 1530s the John Palmer who worked for Thomas Heritage junior in London as a 'servant' (a trusted agent in commercial matters) may have been recruited from the Gloucestershire family.[56]

John Heritage had been absorbed into the social and commercial network of the Palmers, firstly when he married Joan, but more decisively and completely when he moved to Moreton. He was helped in his early years by his brother-in-law and cousins. For example, in 1502 John Palmer of Lemington sold him more than 6 sacks of wool in one of the largest deals of Heritage's career, but no more sales followed.[57] Tensions within the family may have resulted from the social divide between the gentry Palmers of Lemington and the others who were rated as yeomen and husbandmen. The descendants of Robert and Alice were accounted gentry in the late sixteenth century, and acquired local manors such as Bourton on the Hill, and Compton Scorpion in the parish of Ilmington.[58] John Heritage and his brother-in-law Robert Palmer were in direct competition in the wool trade, which could have made for some uncomfortable moments. Just as his brother Thomas encountered problems in dealing with the fellows of Oriel College, John may well have had difficulties with the Palmer cousinage.

A number of the Palmers give the impression of having been 'gallant fellows', 'clothed in mighty colours', and gave a high priority to improving their fortunes. Two incidents suggest that the Palmers gained a reputation for behaving selfishly and even unscrupulously. Robert Palmer of Moreton in Marsh, who died in 1534, left much of his goods and property to his wife Alice (Heritage) and his two sons Robert and Richard.[59] He also looked after his two daughters Agnes and Joan by arranging that half of his 'household stuff' should be divided equally between them, and that each should also receive a burgage in Moreton. They were being treated as equals, except that

[54] L. Toulmin Smith (ed.), *Leland's Itinerary in England and Wales*, 4 (London, 1909), 79.
[55] AB, fos.1r, 84v.   [56] WAM, 12257, fo.29v.   [57] AB, fo.8v.
[58] *VCH Glos*, VI, 200; *VCH Warwicks*, V, 100.   [59] TNA: PRO REQ 2, 3/329.

Agnes was left £20 in cash but Joan received no money at all. His eldest son and sole executor, Robert Palmer of Blockley, was said to have withheld Joan's £20. The interests of this girl, who had reached the age of ten at the time of her father's death, were defended by Thomas Heritage the elder. He was acting as executor for the will of Alice, his youngest sister, who had died soon after her husband, leaving Thomas the responsibility of being Joan's guardian. Thomas, who must have been well informed about the law, took the case to the Court of Requests and demanded that Robert Palmer of Blockley, as his father's executor, should pay the £20 to him as Joan's guardian.[60] Attached to the copy of the will in the register of the Prerogative Court of Canterbury is a statement that Thomas Heritage had seen it, and then is added a sentence: 'Item I give and bequeath to Joan Palmer my daughter £20 of lawful money of England.' This is an afterthought and presumably tells us the words that Heritage thought should have been in the will. A modern observer would assume that the older Robert Palmer intended to treat his daughters equally in every respect, and the bequest of cash to Joan was omitted by accident. He surely could not have formed an uncharitable attitude towards a ten-year-old. The younger Robert was intransigent in the matter, as he must have been given many opportunities to be generous and correct the error in favour of his young and vulnerable sister. He appears to have been acting selfishly and lacking in charity by refusing to budge, even to the point that he incurred all of the trouble and expense of a court case.

In his pleading Thomas Heritage showed that there was no shortage of funds from which to pay the bequest. He alleged that the deceased Robert Palmer of Moreton had goods and chattels worth £1,000. It was in Thomas's interests to exaggerate the wealth of Robert, but he would only have made the estimate if it was plausible, and the military survey of 1522 confirms that Robert was very rich by assessing his goods at £466 13s 4d, which would have been an underestimate.[61] Alice, whose possessions were worth £80, had bequeathed the remainder of her goods to Joan after various specific bequests ('small parcels and sums of money') had been paid, and Alice's favouritism towards her youngest daughter may explain Robert the younger's unsympathetic attitude towards his sister. Alice, however, was no doubt using her will to put right the injustice of the unequal treatment of the two daughters by her husband.

Others thought ill of members of the Palmer family. A few years later a case came before chancery concerning the leases of the tithes of Moreton in Marsh and Bourton on the Hill.[62] John Smyth held the leases for a term of twenty years, but he granted them to be divided between Robert Damport and Richard Palmer, both of Moreton. The document was delivered to Palmer, with the intention that two separate leases be drawn up for the two new tenants, but Richard 'of his crafty mind doth withhold the said indenture', perhaps with the intention of reserving all of the tithes for himself.

---

[60] *ibid.*   [61] *MSG*, 179.   [62] TNA: PRO, C1/976/3.

Before leaving the Heritage family and their associates, a general point needs to be made about their social rank. John Heritage was described as a yeoman in 1507, and this would have been the term applied to most of his relatives and associates. Yeomen are best defined as the top layer of the peasantry, because they lived from their holdings of land and sometimes trade, but had no claim to gentility, which was judged by a number of yardsticks.

As a minimum a gentleman possessed a quantity of freehold land, and ideally was the lord of at least a small manor with a manorial court. John Heritage, his father, his brothers William and Edward, Robert Palmer his brother-in-law, Thomas Palmer his business partner, and John Freman of Batsford with whom he leased the pasture at Blockley, were all accounted yeomen. They were wealthy in terms of their goods and lands – we have heard that Robert Palmer was reputed to have had goods worth £1,000, and we find yeomen from the villages around Moreton with goods valued at £80–£100 in the assessment for the military survey of 1522, including Thomas Palmer of Moreton.[63] A number of them must have had an income from agriculture of £20, which was similar to the income of many gentlemen, but it was not the size of the income but the way in which it was obtained that was all-important. Of similar wealth were merchants such as Thomas Davies and Thomas Alen of Stow on the Wold. All of these people would have sublet land, and collected rents from tenants, but these holdings did not constitute a manor. Although they employed servants, kept households with eight or ten members, and lived in sizeable houses, they still engaged continuously in trade, and may themselves occasionally have worked with their hands – they could have helped to drive sheep at shearing, for example. They found their own level of administrative responsibility, serving in manorial administration as bailiffs and in manorial courts as jurors.[64]

By contrast the gentry that they encountered were manorial lords: one branch of the Grevilles held Upper Lemington, another Sezincote and Meon; the Belknaps had Whitchurch and the Fortescues Ebrington, Hidcote Boyce, one of the Bourton on the Hill manors, and part of Condicote. Their income, which came mainly from rents, was habitually underestimated in the tax returns, but in 1522, to take an example, Adrian Fortescue was assessed on a landed income of £51 per annum from lands in Gloucestershire.[65] The gentry made money as lawyers, notably William Greville of Arle and Lemington, who was a judge, or they were employed as high-powered estate administrators, like John Hornyhold as receiver of the bishops of Worcester. They served the Crown on judicial commissions (Greville and Belknap) or supervised tax collection (John Palmer), which earned them prestige, not an

---

[63] *MSG*, 221 (e.g. Richard Colchester of Lark Stoke £100); 225 (William Kyte of Ebrington £80); 180 (Nicholas Willington of Todenham £100).

[64] R. Almond and A. J. Pollard, 'The Yeomanry of Robin Hood and Social Terminology in Fifteenth-Century England', *Past and Present*, 170 (2001), 54–6; on administrative roles elsewhere: C. M. Newman, *Late Medieval Northallerton: A Small Market Town and its Hinterland c.1470–1540* (Stamford, 1999), 117–24.

[65] *MSG*, 30, 146, 178, 217.

income.[66] Their lifestyle, which involved no manual work, could have included hunting and socializing in Gloucester, Oxford, Warwick, or Worcester when the county court was being held. Most of them simply sold their wool to merchants, though around 1480 William Stonor, a predecessor of the Fortescues in their Gloucestershire manors, was trading on a large scale, both buying wool locally and shipping it to Calais. For him engagement in trade was not regarded as demeaning, though most of his income came from a large landed estate.[67] John Heritage in his account book showed his sensitivity to social distinctions by reserving the title 'Master' for the gentry he encountered: 'Master Greville', 'Master Daston', and so on. He used the same title for the parish clergy, as in 'Master vicar of Longborough', and for the important London merchants such as 'Master Brown'.

THE HERITAGE FAMILY IN CONTEXT

As we have followed the fortunes of the Heritage family, reference has been made to the general history of families in this period, but a more systematic comparison can be made with families living in the countryside and towns around Moreton in Marsh. Questions include the nature of family life, such as the formation and composition of the household, the relationships within families, inheritance, and the structure and stability of the family. The evidence comes mainly from fifty-eight wills between 1491 and 1538 from the Prerogative Court of Canterbury and the diocese of Worcester.

To begin with the formation of the household, John Heritage has been seen to have married in his early or mid-twenties after an episode of education at school and a period when he could have helped to run the Burton farm. In addition to this practical training at home, he might have gone to another household to gain experience as a servant, as did Alice his sister in the household of the Fermors of Witney. This period of preparation for adult life was more formalized in the case of his brother Thomas, who spent his teens and twenties at school and university in anticipation of a clerical career, and Thomas the younger who served a long apprenticeship to qualify as a skinner. Thomas the elder was of course celibate, but the others married only after their period of education and work experience, well into their twenties. Contemporary wills sometimes contemplated an earlier age when children might marry and establish an independent household. Richard Freman of Todenham, in making a bequest to his daughters in 1535, believed that they might marry before they reached the age of twenty. The gentry arranged marriages among very young children, like the contract in 1500 that John Russell would marry Ann Greville from the Milcote branch of the family when she reached the age of fourteen.[68]

[66] C. Dyer, *Lords and Peasants in a Changing Society: The Estates of the Bishopric of Worcester 680–1540* (Cambridge, 1980), 384; *L and P*, I, p. 31, 57, 134; *Calendar of Patent Rolls, Henry VII*, 280, 456, 459, 591.

[67] E. Noble, *The World of the Stonors: A Gentry Society* (Woodbridge, 2009), 96–7.

[68] TNA: PRO, PROB 11/26, fos.26r–26v; Centre for Kentish Studies, Sackville of Knole, U269, T176/6.

As the age of marriage is rarely documented, the frequent recording of servants provides some evidence for regarding the Heritage's pattern of late marriage as typical. The servants are worth considering in their own right as they formed an integral part of households, living with their employers on an annual contract and receiving as a major part of their reward food, drink, shelter, and sometimes clothing.[69] The wills mention servants who were presumably young and expected to marry in the future, like two employees of John Freman of Great Rollright in 1491 who would receive six sheep each when they were married.[70] They could be numerous in wealthier households: Roger Heritage had six, Edmund Bradwey of Blockley in 1493 at least four, and four are named in John Willington of Todenham's will in 1512.[71] They appear in limited numbers in the tax lists, mainly because their lack of wealth set them below the bottom threshold of taxpayers, but nonetheless they appear occasionally in respectable quantities like the eight servants among the twenty taxpayers at Weston Subedge in 1525.[72]

'Servant' was a general term covering a wide range of people. It might include low-status individuals, often young, doing menial or unskilled work, who appear in wills anonymously and who received only a modest reward. We know from elsewhere that they tended to be birds of passage who stayed for a year or two with one employer before moving off in search of something better. People with such transient habits may be included among the five young men at Todenham in 1509 who were aged over fourteen years but were not yet 'sworn into assize', that is, they had not been included in the tithing system which was supposed to maintain good order.[73] One of them was evidently the son of a villager, but the others bore strange names and were probably incomers. The term 'servant' also extended to cover more highly regarded employees, like Thomas Kytlett of Great Rollright who was offered by his master's will £6 13s 4d if he would stay for three years serving his employer's widow. A gentleman testator in 1516 left to a servant of whom he must have had a high opinion a colt and twenty sheep.[74] Service was important in the higher levels of society. The son of a gentleman, Henry Durant of Barcheston, in the early years of the sixteenth century recounted his early career as a ward of Hugh Clopton, mayor of London and a member of a local landed family, from the age of nine until twenty-four, and then as a servant to Sir Robert Throckmorton and after that with the Marquis of Dorset.[75] Below the gentry a servant could be a relative, as in the phrase 'son and servant' found in the poll taxes. If this phrase conveys a picture of a disciplined household, the opposite is suggested by the order in the court at Broadway in 1512 that 'the servants and the sons' of the brewers should not play

---

[69] On this 'life-cycle' view of servants, P. J. P. Goldberg, *Women, Work and Life Cycle in a Medieval Economy: Women in York and Yorkshire c.1300–1520* (Oxford, 1992), 158–202.

[70] Weaver and Beardwood (eds), *Oxfordshire Wills*, 47.

[71] TNA: PRO, PROB 11/10, fo.231v; fo.46r; WRO, BA 3590/2-3, fos. 40v–41v.

[72] *B & GLS*, 419.

[73] WAM 8364 (Todenham court roll). The transient servants in husbandry in later centuries are discussed in A. Kussmaul, *Servants in Husbandry in Early Modern Britain* (Cambridge, 1981).

[74] Weaver and Beardwood (eds), *Oxfordshire Wills*, 47; TNA: PRO, PROB 11/18, fos.271v–272r.

[75] WCRO, CR580/11 (Barcheston deeds).

at gaming boards in the house after noon. Sons could escape, as is apparent from a court case in 1501 when Thomas Taylor of Chipping Norton complained that an ironmonger had induced Thomas Taylor junior to leave his service.[76]

'Servant' took on another dimension in the household of John Heritage and among the employees of his many business contacts. When he paid for wool, and hundreds of such transactions are recorded, he sometimes recorded the person who made the payment or the person who received it (Table 2.1). In twenty-three cases one of his own servants handed over the money, and in twenty-nine cases the money was received by one of his clients' servants. These are probably just a small proportion of the total of transactions involving servants, as in many cases he memorizes the event not by noting the person who made or received the payment, but by recording the date or place for the payment, and servants may well have been involved in some of these. The implication of these records is that servants enjoyed a high level of trust. A creditor must have knocked on Heritage's door, and, in the absence of his employer or his wife, the servant had access to a chest or purse from which a payment could be made. We know the names of John Heritage's servants sometimes – Felpys in 1501–2, Haukis in 1508, and 'my servant Richard' in 1514–16. John provided Richard with a livery gown, perhaps a sign of regard. On the other side of the transactions the wool growers trusted their servants, a few of them young women, to take the cash. Heritage's servants seem to have been young men from a reputable background of similar standing to their employer, like Heritage's 'Felpys' who may have been a member of the prosperous Phelpys family of Batsford.[77] Occasional entries in the account book in a hand other than Heritage's may have been made by a family member, but a literate servant may have assumed that responsibility. These servants were learning a trade before moving on to some more independent position; they may even have begun

Table 2.1. Family and household in John Heritage's business transactions, 1501–20.

	Servant	Wife	Son	Daughter	Brother	Mother	Other	Total
Payments made by John Heritage's family and household	23	16	–	–	–	–	1	40
Family members and servants receiving payments from John Heritage	29	8	37	6	7	2	2	92

Note: The figures relate to the occasions when money was given out by identifiable people other than Heritage himself, and the occasions when money was taken by people other than the suppliers of wool who were being paid in instalments.

Source: AB.

---

[76] TNA: PRO, SC2 210/33 (Broadway court rolls); P. R. Cavill, 'The Problem of Labour and the Parliament of 1495', in L. Clark (ed.), *The Fifteenth Century*, 5 (2005), 143–55, esp. 147.

[77] For the Phelpys family, *MSG*, 216.

to establish their economic independence while still in service, as 'my servant Richard' in 1514 sold enough wool to his employer to suggest that he was keeping forty sheep.[78]

There is nothing here to contradict the conventional view that an episode as a servant formed part of the experience of many young men and women, and marriage was often delayed until after a period of work and training. This beginning in adult life enabled people in their twenties to acquire a skill or a job or that could form a stable basis for a new household. When it came to marriage, Roger Heritage was not the only stern father to demand that his daughters should only marry under close supervision, as Richard Freman of Todenham in 1535 expected his daughters to be 'ruled, ordered and guided' in this important matter.[79]

Marriage provided the means for raising and caring for children, who might themselves in turn give some support to elderly or disabled parents, if they lived so long. The numbers of children alive at the point when their father or mother died, when they were mentioned in wills, is recorded in Table 2.2, which analyses the five Heritage and Palmer families for which we have a will, and the rest of the will makers from the vicinity, excluding clergymen and those who were unmarried or too young to have children. The predominance of sons, which is found in any medieval listing, could have been the result of the omission of some daughters, so a correction has been made to calculate family size on the basis of an equal number of children of both genders. These families are quite large by the standards of the period: occasional listings and other samples based on wills tended to produce an average below three children per family (after correction).[80] The figures presented here are, in the case of the Heritage/Palmer group, distorted by the unusually large number of children reared by Elizabeth and Roger Heritage, but in general reflect the wealth of those whose wills were proved before the court of Canterbury. Children with more affluent parents,

Table 2.2. Size of families, 1490–1538.

Number of families	sons	daughters	total	mean no. children	mean no. children (corrected)
Heritage/Palmer 5	13	9	22	4.4	5.2
Whole sample from Heritage's country 46	78	67	145	3.2	3.4

Source: Prerogative Court of Canterbury wills (TNA: PRO, PROB); Worcester wills; Weaver and Beardwood (eds), *Oxfordshire Wills*; AB, fo. 87v.

[78] AB, fo.60r.
[79] TNA: PRO, PROB 11/26, fos.26r–26v.
[80] E. A. Wrigley and R. Schofield, *English Population History from Family Reconstitution* (Cambridge, 1997), 614; C. Phythian-Adams, *Desolation of a City: Coventry and the Urban Crisis of the Later Middle Ages* (Cambridge, 1979), 221–37.

who lived in large and well-constructed houses, had a better chance of survival because they were better fed and sheltered than the general population.

Households, then, were formed by the union of two people who had experience of life and had the means to support themselves and children born to them. The household among better-off yeomen and traders consisted of a husband, wife, three or four children, and a servant or two. The tendency among modern commentators, conscious as we are of the fractured and discordant nature of many families in our own time, is to regard the pre-industrial household as strong and cohesive, based on strong ties of loyalty. We have already noticed the evidence for bonds of trust and even affection between employers and servants. Analysis of the cash transactions handled by members of Heritage's household and the households of those who supplied him with wool (see Table 2.2) also reveals the participation of wives, sons, daughters, and occasionally other family members in the conduct of trade. Heritage's wife was fully involved, but not his sons, because Thomas was away in London and Richard may not have been at home. The sons of Heritage's clients were obviously expected to take responsibility for the payments when they arrived at the door or in the street or even in the field. One is given the impression of households in which everyone was committed to the common enterprise, and presumably participated in the work of the farm as well as the handling of money.

Women were expected to play their part, whether maids, daughters, or wives. Heritage sometimes uses the positive phrase 'good wife'. Farms and businesses were managed by wives in their husbands' absence, in London for example, and women in widowhood would routinely act as the executors of their husband's will, and would expect to maintain the continuity of family enterprises.[81] Widows did not just manage the farm after their husbands' death, but they also entered into new contracts, together with a son, presuming that he would eventually succeed. So the lease of the Ebrington demesne was granted in 1487 to Marion Kyte and her son William, and Agnes and John Fletcher took on the lease of Upper Swell in 1500. Sometimes the woman acted on her own, as when Alice Willington in 1527 became lessee of the Todenham demesne for twenty years. An exceptional inheritance at Bourton on the Hill in 1512 made Margaret Stevens a tenant of her late husband's holding, but she also took over his office as manorial rent collector. Normally women by custom were not able to occupy such an office.[82]

The records of John Heritage's wool purchases underline the impression of the integration of wives and relations into the family economy. For example, William Hosyar sold his wool to Heritage between 1501 and 1505. In 1506 the wool was supplied by 'Hosyar's wife', and in 1507 by Joan Hosyar. We do not know whether William had died or had become unwell, but his wife seems to have managed the

---

[81] C. M. Barron, 'Introduction: the Widow's World', in C. M. Barron and A. F. Sutton (eds), *Medieval London Widows 1300–1500* (London, 1994), xxvii–xxxiv; M. McIntosh, 'Women, Credit and Family Relations', *Journal of Family History*, 30 (2005), 143–63. On the general point that families played a part in early capitalism, R. Grassby, *Kinship and Capitalism* (Cambridge, 2001).

[82] Devon Record Office, Fortescue papers, 1262M, Glos leases E1; TNA: PRO, SC2 175/77; SC6/ Henry VIII 7238 (Westminster Abbey account).

holding effectively, though the annual yield fell a little from just over 4 tods to just below that amount. Another type of family association brought fathers and sons together as suppliers of wool, after the younger generation had formed new separate households. John Persons, senior and junior, John Nelme senior and junior (of Bourton on the Hill), and various members of the Bumpas, Jurdan, Mansell, and Perte families all suggest that once Heritage had made a contract with one family member, others would follow suit.

Systems of inheritance also strengthen the view that families practised mutual support. Wills, reflecting arrangements among the better off, observe the convention that wives should be provided at least with a house and household goods, and often with land as well. Of thirty non-gentry wills that make provision for widows, thirteen mention bequests of land, and seventeen just goods or cash, or goods and cash. Those who are not specifically bequeathed land or a house may well have received property in accordance with custom, or through some separate arrangement. The wills show that inheritance among the children was partly governed by custom, though they could be modified by the testator. There were thirteen apparent cases of inheritance of land and/or goods by the eldest son, primogeniture, which was an easy choice in four cases because there was only one son. This was apparently the arrangement that gave John Heritage such a good start in life, because he inherited the lease, the farming equipment, and livestock, and his brothers and sisters all received cash. Among the other wills, at least two testators observed the convention that land acquired in the father's lifetime should go to the second son, while the eldest received the land inherited by the father.[83] In at least twelve cases the testator pursued the goal of dividing the inheritance among all the children, perhaps giving preference to one son, but ensuring that each child received at least a small piece of land as well as goods and money. This was the practice of the Palmer family. John Palmer of Moreton in Marsh in 1491 left to his eldest son 'the house in which I live' and nearby land, and a wool house, his main business premises, but also provided all three of the younger sons with property.[84] Some fathers left land to their sons, but cash for the daughters. Sums of money that ranged between £6 13s 4d and £13 6s 8d gave a young woman the basis for negotiating a good marriage.

Most heirs of landed property were members of the nuclear family, who were either part of the household or had lived with their parents for a long period. An example of a more remote relative earning his inheritance was William Wilkes of Blockley, who was granted landed property and the residue of goods and cash by Thomas Wilkes in 1512.[85] Thomas had no surviving children and William, who may have been a nephew, was 'now living with me', and presumably had worked

---

[83] On acquisitions, M. Spufford, 'Peasant Inheritance Customs and Land Distribution in Cambridgeshire from the Sixteenth to the Eighteenth Centuries', in J. Goody, J. Thirsk, and E. P. Thompson (eds), *Family and Inheritance: Rural Society in Western Europe 1200–1800* (Cambridge, 1976), 164–8.

[84] TNA: PRO, PROB 11/9, fos.39v–40r. Caution on using wills as the sole source for inheritance: J. Whittle, *The Development of Agrarian Capitalism: Land and Labour in Norfolk 1440–1580* (Oxford, 2000), 144–50.

[85] WRO, BA 3950/I, ref.008:7, vol.2, fo.46v.

on the holding in the way that a son would have done. Just like a trusted son, William was also nominated as sole executor, with, incidentally, John Heritage as the overseer. Other childless testators made more remote relatives their heirs, like Thomas Davies's 'kinsman' (in 1511) and Thomas Alen's cousin (in 1506). These were both merchants of Stow on the Wold.[86]

Most relatives from outside the nuclear family were not major heirs, but acted as executors, like Thomas Davies's sister in 1511, or they received a small bequest, most remarkably in a will also of 1511 whereby sheep (one to each beneficiary) went to 'everyone in four degrees of consanguinity'.[87] The great majority of the fifty-two lay testators studied here had heirs to succeed them, though in some cases their circumstances are unclear. Three had no children, three had daughters only, and forty-one had sons. The wills show the family could provide a system of support. Husbands looked after their wives, fathers helped all of their children, even practising a form of partible inheritance in a region where that custom was not part of the tradition. The younger generation were sometimes being rewarded for the help that they had given to their parents. This may, however, reflect to some extent the literary genre to which the will belonged, with its many commonplace phrases ('whole in mind, sick in body', for example).[88] Will makers were drawn by convention into expressing positive sentiments about family obligations, and they only rarely revealed some of the tensions and antagonisms.

We need to modify this rather idealistic picture of mutually supportive households in the light of contemporary concern for parental authority and in particular for the rule of the father. We have observed Roger Heritage's meal table, dominated by the occupant of the single chair at the head, and his will, like others of the same period, seeking to control the behaviour of his children from beyond the grave. Thomas More, writing *Utopia* in *c*.1515, advocated ideal households in which wives and children helped the male head, and the young were subordinate to the old.[89] These admonitions were of course necessary because in the eyes of those in authority, children were headstrong and disrespectful, and wives sought excessive independence. There were obvious complexities in families which often had to cope with the premature death of either mother or father. Husbands who had remarried had to decide when they made their wills, as they had presumably done during life, what attention they should pay to stepchildren, and some of their decisions reflect a discrimination that must have caused resentments. Edmund Bradwey of Blockley in 1493 left his goods to be divided equally between his own two sons, but bequeathed to his stepchildren two sheep each, which was at least a better deal than the one sheep each received by his servants.[90] They probably received more

---

[86] TNA: PRO, PROB 11/17, fos.16v–17r; PROB 11/15, fo.192r.

[87] TNA: PRO, PROB 11/17, fo.43v.

[88] M. Zell, 'Fifteenth- and Sixteenth-Century Wills as Historical Sources', *Archives*, 14 (1979), 61–74; T. Arkell, N. Evans, and N. Goose (eds), *When Death Us Do Part: Understanding and Interpreting the Probate Records of Early Modern England* (Oxford, 2000).

[89] G. M. Logan and R. M. Adams (eds), *Thomas More: Utopia* (Cambridge, 1989), 55–9; see Hartman, *Household and the Making of History*, 34–8.

[90] TNA: PRO, PROB 11/10, fo.46r.

substantial bequests from their father's relatives. Family stability depended on standards of conduct normally enforced in the Church courts (but in our case no records survive) and occasionally in the manor courts, which relied for their information on the reports of neighbours. So at Adlestrop in 1501 Thomas Broke aroused the disapproval of his fellow villagers and was told to remove the 'badly governed' Agnes Clerk from his house.[91] Dysfunctional families are more easily discovered among the gentry because they have left more records. The disgruntled Henry Durant, who spent many childhood years away from the parental house at Barcheston, complained in about 1505 that he had never had 6*d* from his father 'as all the country knows'.[92] The only known divorce case in the Heritage circle involved no less a family than the Belknaps, from which Alice, the widow of John Heritage's ally at Burton Dassett, brought a case in the court of Star Chamber when pursuing her separation from John Bridges, her second husband.[93]

There is little evidence for a strong sense of lineage. Leland reports a family legend of the Palmers, and one notes the recalling of earlier generations through the reuse of forenames, so that John Heritage was named after his grandfather. Very rarely a father bequeathed an heirloom, if that is a correct description of a mazer passed to his elder son by Edmund Bradwey in 1493, but will makers showed no consistent attachment to holdings and houses that might have been regarded as family possessions.[94]

The character of family life can be investigated systematically by focusing on inheritance among a wider section of society than is represented by the will makers. The background to this is provided by the discontinuity of village and town populations, which shows that families did not cling to particular holdings of land. In the long term, families either died out in the direct male line, or moved away, resulting in a continuous turnover. To begin with the tenants of Blockley manor, which included eight contiguous villages, a list of 1544 shows not a single name recorded in a survey of 1299.[95] This was not the result of the disasters of the fourteenth century but of instability over a long period, including the decades around 1500. This is demonstrated by the forty-nine surnames recorded in the 1490s in the Westminster Abbey manors of Bourton, Moreton, Sutton, and Todenham, of which only fourteen can be found on a list compiled in 1545, so that thirty-five names, or 71 per cent of the total, had gone in a half-century.[96] The lay manor at Bourton on the Hill had tenants with fifteen surnames in 1487, three of which survived in 1523.[97] Of course, families may have remained longer in the female

[91] TNA: PRO, SC2 175/77.

[92] WCRO, C580/11 (Barcheston deeds).

[93] T. Stretton, 'Marriage, Separation and the Common Law in England, 1540–1660', in H. Berry and E. Foyster (eds), *The Family in Early Modern England* (Cambridge, 2007), 27–8.

[94] TNA: PRO, PROB 11/10, fo.46r. On the land-family bond, R. Hoyle, 'The Land-Family Bond in England', *Past and Present*, 146 (1995), 151–73; J. Whittle, 'Individualism and the Land-Family Bond: A Reassessment of the Land Transfer Patterns among the English Peasantry, c.1270–1580', *Past and Present*, 160 (1998), 25–63.

[95] M. Hollings (ed.), *The Red Book of Worcester*, Worcestershire Historical Society (1934–50), pt. 3, 295–311; WRO, BA 2636, ref.009:1, 18/47765.

[96] WAM 8361, 8383 (court rolls and list of tenants).

[97] TNA: PRO, 175/17 (court roll); SC11/990 (rental).

line, because daughters inherited and their names changed with marriage, but the discontinuity of male succession is still a significant feature of the history of families and communities.

Many families with an apparently stable holding of land in a village lost their connection with the place because sons moved away, and did not claim their rights of inheritance. The generalization can be made that in the Midlands and the western part of England inheritance of land was very common in the period 1270–1348, but it had become less frequent in the fifteenth century. Inheritance almost disappeared for a time on some manors.[98] The holdings of customary land, which are well recorded, fell back into the lord's hand when a tenant gave up or died, and the lord found another tenant, who was often a newcomer from outside the village. Alternatively the land was acquired, either after death or in the lifetime of the tenant, by a member of another family. Inheritance often revived around 1500, so in Heritage's day it was becoming more common for sons to succeed their fathers. Nonetheless young men were still able to find land on their own initiative, and did not wait for their father to die or retire. Many households in the later stages of the tenant's life contained no elder son, or any children at all, as sons and daughter alike would have been in service elsewhere or had set up their own homes.

The sample of land transfers used for this inquiry came from manorial court rolls of six estates, containing a total of fifteen villages, covering the period 1493–1529 (Table 2.3). They record 207 transfers of land, of which eighty-two (40 per cent) show property passing from one family member or relative to another. Twenty-three of these 'family' transactions refer to the succession of a widow on the death of her husband, in accordance with the custom of free bench that was a standard practice under customary tenure. The widow kept the holding for life, or she lost it if she remarried, and then it would pass to the next generation. This leaves fifty-nine changes of tenant, or just over a quarter, in which both parties were related to one another. Many of the new tenants were of course sons, and the substantial minority of holdings that passed to the next generation suggests that family cohesion was recovering.

In about three-fifths of transactions land was transferred from one family to another. The courts were really recording a land market, but maintained the formal structure of tenure by insisting that land was held as a tenancy, and had to pass through the hands of the lord, or under his supervision. In accordance with this customary law the seller of the land appears in the record as an outgoing tenant, and the buyer takes on the tenancy. The procedures in the courts analysed here included surrender and admittance, in which the outgoing tenant surrendered the holding and a newcomer was accepted as a tenant, or alternatively the existing tenant would surrender the land for the use of (*ad opus*) another tenant. The old and new tenant were not always making an arrangement between themselves, as the land could be surrendered to the lord, and would remain 'in the lord's hands' for a period of months until a new tenant took it.

---

[98] Z. Razi, 'The Myth of the Immutable English Family', *Past and Present*, 140 (1993), 27–42.

Table 2.3. Transfers of land from court rolls, 1493–1529, (a) between family members, (b) to members of other families, and (c) in summary.

Places	(a) Transfers between family members					
	Tenant dies, to widow	Tenant dies, to heir	Tenant surrenders to family member	Family member acquires reversion	Lord grants to family member	Total
Bourton, Moreton, Sutton, Todenham	1	3	2	2	–	8
Blockley, Tredington	2	2	–	5	–	9
Adlestrop, Maugersbury, Upper Swell	4	6	6	1	–	17
Blackwell, Shipston	6	6	4	2	2	20
Quinton	3	–	1	–	–	4
Broadway	7	10	4	3	–	24
Total	23	27	17	13	2	82

Places	(b) Transfers to members of other families					
	Tenant dies, to non-family	Holding to lord	Grant by lord	Surrender to non-family	Non-family member acquires reversion	Total
Bourton, Moreton, Sutton, Todenham	–	2	4	4	2	12
Blockley, Tredington	1	–	3	2	-	6
Adlestrop, Maugersbury, Upper Swell	9	13	3	12	4	41
Blackwell, Shipston	5	6	6	5	2	24
Quinton	–	2	5	2	-	9
Broadway	2	11	14	4	2	33
Total	17	34	35	29	10	125

(c) Summary			
	Transfers between family members	Transfers to members of other families	Total
number	82	125	207
per cent	40	60	100

Source: Manorial court rolls in WAM; GA, D1099; WRO, BA 2636, ref. 009:1; TNA: PRO, SC2 175/77, 78; Worcester Cathedral Library, E series; Magdalen College, Oxford, Quinton documents; TNA: PRO, SC2 210/32, 33.

Sixty-nine of the transfers belong to this category of land passing to or from the lord, a number that suggests a lack of fierce demand for land.

Inheritance, however, was coming back into use for a minority of families, not necessarily because of a change in family sentiment, but reflecting the beginnings of a shortage of easily obtained vacant holdings. We can also observe families anxious to promote hereditary succession. Instead of the convention by which the children, and especially the eldest son, waited for the death of the father before taking over the holding, some families transferred the land in the lifetime of the older generation. In 1498 William Goodhyne of Maugersbury surrendered his large holding of 3 messuages and 2 yardlands for the use of his son John Good-hyne.[99] Such arrangements show how partial a picture of inheritance emerges from wills, as William's will, had it survived, would have had no reason to mention this grant. A son who was not yet ready to take over the holding, and a father who was reluctant to hand over the management of the land, could nonetheless enter into an agreement for the reversion of land in the future. Thomas Eddon of Sutton under Brailes in 1507 paid a fine of 20*s* to gain the reversion of his father's holding of a messuage and a cotland, by which the land would go to Thomas when his father died or gave up the land.[100] The delay could be a very long one. In the same village in 1514 Agnes Eddon died and her 4 messuages and 3 yardlands reverted to Richard Eddon by an agreement made in 1499.[101] Richard was prepared to wait so long because the holding was large and desirable, and it is quite likely that Richard was not the heir under the customary rules of succession. Older peasants could bypass the rules and give preference to a younger son or other relative. Another method of binding an heir was to name a son as a joint tenant when a piece of land was acquired. When Thomas and Matilda Nycols took two tofts and a yardland at Coldicote in Moreton in Marsh in 1514 they paid a fine to make William Nichols the third tenant.[102] When they died or surrendered the land, William would take over without further payment.

These methods of securing the succession of land for a favoured member of the younger generation were probably accompanied by a commitment by the heir to render some service to their benefactors, either to help with agricultural work, or to provide for the tenants in their old age. The will of John Harryes of Charing-worth in 1535 makes this explicit, by his expectation that his three sons would remain at home to look after his widow, and more remarkably after her death form a joint household and share equally in the income of the land. This type of family would be called a frérèche in the south of France, and is a rather unexpected find in north Gloucestershire.[103]

Finally, a further reminder of the hidden bonds of family connection arises from inheritance by females. We do not know how many new tenants were married to female heirs. Thomas Bagge of Aston Magna in Blockley in 1520 was succeeded in the tenancy of a substantial 3-yardland freeholding by Richard Roche. We would normally judge him to be an outsider, but the court record tells us that he was the husband of Alice Bagge, Thomas's daughter.[104] This hidden category of heirs does not allow us, however, to overturn the generalization about the limited extent of family succession in the tenure of land, as we still

---

[99] TNA: PRO, SC2 175/77 (court roll).
[100] WAM 8362 (court roll).   [101] WAM 8365 (court roll).   [102] WAM 8365.
[103] TNA: PRO, PROB 11/25, fo.311r; M. Mitterauer and R. Sieder, *The European Family: Patriarchy to Partnership from the Middle Ages to the Present* (Oxford, 1982), 13, 30.
[104] WRO, BA 2636, ref.009:1, 177/92504.

have the phenomenon of the land that lay in the lord's hands, unclaimed by members of the previous tenant's family.

The Heritages and the Palmers reflect the diversity in the behaviour of families in the early sixteenth century. The Palmers distributed their considerable wealth at each generation through a form of partible inheritance, which led to them becoming a formidable network of wealthy landowners and traders scattered over a town and four villages in the same neighbourhood. The Heritages, having accumulated a base in the late fifteenth century at Burton, dispersed over south Warwickshire, the Midlands, and the south of England. John Heritage, though he inherited his father's land, was typical of the age in his mobility, moving from Burton to Moreton, and then to London. The Heritage family still retained a degree of mutual support, evident in the elder Thomas Heritage's help in the education of his sisters' children, and his moves to assist his niece in 1536.

This was an age when patronage counted a great deal. By its very nature, influence was applied informally, but occasional written evidence survives. A letter from the lord of the manor of Chipping Norton, Richard Croft esquire, to the president of Magdalen College, Oxford, which held some land in the town and nearby villages, recommended that the college find a place for Richard Perkyns. The young candidate was the son of one of Croft's tenants, and also his godson, who was 'well disposed to learn'. Perkyns had been admitted to the college by 1496.[105] The example shows not only the value of links which those below the gentry could develop with their social superiors, but also demonstrates the practical value of godparents.

No section of society can demonstrate the role of patronage better than the Church. In the district around Moreton in Marsh there were more than ninety benefices and Church offices, as rectors, vicars, and chaplains, most of them producing incomes between £5 and £15 per annum. The surnames of the clergy reveal a recurrent pattern of gentry families, who often held rights of patronage over their local parish church, appointing relatives to the living. So the Savages were lords of the manor at Aston Subedge, where Roger Savage became rector in 1509, and the Burys at Barton on the Heath appointed Edmund Bury to their benefice.[106] Many livings were controlled by monasteries, but they could be persuaded to appoint the sons of the gentry who acted as their officials and advisers, which presumably explains Evesham Abbey's appointment of William Throckmorton to Broadwell, and John Greville's tenure of the rectory of Todenham, which belonged to Westminster Abbey.[107] The bishops of Worcester used the livings of Blockley and Tredington to support their officials.[108] The upper peasantry and merchants benefited

---

[105] Magdalen College, Oxford, Letter 24; N. Orme, *Education in Early Tudor England: Magdalen College Oxford and its School* (Oxford, 1998), 43, 75.

[106] WRO, BA 2648, ref.b716.093, 8(i), 113 (bishop's register); J. Caley and J. Hunter (eds), *Valor Ecclesiasticus temp. Henry VIII, auctoritate regia institutus*, Record Commission (1810–34), III, 96.

[107] WRO, BA 2648, ref.b716.093, 8 (i), 30 (bishop's register).

[108] *ibid*, 59, 110, 114; Robert Haldesworth, vicar of Blockley from 1509, was vicar-general of the diocese: K. Down, 'The Administration of the Diocese of Worcester under the Italian Bishops, 1497–1535', *Midland History*, 20 (1995), 7.

from patronage also, as the elder Thomas Heritage demonstrates, and Richard Salbrygge at Quinton and John Bonefant of Chipping Campden were both able to secure positions presumably with some help from social superiors.[109] The names of most of the clergy are not instantly recognizable because they came from ordinary families, and the sons of peasants and artisans were able to gain employment in the Church.[110]

Patronage was dispensed at all social levels, for example by an influential member of the upper clergy who could help gentry and merchants. The abbot of Winchcombe, Richard Kidderminster (1488–1525), enjoyed a high reputation far beyond his locality, as he was an able administrator who also intervened in politics.[111] He acted as overseer of the will of Thomas Davies (the Stow merchant) in 1511, and in the following year William Greville thought of the abbot as a safe pair of hands who could be put in charge of his lands at Aston Magna and Dorn.[112] Rich London merchants dispensed favours, like the help given to the impoverished Henry Durant by Hugh Clopton (see p. 42).

Just as the yeomen and merchants such as the Heritages, Palmers, and Alens hoped to gain support from their gentry and mercantile superiors, so they exercised patronage among their equals and those below them in the social hierarchy. John Heritage was chosen to be the overseer of the wills of Thomas Wilkes of Blockley and William Randell (alias Bayly) of Condicote.[113]

Neither the bonds of family life nor the influence dispensed by the social elite determined the life chances of individuals. John Heritage was helped along in his career by the patronage of his landlord, the access to the wealth of his father, and his wife's family. He did not live, however, in a rigidly controlled world, even if some contemporaries wished that this was the case. He was making his own decisions, taking risks, seizing opportunities, and changing his life's course, when he made bold changes at Burton, took an enterprising leap to Moreton, and then left for London.

---

[109] Salbrygge must have been related to John Salbrygge, of Willicote and Alscote, a tenant of the Catesby family, and George Catesby arranged for his appointment as a chantry priest at Tanworth in 1499, WRO, BA 2648, ref.b716.093, 8(i), 17 (bishop's register); in 1505 he became rector of Atherstone (*ibid*, 93). The patron of Atherstone, Tewkesbury Abbey, was the landlord of John Salbrygge at Preston on Stour; Bonefant's will: TNA: PRO, PROB 11/19, fo.232 shows that he belonged to a local family.

[110] R. N. Swanson, *Church and Society in Late Medieval England* (Oxford, 1989), 38.

[111] P. Cunich, 'Richard Kidderminster (*c*.1461–1533/4), abbot of Winchcombe', *Oxford Dictionary of National Biography*, 31 (2004), 534–5.

[112] TNA: PRO, PROB 11/17, fos.16v–17r; PROB 11/17, fos.96r–97v (wills).

[113] WRO, BA 3950/I, ref.008:7, vol.2, fo.46v; TNA: PRO, PROB 11/14, fo.133v (wills).

3

John Heritage's Country

The word 'country' was used in the fifteenth and sixteenth centuries to mean a piece of land with known boundaries (it could mean a county), or a region associated with a particular person. This chapter is about the country in which John Heritage traded and farmed within approximately 8 miles (13 km) of the small town of Moreton in Marsh, so it is based on the town's hinterland, though Heritage would travel further in his quest for trade than most of those who bought and sold in the Moreton market. The diversity of this piece of countryside is not unusual, which gives this discussion significance for the study of territories and regions everywhere. We naturally view Heritage's country from a specialized modern perspective, but we must also try to imagine how it looked for John and his contemporaries. Did it have a coherence and unity, in spite of its divergent elements? Did the inhabitants think of it as a home territory, with which they identified?

Administrative boundaries are an obvious starting point in considering a territorial unit, and Heritage's country was in that respect the most fragmented and complicated in England (Fig. 3.1). A mile and a half to the east of Moreton lies the eighteenth-century landmark of the Four Shires Stone, which marks the meeting point of Gloucestershire, Oxfordshire, Warwickshire, and Worcestershire. This originated far beyond Heritage's day in the early eleventh century when the shire boundaries were decided.[1] It had an older beginning as a meeting of boundaries of earlier territorial units marked by large stones recorded in an Anglo-Saxon perambulation.[2] The parts of the four shires that met near Moreton included a peninsula of Oxfordshire (the parish of Chastleton) and an island of Worcestershire, Evenlode, which had once belonged to the cathedral church of Worcester. The tenurial ties of the great Church estates centred in Worcestershire helped to shape the administrative complexities of the district. Before the formations of the shires, in the eighth and ninth centuries, the minster churches of Blockley, Bredon, and Tredington had ruled over large *parochiae* (large parishes served by a number of clergymen), which then formed the building blocks for the shires. The church of Worcester had taken over the lands of the minsters, and under its influential bishops had a voice during the shire-making process soon after 1000, which ensured that both Blockley and Tredington were assigned to Worcestershire, together with

[1] C. S. Taylor, 'The Origin of the Mercian Shires', in H. P. R. Finberg (ed.), *Gloucestershire Studies* (Leicester, 1957), 17–51.

[2] G. B. Grundy, *Saxon Charters and Field Names of Gloucestershire*, Bristol and Gloucestershire Archaeological Society (1935), pt. 1, 128, which describes the meeting of boundaries marked by four separate stones.

Fig. 3.1. Heritage's country: shire boundaries in *c*.1500. For changes in the nineteenth and twentieth centuries, see above pp. xii–xiii. M marks Moreton in Marsh.

their outliers such as Cutsdean, Daylesford, and Evenlode.[3] At the time of the boundary negotiations the northern part of the county that was later called Gloucestershire formed the separate county of Winchcombeshire, but its existence had long been forgotten in Heritage's day.[4] The shires served as the principal units of local government, and they had important responsibilities to the state in financial, judicial, and military matters.

The hundreds into which the counties were subdivided had limited powers in Heritage's time. Winburntree hundred, part of the Worcestershire hundred of Oswaldslow, brought together Blockley and Tredington, and its court meeting in

[3] S. Bassett, 'The Administrative Landscape of the Diocese of Worcester in the Tenth Century', in N. Brooks and C. Cubitt (eds), *St Oswald of Worcester: Life and Influence* (Leicester, 1996), 166–72; F. Tinti, *Sustaining Belief: The Church of Worcester from c.870 to c.1100* (Farnham, 2010), 176–92.
[4] J. Whybra, *A Lost English County: Winchcombeshire in the Tenth and Eleventh Centuries* (Woodbridge, 1990).

the 1520s elected constables and dealt with stray animals, maintenance of roads and bridges, swearing of newcomers to keep the peace, and the occasional petty crime, but the cases were few.[5] By contrast, the hundred of Slaughter on the southern edge of the area examined here provided an opportunity for private litigation, over debt for example, which had disappeared from many manor courts.[6]

Parishes had an enduring importance, and the former minster churches that dated back before the shires influenced the lives of the inhabitants in the early sixteenth century. For example, the wealthy rector of the huge parish of Tredington was worth £100 per annum in 1535, mainly from tithes collected from an area in excess of 7,000 acres.[7] The rector would have lost these revenues if any of the seven villages in the parish became separate new parishes. They were only allowed to have chapels, which caused most contention at Shipston on Stour. Although this town was founded in about 1260, and the inhabitants campaigned for two centuries, the chapel was not officially allowed burial rights until 1516.[8] Burial was a crucial financial issue because the rector received a mortuary, often the second-best animal or a valuable possession for each corpse.

Blockley's huge parish contained not only the villages of the bishop of Worcester's manor, such as Aston Magna, the Ditchfords, Dorn, Draycott, Northwick, and Paxford, but also possessions of other lords, notably Bourton on the Hill and Moreton in Marsh which only acquired burial rights in 1540 and 1512 respectively.[9] Batsford and Stretton on Fosse also buried their dead in Blockley churchyard, and in 1441 an agreement shows how the Stretton funerals were conducted. The rector of Stretton accompanied the coffin on its 4-mile (6.5-km) journey, but when the procession reached the churchyard gate at Blockley his duties ceased and the Blockley clergy then officiated.[10] The absence of parochial autonomy for the dependent villages caused resentment.[11] Another division in Church government, between the dioceses of Worcester and Lincoln, which coincided with the Oxfordshire boundary, cut through Heritage country. The dioceses were governed through archdeacons, whose rule coincided with the four shires. Blockley and Tredington parishes were separate enclaves of peculiar jurisdiction, which mean that wills were proved in a local court.[12]

The boundaries between parishes, manors, hundreds, shires, archdeaconries, and dioceses were not always sharply defined. A compact lowland parish would

---

[5] WRO, BA 2636, ref.009:1, 177/92504, 92508, 92509 (hundred court rolls).

[6] TNA: PRO, SC2 176/8 (hundred court rolls).

[7] J. Caley and J. Hunter (eds), *Valor Ecclesiasticus temp. Henry VIII, auctoritate regia institutus*, Record Commission (1810–34), III, 257.

[8] WRO, BA 2648, ref.b716.093, 8(i), 238 (bishop's register).

[9] *VCH Glos.*, VI, 204, 248. Burials are known to have taken place without official sanction, from wills, and archaeological evidence of human remains.

[10] Society of Antiquaries of London, Prattinton Collection, 3, 130.

[11] Parochial independence caused a dispute at Ditchford Frary but a century before Heritage's time, R. N. Swanson, 'Parochialism and Particularism: The Dispute over the Status of Ditchford Frary, Warwickshire, in the Early Fifteenth Century', in M. J. Franklin and C. Harper-Bill (eds), *Medieval Ecclesiastical Studies in Honour of Dorothy M. Owen* (Woodbridge, 1995), 241–57.

[12] R. M. Haines, *The Administration of the Diocese of Worcester in the First Half of the Fourteenth Century* (London, 1965), 14–15; Caley and Hunter (eds), *Valor Ecclesiasticus*, II, 452–3; III, 257.

have clearly visible limits, marked by the headlands in the open fields, hedgerows, and merestones. Boundaries were liable to fade into imprecision on the edge of a territory when that consisted of a large area of pasture shared by surrounding villages. The greatest area of intercommoned grazing was the large stretch of hilltop, 'up on Cotswold' as people said, which ran from Aston Subedge in the north to Guiting Power in the south (Fig. 3.2). A section of the hilltop pasture lay, according to the Abbot of Pershore, in the eastern part of Broadway, but three laymen in 1458 alleged that it belonged to Chipping Campden. A much earlier boundary perambulation called a piece of land on the northern edge of this pasture 'no man's land', so the ambiguities of the boundary were not new.[13] The parties in the 1458 dispute were of course arguing about a valuable agricultural asset, but they were also voicing uncertainty about the precise dividing line between the shires, as Broadway belonged to Worcestershire and Campden to Gloucestershire. The nearby pasture of Hinchwick fell in two parishes, Condicote (Gloucestershire) and Cutsdean (Worcestershire).[14] Another large piece of shared land was the heath between Moreton in Marsh and Barton on the Heath, in the centre of which stood the Four Shires Stone (see Fig. 3.2). The pasture was sometimes contested, notably when in 1487–90 Richard Palmer of Moreton (Heritage's father-in-law) with his many sheep invaded the common grazing that lay in Chastleton parish in Oxfordshire.[15] More often the disputed pasture simply served a number of parishes and villages within a single county, like Lyneham Heath that was the subject of a quarrel between Sarsden and Churchill in 1524, in which Lyneham itself also had an interest.[16]

Did the shires or hundreds have much significance for their inhabitants? People below the ranks of the gentry paid their taxes to officials of the hundred and the shire, and might themselves be appointed as taxers. Nicholas Willington, a wealthy husbandman of Todenham, was acting in 1514 as collector of the tenth and fifteenth (the lay subsidy) in Gloucestershire.[17] Dozens of people were drawn into the work of the hundred courts. The juries of the Winburntree Hundred court in the 1520s included members of the Dyde, Fletcher, and Gibbes families, who were well-off husbandmen rather than yeomen, and the constables who they appointed for the whole hundred and for each vill, like Richard Tele of Blockley, were of comparable standing.[18] Serious crimes were the concern of the shire, and occasionally villagers, like those of Blockley in 1506–7, were required to transport a suspected felon to the county jail in Worcester.[19] These duties were infrequent and

[13] Society of Antiquaries of London, Prattinton Collection, 5, 167–75; D. Hooke, *Worcestershire Anglo-Saxon Charter-Bounds* (Woodbridge, 1990), 53.

[14] *VCH Glos.*, VI, 67.

[15] British Library, Harleian Roll B13 (court rolls of Brookend).

[16] TNA: PRO, REQ 2/5/308. On intercommoning H. S. A. Fox, 'Co-operation Between Rural Communities in Medieval England', in P. Sereno and M. L. Sturani (eds), *Rural Landscape between State and Local Communities in Europe Past and Present* (Alessandria, 1984), 119–58.

[17] TNA: PRO, E159/292 (Memoranda Roll).

[18] WRO, BA 2636, ref.009:1, 177/92504, 92508, 92509 (hundred court rolls); *WT*, 183, 184, 195. For the peasant contribution to local courts, R. B. Goheen, 'Peasant Politics? Village Community and the Crown in Fifteenth-Century England', *American Historical Review*, 96 (1991), 42–62.

[19] WRO, BA 2636, ref.009:1, 176/92497 (account roll).

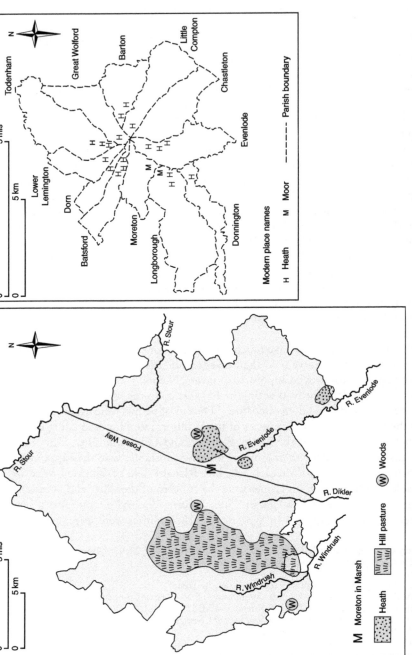

Fig. 3.2. Heritage's country: landscape (woods, pastures, heaths, rivers). In the main map the Fosse Way passes through Moreton in Marsh (M). The large Cotswold pasture occupied the high ground between the rivers Windrush and the Dikler, and various heaths lay near to the valley of the Evenlode. Three major woods are also shown.

The separate map depicts parishes, focussed on the Four Shires Stone east of Moreton, all of which enjoyed a share in the large heath. 'Heath' place names are marked by H. The moor names (M on the map) indicate the Henmarsh from which Moreton takes its name.

irregular, and neither shire nor hundred had a large or continuing impact on the lives of their inhabitants. The gentry were more likely to be involved in challenging administration at shire level, like John Palmer of Lower Lemington, Heritage's cousin, who served as one of the Commissioners for the collection of the subsidies in 1523–7 in Gloucestershire. In a border area like the Heritage country the gentry tended more than usual to hold land and seek marriage partners across county boundaries.[20]

THE LANDSCAPE OF HERITAGE'S COUNTRY

The landscape probably had a stronger influence than shires or hundreds on the sense of identity of the people who lived in and around Moreton. The combination of hills and valleys, pasture and arable, roads and rivers did not just provide people with a source of income, but also influenced their social organization, way of life, and their outlook. The term *pays* sums up the idea that the country can be divided into types of landscape which also had a particular social and cultural character. The woodlands, for example, with their dispersed settlements and pastoral economy, encouraged an individualistic mentality. Heritage's country was of course divided into two *pays*, as it straddled the boundary between the hills and the vale.[21]

Contemporaries referred to land lying 'on the wold', or 'up on Cotswold', meaning the limestone hills that lay to the south-west of Moreton and stretched for almost 20 miles (32 km) to the south to the Thames valley, and further to the west, as far as the Vale of Gloucester (Fig. 3.3). The highest point in the eastern Cotswolds was on the eastern boundary of Broadway, at 1,047 feet (319 m). To the south the hills ended in a gentle slope, but to the north they fell dramatically from an 'edge', hence such names as Aston Subedge for a village located under the quite sharp drop of 250 feet (76 m). The edge continued on the west-facing side of the hills above Stanton and Stanway. On the eastern side the traffic from London and Oxford had to climb up the long steep incline that gave its name to Bourton on the Hill. The edge jutted out to form separate outlying hills, such as Meon Hill and the Ilmington Hills to the north. Once travellers climbed the upland, they found rounded hills of yellowish oolitic limestone, cut by valleys containing small rivers, all running roughly north to south, the Windrush river (rising in Cutsdean) on the west side of the large hill pasture between Aston Subedge and Guiting, the Dikler on the eastern edge of the pasture, which begins at Donnington, and the Evenlode

---

[20] *B & GLS*, xxxvi. On the gentry in local government and specifically in the shire, E. Acheson, *A Gentry Community: Leicestershire in the Fifteenth Century c.1422–c.1485* (Cambridge, 1992), 107–34; on the divisions within a county, C. Carpenter, *Locality and Polity: A Study of Warwickshire Landed Society, 1401–1499* (Cambridge, 1992), 591–6, 609–14. The same work discusses cross-border marriages, 116–19.

[21] On the idea of *pays*, which includes social and cultural as well as physical characteristics, see A. Everitt, 'River and Wold: Reflections on the Historical Origins of Regions and *Pays*', *Journal of Historical Geography*, 3 (1977), 1–19; on woodland characteristics, compared with champion and wold, J. Thirsk (ed.), *The English Rural Landscape* (Oxford, 2000), 97–149.

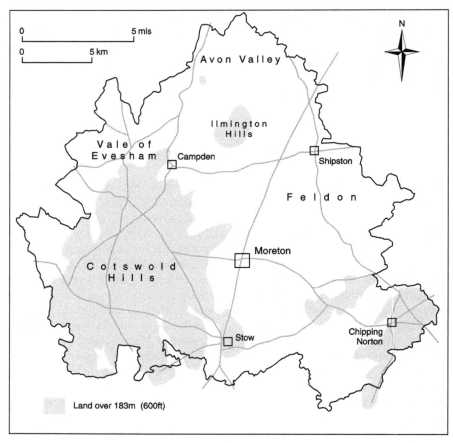

Fig. 3.3. Heritage's country: high ground, main roads, and towns.

that had its origins near Moreton in Marsh. (see Fig. 3.2) The waters of all three rivers flowed ultimately into the Thames. The Cotswold soils include a 'brown calcareous earth' (known to soil scientists as the Sherborne association), which contains many small pieces of broken and weathered limestone, and drains freely.[22] This was potentially quite fertile soil, and indeed much of it was ploughed in the Middle Ages, and at the present day it carries extensive crops of grain and vegetables. Farmers complain in the twenty-first century that the soil can be thin, and now as in the past the height of the hills ensures that the spring comes late and average temperatures are lower than those of the valleys. In Heritage's time a good deal of former arable had been converted to grass. Meadow was scarce in the often

---

[22] J. M. Ragg et al., *Soils and Their Use in Midland and Western England*, Soil Survey of England and Wales, Bulletin no. 12 (1984), 178–81, 189–92; D. C. Findlay et al., *Soils and Their Use in South-West England*, no. 14 (1984), 140–65, 271–4.

narrow river and stream valleys, though quite large meadows lay in the valleys of the Evenlode and the southern end of the Dikler. Large woods were few, notably at Blockley, Bourton, and Guiting, and there were only two parks, the bishop of Worcester's park at Blockley and that of the abbot of Hailes in Lower Swell. The modern landscape parks (at Batsford, Daylesford, Eyford, and Sezincote) occupy former arable land.

With the exception of a scatter of smaller settlements, such as Bold in Lower Swell and Hinchwick in Condicote, most people lived in nucleated villages, and their land lay in conventional two-field systems. The ridges of ploughing, marking the selions in which the land was divided, have now largely disappeared on the hills, partly because of modern intensive cultivation, but they are still visible in protected places such as the park at Sezincote. There were patches of permanent pasture, and mention has been made of the large area of pasture between the Wind-rush and the Dikler.

Off the wold, below the edge to the north and east the land tended to lie around 200 feet (60 m), rising in some low hills above 300 feet (90 m). Only the Stour ranks as a river, and the water drained northwards in such minor watercourses as the Nethercote Brook, the Knee Brook, the Humber Brook, and the Marchfont Brook. All of these emptied ultimately into the Avon, which means that the Cots-wold edge formed a watershed between two major river systems, dividing our district in a rather fundamental way. The predominant soils of the Vale of Evesham and Avon valley were the heavy liassic clays of the Evesham association, but lighter loams, and a very mixed range of soil types, are found.[23] Around Moreton itself the land lay low near the Evenlode, hence the 'Henmarsh' ('wet land with moorhens') that became incorporated into the name 'Moreton in Marsh'. Outsiders betray their ignorance when they call the place 'Moreton in the Marsh'. Originally a number of other villages in the vicinity were named in the same fashion, including Barton Henmarsh that has more recently become Barton on the Heath.

Most of the villages in the lowlands had no connection with heaths or marshes, but instead their clay soils were devoted mainly to corn-growing, with village lands divided between two open fields. Maps drawn before enclosure survive for Ilming-ton, Tredington, Whitchurch, and Great Wolford, all showing the 'lands' as people called the individual strips, or 'selions' as they often appear in the documents.[24] In the clay soils the ridge and furrow is sometimes preserved, with wide high-backed ridges and deep furrows, and large areas were photographed from the air in the 1940s on the eve of its destruction, giving us a visual impression of the landscape of the open fields. Meadow was not plentiful, though it was a feature of some Stour valley parishes. Permanent pasture was also scarce, except on the heaths and par-ticularly the large heath to the east of Moreton, and the largest wood, Wolford Wood, was also located there. Many villages had no more than small groves, which

[23] Ragg et al., *Midland England*, 190–3; Findlay et al., *South-West England*, 169–73, 255, 265.
[24] WRO, BA 5403, ref.b.009:1, 20, WCRO, CR569/261; Z183(L)/2L; Shakespeare Birthplace Trust Record Office, ER 145/435.

were large enough only to provide firewood and fencing material.[25] Nucleated villages housed most of the population, but as on the wolds small hamlets or single farms could be found, such as Coldicote in Moreton and Radbrook in Quinton. This champion landscape – dominated by *champs*, or open fields – is found over large sections of the Midlands and the north-east, but in Warwickshire it was known as the Feldon, which is the same term in English rather than French, and is often contrasted with the wooded Arden.

LINKS AND RESEMBLANCES

Although the contrasting upland and lowland landscapes present us with a number of differences in their relief, drainage, and soils, they also resembled each other in some important respects.

Firstly, as has already been shown, the main settlement form was the nucleated village, with a thin scatter of non-village settlements. The whole district lay within the Midland belt of villages, now commonly known as the central province.[26] Few of the villages were very large. For every Longborough or Mickleton with thirty or forty households in Heritage's time there were a dozen settlements with ten to twenty households. The villages that were administratively important, such as Blockley, Stanway, and Tredington, did not have high populations and stood at the head of a group of settlements of modest size. There is no obvious difference between the upland and lowland villages either in terms of their population numbers or the form of the settlement. Many consisted of a cluster of houses close to the manor house and church or chapel, with dwellings sited close together along a number of curved roads. A few villages such as Broadwell, Kingham, and Little Wolford had a green at the centre of the settlement. At least part of the plan of some settlements has a regular 'street village' element, as at Bourton on the Hill with its rows of houses on either side of the main road, or at Great Wolford. Small villages might simply consist of a single street flanked by rows of houses – in the lowland at Draycott in Blockley and Crimscote in Whitchurch, or on the hills at Cutsdean and Kineton in Temple Guiting. Admington in the lowland had a single row. Some had plans best described as polyfocal, or at least bifocal, as there were two distinct parts of the village, at Lower and Upper Oddington, and at Todenham, where the northern section of the settlement was called Homestall End.

These observations based on modern maps might be questioned because the village plans have changed over the centuries. Archaeological research shows that this is sometimes the case, but we know that settlements could be prone to preserve their plot boundaries once property rights were established.[27] We find the plan

---

[25] S. Wager, *Woods, Wolds and Groves: The Woodland of Medieval Warwickshire*, British Archaeological Reports, British Series, 269 (1998), 13–23, 250–1, 253.

[26] B. K. Roberts and S. Wrathmell, *An Atlas of Rural Settlement in England* (London, 2000).

[27] The problem is discussed in M. Page and R. Jones, 'Stability and Instability in Medieval Village Plans: Case Studies in Whittlewood', in M. Gardiner and S. Rippon (eds), *Medieval Landscapes: Landscape History after Hoskins*, 2 (Macclesfield, 2007), 139–52.

forms observed today fixed in the earthworks of the deserted village sites, such as Compton Scorpion, Norton Subedge, or Middle or Upper Ditchford, which were clustered villages, or a single street at Lark Stoke and Pinnock, which preserves the shape of the settlement in its last phase of inhabitation often within a few decades of 1500. Documents for Oddington and Todenham confirm their bifocal character in the later Middle Ages.

Although there is a scatter of timber-framed houses from the period 1400–1550 still surviving across the villages, the church was the most prominent building, and is often the only structure known to Heritage that still survives. The district covered by this chapter contained forty-nine parish churches in about 1500, which were served by rectors and vicars. There were also at least twenty chapels (both on the hills and in the lowlands), so that the great majority of nucleated settlements had a place of worship, even though some of the chapels were not well endowed with land or income and have not survived. They gave the inhabitants of small settlements a social focus and a sense of pride in the place in which they lived.[28]

Open-field agriculture was a second feature common to both wolds and champion country, and in the heyday of high population and intensive land exploitation before 1350 two-field systems were in universal use in Heritage country. Cotswold cornfields tended to be combined with a stretch of hill pasture, and this was true of a number of townships where we have early maps showing the pre-enclosure arrangements. At Temple Guiting together with its two associated settlements at Kineton and Barton in 1603 the cultivated land lay on the lower slopes of the Windrush valley, and the permanent pastures occupied the high ground to the east.[29] At Bourton on the Hill in 1802 the open fields filled the eastern end of the parish on the lower slopes, and the sheep pastures stretched to the west (Fig. 3.4). Documents combined with field observation suggest that this late evidence still reflects the medieval farming systems. Not all of the upland settlements enjoyed large hill pastures, such as Longborough, and in the valley some might benefit from heathland, like those focused on the Four Shires Stone, but villages like Admington, Todenham, and Tredington had virtually no permanent pasture before the Black Death, and the shortage of common grazing persisted in *c*.1500. The ridge and furrow at Compton Scorpion gives a complete picture of an open-field township that was provided with a limited amount of pasture and meadow (Fig. 3.5).

For all of the regional and local varieties, the possession by each settlement of hundreds of acres of common-field arable gave them important similarities in appearance and organization. Their stubbles and fallows were for all of them an important grazing resource for their sheep and other livestock. No matter how much permanent pasture was available, all villages were concerned by problems of keeping numbers of animals in check. From the period around 1400 their by-laws demonstrate the problems that they faced, but also the strength of their organization to maintain the essential rules of common-field husbandry. Alongside the

[28] N. Orme, 'The Other Parish Church: Chapels in Late Medieval England', in C. Burgess and E. Duffy (eds), *The Parish in Late Medieval England* (Donington, 2006), 78–94.

[29] Corpus Christi College, Oxford, Map 64.

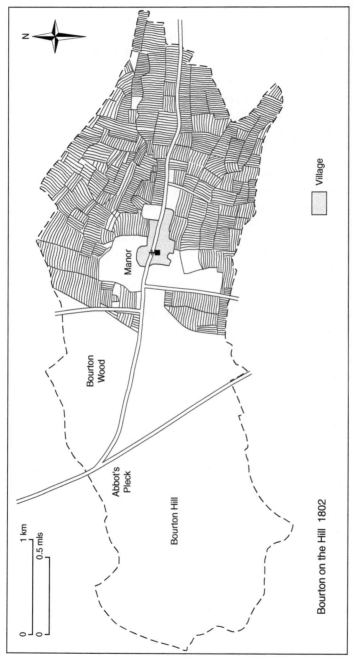

Fig. 3.4. Bourton on the Hill in 1802 (with some information from the enclosure map of 1821). The village, church, and manor house are shown in the centre of the parish. The low ground to the east was occupied by a complex system of open-field strips and furlongs, very similar to those of Heritage's day. The western side contained a large wood and extensive hill pasture, part of which belonged to the demesne, but much of it common for the villagers. A large area of hill pasture is found in a number of north-east Cotswold townships.

Source: GA: PC911; transcription of the 1821 map by G. Gwatkin.

Fig. 3.5. The township of Compton Scorpion, in the parish of Ilmington, with earthworks of ridge and furrow and the village site plotted from aerial photographs. This contrasts with Bourton (see Fig. 3.4) because the arable fields covered about 80 per cent of the territory, with a relatively small area of pasture. This was typical of the Feldon and Vale of Evesham. In Heritage's day this village had been abandoned, and the former arable strips converted to pasture, but most villages were working open fields. P stands for a pond. Source: Warwickshire County Museum, modified by fieldwork by the author and David Aldred.

arable fields and pastures managed by the village communities and manorial courts as communal assets, by Heritage's day the countryside both above and below the edge was dotted with the leasows, that is, large pieces of pasture land, some of them old hillsides or heaths that persisted even through the thirteenth century, and others the product of the retreat of cereal cultivation in the period after about 1320.

Often under the management of individuals, they could be described as several, and therefore outside the common fields.

Thirdly, both upland and lowland were poorly supplied with woods. A few large woods were combined with a scatter of small groves (mainly for firewood) like that near the manor house at Kingham.[30] The parks, though few, yielded an extra source of scarce wood and timber, and the trees growing in hedgerows were so valuable that they were counted and valued in surveys of the 1540s – two hundred elms and ashes at Broadwell, for example.[31] Tenants were sometimes reminded that the larger trees in their hedgerows belonged to the lord, or at least could not be felled for sale without permission. The furze and thorns growing on the commons were an important asset for the villagers, both as fuel and hedging material, and cutting these bushes had to be regulated.[32] Although the trees and bushes of the country around Moreton were carefully managed and protected from misuse, they were still insufficient, with the result that timber was brought in from outside. Leases of the mills at Lark Stoke and Tredington provided that timber for major repairs would come from woods owned by the lord of the manor, in both cases from Bush-wood in Lapworth in the Forest of Arden at a distance of 17 miles (27 km), and the mill at Todenham was to receive timber for repairs from the woodland at Pershore, 20 miles (32 km) away.[33]

A fourth common characteristic can be observed in the social structure of the whole district around Moreton. A very high proportion of the land lay in manors under the lordship of the Church (Fig. 3.6). Some of these lordships were relatively recently founded institutions, such as three Oxford colleges, and there were small plots held by chantries, collegiate churches, and fraternities, but the lion's share consisted of large manors held by major Benedictine monasteries, the archbishopric of York, and the bishopric of Worcester. No fewer than seven of the Benedictine houses (Evesham, Eynsham, Gloucester, Pershore, Westminster, Winchcombe, and Worcester) together with the two episcopal lordships, had been founded before the Norman Conquest, so their authority came from well-entrenched and long-term possession of land and people. The latecomers, established between the late eleventh and mid-thirteenth centuries, notably the Benedictines at Tewkesbury and the Cistercians of Bordesley, Bruern, and Hailes, together with the Knights Hospitaller, had extensive lands and much influence. To reinforce their power as landowners, some ecclesiastical lords wielded an extra layer of jurisdiction through their possession of private hundreds, so they held the hundred courts of Oswaldslow (belonging to the church of Worcester), Westminster (Westminster Abbey), Kiftsgate (Winchcombe Abbey). and in north-east Gloucestershire the hundred of Salmonsbury or Slaughter belonged to Syon Abbey. Within the latter the monks of Evesham claimed that their lands (based on Stow on the Wold) had the status of a

[30] Bodleian Library, Oxford, MS. ch. Oxon. 1403.

[31] GA, D3439/129 (Broadwell lease in Hockaday Abstracts).

[32] TNA: PRO, SC2 175/77 (furze at Adlestrop); WAM 8362 (furze at Moreton); New College, Oxford, 3797 (thorns at Kingham).

[33] WCRO, CR 1911/1; WRO, BA 2636, ref.009:1, 177/92509 (Tredington court roll); WAM, Lease Book, fos.75b–76a.

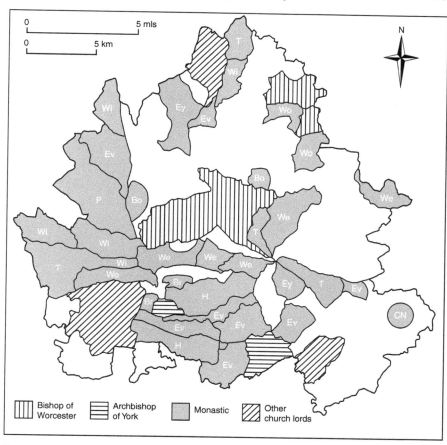

Fig. 3.6 Heritage's country: lords *c.*1500. The shaded and stippled areas were held by Church lords; those left blank were held by a variety of laymen. Abbreviations of monasteries: Bo, Bordesley; Br, Bruern; CN, Cold Norton, Ev, Evesham; Ey, Eynsham; H, Hailes; P, Pershore; T, Tewkesbury; Wi, Winchcombe; We, Westminster; Wo, Worcester.

liberty, with its own jurisdiction, and similarly manors linked to Tewkesbury Abbey formed a liberty within Tewkesbury Hundred.[34]

The Moreton district contained no monastic house, apart from (on its eastern edge) the ill-fated Cold Norton Priory, which was dissolved in 1507. Everyone who lived around Moreton, however, was conscious of the monastic presence, and periodically monks would arrive, like the cellarer of Worcester Priory or the *camerarius* of Evesham Abbey, to hold the manorial courts and check on the state of their manors. No doubt the abbot of Hailes would on occasion have hunted in the park of

[34] *VCH Glos.*, VI, 4–7, 188, 238–9.

Lower Swell. Difficult decisions about the transfer of property or points of customary law would be referred to monastic councils meeting in Pershore, Westminster, or Worcester, and local people would have visited the monasteries themselves to deliver animals (taken as heriots), letters, and cash. The large monasteries may have been old but they were still active, of which one material reminder is the still-standing bell tower of Evesham Abbey, which was a new venture of the early sixteenth century (Fig. 3.7). The local bishops were less likely to take initiatives. The most remote of

Fig. 3.7 The bell tower of Evesham Abbey, built in the early sixteenth century, which was partly funded from the profits of the monastery's landed estates, including seven manors located in Heritage's country. Wool sales enabled the abbey's tenants to pay rents, part of which was spent on this lavish building – its height of 110 feet (33 m) was making a statement about the continued importance of a great monastery on the eve of the Dissolution (photograph Sue Campbell).

the Church lords were the archbishops of York, who, particularly when Thomas Wolsey was appointed in 1514, were preoccupied with more important business than the administration of their Gloucestershire estates. Silvestro de Gigli, bishop of Worcester in 1498–1521, lived in Italy and left the secular affairs of his see to a proctor-general in London and various officials in the diocese.[35]

Interspersed among the Church manors, on upland and lowland, were lay properties, mostly held by gentry, a few of whom were residents and therefore were more visible representatives of lordship than the absentee churchmen. There were more manors under lay lordship towards the eastern edge of the district, in south Warwickshire and around Chipping Norton in Oxfordshire.

The manors had a remarkably uniform structure of tenancy. This was of course an inheritance from before the Norman Conquest, which is first fully documented in the thirteenth and fourteenth centuries. Almost all land was held in standard units of a yardland (or virgate), half yardland, or quarter yardland, as was the case in many parts of Midland and southern England. However, unlike many other regions, in the Cotswolds a relatively high proportion of holdings were, even at the height of population pressure and demand for land in the late thirteenth century, kept as whole yardlands. Peasant families must have wished to divide inheritances between their sons, and the lords would have appreciated their advantage in having many tenants paying as much rent as possible, but they must have arrived at a decision to leave holdings complete because they feared that fractions of yardlands would have not been viable as support for a family, and impoverished tenants would have been unable to pay much rent or buy and maintain the ploughs, carts, and draught animals that could do labour services on the lord's demesne. In some parts of the Cotswolds, and in the Severn valley to the west, the yardlands were large, with 40 acres or more of arable land, which makes the lack of subdivision seem strange, but in the Moreton area the yardlands were much smaller. A 48-acre yardland can be found, at Sutton under Brailes, but at Moreton itself they were as small as 12 acres, and elsewhere the median size often ranged between 20 and 30 acres.[36] Fractions of such relatively small units evidently were not regarded as sustainable, and for the same reason there was a low proportion of cottagers or smallholders, below the ranks of the quarter-yardlanders. We find in the late thirteenth century villages consisting largely of yardlanders, with no more than a handful of cottagers. There was evidently no great demand for hired day labourers, as cottagers normally gained only a fraction of their subsistence from their few acres of land, and earned wages to buy the rest of their food. This was not a countryside with much industry that could provide alternatives to agricultural employment.

---

[35] M. Creighton, 'The Italian Bishops of Worcester', in M. Creighton, *Historical Essays and Reviews* (London, 1902), 202–34; K. Down, 'The Administration of the Diocese of Worcester under the Italian Bishops, 1497–1535', *Midland History*, 20 (1995), 1–20.

[36] The figures are recorded at different periods; the yardlands were not uniform; some of the acreages may be in customary or field acres rather than statute acres: Moreton 12 ac.; Lower Swell 15–25 ac.; Broadwell 20 ac.; Talton 22 ac.; Barcheston 22 ac.; Bourton on the Hill 24 ac.; Oddington 25 ac.; Blockley 24–40 ac.; Todenham 27 ac.; Little Compton 28 ac.; Hidcote Bartrim 31 ac.; Condicote 32 ac.; Ilmington 35 ac.; Adlestrop 40 ac.; Admington 40 ac.; Little Wolford 45 ac.; Sutton under Brailes 48 ac.

By Heritage's day, as the numbers of villagers and the demand for land declined, tenants with a single yardland had diminished to less than a tenth of the total, and multiple holdings with two and three yardlands or even more had become commonplace, accounting for two-fifths of all holdings (Table 3.1a). Smallholdings, those below the quarter-yardland level, accounted for a fifth of the total. There were variations of course, with a higher proportion of smallholders at Adlestrop or Quinton, but the 2- or 3-yardland holding had almost become standard throughout the district. If landholding is analysed in terms of the proportion of land in different units of holding, rather than the number of holdings, the importance of the larger units of tenure is re-emphasized. No less than 67 per cent of the acreage lay in the hands of those with 2 or 3 yardlands and above (Table 3.1b).

Although the yardlands had been combined into larger units, they were still used to describe the size of the holding, and rarely were they allowed to disintegrate into parcels measured in acres. The survival of the yardland into the early sixteenth century, albeit incorporated into double or triple holdings, was a remarkable tribute to a conservative society, in which custom exercised a continuing control over landholding. In theory the tenants in such a society would have been heavily burdened with rents and exactions. Free tenants were few in number, so that seven-eighths of the recorded rural households were those headed by customary tenants, holding by copy of court roll, who were descended from the serfs or villeins of the period 1250–1350. They had then often owed regular labour services, as much as three days per week, together with cash rents and various dues and occasional payments. Those taking a holding for the first time owed entry fines of 30s–80s for a yardland.

By about 1500 the labour services everywhere had been converted into money rents, and most of the extra dues had either lapsed or been reduced to tokens. Entry fines rarely exceeded 30s for a yardland, and were often charged at 6s 8d. Annual rents, calculated for a sample of thirteen manors, varied between 7s and 20s per yardland, with 10s as the median of all of the examples (Table 3.2). A rent of 10s per annum, or 4d–6d per acre, cannot be regarded as very oppressive at a time when land in eastern England could still command rents in excess of 6d–8d per acre. Some of the old oppressions survived. In particular, while villein tenure, long regarded as degrading, had evolved into copyhold that was not very different from freehold, the personal status of servility still persisted, and a small minority of tenants were still described in the documents as *nativi de sanguine*, best translated as 'born serfs by blood'. As late as 1534 serfs belonging to Oddington were reported to the manor court for leaving the manor without the lord's permission.[37] This reminds us that lordship could still stir up resentment by imposing an outmoded status on its subordinates, but the financial cost of personal serfdom was negligible, and the quite low rents attached to customary holdings reflected the productivity and profitability of the land, the local customs that restrained lords,

---

[37] GA, D621/M3 (court roll).

Table 3.1(a). Size of tenant holdings, 1496–1540 (yl is a yardland of c.30 acres).

Size (acres)	below ¼ yl	¼ – below ½ yl	½ yl – below 1 yl	1 yl	between 1yl & 2yl	2yl	between 2yl & 3yl	3yl	above 3yl	Total
	0–6	7–14	15–29	30	31–59	60	61–89	90	90+	
Adlestrop 1498–1520	7	–	–	3	1	2	7	1	–	21
Admington 1540	1	–	–	1	5	2	2	–	–	11
Bourton on the Hill 1523	5	–	2	2	3	–	–	–	–	12
Broadwell 1540	3	1	1	3	4	5	3	8	1	29
Brookend in Chastleton 1499	–	–	–	–	–	2	1	1	–	4
Churchill 1518	4	1	2	3	3	9	–	6	3	31
Compton, Little 1540	–	–	1	–	7	7	–	1	–	16
Ilmington 1496	2	1	6	10	7	3	–	1	1	31
Kingham 1499	2	–	–	4	4	1	1	–	–	12
Longborough 1540	6	–	4	6	–	8	–	3	–	27
Maugersbury 1498–1520	2	–	1	–	–	7	–	4	–	14
Preston 1540	–	–	4	1	4	–	2	–	–	11
Quinton 1517–18	7	1	2	–	1	3	4	–	–	18
Shipston 1502	14	4	7	2	10	3	1	–	–	41
Swell, Lower 1540	4	–	1	–	1	–	–	–	–	10
Swell, Upper 1498–1520	–	–	–	1	–	4	–	2	1	10
Talton 1540	–	1	3	1	3	–	5	2	3	17
Total	57	9	34	38	53	56	26	30	12	315
	18%	3%	11%	12%	17%	18%	8%	9%	4%	100%
		21%			40%			39%		

Table 3.1(b). Distribution of tenanted land among holdings of different size, 1496–1540.

Size (acres)	0–6	7–14	15–29	30	31–59	60	61–89	90	90+	Total
Number	171	90	748	1140	2385	3360	1950	2700	1200	13744
%	1%	1%	5%	8%	17%	24%	14%	20%	9%	100%
							39%			

Sources: TNA: PRO, SC2 175/77, 78 (Adlestrop, Maugersbury, Upper Swell); SC6 Henry VIII/1240 (Admington, Longborough, Lower Swell); SC12 7/67 (Bourton on the Hill); SC6 Henry VIII/4047 (Broadwell, Talton); SC11 683 (Ilmington); BL, Harleian Rolls B14 (Brookend); Northamptonshire Record Office, FH 363 (Churchill); GA, P329/1 (Little Compton, Preston); New College, Oxford, 3797 (Kingham); Magdalen College, Oxford, Quinton 357 (Quinton); Worcester Cathedral Library, C787 (Shipston).

Table 3.2. Rents per yardland held by custom of the manor.

Place	Date	Median rent recorded
Adlestrop	1498–1517	9s 0d
Bourton on the Hill	1494	17s 0d
Broadwell	1540	8s 0d
Churchill	1518	12s 0d
Compton, Little	1539–40	9s 8d
Donnington	1533	6s 8d
Ilmington	1496	11s 8d
Kingham	1499	14s 0d
Longborough	1540	13s 4d
Maugersbury	1498–1515	10s 0d
Oddington	early 16th cent.	6s 10½d
Quinton	1517–18	20s 0d
Swell, Lower	1540	8s 0d
Swell, Upper	1498–1515	5s 0d
Talton	1540	12s 0d
Median of medians		10s 0d

Source: As for Table 3.1, with the addition of GA, D621/M8 (Oddington).

and the active resistance of tenants over many generations which helped to define customary payments.

To sum up, the inhabitants of the countryside around Moreton, both on the wold and in the valleys, lived in compact villages, farmed in open fields, belonged as tenants to ancient Church estates, and had developed a landholding structure in which a majority of tenants held 1, 2, 3, or more customary yardlands. People from different villages would have found it very easy to relate to one another. They would share in the same way of life: they were aware of both the merits and the frustrations of living in a community, they valued meeting as a congregation in a church or chapel, the importance of custom, and the skills needed to deal with a remote and conservative lord. These characteristics were shared with a broad swathe of countryside across the Cotswolds and the vales below the hills, so one cannot claim that our district was unique. To these similarities must be added the links that emphasize the way in which different parts of the district complemented one another.

The first connection between upland and lowland was sometimes achieved at local level by the inclusion in parish, township, or manorial boundaries of different types of land that allowed the inhabitants access to a balanced range of resources. A series of parishes straddled the western and northern edge of the Cotswolds from Stanway in the west to Ilmington in the north, so as to include pasture on the hill, slopes that might have some woodland, arable land at a lower level, and some meadow at the lowest point on the banks of a stream. On the eastern side of the region the hills are not so high, and lack a sharp edge, but nonetheless parishes like Cherington and Stourton extended across a valley, taking in hills both on the northern and southern boundaries, and containing at mid-point the best arable and extensive riverside meadows. The Oxfordshire parishes of Churchill and Kingham ran from hills to the north-east down to the Evenlode, so as to include good meadow land. The same anxiety for as many villages as possible to get a share of pasture led to the extraordinary intrusion of ten parishes into the heath to the east of Moreton, all meeting at or very near to the pasture's central point (see Fig. 3.2), and in the same fashion ten parishes held part of the hilltop pasture that lay between the valleys of the Windrush and the Dikler.

A second type of territorial organization was used to deal with problem of imbalances of resources. Some villages either lacked access to broad stream valleys with adequate areas of meadow, or they had taken a decision to plough up their pastures and use most of their land for arable. Pieces of meadowland would be attached to a village some distance away. For example, the meadows and pastures of the Evenlode valley were shared out among more remote settlements.(Fig. 3.8) Condicote, which was sited at a great height on the hills, included in its boundaries a detached meadow of 23½ acres at Horsenden on the eastern side of Longborough. Villagers going to mow the hay in this meadow drove their carts 2½ miles (4 km), mostly

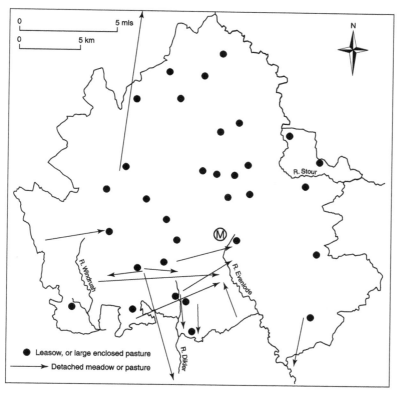

Fig. 3.8. Heritage's country: leasows and other large pastures, and connections between estates and farms and detached pieces of meadow or pasture.

through Longborough's territory. Longborough itself took in fields at Heath End in adjoining Evenlode. Broadwell, which had especially extensive meadows, had part of them allocated to the adjoining parish of Oddington, and some meadow was attached to Temple Guiting, which was situated 6 miles (9.6 km) away in the narrow valley of the Windrush where meadow was in short supply.[38] Meadow at Evenlode, and at Hyde Mill on the Dikler, was also attached to Upper Swell, and Eyford, placed high on the wolds, obtained hay from meadows again at Evenlode and also on the Dikler at Bourton on the Water. The latter village lies outside Heritage country, as does Welford on Avon, but the monks of Bordesley Abbey who held Coombe Grange on the hills above Chipping Campden also had property at Welford, presumably for the sake of its meadow.[39]

These attachments of meadow to the main village territory were often very old. They might have been recorded for the first time in Heritage's day or even later, but they went back to lords' purchases in the thirteenth or fourteenth centuries, or to territorial arrangements before the Conquest, and had become part of the institutional structure of the countryside. On a larger scale one can see how estate structures extending far beyond the narrow confines of the Moreton district could help to maintain balances in land and produce before 1400. Bourton on its hill was naturally twinned with Moreton in its low marsh, and both should be seen in the context of the west Midland estate of Westminster Abbey that held the bulk of its land in the mixed farming and woodland manors of the Severn valley. Likewise Blockley contributed sheep pasture to the bishopric of Worcester's estate with much corn in the Avon valley and wood in the forest of Feckenham.[40]

Complementary landscapes could be used effectively by moving animals between pastures. Traditional transhumance was practised on the hills by driving flocks of sheep to higher ground in the summer (usually from May to early November) when the grass was growing and the weather kind, and then moving them in the winter to more sheltered pastures where the grass was more likely to keep growing, and where the hay was conveniently stored. Some hardy sheep, usually the tough adult wethers that grew the heaviest fleeces, remained on the hills, where they were sheltered in sheepcotes and were fed in bad weather from lofts full of hay and sheafs of grain, peas, and beans.[41] The high pasture of Hinchwick in Condicote was estimated to accommodate five hundred sheep in the summer and three hundred in the winter. Hill pasture had a scarcity value at Snowshill, and was recorded in 1535 as capable of feeding five hundred sheep at 4d per sheep in the winter, whereas in the summer one thousand sheep could be accommodated and their pasture was worth 1d each. Sheep were sometimes moved to graze the stubbles of cornfields, like the flocks from Condicote that were customarily driven (according to a record

---

[38] *VCH Glos.*, VI, 68–9; TNA: PRO, SC6 Henry VIII 1240 (Longborough account, 1540); *VCH Glos.*, VI, 53.

[39] TNA: PRO, SC2 175/77 (Upper Swell court rolls, 1500, 1512); Caley and Hunter (eds), *Valor Ecclesiasticus*, II, 252 (Eyford); 272 (Combe Grange).

[40] B. F. Harvey, *Westminster Abbey and its Estates in the Middle Ages* (Oxford, 1977); C. Dyer, *Lords and Peasants in a Changing Society: The Estates of the Bishopric of Worcester, 680–1540* (Cambridge, 1980).

[41] C. Dyer, 'Sheepcotes: Evidence for Medieval Sheep Farming', *Medieval Archaeology*, 34 (1995), 136–64.

of 1517) through intervening Upper Swell to reach the fields of Temple Guiting.[42] The sheep at Condicote and Snowshill were being taken no more than a mile or two up and down the hills, though in the heyday of the great estates before 1400 flocks would regularly be driven 10 or 20 miles (16 or 32 km), from the river valleys to the Cotswold heights. In Heritage's day estates based on leaseholds tended to be smaller and more self-contained, though it would be tempting to think that William Willington, for example, when he held the pasture high up on Upton Wold in Blockley, would have taken sheep there in the summer from his Stour valley pastures at Barcheston. The tenants of lesser holdings who were accused at Maugersbury and Churchill of misusing common rights by taking in the flocks of outsiders were providing the facilities for small-scale transhumance, and Heritage's account book refers quite often to the 'summering' and 'wintering' of small numbers of livestock.[43] There were many contentions about the practice of transhumance, but everyone appreciated that differences in the landscape could be used in a complementary way, and gave people who lived on or near the hills a sense of an integrated economy based on combining assets.

The third connecting web that stretched across Heritage's country came from the social and institutional bonds which brought people together through official duties, ownership of property, and more informal social connections. The people of Lower Lemington were obliged to attend a court at Stanway, involving a journey of 10 miles (16 km), for their lord's convenience. For the same reason the tenants of the Westminster manors of Bourton, Moreton, Sutton, and Todenham met at a court held at Moreton. Other groups of villagers, not all of them living near one another, were supposed to be present at the hundred courts. The annual audit of manorial accounts brought together the bailiffs of the Westminster estate. Some gentry lords, such as the Fortescues of Ebrington, held manors scattered across the district, which must have pushed the tenants into contact. Leaseholders also made connections between settlements, like John Bradwey of Chipping Campden who was a tenant at Norton Subedge and Barcheston, and William Porter of Chipping Campden who held a farm at Mickleton. People created their own associations without the encouragement or compulsion of lords. A group of deeds from Hidcote Bartrim on the north-western edge of Heritage's country show free tenants transferring land in the period 1484–1523. The parties to the transactions, that is the buyers and sellers of land, came from Hidcote itself, Mickleton, Evesham, Foxcote (in Ilmington), and Rollright in Oxfordshire. In the more detailed descriptions of parcels of land we are told of the owners of adjacent properties, who came from Ebrington, Evesham, and Ilmington. The witnesses included people from Hidcote and Mickleton. The association between these people was not just based on commerce, as the choice of a witness, for example, arose from the regard in which individuals were held.[44] Buyers and sellers of land were connected by

[42] Caley and Hunter (eds.), *Valor Ecclesiasticus*, II, 203, 457; TNA: PRO SC2 175/78.
[43] TNA: PRO, SC2/175/77 (court roll of 1504); Northamptonshire Record Office, FH 365 (court roll 1520); AB, fos.23r, 35r, 35v, 40v, 45r, 50r, 53v, 57v, 58r, 62v.
[44] GA, D5358/4, 5, 6, 7 (deeds).

marriage, family, friendship, or membership of a religious fraternity, and these connections brought the inhabitants of scattered villages and towns together.

These links suggest that the different parts of the country around Moreton were in contact with one another, their resources complemented one another, and they were bound together by ties of mutual support. Their main connections, however, depended on the network of towns.

TOWNS AND COMMUNICATIONS

Necessarily at some length, we must consider the flow of commerce within and beyond Heritage's country, which could be both unifying and divisive. Much of that trade was focused on five towns, Moreton in Marsh being Heritage's home town, and in a ring around it Chipping Norton, Stow on the Wold, Chipping Campden, and Shipston on Stour (Fig. 3.9). On the horizon, and exercising an

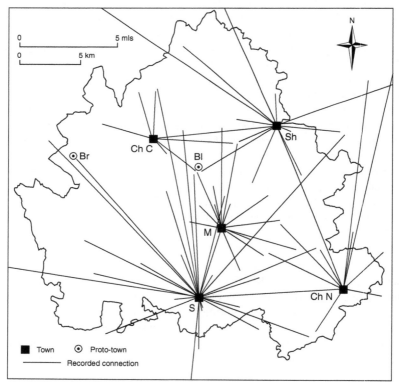

Fig. 3.9. Towns and hinterlands. Each town is shown together with lines indicating connections arising from tenancy, trade contacts, migrations, debts, and other links. Abbreviations: Bl, Blockley; Br, Broadway; Ch C, Chipping Campden; Ch N, Chipping Norton; M, Moreton in Marsh; S, Stow on the Wold; Sh, Shipston on Stour.

influence on the district, were Banbury, Burford, Evesham, Stratford upon Avon, Tewkesbury, and Winchcombe. Even more remote, but still having occasional contacts, were large and important towns, notably Worcester, a centre of shire and diocesan government, and a hub of trade because of its river port and bridge, and two other shire towns, the port of Gloucester, and Oxford with its landowning colleges (see Fig. 1.1). The regional capitals of Bristol and Coventry had many points of contact with Moreton's district, and of course the powerful looming presence of London was always felt.

Towns were dense and permanent settlements in which most of the inhabitants had non-agricultural occupations. The concentrated built-up urban space can be observed in the layout of carefully planned settlements. All five towns in Figure 3.9 had been founded deliberately in the twelfth and thirteenth centuries, and that creative process left them with a legacy of either a single street which was wide enough to accommodate a market, as at Campden, Moreton, and Chipping Norton, or a more complex cluster of streets around a marketplace, as at Shipston and Stow.[45] For modern observers, and for people in the centuries immediately following their foundation, these planned settlements looked different from even the largest and most regular villages (Figs. 3.10 and 3.11). The continuous congested rows of houses facing the main streets and marketplaces, the long narrow plots running from the backs of the houses, the marketplaces partly occupied by permanent stalls, and the occasional public building or market cross all demonstrated the special character of the urban environment. Anyone entering a town in Heritage's day would have been confronted with rows of two-storey houses, with their upper floors jettied over the street, often containing shops on their ground floors, which during the day had boards jutting out to display goods. Signs, including stakes to advertise alehouses, bristled out of the street frontages at first-floor level. There were also compact lines and blocks of shops and permanent stalls, such as the 'butchers' selds' at Stow and the 'shoprow' at Shipston, which had chambers above them. At Shipston the shop row still exists, constricting parts of a once wide street into narrow alleys perpetually in the shade. The density of commercial space is only too apparent.

A majority of non-agricultural occupations was anticipated in some towns by their founders, who carved out a small patch of land that could not have provided much scope for farming. Stow's resources amounted to 33 acres, and landholding at Chipping Campden was restricted by the pre-existing agricultural settlements of Berrington and Westington.[46] Towns could not feed their own population from the land allocated to them: instead it was always intended that they had to find

---

[45] The town plans are presented in R. Leech, *Historic Towns in Gloucestershire*, Committee for Rescue Archaeology in Avon, Gloucestershire and Somerset, Survey no. 3 (1981), 12, 55, 79; K. Rodwell (ed.), *Historic Towns in Oxfordshire: A Survey of the New County* (Oxford, 1975), 89–92; M. Aston and C. J. Bond, *The Landscape of Towns* (London, 1976), 93; T. R. Slater, 'The Analysis of Burgages in Medieval Towns: Three Case Studies from the West Midlands', *West Midlands Archaeology*, 23 (1980), 57–9.

[46] H. P. R. Finberg, 'The Genesis of the Gloucestershire Towns', in H. P. R. Finberg (ed.), *Gloucestershire Studies* (Leicester, 1957), 68–9; M. Beresford, *New Towns of the Middle Ages* (London, 1967), 438.

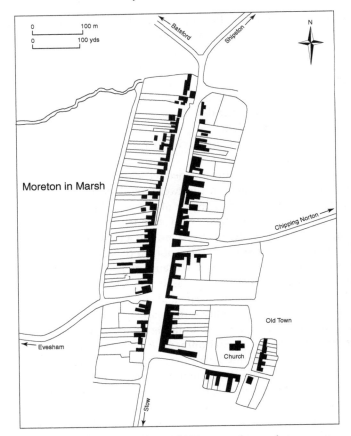

Fig. 3.10. Moreton in Marsh town plan. Old Town to the south-east represents the pre-urban settlement. The layout of the High Street as a broad marketplace along the Fosse Way, with the burgage plots and back lanes, dates from the thirteenth century. Heritage's house occupied a burgage plot and faced onto the marketplace. Source: R. Leech, *Historic Towns in Gloucestershire* (Committee for Rescue Archaeology in Avon, Gloucestershire and Somerset, Bristol, 1981), 55–7.

other ways to make their living. Some evidence for occupations comes from Stow, where we find a baker, butcher, a capper, an innholder, a shearman, a slater, and woolmen. Well-documented Shipston had representatives of the distributive trades: draper and spicer; people who made cloth and clothing (fuller, tailor, and hosier); those involved in preparing and working leather (tanner, skinner, and shoemaker); those who processed and sold food and drink (baker, butcher, brewer, and tippler [retail seller of ale]); and representatives of the metal trades (ironmonger and smith). A wider range of occupations is found in large towns, where merchants tended to congregate, but our five towns, with the possible exception of Shipston, each provided a living for two or three merchants. There are also hints

Fig. 3.11. High Street, Moreton in Marsh, planned as a wide space for a market, looking north. The left-hand (western) side, filled with cars, was occupied in the Middle Ages by market stalls, some of them permanent structures (author's photograph).

of specialities, such as trade in horses at Stow and sheepskins (wool fells) at Stow and Chipping Norton.[47]

The best sense of the differences between towns can be gained from comparing their size, and Table 3.3 summarizes our knowledge of the urban populations. None of them were very large, not even by the standard of market towns, which exceeded a thousand people in many cases, such as in the nearby centres at Banbury, Evesham, and Stratford. A clear hierarchy is apparent, which placed Moreton at the bottom and Campden in a superior position. Two rural settlements have been included because they had some urban pretensions. Broadway had been founded as a new town, but does not seem to have developed its potential, though it had a chartered market, and Blockley was a centre of trade, both in local retailing of foodstuffs and more widely through its fair. Blockley, like most of the villages of the district, was smaller than the towns, but Broadway was a large settlement with enough peasant and labourer households to outstrip the smallest of the

---

[47] Occupational studies of an earlier period are R. H. Hilton, *The English Peasantry in the Later Middle Ages* (Oxford, 1975), 78–9; C. Dyer, 'Small Town Conflict in the Later Middle Ages: Implications of Events at Shipton-on-Stour', *Urban History*, 19 (1992), 1–28; the information for the occupations at Stow and Shipston given here for the period 1495–1520 come from deeds, court rolls etc.; TNA: PRO, SC2 175/77 (court roll of Maugersbury, 1499); A. Hanham (ed.), *The Cely Letters 1472–1488*, Early English Text Society (Oxford, 1975), 155, 158.

Table 3.3. Urban populations in the early sixteenth century.

Chipping Campden	500–600
Chipping Norton	400–500
Stow on the Wold	300–400
Shipston on Stour	200–300
Moreton in Marsh	200
Broadway	*350*
Blockley	*150*

Source: J. Sheail, *The Regional Distribution of Wealth in England as Indicated in the 1524/5 Lay Subsidy Returns*, List and Index Society, Special Series, 29 (1998), 2, 110, 113–15, 259, 392–4; *B & GLS*; *MSG*; *WT*; J. Maclean, 'Chantry Certificates, Gloucestershire', *Transactions of the Bristol and Gloucestershire Archaeological Society*, 8 (1883–4), 271, 278–80; A. Dyer and D. M. Palliser (eds), *The Diocesan Population Returns for 1563 and 1603*, Records of Social and Economic History, new ser., 31 (Oxford, 2005), 167–9, 292–3; Worcester Cathedral Library, C787; WAM 8383.

market towns. This emphasizes the importance of urban functions and occupational diversity in defining a town, rather than putting too much reliance on size.

A useful way of seeing the towns operating in a region is to regard them as a network, forming connections to their mutual benefit. The traders in towns tended to buy from or sell to counterparts in other towns. Heritage in the course of his operations visited not just Campden, Chipping Norton, Shipston, and Stow, but also Banbury, Evesham, and Stratford. Market stalls in Shipston in 1500–10 were rented by traders from the aspiring towns of Bidford, Blockley, and Brailes, and from a wide range of larger towns at Campden, Chipping Norton, Gloucester, and Stratford.[48] The markets, by a well-established convention, tended to be held on different days, so that traders could circulate from Broadway on Tuesday, to Campden on Wednesday, to Stow on Thursday, and, because one clash had been allowed, to either Moreton or Shipston on Saturday.[49] This was a world dominated by middlemen, who acquired goods from a considerable distance and then distributed them in smaller quantities to local customers. Robert Downford can stand for many others. A draper of Chipping Campden, keeping a market stall at Shipston, he presumably bought his cloth in 25-yard lengths from other drapers in larger towns and then cut these into smaller pieces for the customers who came to him during the week at Campden, and on Saturdays in Shipston.[50] He would be selling to the people who would wear the cloth, but also to tailors or lesser drapers who would be engaging with the consumers. Similarly, ironmongers sold to smiths, and tanners to shoemakers. Sometimes a glimpse can be gained of a transaction with a consumer, such as a sale in 1518 by William Reynolds of Stow to a well-off client, Richard Gerves, of 4¾ yards of violet woollen cloth and 5 ells of linen for 23s 4d.

[48] Worcester Cathedral Library MS A6 (2), fo.12 (record of new stalls, 1500); C788 (rental of stalls 1509–10).

[49] S. Letters, *Gazetteer of Markets and Fairs in England and Wales to 1516*, List and Index Society, Special Series, 32 (2003), 141, 146, 148; 33 (2003), 362, 380.

[50] Downford is recorded in the Worcester Cathedral Library rental, C788.

The cloth was clearly of high quality, costing between 3s 0d and 4s 0d per yard, which was appropriate because Gerves was (by 1525) the second richest man in Stow.[51]

Most urban trade was in mundane agricultural produce. The towns had a role in the exchange of crops, livestock, dairy produce, and sometime labour between its varied landscapes. The Stour valley had a surplus of wheat, while barley was grown in quantity on the hills. Cattle were kept in greater numbers in the lowlands, and the hills had more sheep. Woodland products from the district mostly came from the hills, but more often from longer distance sources in the woodlands to the north and east. Of the five towns, four lay on the edge of the high ground, and Broadway and Blockley, the two aspirant towns, were similarly placed. Only Shipston was located in the midst of lowland champion country in the Stour valley. There was a notable gap between towns on the high ground, to the west of Stow, perhaps because people who made their living in an homogeneous rural economy did not need the services of a town to make exchanges with one another.

The hinterlands served by each town demonstrate competition, as well as showing how the urban market assisted in the interchange of goods between complementary landscapes (Fig. 3.9). We lack the numerous and detailed records of debts that are the best indication of a town's 'sphere of influence'; there are enough indications of the range of contacts from such indirect evidence as tenancy of land, references in wills, and occasional records of debt.[52] These do not show neatly defined territories around each town, though an inner ring of contacts within a radius of about 6 miles (9.6 km) can be detected. Quite often the tenant or debtor lived 10 miles (16 km) or more from the town. One can see that Stow on the Wold had more of these relatively long-distance connections than did Moreton in Marsh, which suggests that Stow had greater success in building up a network of contacts and in attracting trade. Towns reached across the commercial territory of a rival, and encroached on its 'natural' customers, as when Stow had links with Lemington, on Moreton's doorstep, and Chipping Norton attracted a customer from Barton on the Heath, which lay quite near to Moreton.[53]

The differences between towns are most obviously displayed when we consider those that failed to develop. Broadway is the clearest case, as it was granted a market and a fair in 1251, and its lord, Pershore Abbey, founded burgage plots along the road between Worcester and London. It had a special court in the fourteenth century suited for dealing with the legal business of a town, a portmoot. Burgages were regularly being conveyed in the 1490s and early sixteenth century, but in groups of two, three, and four, sometimes in association with agricultural land, rather as cottage holdings might be part of a composite holding in a village.

---

[51] TNA: PRO, SC2 176/8 (Slaughter Hundred court roll, 1521).

[52] On these general questions of urban location, urban hierarchy, and 'spheres of influence', see for example J. A. Galloway (ed.), *Trade, Urban Hinterlands and Market Integration c.1300–1600*, Centre for Metropolitan History Working Party Series, 3 (London, 2000); J. Laughton, E. Jones, and C. Dyer, 'The Urban Hierarchy in the Later Middle Ages: A Study of the East Midlands', *Urban History*, 28 (2001), 331–57; J. S. Lee, *Cambridge and its Economic Region, 1450–1560* (Hatfield, 2005).

[53] TNA: PRO, PROB 11/15, fo.192r (will); *Calendar of Patent Rolls*, Henry VII, 153.

The food and drink trades were quite prominent, and there were usually four brewers, a butcher, and an innkeeper, but no sign of varied crafts and other occupations.[54] At Blockley a burgage is recorded in the fourteenth century on land belonging to the church, so the initiative in founding a town may have come from a rector. The bishop also contributed by founding a fair, and in our period the fair (held at Michaelmas, 29 September) was attracting a respectable amount of trade (see p. 200), and there seems to have been an unofficial market. A shop was built on to a house in 1506–7, and a butcher built a stall in the street near the church in 1529. In the 1520s a concentration of food and drink traders – bakers, butchers, and brewers – plied their trade at Blockley, apparently supplying the needs of the other nearby villages of Draycott, Aston Magna, and Northwick. Cloth must have been made there or nearby, as one of Blockley's mills worked as a fulling mill.[55] But while this evidence suggests that Blockley might have had a chance of becoming a town, there is no suggestion that this potential was realized.

So these were two 'might have been' towns, and we are left with five that all had very visible urban roles in the early sixteenth century, and which have functioned effectively from the time of their foundations in the thirteenth century until the present day. Why were some more successful than others? A possibility lay in the varying degrees of influence and encouragement given by lords, as all of our towns were 'seigneurial boroughs' living under the government of various landed estates. Lords played a vital part in founding the towns and provided an institutional framework by granting land by burgage tenure, that is, a privileged free tenure which allowed the tenants to do as they wished with the property, on payment of a modest cash rent of between 12*d* and 16*d*. They were often governed by bailiffs, catchpolls, or other officials who were themselves townsmen, and in all cases there was at some stage of the town's development a special court, such as a portmoot or a piepowder court. Lords generally favoured a compromise by which they had ultimate control of the town, and drew from it a regular income in rents, tolls, and court profits, but the townsmen ran their own affairs from day to day.

Occasionally a lord helped the town long after its foundation, as when Evesham Abbey arranged a new fair charter for Stow in 1476, under which the date was moved from early August to 1 May and 13 October.[56] The townspeople could express their sense of community, and take a hand in running their own affairs, by organizing themselves as fraternities or feoffees running a chantry, chapel, or school, which had a religious purpose but could also deal with secular matters of common interest. These institutions were sometimes shadowy and poorly recorded. Moreton's guild is known from a single reference in 1522 to its property holding in the village of Greet.[57] The group of Shipston townspeople who administered

---

[54] Birmingham Archives and Heritage, DV20a 167575, DV 19a 16574 (deeds); Barnard 223 (court roll); TNA: PRO, SC2 210/32 (court roll).
[55] Worcester Cathedral Library, E54 (court roll); WRO, BA 2636, ref.009:1, 176/92498; 177/92504; 177/92509 (account rolls); 37(iii), 43806, fo.28r.
[56] Letters, *Gazetteer*, 148.   [57] *MSG*, 211.

their chapel were only recorded when their activities were curtailed on the initiative of the rector of Tredington, who felt threatened by them. In the course of this dispute it was revealed that they had a common seal. Shipston was the only town where the lord took a continuing close interest, which was to the town's political disadvantage, in that Worcester Priory, stung by acts of insubordination, cancelled the townspeople's burgage tenure in the early fifteenth century. This meant that in Heritage's time the tenants of Shipston held a 'messuage and a curtilage' by customary tenure, not a freehold burgage as was the case in all of the other towns. Transfers of land and other matters were recorded in a conventional manor court, not in a borough court or portmoot, and Shipston burgages paid a variable entry fine, just like customary holdings of agricultural land. But the Priory was still prepared to invest in the town, building a new row of sixteen shops in 1500, which were added to the existing forty. Within its modest expectation of achievement, Shipston seems to have had a lively economy, in view of its rapid recovery from a disastrous fire in 1478.[58] Moreton was notably less privileged than other towns, in that its affairs came before the manor court held for the surrounding villages of the Westminster Abbey estate. Transfers of burgages were reported to the court, and they paid a relief to the lord of one year's rent.[59]

Our two smallest towns lacked autonomy and were governed as part of a manor, which may have given them disadvantages when competing with their rivals. Location was probably a more important influence on the towns' varied fortunes. There was not enough trade or demand for manufactures to support a high density of towns, and among our failures Blockley was clearly too close to Moreton and Campden. Some were placed on major roads that gave them the role of 'thoroughfare towns', which is often indicated by the number of inns. Broadway, Moreton, and Chipping Norton lay on the main Worcester to London road, but Broadway was too near to Evesham for it to be a major stopping place, while Moreton was ideal for travellers who had set out from Worcester, Evesham, or Oxford, and it had two inns. It also served the Fosse Way, but Stow on the same road sat at a point where a branch of the London road, two other routes from the south-west, and the road to Burford all met – and it seems to have attracted more travellers, as we know of four inns, the Bell, the Crown, the George, and the Swan.[60] Chipping Campden's place on the junction of the roads that joined Banbury to Evesham, and Stratford to Winchcombe and Tewkesbury, attracted travellers. A duty of the farmer of the demesne at Cutsdean was to pay the expenses of the steward of Worcester Priory on the long journey to outlying Cutsdean, and Campden was regarded as the ideal location for a meal.[61] Shipston stood on the road that took travellers from Campden to the minor borough of Brailes and then to Banbury, but though near to the Fosse Way it lay on the north-south road from Stratford to

[58] Dyer, 'Small Town Conflict'; C. Dyer, 'The Great Fire of Shipston-on-Stour', *Warwickshire History*, 8 (1992–3), 179–94.
[59] WAM 8383 (Moreton court roll).
[60] WAM 8383; *VCH Glos.*, VI, 149.
[61] Worcester Cathedral Library, A6(2), 51v (Priory register).

Chipping Norton. It was not as well placed as its rivals, but still in 1518–19 was equipped with two inns. The character and capacity of one of these small-town inns can be glimpsed from the surviving structure embedded in the modern White Hart at Chipping Norton. It occupied a plot that was 17 metres wide at the front, and stretched back for 120 metres. In *c.*1500 there would have been stables and outbuildings at the back of the plot, but the accommodation for travellers in a range running back from the street was provided with a first-floor gallery 21 metres long, giving access to a series of chambers. Traces of the original colour scheme, with red and green paint, could still be seen when modern restoration exposed the structure of the gallery.[62]

If long-distance roads determined the wealth and size of a town, then Stow and Moreton would have occupied a high point in the hierarchy, and also important was the dense network of local communications that delivered goods and people to Chipping Campden and Chipping Norton. These towns lived on local trade in agricultural produce and cheap manufactured goods, and so short journeys to many villages contributed much to the urban economy. Stow and Moreton inn-keepers welcomed a cart loaded with a barrel of wine landed from the Severn at Gloucester or Tewkesbury because the driver would buy a meal for himself and fodder and stabling for his horses, but the wine would proceed on its journey to be sold at a larger town. Small-town traders gained much more from the arrival of a cartload of barley from a village a few miles distant, because as well as servicing the driver and the horses, the grain could be sold in the market, malted locally, and used to brew ale for sale to dozens of customers in the alehouses of the town. Local trade also allowed the town markets to profit from the divergent landscapes of their hinterland. Again Chipping Campden and Chipping Norton were located on significant frontiers between upland and lowland.

Towns depended on trade, markets, and manufactures, but their inhabitants and their visitors took a strong interest in the institutions that had often played a part in the early stages of the town's growth, and which developed as part of civic, social, cultural, and religious life. There is a close correlation between the size and number of these institutions and the scale and importance of the town. Chipping Campden is still dominated, as it was in Heritage's time, by its tall church tower, which like much of the rest of the church had been rebuilt in the late fifteenth and early sixteenth centuries. The size and quality of the structure, and its furnishings and decoration, of which monumental brasses and pieces of embroidered vestments still survive, reflect the wealth and enthusiasm of the parishioners. The rectory had been appropriated by Chester Abbey, but the living of the vicar at £20 was a good one, and there were four chantries. So at least five clergy lived there, and in addition a schoolmaster taught in a grammar school, which was founded in 1443 and was said to be teaching sixty pupils a century later.[63] Chipping Norton church was also provided with a

---

[62] Worcester Cathedral Library, E95 (Shipston court roll); for Chipping Norton: E. Simons, J. Phimester, L. Webley, and A. Smith, 'A Late Medieval Inn at the White Hart Hotel, Chipping Norton, Oxfordshire', *Oxoniensia*, 70 (2005), 309–25.

[63] Caley and Hunter (eds), *Valor Ecclesiasticus*, II, 502; J. Maclean, 'Chantry Certificates, Gloucestershire', *Transactions of the Bristol and Gloucestershire Archaeological Society*, 8 (1883–4), 278–80.

clutch of institutions, three chantries, a guild dedicated to the Holy Trinity, and a St Nicholas Guild. A school was founded in 1450, and a hospital or almshouse in 1513. The medieval church tower has gone, but the late fifteenth-century nave is as impressive as that at Campden, and brasses commemorating wealthy townspeople are similarly the main survival of the church's interior furnishings. A will of 1501 lists ten lights that were kept burning in the church.[64] Stow stands next in the hierarchy, with two chantries and a fraternity of the Holy Trinity that was richly endowed with land in the late fifteenth century. Its architecturally complex church includes a tower and windows, including a clerestory in the nave, all of the fifteenth century. The tower stands next to the marketplace, so the clock and chimes for which money was bequeathed in 1511 by Thomas Davies, a friend of Heritage, must have served a useful civic purpose in signalling the correct times to begin and end selling. Stow was also provided with an almshouse and a school.[65]

Chipping Campden, Chipping Norton, and Stow had rich and old churches, which are likely to have been minster churches in the pre-Conquest period. In the early Middle Ages they acted as a point of attraction for traders and artisans, because the clergy were themselves wealthy consumers, but they also gathered crowds from a large parish, who assembled in and around the church to buy and sell as well as worship and pay church dues. These churches helped to determine the site of early market towns. Blockley and Broadway had also been minsters, and as we have seen these embryonic towns did not mature into sustainable urban communities. Instead urban functions developed in relatively minor settlements at Moreton and Shipston, within a few miles of the former minster (Blockley and Tredington). The ecclesiastical facilities of these new small towns were poorly endowed and of low status. Both were provided with chapels without legal burial rights until the early sixteenth century, though we know that both already had churchyards. But if they had not inherited important churches, the townspeople made of the chapels as much as they could. Shipston had endowed its chapel with landed income, and around 1400 the town had a school, which may have persisted a century later. Moreton's chapel presumably housed the altar of its fraternity, and John Palmer in 1491 bequeathed the large sum of £5 towards the cost of a 'great bell' that would be hung in a new tower.[66] No medieval church building survives either at Moreton or at Shipston because they were later rebuilt.

This examination of urban institutions and buildings demonstrates that towns were in a variety of ways important places for their inhabitants and for people in their surrounding countryside. The churches of the larger towns made a visual impact, and the buildings and fittings impressed visitors with their richness. The clergy provided religious services, and officiated at the masses for the dead that were funded by the chantries and fraternities. The churches brought colour, light,

[64] Caley and Hunter (eds), *Valor Ecclesiasticus*, II, 180; J. R. H. Weaver and A. Beardwood (eds), *Some Oxfordshire Wills*, Oxfordshire Record Society, 39 (1958), 69–70; TNA: PRO, PROB 11/22, fo.75r–75v.
[65] *VCH Glos.*, VI, 160–2, 163; TNA: PRO, PROB 11/17, fos.16v–17r; Caley and Hunter (eds), *Valor Ecclesiasticus*, II, 436.
[66] TNA: PRO, PROB 11/9, fo.39v–40r.

music, drama, and ritual into the lives of all those with humdrum daily lives. The concentration of clergy gave urban society a special character: they were often not local in their origins and connections, and they brought the laity into contact with a literate world, not just because they themselves owned and read books, but because they educated local children.

Towns were commercial centres, but they had no monopoly on trade. The transactions of individuals help us to see how exchange worked at a local level in the countryside. For example, John Robert died in 1542, some years after the period of main interest to us, but his connections were likely to reflect well-established patterns that went back many decades. He had lived at Stanway, on the western edge of our district. He was a peasant cultivator, who owned a plough, horses, cattle, and sheep. His sheep moved up and down the hill above Stanway, as he owed a man from Wood Stanway for the winter pasture of forty-five sheep (that was specified as lasting from 11 November to 25 March), and in turn had sold summer pasture to a man from Church Stanway and winter pasture to a man from Ford in neighbouring Temple Guiting parish. These movements of animals were not ancient customs, but show that access to grazing was bought and sold – 2*d* per sheep for summer pasture, for example. Most of Robert's debts arose apparently from trade in goods or animals, and they divided almost equally between people living in the lowland to the west of Stanway and those farming on the hills to the east. He had bought malt and a horse in the valley, and sheep and another horse from the hills at Cutsdean. Only once was a town mentioned, because he owed money to the king's bailiff of Winchcombe, which was probably a rent rather than the price of a purchase.[67]

William Gibbes of Stretton on Fosse, who made his will in 1529, also lived on the edge of the hills, on the northern side, and also owned many sheep. Of the twenty-one debts owed to him, at least ten came from the lowlands mainly to the north of Stretton, in villages such as Blackwell and Honington, and five from the higher ground towards Chipping Campden. Three of his debtors lived in towns – Campden, Moreton, and Shipston – so the majority, as in the Stanway example, apparently arose from deals done directly between country dwellers.[68] We will see that John Heritage also negotiated his purchases directly with his suppliers in the country.

A road system was essential to the many links and connections identified here, whether agricultural, commercial, or religious. The most important routes connected towns, like Banbury Way, Burford Way, and Woodstock Way, that were all used to define boundaries of parcels of land in a Chipping Norton terrier (survey of land) of about 1500.[69] Most roads, however, were part of a network of routes that gave the local population access to fields, pastures, mills, and churches, like

[67] GA, D3439/349.
[68] WRO, BA 3590/I, ref.008:7, wills vol.2, fo.104; on the general tendency for buying and selling to happen in the country, C. Dyer, 'The Hidden Trade of the Middle Ages: Evidence from the West Midlands', in *idem, Everyday Life in Medieval England* (London, 1994), 283–303.
[69] Magdalen College, Oxford, Adds. 92.

the common way at Draycott in Blockley in 1520, on which animals were grazed.[70] At Barcheston a causeway led from the church towards a crossing of the river Stour, which is recorded because it was damaged by local people digging out stones.[71] If well-used roads were impeded, then conflict followed. At Kingham the Church-way at some time before 1516 was blocked when the farmer of a local lay landlord built his house across the road, preventing, as the parishioners complained, the carriage of dead bodies to the churchyard.[72] On the boundary of Longborough and Evenlode the abbot of Hailes was supposed to maintain the Stratford bridge across the Evenlode river, which gave access to the Heath End pasture, and that route is only one example of the many roads that converged on areas of pasture, such as the heath to the east of Moreton or the Ilmington Hills.[73]

Road building and maintenance at such villages as Bourton, Broadway, and Moreton required tenants to carry cartloads of stones to mend the carriageway. At Evenlode the word 'pavement' was used to describe the stone road surface. The duties of villages included repair to bridges, such as that on the road between Blockley and Shipston which was supposed to be maintained by the village of Northwick. Villagers were evidently maintaining quite important 'main roads', or the king's highway, which carried long-distance traffic as well as local carts and draught animals. At Broadway an important road, the main route from Worcester to London, ran for 2 miles (3.2 km) through the parish. Tenants and inhabitants were ordered seven times between 1494 and 1513 to mend the common way or the king's way. On one occasion each tenant was expected to contribute a wainload of stone; another time it was proposed to raise money at a rate of ½d per yard-land.[74] Local communities were contributing to the travelling convenience of the whole kingdom, no doubt after higher authority put pressure on them.

The major roads took people and goods out of Heritage's country to the regional centres, such as Worcester, where the Fretherne family lived, who also held property in Moreton; to the large town of Coventry, the place of origin of Robert Tate, who also had strong links with Stow; and to Bristol, from which came Robert Beysond, a landowner in Shipston.[75] In fact, the journey to Bristol would have involved only a relatively short trip by road, to the river ports at either Tewkesbury or Gloucester, and then down the Severn. The road through Moreton to Chipping Norton was the main route to London, and that journey was often made. The officials of the manors based on Moreton were in regular communication with Westminster Abbey, their lord. Estate administrators and occasionally monks visited the manors, but the accounts of the abbey's receiver for the west Midland manors in 1497–8 reveals that John Payne, the abbey's local representative, sent cash to London by a Worcester carrier, who then took letters back. We know

[70] WRO, BA 2636, ref.009:1, 177/92504 (court roll).

[71] WCRO, CR 580/8 (court roll).

[72] New College, Oxford, 3797 (court roll).

[73] WRO, BA 2636, ref.009:1, 177/92509 (court roll).

[74] WRO, BA 2636, ref.009:1, 177/92509 (court roll); TNA: PRO SC 2 210/32, 33 (court rolls).

[75] Tate appears in a court roll as a property holder in Stow: TNA: PRO SC2 175/77 (court roll). See also A. Sutton, *A Merchant Family of Coventry, London and Calais: The Tates, c.1450–1515* (London, 1998); Beysond is in the 1502 rental, Worcester Cathedral Library, C787.

from other early sixteenth-century sources that a Worcester carrier regularly took his cart to London, probably with loads of cloth for the capital, and returned with goods such as spices for wealthier Worcester consumers.[76]

The administrators of the bishop of Worcester's estate also needed to send money and information to London, where Giovanni Paolo de Gigli, the brother of the bishop Silvestro de Gigli, was occupying the bishop's house on the Strand, and collecting money for transmission to Italy. The messengers included John Freman of Blockley, two Stow merchants, Thomas Alen and Thomas Davies – and John Heritage. Like the Worcester carrier, they needed to go to London for their own business, and saved the estate the trouble and expense of sending a messenger solely for that purpose.[77] Secular lords and their officials also made the journey back and forth, like William Belknap's bailiff at Whitchurch who had his master's accounts audited in London. Again he doubtless carried cash with him.[78]

Mention has been made of Stow merchants who travelled to the capital, and a London mercer and one-time mayor, Robert Tate, owned a house in Stow. A London skinner endowed a Stow chantry with property in Southwark. The clergy had London connections also, like John Molder, vicar of Great Wolford, who allowed in his will of 1524 that if he died in London, he should be buried in the church of St Mary Wolnoth in Lombard Street.[79] More examples are unnecessary, as they would merely reinforce the impression that traders, officials, clergy, and other wealthy and important people had regular contacts with the capital, but that should not be surprising as we have already seen that John Heritage's brother and son were Londoners, and his nephews were educated in schools in or near to the city.

CONCLUSION

What conclusion or generalization can emerge from this examination of Heritage's country about the perspective and local consciousness of those who lived in an 8-mile (13-km) radius of Moreton? To some extent the whole concept of this district is an artificial creation based on the business contacts of one man. But the other inhabitants of the town, and many people who lived in the surrounding villages, must have worked within the framework of Moreton's hinterland. There were hundreds of people who habitually bought and sold in the town's market, and through that activity they grew to know a circle of people who they felt could be trusted, and others they regarded with suspicion. They drank together in the alehouses, gossiped on the street, and no doubt met potential marriage partners. At the same time people went to other towns, attracted by the better opportunities for sale they enjoyed in those markets, or the wider range of goods and services that were available in the larger and busier urban centres.

[76] WAM 24482 (receiver's account, 1497–8);E. S. Fegan (ed.), *Journal of Prior William More*, Worcestershire Historical Society (1914), 208, 260.

[77] WRO, BA2636, ref.009:1, 192/92627 5/12.

[78] Northamptonshire Record Office, Temple of Stow, Box 6/2 (bailiff's account, 1480–1).

[79] GA, D1375, XII 17 and 18; TNA: PRO, PROB 11/21, fo.224v.

They identified with the people who came from the same landscape, but the people of the wolds, or the people of the clay lowlands, would have belonged to a much larger area than was contained within the boundaries of Moreton's hinterland. The Warwickshire Feldon and the oolite uplands stretched for many miles. But the group of villages that we have been examining, as well as their nucleated settlements and economies based on two-field systems and sheep and corn husbandry, with not much wood, shared the peculiarly strong presence of monastic estates, and a tenurial structure based on the yardland, which at the same time was not burdened with a very onerous charge of rent. Their inhabitants must have appreciated the advantage that they enjoyed from living on or near to the edge of the hills, which made it easy for them to exchange crops, animals, foodstuffs, and raw materials that were produced in greater abundance on one side of the border and could be profitably carried to the other side.

One doubts whether anyone identified strongly with the hundreds, but the necessity of involvement in some aspects of government, such as tax collection and law enforcement, meant that people were conscious of being attached to one of the four shires. The complexity of the boundaries made it difficult for anyone to regard Gloucestershire or any of the other shires as a separate entity deserving loyalty from its inhabitants – the shire was just a fact of life. The diocese, especially the diocese of Worcester, must have made contemporaries aware of an area larger than a shire, looking to a great cathedral, and it is this combination of Gloucestershire with much of Worcestershire and Warwickshire, focused on the Severn and its tributaries, that has been claimed as a coherent region. People of the early sixteenth century must always have reserved their strongest sense of attachment to their village or parish, which was not without its controversial dimensions. Firstly, they belonged to more than one village in view of the federal structure of the larger villages and parishes, such as Blockley. The inhabitants of a village such as Aston Magna (or Hanging Aston as it was known) must have felt some connection to Blockley, with its mother church and centre of administration, but were perhaps frustrated that their own settlement had only an underprivileged chapel, and were subordinate to Blockley in such matters as the holding of the court leet (view of frankpledge). Secondly, many individuals were not committed entirely to their community, as they were ready to move from their native village in pursuit of land, employment, and marriage partners.

Finally, as the strength of the London connection makes clear, everyone was aware of the kingdom, and their obligations to it. The military survey of 1522 identified the 'able men' who owned military equipment that could be put at the king's service, and they included people who were known to John Heritage, like William Mansell junior of Bourton on the Hill who was equipped with 'harness for a man', meaning a set of armour, and John Harrys the demesne farmer of Condicote who had a 'sallet', a helmet, and a bill. Among the villagers a few were recorded with a bow and arrows.[80] These people felt that it was their duty to be

---

[80] *MSG*, 178, 217.

prepared to defend the kingdom, and there was a grudging acceptance that they should contribute through their taxes to the costs of the king's wars. If identity was based on shared values, then these were not confined to any specific locality: respect for the Crown, loyalty to the Christian religion, the ideals of freedom, honesty, and trustworthiness, were shared by most people in England. An attachment to the values of the substantial peasants, which meant honouring custom, upholding the rules of husbandry, acting responsibly as governors of the village, and resisting threats from outsiders, including an oppressive lord, was not peculiar to a single country or region.

We can conclude that John Heritage belonged to a country held together by many territorial and commercial links, and those who lived there had common experiences of landscape and society. At the same time contrasts in the countryside helped to pull people into a variety of associations and communities, such as those who used the same urban market, or who shared in the use of a large common pasture, or who attained a similar level of wealth and social standing. Their outside contacts made them conscious that they belonged to the nation. We cannot talk of the people of Heritage's country as having a sense of identity, but rather they experienced a number of divergent and overlapping identities.

4

John Heritage's Wool Business

The early sixteenth century is sometimes represented as a period when England became a capitalist country, but on the other hand it continued to produce and trade in a style that had been established over the previous two centuries. Heritage's account book gives us an opportunity to look into his business dealings and ask whether he had a capitalist mentality. The book also reveals a network of buying, selling, and credit, and we can explore the business world in Gloucestershire and London. How was trade conducted, and how efficient were the methods? Was this the scene of greed, selfishness, and dishonesty that commentators said threatened the common good? How successful was Heritage, and does his career serve as a window on to the trading economy in general?

ACCOUNTING

When John Heritage, in 1501 on one of his regular visits to London, bought a new paper book with ninety-six leaves, he must have been intending to improve his business administration. Perhaps in earlier years he made records of his purchase and sales on loose pieces of paper and parchment, and relied a good deal on memory. In his relatively short career since inheriting the Burton Dassett farm in 1495 and getting started in the wool trade in Moreton in Marsh in about 1498, he may not have conducted enough transactions to fill a whole book. Or a book had been used for a miscellany of farming, trading, and household matters, and the benefits of dividing records into compartments became clear. From his existing records he was able to enter on the first leaf of his new book a total of wool purchases and a sum of money that must relate to his activities in the year 1500. He may have known that in the coming year he would be dealing with some important clients, and felt the need to adopt a more systematic and business-like approach in the style of the London merchants he knew. He may have experienced a problem in which an oral agreement had been disputed, and the value of a written record was impressed on his mind.

Various accounting methods were available in England in 1501. The oldest and best established was that developed for the royal exchequer and then widely adopted for the management of manors and landed estates. In this relatively simple calculation the official presenting the account added together rents and sales for the year, together with any money owed from the previous year (all of these items became the charge) and then arrived at a total of the discharges, consisting of expenses and any money that had been paid over to the lord or the central estate administration. If the discharge was subtracted from the charge, a sum of money often remained that was owed to the estate. This method was originally designed to ensure that officials who had used the receipts legitimately and handed over any surplus would be found at the end of the process to owe nothing and would be 'quit'. The process of auditing was also a check on their honesty and efficiency.[1] Such accounts were being compiled around Heritage every year, for the manors with which he was very familiar, both those belonging to large church institutions at Blockley and Bourton on the Hill, and those held by lay lords such as the Fortescues of Ebrington and the dukes of Buckingham at Great Wolford. Heritage knew well some of the officials who presented the accounts for these manors, such as John Freman the bailiff of Blockley, John Stevens the rent-collector of Bourton, and William Messenger who was farmer of Great Wolford.[2]

The charge/discharge accounting system allowed profit to be calculated, and often led to estates assigning an annual 'value' to a manor, but it was best suited to an official who was justifying his conduct to some higher authority. In choosing his accounting method, Heritage followed the example of other merchants. Sophisticated Mediterranean techniques were known to English traders, probably through their numerous contacts with their Spanish counterparts.[3] As early as 1517 Thomas Howell of London, who was a member of the drapers' company and engaged in the Spanish trade, was using double entry, but he was a pioneer.[4] In 1501 Heritage may not have heard of this important development, or if he had done so, preferred a less complex procedure. In any case, as he was not involved directly in international trade, and as he did not enter into formal partnerships he had no need of such an elaborate systematic innovation.

A variety of accounts were kept by other merchants around Heritage's time. William Mucklow of Worcester, who he may well have known, in 1511 had adopted a type of charge/discharge account, with lists of sales of woollen cloth in the Low Countries, followed by lists of purchases, after which he could strike a balance.[5] John Smythe of Bristol, whose surviving accounts begin in 1538, entered debits and credits on opposite sides of the ledger. This was known as 'venture accounting', as practised in Italy, but fell short of the fully developed double-entry method.[6] These examples were more neatly written and systematic than Heritage's effort, which falls into the category castigated by a contemporary advocate of more

---

[1] The best guide to this system is P. D. A. Harvey, *Manorial Records*, British Records Association, Archives and the User, 5, revised edn. (London, 1999), 25–40. Calculations of profit and compilation of valors developed in the fifteenth century: T. B. Pugh (ed.), *The Marcher Lordships of South Wales, 1415–1536: Select Documents* (Cardiff, 1963), 154–83.

[2] Blockley under John Freman: WRO, BA 2636 ref.009:1, 157/No number (1505–6 account), 170/92389 (1514–15 account); Bourton on the Hill under John Stevens, e.g. WAM 8350 (1496–7); for Fortescue: TNA: PRO, SC6 Henry VIII/1095 (1522–3); for Wolford under William Messenger: Staffordshire Record Office, D641/1/2/277–279 (1497–1509).

[3] J. Vanes (ed.), *The Ledger of John Smythe 1538–50*, Bristol Record Society, 28 (1974), 16–19.

[4] G. Connell-Smith, 'The Ledger of Thomas Howell', *Ec. HR*, 2nd ser., 3 (1951), 363–71.

[5] Birmingham Archives and Heritage, M5 3688, Z Lloyd 51/1.

[6] Vanes (ed.), *John Smythe*, 18–19.

advanced techniques as 'grossly, obscurely and lewdly kept'. It consisted of memoranda and 'reckonings', like the accounts compiled by the London ironmonger of the 1390s, Gilbert Maghfeld, and the book kept at Ipswich from 1521 by Henry Tooley, who was involved in overseas trade.[7]

Among those who kept accounts and were not merchants, memoranda and statements of the finances of agricultural activities were kept by Sir John Pennington, a Lancashire landowner from the 1490s until his death in 1512, which contain records of sales of wool and animals, receipt of rent, and much else. Much less systematic were the financial notes included with a great variety of material in the commonplace book of a Cheshire gentleman, Humphrey Newton.[8] Monastic officials would keep jottings, which only occasionally survive, of day-to-day expenses, such as accounts from Maxstoke Priory in Warwickshire in Heritage's time.[9] Like Heritage's accounts, they were kept in a book with other notes and memoranda. At the end of the year these notes could have contributed to compiling formal accounts that would have been subject to audit, but for Heritage this next stage was unnecessary. A feature he shared with other account keepers at this time was his use of English. These were often direct, immediate, and functional records that were best kept in the language in which the business itself was conducted, and with which the merchants felt most comfortable.

It would not be accurate to describe Heritage's accounts as mere jottings and memoranda, as he arranged his material in a logical fashion, and one can see that his method was systematic enough to be useful to him. He began each year on a new page and entered the name of each supplier of wool, leaving sufficient space for a paragraph for each person (for sample pages see Appendix 1). The transactions during the year would be recorded, beginning with the total price agreed for the wool, and then noting the successive instalments of the money payments made by the merchant to each supplier. The first item in 1501 related to a bargain made with William Bayly of Condicote. Heritage entered the quantity of wool, 2 sacks and 16 pounds in weight, and the price of 10s 8d for each tod of 28 pounds, giving a total of £14 3s 4d. Then follows two of the payments, 23s 4d in 'earnest money' and £5 paid 'by the hands of Fylpys', who (as noted earlier) was Heritage's servant.[10] The record was being updated as money was handed out, though unfortunately Heritage neglected to include every payment, and as in the Bayley case we are left to wonder whether the remaining £8 was ever paid, or whether the recording was neglected – the latter is most likely. He needed to keep his memoranda as he was constantly handing out sums of money, often one suspects when he met his creditors by chance. He might make a number of payments on

[7] P. Ramsey, 'Some Tudor Merchants' Accounts', in A. C. Littleton and B. S. Yamey (eds), *Studies in the History of Accounting* (London, 1956), 185–201; M. K. James, *Studies in the Medieval Wine Trade* (Oxford, 1971), 196–217; J. G. Webb, *Great Tooley of Ipswich: Portrait of an Early Tudor Merchant* (Ipswich, 1962).

[8] TNA: PRO, E101/691/41; Cumbria Record Office, Carlisle, D/Pen/200; D. Youngs, *Humphrey Newton (1466–1536): An Early Tudor Gentleman* (Woodbridge, 2008), 177–200.

[9] A. Watkins, 'Maxstoke Priory in the Fifteenth Century: The Development of an Estate Economy in the Forest of Arden', *Warwickshire History*, 10 (1996), 3–18.

[10] AB, fo.2r.

a single day, for example on 9 October 1504, when he encountered three separate suppliers, and sixteen on 29 September (Michaelmas) 1508.[11] Other payments may have slipped his mind when he sat down with his book, which should have happened every five or six days according to sixteenth-century accounting textbooks, but his errors of omission suggest that he did not always follow this good practice.[12] It was important that the earnest money be committed to paper, because by custom that initial payment made the contract binding. It was understood under some customary rules that if the seller did not deliver, he had to pay back double the earnest money.

Memory was central to the account book, as it was compiled by recording events, that is, the payments of money to those who sold the wool, and its purpose was to aid recall. Commonly, but inconsistently, records of payments were accompanied by a detail that would help to impress on the mind the moment when the money was handed to the supplier. In a sample of 125 payments made in 1513–14, 20 (16 per cent) were given a date, either according to the calendar (10 November) but often by an easily remembered feast day, such as Michaelmas. A place (at Campden, at Blockley) was mentioned in 8 per cent of cases, and two payments took place on an important occasion in a significant place, at Stow Fair and at Stratford Fair. The Michaelmas payments, like the large number noticed above for 1508, were almost certainly made at Blockley Fair, or on the way to or from the important local event held at that time.[13] Twenty-three (18 per cent) were recorded as having been paid by someone in Heritage's circle ('by Hawkins', 'by Bumpas'), or Heritage had given the money to someone other than the creditor himself ('to his son', for example). The money itself might have been memorable ('in gold') or instead of cash, payment was made in kind, in the form of a barrel of tar or a horse. It was often useful to record the purpose of the payment: in 34 cases among the 125 (27 per cent) it was earnest money, and six times the payment was made 'on delivery' when the wool arrived at the woolhouse on the main street of Moreton. Only 20 transactions of 125 were not identified by reference to a date, a place, a person, a coin, a type of payment, or some other aid to memory. Sometimes when no instalments were recorded, because the full purchase price was handed over, it was not even necessary to know the seller's name. On one occasion 21*s* 8*d* was paid to 'a man of Adlestrop'.[14]

The entries are often found to be incomplete, as in the first entry in the book that we have already seen. From a hundred transactions in 1507 and 1508, thirty-eight were settled in full, or at least the recorded payments came within a few pence of the agreed price. A rather greater number, forty, were incomplete in the sense that two-thirds or more of the money was paid, and in the remaining twenty-two the shortfall was more serious, and less than two-thirds of the sum had been

---

[11] AB, fos.13v, 35r, 36r–38r.   [12] Vanes (ed.), *John Smythe*, 18.
[13] S. Letters, *Gazetteer of Markets and Fairs in England and Wales to 1516*, part 1, List and Index Society, Special Series, 32 (London, 2003), 140.
[14] The relationship between financial accounts and memory is explored in P. Quattrone, 'Books to be Practiced: Memory, the Power of the Visual, and the Success of Accounting', *Accounting, Organizations and Society*, 34 (2009), 85–118.

recorded as settled. The gap between debt and payment sometimes seems very large. In 1508 Alexander Hunden delivered wool worth £25 16s 6d, but is said to have received only £17 16s 2d, leaving £8 outstanding.[15] We take it that we are observing bad record-keeping, not a persistent failure to pay, which would have ended Heritage's business career. Nonetheless the long series of instalments sometimes reveals some continued negotiation of the price during the payment process. The merchant added a note to Thomas Powle's entry in 1508: 'paid all saving 26s 8d' but according to conventional arithmetic he still owed £2 6s 4d, suggesting that almost a pound had been forgotten or forgiven. A sum of 10s 8d was, according to our calculations, still owing to William Robyns in 1508, but Heritage felt able to write 'paid all' and close that part of his accounts.[16] For some suppliers their sales of wool to Heritage formed one element in long-running business connections, so that a payment to William Bumpas, Thomas Fletcher, or Thomas Palmer might be lost as the result of some reciprocal service or favour that could not conveniently be entered on the formal account.

The account book therefore was defective in that it omitted relevant payments of money. To add yet more scepticism about the precision of the calculation, one cannot fail to notice that in a suspiciously high proportion of transactions, such as 36 out of 156 in 1503–5, the weight of wool was given as exactly 2, 3, 4, or more tods. The tod contained two stones, or 28 pounds, and it was convenient for the total to be a round number because wool was priced in tods. One supposes that Heritage or his servant stood at the balance and said to the seller, 'let's call it 4 tods' (or rather the equivalent expression in the English of the day), and that amount was written in the book. Perhaps the decision to round up or down depended on factors such as the quality of the wool or the state of dealings between the woolman and the client on other matters.

The account book had a primary purpose of keeping track of individual records of each purchase, but it had a more strategic function of allowing the woolman to be aware of the progress and scale of the business, as he maintained a systematic series of totals throughout the accounts. This was evidently one of the purposes of the book from the beginning, because at the foot of the first page the quantity of wool (7 sacks 1 tod 17 pounds) was calculated, together with the total of money that had been agreed (£49 13s 10d). Heritage's method of dealing with these totals evolved over the years. In 1501 he arrived at an interim total of wool, just over 24 sacks (and money) after four pages, which marked roughly the mid-point of the year. Three pages later he came to another interim total (19 sacks) and then made some rough jottings about wool sales.[17] This was evidently the end of the accounting year, because 1502 appears as a subheading on the next page. After that tentative year, in 1502 and all subsequent years, there was an annual total of the quantity of wool bought, together with the sum of money that had been committed to buy it. An interim total shows sometimes that Heritage was keeping a check on progress. Gradually he included more and more information, especially in the calculations

[15] AB, fo.37r. [16] AB, fo.38v. [17] AB, fos.2r, 3v, 6r, 6v.

at the end of each year. In 1505 the precise date of the start of the year was given for the first time: it was on 30 April, and in subsequent years, although a preference was shown for 1 August, the date could slip to 14 August, 18 August, 31 August, or 1 September. This confuses the modern reader because Heritage's trading year straddled two calendar years (using our convention of starting the year at 1 January, which was used in some circles in Heritage's day), and most of the year labelled by him '1511' was actually in the calendar year 1512. The years varied in length, so that 1505 was a short year and 1506 a long one, which enabled the brogger to acquire an unusually large quantity of wool. There was a good practical reason for beginning the year in late summer, because the shearing season in June had been completed, and during the following weeks the wool had been collected in Heritage's woolhouse. The financial year, however, had really begun with the payments of earnest money before shearing.

Heritage kept a tally from 1505 at the beginning of each year of 'Money delivered for wools', which later was changed to 'Earnest paid upon wool'. This list consisted of the names of the suppliers, with a sum of money for each: 'William Bumpas 13s 4d', for example. The names do not always appear in the detailed accounts of wool purchases, nor are the sums of money the same when the earnest money is recorded as the first of the payments in individual transactions. The inconsistencies suggest either errors in the bookkeeping, or changes of mind which show that payments of earnest money did not always seal the bargain. An explanation of at least some of the discrepancies is provided by the new heading for the list of payments towards the end of the account book. In 1519 the list appears under the title 'Money lent upon wool', which is a correct description of the list throughout, because the earnest money payments were advances, that is, loans made in expectation of the eventual delivery of the wool. The final list is headed 'Money lent in 1520', and one realizes that sometimes the earnest money was advanced, and repaid in cash rather than wool, which reveals that Heritage had a role as a moneylender in addition to his other activities. In the thirteenth and early fourteenth centuries merchants, many of them Italian, but not all, would make contracts with large-scale producers, especially monastic houses, to buy their wool a long time ahead, sometimes as much as twenty years. This was moneylending on a large scale, involving many complexities over such matters as non-delivery, and has been likened by some historians to an early version of a 'futures' market. One of the purposes of these dealings was simply to seal a contract, and that was undoubtedly the main purpose of Heritage's much more modest and short-term payments of earnest money.[18]

To sum up, for most years between 1505 and 1519 Heritage can be seen to have been keeping an eye on earnest money payments, and on the total of wool that was coming in from the consignments he 'gathered' in the district, as well as his own wool from his flocks at Ditchford, Moreton Heath, Burton Dassett, and other pastures. The totalling exercise between 1507 and 1518 was completed each year

---

[18] AB, fos.73r, 76r record the money loaned. On the earlier purchases, A. Bell, C. Brooks, and P. Dryburgh, *The English Wool Market c.1230–1327* (Cambridge, 2007).

in a table, using symbols for sacks and cloves, which evidently recorded the wool that was sold in London. This is revealed in 1509 when the calculation was headed 'Wool delivered at the king's beam', which refers to the Great Beam housed in Cornhill that was used by London merchants to weigh heavy commodities.[19] The symbols were evidently in general use among the London wool traders, and we find them in the papers of the Cely family in the 1480s.[20] It was the custom in London to divide the sack of wool into the clove or nail of 7 pounds, which was a half stone and the fourth part of a tod. The weights were given for sarplers, which were containers made of canvas holding about 2½ sacks, each of which was given a number. The wool was carried from Gloucestershire to London in these sarplers, and then by ship to Calais. The Celys would keep track of each numbered sarpler, and if one of them needed to be repacked, or wool from one of them had been damaged by saltwater, or some other treatment was necessary, they could readily identify the sarpler concerned.[21] They could even make use of the number to identify the packer of the sarpler, and blame him if the quality of the wool was being questioned at Calais.

Heritage's account book seems to be arranged rather haphazardly, with its apparently random subtotals, inability to keep to a year lasting twelve months, and its memoranda and other oddments slipped on to the page in a fashion that is confusing for us, but no doubt convenient for the woolman. Some method, however, can be discerned behind the apparently undisciplined entries. The annual totals of wool gathered by Heritage hovered around 40 sacks between 1500 and 1505, wavered uncertainly between 28 and 58 in the next four years, then settled down to about 20 in 1510–12, and moved between 10 and 15 in the remaining years (see Appendix 2). The similarity of the quantity acquired in successive years, for example in 1510, 1511, and 1512, suggests that the brogger had decided on a target, and the accounting system had allowed him to adjust his purchases to meet a total. In his later years the total may have declined because his energy and negotiating skills failed to match those of his competitors, but in view of the consistency from year to year in 1516–19 it seems more likely that the fall in quantity resulted from a deliberate decision to reduce the scale of his trade.

The pages at the end of the account book were set aside for items other than the regular recording of wool purchases, and cannot impress us with their systematic organization. They record aspects of Heritage's livestock husbandry, with total numbers of sheep being calculated at different times. They seem to be in no clear chronological order, nor were flocks counted at the same time of year. The pages also contain lists of debts, references to tithe collection, church rents at Moreton in Marsh, and contributions to the lay subsidy at Burton Dassett. A few of these

---

[19] C. M. Barron, *London in the Later Middle Ages: Government and People 1200–1500* (Oxford, 2004), 57; P. Nightingale, *A Medieval Mercantile Community: The Grocers' Company and the Politics and Trade of London, 1000–1485* (New Haven, CT, 1995), 521–2.
[20] A. Hanham, *The Celys and Their World: An English Merchant Family of the Fifteenth Century* (Cambridge, 1985), 120.
[21] *ibid*, 132–3.

miscellaneous items are also included with the records of wool purchases, and in particular the occasional 'reckonings' are appropriately included with the wool accounts as they often began with payments for the supply of wool. The custom of 'reckoning' refers to a procedure by which two parties who had a number of reciprocal dealings, for which no immediate payment had been made, met to settle their affairs by offsetting each sale, service, debt, or obligation against another. In 1514 Heritage sat down with William Mansell and reviewed their various exchanges probably over a number of years, and reached the conclusion that Heritage should pay Mansell 20s.[22] When Thomas Palmer reckoned with Heritage in 1507, part of Heritage's payment to Palmer consisted of 3 loads of peas and 4 sacks of oats, and in 1509 it was conceded that Palmer could put his lamb flock onto Heritage's summer pasture, four cows were allowed to graze at Coldicote in Moreton, and a colt was put onto a winter pasture, all of which were substituted for money owed to Palmer, mainly for wool.[23]

We have seen then how the account book was arranged and appreciated its value for its compiler. It deserves attention because no other Cotswold wool merchant of the period has left records of this kind, and this perhaps creates the impression that Heritage was a special case. In fact, the wills of traders and farmers show that they kept written records because they make reference to 'books of debts', which their executors could use to pay money owed and to collect the sums that were due to them. A few short documents listing debts are known.[24] The unusual feature of Heritage's book is not the fact that it was compiled, but that it has been preserved until the present time. A number of account books from the archive of the Heritage family have survived, which must be explained by some unknown circumstance rather than mere coincidence. Thomas, John's son, kept a book of accounts on behalf of his uncle Thomas (John's brother) when he was clerk of works for Whitehall Palace, and another set of accounts also for sums of money received from his uncle.[25] The tradition of record-keeping and preservation persisted into the next generation because Peter Temple took over a book of accounts of Thomas Heritage junior and used it for his own dealings, beginning in 1541.[26] Three of the books came into the hands of Westminster Abbey, which helps to explain why they were kept, but that does not explain why someone (most likely Thomas the younger) handed them to the Abbey in the first place. Both he and John had been tenants of the Abbey in Moreton and perhaps in London, but why should they uniquely among thousands of tenants have deposited their account books? Many thousands of similar accounts were destroyed because they had no practical value after the transactions had been completed, and executors had wound up the affairs of the merchant or farmer. These few

---

[22] AB, fo.61v.　　　[23] AB, fos.33v, 40v.
[24] C. Dyer, 'A Suffolk Farmer in the Fifteenth Century', *Ag. HR*, 55 (2007), 10; on the 'bills' of farmers in Romney Marsh, G. M. Draper, 'Writing English, French and Latin in the Fifteenth Century: a Regional Perspective', in L. Clark (ed.), *The Fifteenth Century*, 7 (Woodbridge, 2007), 213–35.
[25] WAM 12257; 12257*.　　　[26] *WGLS*, 1–5.

books, to our great benefit, escaped the flames. In spite of our good fortune in being able to read and analyse John Heritage's calculations, this must represent a very incomplete record of his dealings, and he may have had 'a book of husbandry' as well as the 'wool book' that has survived. His most precious documents, deeds of his Moreton house, and the indentures recording his leases of Burton Dassett and Upper Ditchford, were put into safe keeping according to a memorandum written before 1511.[27] They established his legal title to his woolhouse and pastures, whereas the accounts were ephemera, which would not carry much weight in common law.

The point has already been made that account books were connected with memory, but they also tell us about other dimensions of the minds of the people who made them and used them. Historians have often linked double-entry bookkeeping with capitalism, not just because this was the technology that made it possible to calculate profits, but also because it revealed a mentality that approached trade and business in a methodical fashion.[28] If double entry is the main litmus test for regarding someone as a capitalist, then Heritage fails to be included in the category, but he would be in the company of many contemporary and later businesses, including such leviathans of the period as the Fuggers of Augsburg.[29] In a number of ways, however, his activities and outlook resemble those of capitalists broadly defined. He produced wool and animals for sale in a specialized agricultural operation, and he must have invested in fencing, buildings, and other capital assets to enable that production to be conducted effectively. He was part of an innovating tendency in farming, because he participated in the enclosure of Burton Dassett and the conversion of large areas of arable into pasture, and at Upper Ditchford divided the land into hedged parcels. He was not a landlord and cannot be regarded as a member of the gentry, and his main landed assets were held on lease or rented more informally. It would not be possible to regard him as a peasant because of the large scale of his farming, his dependence on the market, and the apparent absence of self-sufficiency in his household economy. He made most of his money by commerce, taking advantage of opportunities to buy and sell, in which he was evidently reasonably successful as he continued in business for more than twenty years. His two profitable enterprises, as an agricultural producer and merchant, were integrated and complemented one another. He was not a conventional merchant like his London contacts, because he lived in a small town and had very strong rural interests. Contemporaries, with a limited vocabulary of social description, called him a yeoman, but for us to describe this entrepreneur as a capitalist would not be inappropriate.

---

[27] AB, fo.92v. This records that he had left nine documents 'in keeping in the hands of Thomas Davies of Stow'.

[28] R. Grassby, *The Idea of Capitalism before the Industrial Revolution* (Lanham, MD, 1999), 25–6, reports the equation of accounting techniques with capitalism, and expresses scepticism.

[29] A. W. Crosby, *The Measure of Reality: Quantification and Western Society, 1250–1600* (Cambridge, 1997), 219.

MAKING CONTACT WITH THE SUPPLIERS

Heritage's business was not the result of a cold calculation of economic advantage. He depended on knowing a neighbourhood, and the people of his country seemed to know him and put some trust in him. We could use scientific language to describe the geographical area in which he operated as the hinterland or sphere of influence of the town of Moreton in Marsh.[30] If we use a term like 'marketing zone' we would make Heritage's network sound impersonal and distant, whereas he depended on contacts that arose from a variety of encounters and acquaintances. Most of his business dealings lay within 8 miles (13 km) of Moreton (Fig. 4.1). The outer edge of his connections was marked by the ring of towns all situated within 5 to 7 miles (8 to 12 km) of Moreton, where he visited markets and fairs in

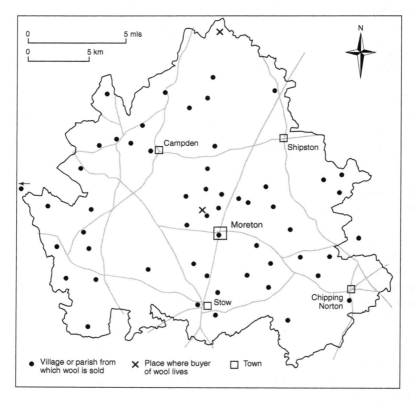

Fig. 4.1. Suppliers of wool to John Heritage. This locates the places from which Heritage bought wool, some of them with more than one supplier. The main roads along which wool was carried are depicted. The locations of wool purchasers are also shown.
Source: AB.

[30] The idea is outlined in H. Carter, *An Introduction to Urban Historical Geography* (London, 1983), 89–94. An example of its application is M. Kowaleski, *Local Markets and Regional Trade in Medieval Exeter* (Cambridge, 1995), 279–324.

particular: Shipston, Chipping Norton, Stow, and Chipping Campden, though he sometimes travelled to Evesham, Stratford, and Winchcombe. He would have encountered potential customers on these visits, and meetings at fairs may explain his longer-distance ventures to villages such as Taddington between Evesham and Winchcombe.

In his first two recorded years, 1501–2, Heritage achieved some notable successes in buying large quantities of wool from the landed gentry. In the case of these leaders of society one supposes that he depended on a recommendation, perhaps by enlisting the help of some patron, though the network may have worked through the senior officials of these substantial landowners, that is, the stewards and bailiffs who would have been able to suggest a suitable buyer to the lord. His dealings with the gentry were, however, unsuccessful. He bought what was probably the whole clip of 8 sacks (about 1,600 fleeces) from William Greville of Upper Lemington in 1501, but in the next year he negotiated a purchase of only 3 tods, and had no subsequent dealings with this very wealthy and important local figure.[31] Heritage gained and lost the custom of two other gentry wool producers in the following year, John Daston of Dumbleton who sold him 5 sacks, and Heritage's socially elevated cousin, John Palmer of Lower Lemington, with 6 sacks.[32] To be deprived of a potential delivery of almost 20 sacks per annum from these major flock owners was a considerable blow to his business. The wool from these three gentry producers together was equivalent to a half of the total that he handled each year, and we might suppose that there was a great advantage in time and costs in making three large purchases, rather than arranging bargains with a dozen lesser producers.

Why did these three estates have dealings with Heritage only once? Did they find him unsatisfactory, or did he decide for some reason that their business was not to his advantage? Perhaps they were dissatisfied with his arrangements for payment, or they were offended by his assessment of the quality of the wool. A point of potential friction was the amount of wool judged to be substandard, which could reflect on the quality of the livestock, their washing and shearing, or the preparation of the fleeces for sale. One would expect, however, that large producers with a well-organized hierarchy of officials and access to an adequate labour force would have been able to maintain high standards of care for the sheep and their wool. This leads us to believe that the dissatisfaction was felt by Heritage, and the size of the earnest money payments must have been the main problem. Often suppliers were paid between 5 per cent and 40 per cent of the total agreed price in earnest money, but Daston received a half and Greville two-thirds. To give £41 in earnest money to Greville well in advance of gaining any return from the wool would have been very hard for Heritage to bear. Perhaps the decision not to return to these large suppliers was made by Heritage, as he had to struggle to raise the cash

---

[31] AB, fo.4r. Greville kept sheep on pastures at Puckham in Sevenhampton as well as Upper Ditchford, Coldicote in Moreton in Marsh, and Broad Campden: TNA: PRO, PROB 11/17, fos.96r–97v; J. Rhodes (ed.), *A Calendar of the Registers of the Priory of Llantony by Gloucester*, Gloucestershire Record Series, 15 (2002), 74.

[32] AB, fos.7r, 8v.

to pay them. A speculation might be that Greville and Daston took advantage of a new and relatively young arrival who was inexperienced in negotiating such large sums, particularly if he felt intimidated by social superiors and their officials. In the long run their business would have been better handled by a well-established merchant who was practised and confident enough to persuade them to reduce their demands, and who, if the sellers insisted on large sums 'up front', had access to substantial amounts of cash.

Heritage had a much better experience of dealing with demesne farmers, who like the gentry kept large flocks, but did not drive such hard bargains on earnest money. A number of them came back to him in successive years, notably William Robyns of Donnington, who sold 4–5 sacks (800–900 fleeces) in 1503, 1504, 1506, and 1507, and a similar record with occasional missed years is found in the case of Thomas Kyte of Broadwell and Thomas Fletcher of Chastleton. These three all held farms in the vicinity of Stow on the Wold, and they must have had good reason to prefer to sell wool to Heritage rather than a brogger from that town. Commitments were very unpredictable, as we might expect to find that Thomas Wilkes, who held a share of the lease of Upper Ditchford before Heritage, would have regularly sold wool to Heritage, but this is recorded only once; just as Heritage's son-in-law, Richard Fretherne, sold him 7 sacks in 1504 and 4 in 1505, but only small quantities in subsequent years.

Much of Heritage's trade was conducted with relatively small-scale producers who kept flocks of a hundred sheep or less. Many of his suppliers came from Moreton itself, and three large parishes to the west of the town in Blockley, Bourton on the Hill, and Longborough. These included people who knew him very well, including his wife's relatives. As he lived in Moreton and held pastures in both Moreton and Blockley he must have met potential sellers of wool from these parishes constantly through the normal routines of churchgoing, attendance at manor courts, gatherings for weddings, visits to market, negotiations over the repair of fences and straying animals, and the hiring of labour, both for work on the land and for more specialist tasks such as shoeing horses. Some of these neighbours could be very faithful in returning with their fleeces in successive years, like William Nycols of Moreton who sold 1 or 2 tods, from perhaps twenty to thirty sheep, each year between 1503 and 1508; and Thomas Palmer, one of the clan into which Heritage and his sister had married, whose flock numbered two to three hundred judging from the quantity of wool that he sold each year between 1501 and 1513.

How did Heritage make contact with those living further afield? An insight into his methods comes from the details recorded in the accounts of the places where payments were made. We have seen that he used a number of aids to memory when writing down his record of payments, so places were mentioned almost at random. He probably made most of his payments in or near his house on the main street of Moreton, in the hall where guests would be received, or in his counting house where the book was kept, open at the current page. Sometimes the payment was made in the woolhouse, the building at the back of his dwelling house where the wool was received, sorted, packed, and stored. In Moreton he would pay an instalment for wool in a public place – 'in the church green', or 'in the church yard', perhaps on a Sunday or after a service on a feast day. He often paid in the villages where his suppliers lived, especially in Blockley and Bourton, but also occasionally at Batsford, Broadwell, Condicote, Dorn, and Wolford. The striking feature of the records of payment is that the majority, about two-thirds, took place in towns. Heritage was clearly making regular journeys to Stow, Campden, and Shipston, perhaps on market days, and there meeting those to whom he owed money (see Figs. 4.2 and 4.3). Perhaps these encounters were prearranged? More likely he and the various farmers and better-off peasants with whom he had dealings visited the market towns for a whole range of reasons – social as well as economic – and were likely to encounter one another. Heritage went to towns because he was selling wool that was not good enough for his London buyers, or he was taking sheep to market, or the tar, fish, and other goods that he brought from London, or he was making purchases for his household. Some of these meetings happened at fairs, and Heritage and his acquaintances were prepared to travel further on those occasions, to Stratford and Evesham as well to fairs in the nearby towns. His payments at Burford, Tewkesbury, and London were more likely to have been the result of chance meetings. In the capital Gloucestershire men tended to gather at such places as the great beam in Cornhill.

Fig. 4.2. Stow on the Wold marketplace occupies a very large space in the centre of the town, where once permanent stalls occupied an area on which the Victorian public building now stands. Heritage met many of those who sold him wool here, and settled some of his debts (author's photograph).

Fig. 4.3. Shipston on Stour marketplace, looking north towards the shop row, of which a part, now a bank, is visible at the far end. This was also a meeting place for Heritage and his creditors (author's photograph).

When the account book tells us that a payment was made in open country, such as 'in the Heath', it was likely that Heritage encountered his creditor on the road that passed through these places. The main route leading east out of Moreton crossed the Heath, and skirted Wolford Wood, where one payment was said to have been made. The meeting also took place on the Roman road that took the traveller to the north and south of Moreton, as one payment occurred on 'The old Fosse' and another at Stow Bridge, which was a landmark on the Fosse Way between Moreton and Stow. A payment in 1510 'upon Cotswold', which was made to John Randall of Longborough, is likely to have been on the road that crossed high ground between Blockley and Stow, rather than on some windswept pasture.[33] 'In the meadow' probably refers to a meeting not on a road but in a really agrarian setting, when Heritage and his neighbours were haymaking in one of the Blockley or Moreton meadows.

The many references in the accounts to towns, fairs, and roads shows that the woolman was often on the move. Those to whom he owed money must have been pleased to meet him on the road or in the marketplaces of Stow or Campden, and he must have expected that they would be there and so took with him a full purse.

---

[33] AB, fos.45v; for a similar pattern of transactions outside marketplaces, see M. Mate, *Trade and Economic Developments, 1450–1550: The Experience of Kent, Surrey and Sussex* (Woodbridge, 2006), 26–9.

If he met too many of these importunate wool growers, he would have to disappoint latecomers with the explanation that the cash had gone to those who saw him earlier in the day. He moved along the roads for other reasons, including inspecting his own sheep on the Heath or at Ditchford, and to see his shepherds. The same errand would take him out of the Moreton district to Burton Dassett. He would have good reason as he rode to cast an eye over everyone's sheep, as he was seeking wool to buy. On these journeys he would pause to rest his horse and refresh himself at inns, at Broadway on his way to Evesham for example, and there gather useful information. He would have needed to become an expert on the agricultural producers of his territory, large and small, and be a good judge of sheep and their fleeces.

Having found out about suitable producers and approached them, suppliers would recommend relatives, friends, and neighbours. Through these webs of contacts the brogger could hope to develop a clientele. One sees him achieving this in Oxfordshire in 1501–2 when he bought wool at Chastleton, Little Rollright, and Chipping Norton.[34] Heritage ventured into Warwickshire in the 1510s by making purchases in Cherington and Stourton.[35] Perhaps he was recommended by one villager and was able to add to his list of suppliers in the neighbourhood. In 1501 Nicholas Rose of Great Wolford sold him wool, followed within two years by a presumed relative, Robert Rose, and two other wool producers in the same village, John and Thomas Jurdan.[36]

Heritage was not entirely successful in developing loyal networks of wool growers, as is apparent from the gaps in the records. Most of the people who sold him wool did so intermittently. Even an apparently faithful producer would be absent from the accounts in occasional years, and many would sell for a year or two and then disappear from view, which means that the list of those owed payments was markedly different from one year to the next. Those who kept sheep did so continuously, and would have wool to sell each year, even if the quantity and quality varied with disease or the weather. The discontinuity in their sales resulted from their decision to transfer to different merchants, and one realizes that Heritage was competing with many rivals who could offer advantages to the growers. They might be tempted to sell their wool to the Palmers of Moreton and to merchants from other towns, such as Thomas Davies of Stow, John Bradwey of Campden, and Thomas Busshe of Northleach. No doubt merchants from more distant towns such as Stratford and Winchcombe made sorties into Moreton's hinterland. They would be approached also by merchants based in the country, such as William Willington, originally of Todenham and later living at Barcheston. As a merchant of the staple he could export wool bought in the locality through London and gain more profit. Merchants of the staple based in rural settlements, who really were 'country merchants', and had no need of middlemen like Heritage, are found throughout the country, for example in Berkshire.[37]

---

[34] AB, fos.2r, 2v, 5r, 6v.   [35] AB, fos. 59v, 62v, 64v.   [36] AB, fos.4r, 5v, 6r, 7v, 10v, 12r.
[37] M. Yates, *Town and Countryside in Western Berkshire, c.1327–c.1600: Social and Economic Change* (Woodbridge, 2007), 197–200.

If the account book's entries are compared with wool production in the territory around Moreton known from other sources, other gaps become apparent, such as the lack of any reference at all to the farmers of the most extensive pastures and the great estates that were keeping the largest flocks. Where did the big monastic lords such as Winchcombe Abbey sell their wool? In the 1530s, and presumably earlier, a thousand sheep were kept by the abbey on the pastures of Snowshill. In the fifteenth century the monastery gathered all of its wool at its manor of Sherborne, and sold it probably through Northleach, where at that time there were local broggers such as the Midwinters, or the clip went to visiting Italian merchants.[38] Nearer to Moreton lay a number of large enclosed pastures, or leasows, which were in the hands of farmers, but neither their names nor those of the lords of these places figure in the account book: these include Upton Wold, Middle Ditchford, and Weston juxta Cherington. Moving down the ladder to the lesser producers, who were cumulatively important to Heritage's business, some villages seem to have been closed to him, so there are few references to tenants from Todenham, presumably because the Willingtons had a strong influence there. Heritage had many contacts in villages to the north and east of Stow, but not in Lower and Upper Swell on the western side.

Heritage's book contains a record of only a fraction of the wool production and sales of Moreton's hinterland. He was in competition with other buyers, and his suppliers would be negotiating with a number of traders. Heritage also exercised choice, and may well have avoided some small wool growers after a bad experience, in the same way that we have speculated that he decided not to handle the large quantities of fleeces produced by the gentry. If the account books kept by his contemporaries had survived, they would have depicted the same uneven pattern of discontinuities and gaps, which means that Heritage's book was not recording an unsuccessful business, but a characteristic one. Of one point we can be certain, that in the wool markets there was no question of monopolies, nor even of custom and loyalties to family or neighbour having a decisive influence. Both sellers and buyers could exercise choice. The supplier who moved from one brogger to another may not have found that there was a great deal of difference between them in price or speed of payment, but their mobility helped to ensure that no brogger took anyone's custom for granted, and was careful to ensure that his prices and service were competitive.

Much depended on the information system that Heritage and his suppliers could employ to establish contacts. To a modern reader the constant riding and conversation that filled much of the woolman's life must seem wastefully time consuming, yet it was the only way that he could find out about producers and meet them. He must have negotiated each year with dozens of potential partners, only to fail eventually to persuade them to accept his services. Heritage's trade confirms the importance of towns as nodal points for commerce. Although

[38] J. Caley and J. Hunter (eds), *Valor Ecclesiasticus temp. Henry VIII, auctoritate regia institutus* (Record Commission, 1810–34), II, 457; R. H. Hilton, 'Winchcombe Abbey and the Manor of Sherborne', in H. P. R. Finberg (ed.), *Gloucestershire Studies* (Leicester, 1957), 89–113, especially 112–13.

many of the crucial decisions of his business were made leaning on gates and fences in the countryside, his base was in the town of Moreton, well served by roads radiating out to the villages and fields where the wool was grown, and he often met his creditors to make payments in towns such as Stow. Towns, and the markets and fairs held in them, by serving as convenient meeting points reduced 'transactions costs'.

BUYING AND SELLING WOOL

How did a wool brogger set about his work of acquiring wool and then selling it? Middlemen are often shadowy and anonymous figures, but here we have a well-documented example. The best way to investigate Heritage's activities is to follow him through the various stages in the trading year. We might expect that the starting point of Heritage's wool purchases would have been each June, when on peasant holdings, farms, and manors throughout the Moreton district, piles of fleeces after shearing became available to be weighed and priced. The crucial bargain, however, judging from a list of dated earnest money payments for 1506, was struck earlier in the year, in February, March, April, and May, though occasionally they were made after shearing.[39] In many cases the decision that the wool would be sold to John Heritage was made while the commodity was still on the backs of the sheep, which presumably followed an inspection by the brogger or his servant, when the number of animals was known, and the weight and the quality of their fleeces could be estimated. One imagines Heritage and the grower standing in the pasture with the sheep grazing around them, with the grower hoping that the merchant would not notice any grubby and sick animals which would yield fleeces of inferior quality. The price would be predicted, on the basis of the current amount per tod, and the earnest money handed over, or at least promised for the near future. This assumption that the sales were agreed early in the year is reinforced by references in the accounts to the payment following the earnest money being 'on delivery', so the first payment was made before shearing and the second when the wool came into the woolhouse.

The practice of buying wool before shearing was mentioned in a parliamentary statute in 1488/9, when buying or bargaining 'wool unshorn' was forbidden, except for those who were buying wool to be made into yarn and cloth 'within the realm'.[40] This piece of protectionist legislation was motivated by the belief that the English cloth industry was hampered in gaining its raw material because those buying wool for export were securing their supplies before the wool reached the open marketplace. The practice could be classified as a variation of the offence of forestalling that agitated the authorities in towns. They were concerned that traders would intercept commodities such as grain, fish, or hides before they reached the market, and sell them at a profit. This pushed up

---

[39] AB, fo.23v.
[40] *Statutes of the Realm*, 11 vols., Record Commission (1810–28), II, 535–6.

prices and did not give all traders, or consumers, a chance to buy.[41] It was precisely the activities of people like Heritage that the law sought to curb, but the
law lapsed after ten years, and in any case like most legislation on economic
matters, it was ineffective (see pp. 202–3).

The agreement that Heritage made with the grower began with setting the price.
A guide price in the range of 11s–13s per tod reflected the state of the national and
international market, within which Cotswold wool enjoyed a well-known position
near the top of the range. The decision on the exact price must have been based on
a judgement as to the quality of the wool, which varied from flock to flock. In
1506, from a total of seventy-seven transactions, thirty-seven were based on a price
of 11s, with only two above that level and the rest below, mainly in the range
between 10s and 10s 10d. Two patterns stand out, firstly that small producers,
those selling less than a tod, had their wool priced below the guide price, which
may reflect its quality; secondly, the price dipped towards the end of the season,
when a clutch of sellers had their fleeces valued at 10s per tod. In the following year
prices did fall slightly, confirming the trend.

The bargaining must also have concerned the speed of payment and the problem of poor-quality fleeces. On the speed of payment, the customer wished to
receive a very large sum of earnest money, with the remainder of the agreed sum
arriving quickly, which the merchant had difficulty in providing, because of the
limited and uneven flow of cash into his hands. If his payments were slow, the
dissatisfied wool grower would in the following year make his bargain with a
dealer who would promise to deliver the money more promptly. In some cases no
earnest money was paid at all, as we have seen. Sometimes small amounts of wool
were being traded, and the merchant could pay immediately, but one of the regular suppliers, Nicholas Rose of Great Wolford, did not receive any earnest money
payment, but we do not know why this was the case. The great majority were
given this advance payment of credit before delivery. We have already seen that it
varied greatly between 5 per cent and more than 50 per cent of the total price, and
the size of this payment must have been the subject of some intense negotiation.
Perhaps the amount of earnest money was based on an inaccurate estimate of the
quantity of wool, but the merchant was very experienced, and unless there was an
outbreak of disease, or the grower sold part of his flock before shearing, one suspects that the estimate was not too far from the eventual result. But the main
reasons for variations in the size of the earnest money payment must have been
careful calculations of advantage on both sides. If Heritage wished to ingratiate
himself with a potentially valuable supplier, he might offer a high earnest money
payment of about 20s, but if he distrusted the supplier, and was unsure about the
quality of the wool, he might pay a few shillings. On the question of quality, the
merchant was very concerned about the inferior wool, the *remys*, which he wished
to keep to the minimum or eliminate entirely. On their side the wool growers

---

[41] R. H. Britnell, 'Price-Setting in English Borough Markets, 1349–1500', *Canadian Journal of
History*, 31 (1996), 1–15, especially 10–13; J. Davies, *Medieval Market Morality: Life, Law and Ethics
in the English Marketplace, 1200–1500* (Cambridge, 2012) 254–6.

varied in their degree of confidence, and might make a strong demand for high payment or be content with a small sum. We are not given enough information about the subsequent instalments and their date to check on the subsequent payment history, but perhaps a low initial outlay was followed more quickly by the remaining sums of money.

Buyer and seller negotiated at a number of times as the bargain was initiated and gradually completed: at the door of the grower's house, or in his hall, after the sheep had been appraised by Heritage; then in the Moreton woolhouse after the wool had been delivered, weighed, and judged again; at further encounters at Stow or Blockley fairs and elsewhere when money was being requested and often paid. The conversation must often have focused on the date and size of the next payment, but often it would have revolved around the issue of *remys* wool. This is indicated by the obscure system of rebates operated by Heritage. In 1501, for example, William Colchester, a relatively large producer with about 200–250 sheep, sold 12 tods 16 pounds to Heritage. Heritage took a rebate of 4 pounds, which meant that he did not pay for that amount of wool, and Colchester received (or rather was promised) £6 12s 6d rather than £6 14s 1d.[42] He was valued as a customer, however, or alternatively he negotiated assertively, as he was given £4 in earnest money, so unusually he received more than 60 per cent of his total before shearing. On very large purchases of wool the rebate could amount to a tod (of 28 pounds) worth 11s or 12s in most years. More often it was just a modest number of pounds, as in the examples given, and very commonly a fleece or two, valued at 8d each. More rarely the rebate was expressed in cash, at 12d in one case and 6s in another.

Why did Heritage feel that he was entitled to a rebate, and why did the seller accept the reduction in the amount that the merchant paid? In 1503 he said in explanation of part of a rather involved negotiation, 'for the lack of weight it is agreed that I should be recompensed at the last payment', and indeed 6s was deducted from one of the instalments.[43] The rebates cannot, however, usually have been an adjustment made necessary by the difference in weight between the estimate made in the field and the result obtained from the brogger's scales in the Moreton woolhouse. The pre-shearing anticipation of the weight of wool, no matter how experienced the merchant or servant making the estimation, must have differed from the weight of the shorn wool, and the most likely way of dealing with this was to enter the weighed total in the account book rather than the estimate. The main reason for the rebate system was probably the vexed question of *remys* wool. Every batch of wool collected after shearing consisted of the fleeces of healthy and relatively clean animals, together with 'locks', which were odd strands of wool trimmed from the legs and head of the sheep, and the shabbier substandard fleeces. Heritage and the other wool dealers divided the product into good, middle, and *remys*, and bought them at different prices. The inferior wool could not be so

[42] AB, fo.3r.
[43] AB, fo.12v. The supplier was John Saunders, who was selling 4 sacks 3 tods.

readily exported to Calais, so it was routed through other traders for the English cloth makers who did not aspire to match the high quality of their Flemish or Italian counterparts. In 1509 according to the account book a sum of 6*s* 8*d* was taken from a supplier's money as 'further rebate 7lbs for *remys*'.[44] So the rebate was being taken to compensate the merchant for the poor quality of wool in the consignment.

In 1505 Heritage became more urgently concerned with the problem of *remys*, perhaps because a London merchant or even a purchaser in Calais had complained about the quality of the wool in his sacks. In that year he calculated that from the total of 9 sacks and 11 pounds of wool in the woolhouse, 17 tods 15 pounds was '*remys* wool and middle wool', that is about 15 per cent of the wool to be sold.[45] Various forms of words were used in the account book, which all seemed to have a similar meaning. In 1505–6 we find 'And to rebate 14 pounds for that is given in', or Heritage could say 'and to give a fleece', or 'in *remys* 6 fleeces' or 'to *remys* 4 fleeces', or 'rebating in all 5*s*'. He could also instead make the comment that the suppliers had 'put out the *remys*', that is, they had removed the inferior wool and sold it elsewhere, leaving Heritage with the best of the batch. Sometimes he bought the inferior wool, delivered separately, at a lower price: the vicar of Lemington who was selling his tithe wool received 4.7*d* per pound for 1 tod 20 pounds of good wool, and 2.5*d* per pound for 8 pounds of *remys*.[46] More often *remys* was priced at 7*s*–8*s* per tod, when good wool fetched 11*s*–12*s*. This separate delivery and pricing revealed that the *remys* accounted for a high proportion of the total sent – in 1512 Heritage noted that one delivery contained 9 tods 19 pounds of good wool worth 10*s* per tod, and 4 tods worth 8*s*, representing about 30 per cent of the total.[47]

An alternative course in the negotiation over the inferior wool with individual growers was for Heritage, presumably to secure a particular deal, to offer to ignore the *remys*, and to demand no rebate, but instead to 'take all'. The long-term solution to the problem seems to have been, by 1510, not to make much mention either of *remys* or rebates. Heritage, in line with general market conditions, was paying above 12*s* per tod. Perhaps he expected that his suppliers would 'put out the *remys*', or alternatively the price per tod made an allowance for a proportion of *remys*, and there was no need for complicated fine-tuning of the price through rebates.

Another possible explanation of the rebates, to add a further complication, relates to the payment of earnest money as a form of credit. As Heritage was loaning money before delivery, the rebate might have been a way of taking interest, or at least making a charge for moneylending. This seems an unlikely explanation, as all of the earnest money payments were loans, yet rebates appear inconsistently. Although Heritage sometimes lent money in transactions that were not connected to wool sales, we do not know how he obtained interest, which is not surprising as lenders were wary of the prohibition on usury, and would not wish to be too open about the methods that they used to take profits. In his wool transactions, however, during the course of the year the credit balance was reversed – he lent cash to

[44] AB, fo.41r.　　　[45] AB, fo.19r.　　　[46] AB, fo.12v.　　　[47] AB, fo.53v.

the growers as earnest money, but after delivery he became a debtor, and they were in effect advancing money to him. Rather than the buyer charging interest for the first few months of the contract, and the sellers charging it at the end, the best solution was perhaps to assume that the two phases of borrowing and lending cancelled each other out.

Heritage could sometimes reward producers, perhaps those who were delivering good wool, by giving them extra payments – instead of a rebate he gave a premium. In 1504 John Mansell was allowed 16*d* in addition to the 11*s* per tod for 6 tods that had been agreed, and Thomas Mansell also received the same sum of 16*d* to add to the £3 17*s* 0*d* that had been promised for his 7 tods. In the following year John Fretherne, who was not, unlike the Mansells, a regular, was rewarded with an extra 6*s*, perhaps in the hope that he would come again.[48]

Discussion of the finances and the fixing of prices has taken us well beyond the first encounters between Heritage and the owners of the sheep, and we should return to the pastures to follow through the shearing and delivery of wool. The animals would have the benefit of the new growth of grass in the early summer, and the ewes would recover from lambing. The previous year's lambs would be growing their first fleece. Managers of larger flocks might cull their flocks at this time and sell inferior and elderly animals, which would reduce the volume of wool to be sheared, but might improve its overall quality.

The first stage of shearing would be washing the sheep, so that the fleeces would be cleaned while they were still on the backs of the animals. Shearing would follow immediately, so the ideal location for the whole shearing process would be near a stream with a good flow of clean water. Heritage's own sheep at Upper Ditchford would have been driven down to the Knee Brook for this purpose. After shearing, the wool would be packed for delivery. The detailed accounts of the whole process of washing, shearing, and packing at the manor of Blockley, when it was under the direct management of the bishop of Worcester in 1384, was carried out by men and women hired for the purpose and paid by the day.[49] They were supplementing the efforts of the permanent staff of Blockley manor, and shepherds from other manors who were staying at Blockley with their charges during the season of summer grazing, making about five shepherds in all. Estimating from the wage bill of 17*s* 1*d* (which is not itemized), the whole series of tasks took a little more than one hundred days of labour, during which time 1,110 sheep were washed and sheared at a rate of about ten sheep per person per day, and their wool was sorted and packed. Heritage's suppliers more than a hundred years later would be using similar methods, and the equipment, essentially iron shears, had not changed either. The pressure might be applied to the shearers to deal with more sheep each day, but they were slowed down by the need to cut the wool as long as possible, that is, near to the skin, without harming the sheep. Few of Heritage's suppliers had as many as a thousand sheep, though the three gentry graziers who sold him wool in 1501–2 exceeded that figure. The majority, those who kept smaller flocks of sheep, if they

---

[48] AB, fos.14v, 20r.
[49] WRO, BA 2636 ref.009:1, 157/92007 (manorial account).

achieved the same level of productivity as the bishop's employees, would have needed ten days' labour to process a flock of a hundred sheep, which was well within the capacity of an average peasant family.

The Blockley wool in the fourteenth century was weighed at the shearing site and handed over to the merchant who organized his own transport, and perhaps the Daston, Greville, and Palmer wool in the early sixteenth was treated in the same way; but it was not worth carrying the 'balance' (the word used in 1384 for the scales) around the countryside for relatively small quantities of wool. The normal procedure then was for the grower to bring the wool to Moreton, which would be done soon after shearing, in June or July, because many of those owning sheep were mixed farmers with a grain harvest that would keep them busy in the late summer. A further incentive for the wool to be taken early to Heritage was the common practice for Heritage to pay an instalment of cash 'on delivery'. The amount that he paid at this stage was as variable and unpredictable as that paid 'in earnest'. It could be as little as 2*s*, or as much as £5. In a sample of forty-three transactions when both earnest money and delivery money are recorded, the payment was equal in six cases; in nineteen cases delivery yielded more money than earnest, and in eighteen earnest money involved a larger sum than was paid on delivery. The encounter would not always have been a very harmonious and happy occasion, as no doubt there would be disagreement about the quality of the wool, and Heritage could have been reluctant to commit himself on the vexed question of the time and amount of the next instalment. Stow Fair on 13 October was often the occasion for a payment, and one can imagine him offering to meet his creditors there, hoping that in the following three or four months he might have scraped together some more cash.

The building in which these discussions took place, the woolhouse, has not survived, nor has any other in Moreton as far as is known. From elsewhere there are woolstores still standing, or they are described in documents. Not just merchants, but others who produced or used wool on a large scale, such as gentry with extensive flocks, or clothiers, often used rooms in their houses as woolstores, called a wool loft or wool cellar, which were often of modest capacity. Rooms for this purpose in houses built for clothiers in the late fifteenth and sixteenth centuries near Halifax measured approximately 5 metres by 5 metres (16 feet by 16 feet).[50] Woolhouses of the type that Heritage probably used have been identified tentatively in the Cotswold towns of Burford and Northleach, standing in courtyards at the back of the merchants' houses.[51] They were barn-like structures, in one case with slit windows that provided ventilation without compromising security. The example at 'Calendars' in Burford was a timber-framed structure of three bays, about 15 metres long and with sufficient height to be converted later (with some modification of the roof) into a two-storey dwelling (Fig. 4.4a, b).

[50] A. Quiney, *Town Houses in Medieval Britain* (New Haven, CT, 2003), 239–40.
[51] A. Catchpole, D. Clark, and R. Peberdy, *Burford: Buildings and People in a Cotswold Town* (Chichester, 2008), 42–3, 67, 202–3, 205. I am very grateful to David Clark for showing me the Oxfordshire Buildings Record Report (OBR 116) on Calendars.

Fig. 4.4a,b. Calendars, Sheep Street, Burford, Oxfordshire. As no woolman's house survives at Moreton in Marsh, this house represents the style of building appropriate for John Heritage. The main dwelling faces the street, and combines stone walls and a timber-framed upper floor, with close studding and a jetty. The building (below) thought to have been a woolstore, also timber framed but with a low plinth of stone, is located behind the house in a west wing facing onto a courtyard. Timbers from both parts of the house were felled in 1473 (photographs by David Clark; copyright University of London).

Emota Fermor (also known as Richards), who was known to John Heritage as his sister's employer, must have been one of the largest wool traders in the southeast Cotswolds in the late fifteenth century. Her probate inventory of 1501 shows that she had a wool chamber in her house at Witney, containing 7 sacks of refuse and some yarn (the refuse being the same grade of substandard wool that Heritage called *remys*), while her woolhouse in Northleach contained 29 sacks (4 of them refuse). Her main store was again at Witney, containing 85 sacks of wool, a beam, two scales and various weights.[52] This last building would have resembled the surviving example at Burford. A stack of 85 sacks in a single pile would have measured about 5 metres by 5 metres, reaching a height of 6 metres, but in order to provide ventilation, and to allow the merchant's servants to move among the sacks, the sacks would have been arranged in a number of piles with spaces between them. With the wool spread out over a floor area considerably larger than 25 square metres, and with space for the weighing equipment, Fermor needed a 5 metres by 15 metres building, while Heritage's smaller business, which accumulated 64 sacks in its peak year, and usually handled no more than 45 sacks, could have been accommodated at Moreton in a two-bay woolhouse of 5 metres by 10 metres.[53]

Like most medieval storage and working space, the woolhouse formed part of the complex of structures belonging to a dwelling house. Access to the woolhouse would have been through an entry from the street – a gateway wide and high enough to allow carts burdened with wool to be driven into the courtyard for unloading by the doors of the woolhouse, and later in the year the carts loaded again would rumble across the yard and through the entry on their way to London. An entry can still be seen in the house of William Greville, the Chipping Campden wool merchant who flourished in the last two decades of the fourteenth century. A wool merchant's house needed ideally a large curtilage or plot to accommodate the entry, yard, and outbuildings, which could be achieved by combining two or three of the traditionally narrow burgage plots. At Northleach three major woolmen's houses survived until modern times, of which one, likely to have been the base of the Midwinters' operations, occupied three burgage plots, while the Antelope, so called because it became an inn after serving as a woolman's house, was built on 2½ burgages, with four bays of building (20 metres long) at the rear at right angles to the dwelling, which faced the main street. The Great House that belonged to Thomas Busshe in the early sixteenth century stretched back 50 metres from the street, with a galleried range and courtyard amply provided with stables and storehouses.[54] At Burford the house in Sheep Street now called Calendars was once known inappropriately as the Little House. It occupied a plot 20 metres wide and 150 metres long. The front range included domestic rooms such as a parlour, with a ground floor built of stone and timber, and a jettied upper storey. A range of buildings at the rear included the apparent woolstore. Timbers from the main building phase have been dated to 1473.

---

[52] TNA: PRO, PROB 2/465.

[53] Hanham, *Celys*, 118 gives the dimensions of a bale or sack, 40 by 27 by 27 inches; an oddity of Heritage's account is that at an unknown date he pays rent for his woolhouse (AB, fo.93r), at 2s. 6d., 3s. 4d, and 5s. per annum. This may mean that it was not attached to his house.

[54] *VCH Glos.*, IX, 111–13.

Turning to Moreton in Marsh, the combination and amalgamation of plots was often easier to arrange on the edge of the town, and Richard Palmer's woolhouse (recorded in 1496) was situated near to the end of the High Street, as was Richard Palmer the younger's, inherited in 1491. John Fretherne owned a plot of three burgages (in 1494) in the north-west corner of the built-up area, near to the junction of the main street with the road to Batsford (see Fig. 3.11).[55] Another advantage of finding a site away from the centre of the town would be to escape congestion, such as that caused by stalls on market days, which might obstruct easy access to the entry.

In the woolhouse, which would be at its busiest in the delivery season in June and July, the wool would be weighed and the precise price agreed – previously both parties were depending on an estimate of the quantity and quality of the unshorn wool. It was subjected to a new sorting process, as Heritage had to maintain a reputation for quality among those who bought from him. Sometimes he included the cost of winding, about 2*d* per tod, among the payments that he made to his suppliers, charging the process to them. Winding must refer not just to a procedure for putting the fleeces in good order for packing into sarplers (canvas containers), but also separating the good, middle, and *remys* wool. This was only charged to the supplier in a minority of cases, and it may be that the normal procedure was for the suppliers to do some preliminary sorting and grading before delivery. If the rebate payments were connected with the identification of the amount of *remys*, they must have been fixed at the packing stage.

Wool packing was very controversial, and wool packers were seen as dishonest, and potentially damaging to the reputation of the trade. Packers were accused of putting stones in the sarplers, and even dung, to increase the weight. Other sharp practices included a failure to remove defective fleeces, such as those matted with tar, and mixing together inferior wool with the best. Packers were alleged to be in alliance with dubious merchants, notably Italians, and arranging for wool to be smuggled, avoiding the Calais staple. Like many trades linked with fraud, packing was a skilled job with much influence, as the grading chosen by the packer in effect fixed the price of each consignment of wool. They were quality controllers, whose judgement was distrusted and questioned. They were employed by woolmen, like Heritage, and the staplers in London were so concerned about the abuses of the procedure that they might insist on attending the packing themselves, or having the sarplers repacked in London. A statute in 1473 forbade packers from dealing in wool, and this was being enforced in Heritage's day. In 1506 a woolpacker from Fulbrook near Burford was brought before the courts, as were various London packers in other parts of Oxfordshire.[56]

The wool was then carried to London, but at this stage we ought to pause in following its progress outside Gloucestershire to complete the story of Heritage's payments to his suppliers. He usually paid between three and seven instalments,

[55] TNA: PRO, PROB 11/10, fos.41r, 67; PROB 11/9, fos. 39v–40r.

[56] E. Power, 'The Wool Trade in the Fifteenth Century', in E. Power and M. Postan (eds), *Studies in English Trade in the Fifteenth Century* (London, 1933), 56–60; Hanham, *Celys*, 116–17; TNA: PRO, E159/284.

often, as we have seen, beginning with earnest money, and then a payment on delivery, and then further sums through the autumn, winter, and early spring. From a sample of dated payments in 1503–8, most were made between September and April. Heritage usually provides only one piece of information about each payment, which therefore excludes almost all sums paid in earnest or on delivery, as those descriptions were sufficient to identify them and they were undated. If he records a payment as having been made at a fair, no date was given as he knew when the fair was held. This means that October would have been a month of many more payments than are recorded here, as Stow Fair was held in that month. He was therefore working on an annual cycle of credit, which meant that he did not reach a point when his debts were all settled, as he was still making his last payments when he had to begin a new round of earnest money agreements. Presumably suppliers expected full payment before entering into a new contract and their frustration at his slowness helps to explain why so many of them moved on to another merchant.

The cycle of payment was related to a ritual calendar as well as the merchant's flow of cash. In Heritage's choice of payment days one sees the landmark feasts and commemorations that punctuated the routines of farmers and traders. The significant dates included Goodtide Tuesday (Shrove Tuesday) at the beginning of Lent, Easter week, Whitsun (six weeks after Easter), Michaelmas (29 September), Martinmas (11 November), and Christmas (25 December). These days were so well known that it was convenient to mention a prominent festival in making promises of payment: 'I will pay you by Christmas …'. Those who bought his wool paid him money on feast days that included, as well as Whitsun and Martinmas, Lady day (25 March), Midsummer, St James's day (25 July), the Assumption of the Virgin (15 August), St Bartholomew's day (24 August), and Holy Rood day (14 September). Some of these were significant days in the calendar of Londoners, especially Midsummer, which was an occasion for bonfires and processions. General festivities as well as a great fair were held on St Bartholomew's day.[57] There were practical reasons everywhere for choosing these days for payment, as they were moments when people gathered, and cash was circulating in purchases of foodstuffs and other goods. Some of them were customary days for the payment of rent and wages, notably Michaelmas, so Heritage's suppliers would be anxious to obtain their rent money. Feasts were also times of conviviality and goodwill, when the atmosphere was conducive for settling potentially contentious issues. So we find John Heritage and William Robyns holding a meeting at Christmas 1506 to resolve payments for a large quantity of wool.[58]

From the late summer onwards, when the wool had been collected in the woolhouse and the winding was complete, the wool was put into sarplers of canvas that contained the equivalent of about 2½ sacks (33 tods) and loaded into carts. Each cart would have a capacity of less than 2,000 pounds, so it could take 2 sarplers

---

[57] S. Lindenbaum, 'Ceremony and Oligarchy: The London Midsummer Watch', in B. A. Hanawalt and K. L. Reyerson (eds.), *City and Spectacle in Medieval Europe* (Minneapolis, MN, 1994), 171–88.
[58] AB, fo.29v.

each weighing just over 900 pounds. The journey to London, through Chipping Norton and High Wycombe, would take four to five days, and cost about 3*s* 6*d* per sack or 9*s* per sarpler, judging from the 18*s* 9*d* paid by the Celys to carry 2 sarplers from Northleach to London around 1480.[59] John's son Thomas spent 46*s* 8*d* to send 12 sacks of wool (at almost 9*s* 4*d* per sarpler) from Burton Dassett to the capital in 1533, though costs had risen after a period of inflation.[60] The money was spent on hiring the carts and carters, a service that would be available in most small towns, and the expense of overnight stops. They would stay in inns for security and for the services that they provided: fodder for horses, including loaves of horse bread, and incidental costs such as shoeing the horses. There is a possibility that the Londoners played a larger role, and at an earlier stage, than has been suggested here. The best sources available to us, the Cely letters, show that in the 1480s the London exporters travelled often to the Cotswolds, and together with woolmen such as William Midwinter supervised the packing. They paid for the carting of the sarplers. There is no hint in the account book that Londoners were visiting Moreton or playing a direct role in packing or carrying the wool, which suggests that Heritage arranged his own transport and met with the London merchants on their home ground.

John Heritage could have ridden down to London with the carts, but because they travelled slowly he would perhaps have followed later. His acquaintance with London merchants may have begun in his Warwickshire days, when he and his father were selling the Burton Dassett wool, or he could have been introduced to Londoners by his Palmer in-laws, or by the Fermors of Witney who employed his sister as a servant. Another point of contact would have been provided by the Stow on the Wold merchants, and as we have seen, Londoners had connections with Stow and other Gloucestershire towns. Heritage sold his wool in 1501 to at least four men, of whom the two most important were 'Basforde' and 'Browne'. The first was presumably Christopher Basford, a merchant of the staple, who paid Heritage £60, and the other William Brown, a mercer, who bought wool for £45.[61] There were two Browns, the elder of Mark (or Mart) Lane, and one who in 1522 was living, like Basford, in Cripplegate ward. A merchant called Brown continued to buy Heritage's wool in 1509 and was doing business with him sometime after 1514.[62] Other buyers of wool, presumably in London, were 'Master Morris', 'Master Ade', and Nicholas Tycull, all in 1509, and merchants called Nychyls, Pargeter, and Spryng. The last two are presumably the merchants of the staple called Thomas Pargetter and Thomas Spring, the second of whom was the famous merchant and clothier of Lavenham in Suffolk.[63] At some stage of the negotiations with the

---

[59] Hanham, *Celys*, 119. [60] *WGLS*, 115.

[61] AB, fo.5v; *Calendar of the Patent Rolls, Henry VII (1494–1509)*, 447–50; TNA: PRO, E179 251/15B, fos.57v, 58v; A. Sutton, *The Mercery of London: Trade, Goods and People, 1130–1578* (Aldershot, 2005), 524–6.

[62] AB, fo.39r, 84v.

[63] *Calendar of Patent Rolls*, 447–50; M. Bailey, *Medieval Suffolk: An Economic and Social History 1200–1500* (Woodbridge, 2007), 274–5; D. P. Dymond and A. Betterton, *Lavenham: 700 Years of Textile Making* (Lavenham, 1982), 12–13, 26.

London buyers the wool would have been weighed on the official scales called the king's beam, situated in Cornhill, before being taken to the warehouses of the exporting merchants. The weight would finally decide the precise sum that Heritage would receive. The sale of wool to a number of London staplers, and their practice of buying wool from a number of broggers, could well have been a precaution to spread the risk against business failure or some other misfortune.

Lesser quantities of wool were sold locally. Amounts of wool much smaller than the sacks and sarplers supplied to London, between 4 tods and 20 tods, were bought by a variety of middlemen, such as John Doclyng from Evesham, the parson of Batsford, and a rural trader, identified as 'Grene of Preston', a member of the Green family of Preston on Stour that was represented by Edward and Thomas Green in the early 1520s, who were relatively but not spectacularly wealthy.[64] These and others like William Walgrave and 'Master Payne' were buying *remys* wool, which was relatively cheap at 7s to 8s 8d per tod in 1502–3, when the better wool was fetching 11s or 12s. This lesser grade of wool was not suitable for export, and was being woven into cloth in England. A very large and famous cloth industry was located in Essex, and among the list of purchasers one name stands out: Robert Pekecoke of Coksale, as Heritage calls him, was the brother of Thomas Paycock of Coggeshall, one of a celebrated line of clothiers.[65] He bought more *remys* wool in 1502–3 than any of the other traders, amounting to 2 sacks and 3 tods at 7s per tod. He paid £3 and promised the remainder of the £10 3s total in the following August. Presumably this sale was negotiated in London. None of the purchasers can be identified as having a connection with the very productive south Gloucesterhire clothmakers around Stroud, but they did not weave from Cotswold wool, and usually obtained their supplies from Leicestershire, Northamptonshire, and Warwickshire.[66] An exception that does not come from Heritage's book but from a legal dispute was the sale of wool by a Stow on the Wold woolman to a clothmaker at Wickwar in south Gloucestershire, and later in the sixteenth century wool from Aston Magna in Heritage's home territory was being supplied to the Wiltshire clothing industry.[67]

As the Paycock contract shows, Heritage's financial dealing with those who bought his wool resembled his method of purchasing from the growers. He expected to receive some money when he made bargains in London, and the obligation of the staple merchants is well represented by Richard Cely who in 1479 remarks in a letter 'I look daily for the men of Cotswold to weigh at Leadenhall [the then equivalent of Cornhill] and then I must have money for them'.[68] Heritage received initial earnest money payments, and was kept waiting for the later instalments. One purchaser of *remys* wool expected to pay him at midsummer and Martinmas (21 June and 11 November), and another buyer promised the money

---

[64] AB, fo.89v, 90r; *MSG*, 176; *B & GLS*, 439.

[65] E. Power, *The Paycockes of Coggeshall* (London, 1920), 27 and Appendix I.

[66] P. J. Bowden, *The Wool Trade in Tudor and Stuart England* (London, 1962), ch. 2.

[67] TNA: PRO, C1/370/96; G. D. Ramsay, *The Wiltshire Woollen Industry in the Sixteenth and Seventeenth Centuries* (Oxford, 1943), 6–13, especially 7.

[68] A. Hanham (ed.), *The Cely Letters, 1472–1488*, Early English Text Society, 273 (Oxford, 1975), 48.

on 15 August (the Assumption of the Virgin) and 29 September (Michaelmas).[69] In view of these delayed payments it might be expected that Heritage was owed money by the Londoners, but one undated entry in the book reminds him that he owes £66 13s 4d to 'master Browne of Marke Lane' and £60 to 'Master Nychyls'.[70] This must represent another strand in the tangled web of credit in which Heritage was enmeshed. We can expect that in the season when earnest money had to be paid, in the spring, he would borrow money from his London clients, confident that within a few months, in late summer, he would be sending them enough sarplers of wool to settle the debt. In other words, he was receiving earnest money in order to pay earnest money. It was not, however, as simple as that, because if the initial payments for the wool in London was swallowed up by existing debts, where was the brogger to obtain the money to pay instalments of cash at Stow fair in mid-October?

The Londoners' position was not dissimilar from the broggers in that they were also waiting for payment. They were assembling cargoes of wool in the later part of the year, and their ships (sometimes formed into convoys for security, which took time) sailed to Calais throughout the year. The first instalment of the new season's wool went in September and October, but more followed in spring and summer. They attempted to avoid midwinter, but that was sometimes necessary, and so they sent their ships and hoped for calm seas. The staplers in Calais were not able to negotiate sales of a considerable proportion of their wool to their continental customers, and to secure money from them, until the early months of the new year.[71]

One more episode in the continuing narrative of Heritage's year needs to be completed. We have left the cart or carts in London, which had delivered their wool and were preparing to return to Gloucestershire. Their carrying capacity could not be wasted, and Heritage would make sure that bulky commodities would be loaded for eventual sale in Moreton and its surroundings. These included barrels of tar, ultimately imported from Scandinavia and brought to London by Hanseatic merchants, barrels of preserved herring, sprats, and consignments of dried white fish (ling). There would be room on the carts also for less heavy luxury goods such as hats, gunpowder, and a pewter salt cellar.[72] Once these goods had arrived in Moreton, Heritage might be involved in small-scale retailing, of which he kept a record in the case of one barrel of herring, from which 60 went to Thomas Swayneston, 9 to 'Nelme', 33 to Joan Nycols, and many more. Typical of his age, Heritage had a specialism in wool, but was drawn into trading in general merchandise.

We can describe the method of trading, but it is difficult to make a judgement on its effectiveness. Heritage and his fellow traders were faced with various

---

[69] AB, fos.89v, 90r.   [70] AB, fo.84v.
[71] Hanham, *Celys*; *idem* (ed.), *Cely Letters*, have much information about this.
[72] AB, fos.11r, 17r, 33r, 37r, 93r (tar); 1r, 23r, 93r (herring); 37r (ling); 93r (sprats); 7r (gunpowder); 62v (bonnet and salt cellar). In the same way cloth exporters brought back miscellaneous cargoes of silk, spices, dyestuffs, linen, etc.: C. Brett, 'Thomas Kytson and Wiltshire Clothmen 1529–1534', *Wiltshire Archaeological and Natural History Magazine*, 97 (2004), 35–62.

problems, such as the maintenance of quality in the product, and in the funding of trade in which it was quite impossible to pay for goods immediately on receipt. They found solutions to these problems, including the complexity of the rebates, and the constant round of credit and the payment in instalments, but the price that they paid for their ingenuity was a high level of transaction costs, in which many people travelled about in search of the money that they were owed. As we have already seen, a note of efficiency was introduced into the system by the role of the towns as recognized meeting places, and their fixed market days and fairs that made encounters between debtors and creditors more predictable.

PAYING FOR COMMERCE

All of these operations were based on the credit arrangements that lie behind many of the calculations in the account book. Heritage was juggling the money that he lent to the growers initially, and the money that he owed to them as the year unfolded, with his obligations to the purchasers, and the need to persuade them to pay promptly after the sarplers of wool had been delivered to them. Heritage and the wool trade were not exceptional in this respect, as the whole trading system worked on the basis of delayed payments and an interlocking web of debts and loans. Capital was essential, and traders presumably expected to accumulate profits that could be put back into the business, or loaned to others. Heritage's capital must have come from agriculture, as at the point when he began his Moreton enterprise he had spent a few years managing the farm of the demesne at Burton Dassett. Throughout his career as a merchant he had in reserve some land and one or two thousand sheep, which generated profits that did not depend on the financial balancing act of a middleman located precariously between the provincial growers and the metropolitan tycoons.

Heritage's main source of initial capital came from his family, but they also required expenditure. His father's will recorded that John owed him £7 6s 8d, so he had been helped in some way before Roger died. Although he gained the farm with its livestock and crops in 1495, John had to pay his father's debts (£34) and find over the next few years the £66 13s 4d that Roger left to his children.[73] John finally settled with his brother Thomas in 1504, nine years later, when it was revealed that he was also managing the bequests of his grandfather, John Heritage the elder.[74] Perhaps, like his brother Thomas, Heritage attracted patronage and could even borrow money from the Belknap family, or from his new allies at Moreton, the Palmers, which helped to fund his early years in the wool trade. London merchants in the early sixteenth century resembled John in their credit problems, as 46.5 per cent of

[73] TNA: PRO, PROB 2/457; PROB 11/10, fo. 231v.

[74] AB, fo.95v: statement by Thomas Heritage (the elder) that John had 'at diverse times' paid £28 of bequests 'by my father' (Roger Heritage) and grandfather (John Heritage the elder) to him (Thomas). As John's father left him £13 6s 8d, the grandfather must have bequeathed £14 13s 4d. On the problem of capital and credit, see M.Zell, 'Credit in the Pre-Industrial English Woollen Industry', *Ec. HR*, 49 (1996), 667–91.

their assets at probate consisted of debts, but many of them had been able to buy property, and there is no evidence that Heritage was able to do that, unless he bought the house in Cripplegate in London in which he lived after retirement.[75] In his twenty years of trading he seemed to have lived a hand-to-mouth existence.

The credit system was closely connected to the shortage of coins. A high estimate of the amount of ready money in circulation towards the end of the fifteenth century is £900,000–£1 million, compared with about £1.5 million in the early fourteenth century.[76] The size of the currency was increasing during the period of Heritage's active life as a merchant and had returned to a million and a half pounds by the mid-1520s.[77] As the population was relatively small around 1500, the amount of cash per head had increased from about 6s in the early fourteenth century to 8s, but these sums were still inadequate for a society in which there were a half-million households with an average annual income in excess of £4. For more than a century before Heritage's time western Europe as a whole suffered from a shortage of silver, as mines such as those in Germany were not very productive, and bullion was constantly draining to the east to pay for luxury goods.[78] Gold, much of it from Africa, was becoming from the end of the fifteenth century more readily available, with the consequence that gold coins accounted for 76 per cent of the output of the English mint in the period 1485–1526. To be precise, gold coins with a value of £1,272,000 were produced out of a total of coins worth £1,667,000.[79]

The everyday use of money was made more difficult when the traditional penny coinage was reduced as a proportion of the total of coins in circulation after the early fourteenth century. There had been consistent complaints that even the silver penny was too high a denomination for convenient use when a loaf of bread cost a farthing, and there were demands for the numbers of minted halfpennies and farthings to be increased. Consumers of currency made their own money in the sense that they cut the penny coins into halves and quarters. A cut farthing of the thirteenth century was found among the debris of an abandoned house at Upton in Blockley. Such a tiny coin was easily mislaid and hard to recover.[80]

No one would wish to lose the gold coins that circulated in the fifteenth and early sixteenth centuries, as they carried a considerable value. The noble, which had been the standard gold coin until 1465, and the angel, which was most numerous subsequently, were each worth 6s 8d.[81] This was quite a large sum, and even the half-angels in circulation were equivalent to two weeks' wages for a labourer.

[75] J. Oldland, 'The Allocation of Merchant Capital in Early Tudor London', *Ec. HR*, 63 (2010), 1,058–80.

[76] M. Allen, 'The Volume of the English Currency, 1158–1470', *Ec. HR*, 54 (2001), 595–611, especially 606–8; N. Mayhew, 'Population, Money Supply and the Velocity of Circulation in England, 1300–1700', *Ec. HR*, 48 (1995), 238–57, especially 243–5.

[77] P. Nightingale, 'Gold, Credit and Mortality: Distinguishing Deflationary Pressures in the Late Medieval English Economy', *Ec. HR*, 63 (2010), 1,081–04, especially 1,099.

[78] P. Spufford, *Money and its Use in Medieval Europe* (Cambridge, 1988), 343–62.

[79] C. Challis, *The Tudor Coinage* (Manchester, 1978), 232.

[80] R. H. Hilton and P. A. Rahtz, 'Upton, Gloucestershire, 1959–1964', *Transactions of the Bristol and Gloucestershire Archaeological Society*, 85 (1966), 124–5.

[81] J. J. North, *English Hammered Coinage, II, 1272–1662* (London, 1960), 11; P. Grierson, *The Coins of Medieval Europe* (London, 1991), 200–1.

Wages would normally have been paid in pennies, groats (worth 4*d*), and half groats. The ryal, which was introduced at the same time as the angel, was worth 10*s*, but thereafter was not minted for more than twenty years. Henry VII brought the 10*s* ryal back, in the form of a coin that contemporaries called the 'rose noble', from the image of the Tudor rose that it carried. The angel, still the most plentiful gold coin, would buy three or four sheep, or a cow, and a peasant household could have used it to pay a quarter's rent if they had a large holding of land (such as 2 yard-lands), but such a clumsily valuable currency could not be used for everyday purchases. Heritage's payments to wool growers, which were usually in excess of 3*s* 4*d*, were well served by gold coins, and he sometimes states that a sum of 6*s* 8*d*, 13*s* 4*d*, 20*s*, or 40*s* was 'paid in gold'. The sums of 6*s* 8*d* and 13*s* 4*d* would have consisted of angels, but in 1518 he paid 20*s* in 'ryals' (that is, two coins) to Thomas Peryn at Campden Fair, and he once refers to £10 paid to William Robyns in 1503 'in nobylls and ryalls'.[82] The nobles mentioned cannot have been the pre-1465 coins, which were no longer in circulation. Perhaps it is a reference to rose nobles.[83]

Unfortunately, Heritage was not consistent in recording his payments in gold, because as we have seen the medium of payment was just one of the many ways that he remembered a transaction, and the alternative was to identify the event by a place, or a date, or a person. Only once did he mention silver coins, when he paid £2 'in pens' in an instalment to Thomas Fletcher in 1508.[84] The most likely reason for some payments in gold to be memorable was that although Heritage often handled gold coins, he normally paid his suppliers with a combination of gold and silver, and it was the payment of gold alone that stuck in his mind. The same could apply to the £2 in pence, which might have been unusual because he gave a bag of 480 penny coins rather than a combination of pennies, groats, and half groats, but more likely he would usually have included an angel or two in the mixture of coins that made up a relatively large payment. He mentions ryals, which were quite scarce, and does not refer to angels because they were commonplace.

The references in the account book to payment in gold are made sparsely, only about once or twice a year, but a notable small flurry of five records of gold payments occurred in 1507. It may be a coincidence that from 1505 the London mint was stepping up dramatically its production of gold coins, which may therefore have been more plentiful in the provinces shortly afterwards.[85] The inconvenience of gold coins might have led to recipients asking for silver, but perhaps they had little choice. Our expectation would be that the gold would go to the wealthier farmers, who were selling wool worth £10 or more, in line with the view of some historians that there was a two-tier economy, based on gold for the rich, and silver for the peasants, some of whom, it has been said, would hardly ever handle a gold coin.[86] Heritage's records do not fully support that view, as twelve of fourteen gold payments went to suppliers whose wool was worth less than £10, of whom three

[82] AB, fos.72r, 9Av.
[83] I am grateful for Nicholas Mayhew's advice on this and other numismatic matters.
[84] AB, fo.37v.   [85] Challis, *Tudor Coinage*, 250.
[86] Nightingale, 'Gold, Credit and Mortality', 1,096, 1,100–1.

were owed sums below £2, who can certainly be categorized as peasants. Evidently peasants could make use of an angel or half-angel for major purchases of livestock or for rent, and we should not think of them as excluded from the gold economy. This is supported from an earlier period by one of the rare finds of a gold coin (a quarter-noble of the 1360s) in a peasant house in Wiltshire.[87] Peasants mainly acquired and spent silver pennies and groats, but were not averse to the occasional half-noble or half-angel, while Heritage found gold a very convenient way of transferring money, especially when he received sums as large as £40 and £60 from London merchants. A clue to the contents of Heritage's purse on his return from London comes from a hoard recovered from Asthall near Burford (Oxfordshire), which consisted of 195 angels and 15 half-angels, making £67 10s 0d, deposited in 1526. (Fig. 4.5) One explanation for this accumulation is that it represented a substantial part of a woolmonger's gains from the London staplers, but there are many other reasons for a bag of gold to be collected.[88]

Fig. 4.5. Gold coins from Asthall, Oxfordshire. This hoard of 210 gold coins deposited in about 1526, was discovered in 2007 at Asthall near Burford. It contains the type of coins used by Heritage, and its value corresponds to the sum that Heritage and other woolmen could have brought back from London. The coins were called angels because they carried an image of the archangel Michael slaying a dragon (Ashmolean Museum, University of Oxford, HCR8102).

[87] J. Musty and D. J. Algar, 'Excavations at the Deserted Medieval Village of Gomeldon, near Salisbury', *Wiltshire Archaeological and Natural History Magazine*, 80 (1986), 152–3.

[88] J. Baker, 'The Asthall Hoard of Late Medieval and Early Modern Gold Coins', *Ashmolean Magazine*, forthcoming. Most hoards are much smaller than this, though they show the importance of angels: M. Allen, 'English Coin Hoards, 1158–1544', *British Numismatic Journal*, 27 (2002), 24–84. The average hoard with gold coins was worth £2 6s 0½d.

Various forms of barter played an important part in Heritage's trade, and no doubt in the economy as a whole. Heritage had many goods and assets that he could exchange in place of scarce money. He owned plenty of sheep, and on six occasions used them to settle debts. Once he sent thirty-one sheep, which were valued at 45s, that is, thirty worth 18d each, with one for free ('to give one in') as a goodwill gesture.[89] Other livestock used in payment included a bull, a colt, and a horse. On twelve occasions he provided summer grazing for ewes or lambs (probably at Ditchford) or grazing for a fixed number of cows (between four and seven) at Coldicote in Moreton. He also paid in grain, hay, and firewood. Barrels of tar (worth 5s or 6s), which figured among items he brought back from London, were also given in place of money, and other items from the capital including fish, a 'bonnet for his wife', and gunpowder.[90]

Heritage could become drawn into complex financial transactions when he took over obligations and debts of his wool growers. He did this twice when a supplier died after the wool had been delivered. In 1517 he covered some of the funeral expenses of Thomas Swayneston, such as buying wax for candles, and after Alison Wylcox's death in 1518 he provided bread and ale and rewards for the clergy who attended, her shroud, and the expenses of proving her will.[91] John Mansell, who had sold him wool, evidently had a relative who had died, and under the terms of the will £4 13s 4d had to be found for a chantry priest to say masses for a year, so Heritage shouldered the cost instead of paying the money to Mansell.[92]

When Heritage paid money to third parties to whom the supplier owed money, he was becoming a financial agent. An example would be the sum of £8 6s 8d paid to Robert Dermand in part settlement of a sum of £33 16s 8d that the woolman owed to Richard Fretherne.[93] If this was in response to written instructions from Fretherne, it bears some resemblance to the means of payment employed at the exporting end of the wool trade, by which those who bought wool in Calais arranged for the money to be paid to the English merchants in London.[94]

Most of the payments in kind provided a remedy for the shortage of cash in Heritage's dealings with neighbours he knew well, who could take advantage of the offers of pasturage and hay. For most of those trading with Heritage, who were well used to self-sufficiency in supplying foodstuffs to their own household and in payment of servants in kind, their wool was important to them as a source of cash. They would have used their wool money to pay their rent, for example, which was due at fixed terms during the year. Heritage had to respond to the demands for coins by delaying payments, persuading his suppliers to be patient, and keeping

---

[89] AB, fo.69v.

[90] See note 72. Handguns were just beginning to appear in the English countryside by 1502, the date of Heritage's reference to gunpowder, but they were not in common use: S. Gunn, 'Archery Practice in Early Tudor England', *Past and Present*, 209 (2010), 73–7. The gunpowder went to William Bayly, farmer of Condicote, a man of some wealth.

[91] AB, fo.69v, 70r, 71v. Both Swayneston and Wylcox reappear in the account book in 1518, perhaps because their sheep were still producing wool for their executors.

[92] AB, fo.65v, 68v.   [93] AB, fo.22v.   [94] Hanham, *Celys*, 195–202.

pressure on those who were supposed to pay money to him. Everyone he encountered knew only too well the difficulty of running a money economy in an environment starved of coins.

Much depended on trust. The main written records were the imperfect and often incomplete records entered in the book. Accounts had no standing in common law, but the court of Chancery, which was more flexible in its methods, would recognize an entry in an account book as evidence.[95] Occasionally he noted the presence of a witness: 'Paid in the presence of Robert Wels' (or Welys).[96] He sometimes used written bonds, referring in an undated note to 'an obligation of mine of £4' to John Freman, and another memorandum states 'my cousin Palmer owes to me 40s. whereof he has paid to my attorney for the rest of an obligation'.[97] These documents were unusual: apparently his archive described shortly before 1511 contained only one obligation, and a writ is mentioned once.[98] Agreements were made by word of mouth, and maintained by mutual trust reinforced by community sanctions, which ensured that anyone who failed to pay 'lost credit' in both the literal and metaphorical sense. As he conducted business with many people who were known to him personally, and who he met regularly, Heritage was bound to maintain a reputation for fair dealings and honesty. There was a rich medieval moralistic tradition of condemning cheating and the manipulation of prices and quality by dishonest traders, and this was no doubt possible in the anonymous commerce of a large city, or at a large gathering of strangers at a fair. In the small town and rural world of John Heritage the intertwining of trade and personal relations is perfectly summed up in the record in 1509 that he had paid 13s 4d to John Nelme 'at his wedding'.[99]

Any study of late medieval trade finds the universal use of informal credit, whereby the seller allowed the buyer a long time to pay off the cost of commodities, or of services, or of the purchase of land. The practice is found among the Yorkshire merchants based at Beverley, Hull, and York, and in the south-east of England by those trading in grain and livestock. Women who sold ale and food in London kept a running record with notches on a wooden tally stick, and after a delay demanded payment.[100] The unusual feature of Heritage's book is that it gives us a glimpse of the scale of credit transactions, which ran into many hundreds in his case, but are connected with thousands more payments for sheep, transport, tar, fish, and so on. The whole edifice depended on a web of mutual trust and obligation, sealed by spoken words and gestures, which is first recorded in detail in the sixteenth and seventeenth centuries.[101]

---

[95] Webb, *Great Tooley*, 110. [96] AB, fo.11r. [97] AB, fo.84v.
[98] AB, fo.92v. This is the collection of nine documents that were kept by Thomas Davies of Stow.
[99] Davis, *Market Morality*, 68–83; AB, fo.40v.
[100] J. Kermode, *Medieval Merchants. York, Beverley and Hull in the Later Middle Ages* (Cambridge, 1998), 231–3; Mate, *Trade and Economic Developments*, 33–4; M. K. McIntosh, *Working Women in English Society 1300–1620* (Cambridge, 2005), 88–9.
[101] C. Muldrew, *The Economy of Obligation. The Culture of Credit and Social Relations in Early Modern England* (Basingstoke, 1998).

The late fifteenth and early sixteenth centuries also saw a flourishing in written records of debt, in the form of bonds, obligations, and recognizances. In the twenty-seven deeds and allied documents in the archives of William Willington of Barcheston dated 1497–1520, four were bonds, which sought to ensure by the threat of financial penalties that various acts, mostly property sales, were completed.[102] Recognizances were being brought into estate administration by the Duchy of Lancaster in the late fifteenth century, and it is suggested that it was from this example that Henry VII used them to hold his subjects to promises to keep the peace and carry out services to the Crown.[103]

Records of debt in the state archives, especially the certificates of debt under Statute Merchant, declined in number and value in the mid-fifteenth century, together with extents of debt. They offer an index for the great depression of that period. Those merchants and other wealthy people who needed the protection of a written record of money advanced or loaned were diminishing in number, but then increased from the 1490s. The amounts of money covered by these certificates increased fivefold between the mid-fifteenth century and 1520, most of the increase being concentrated in the last thirty years.[104] Was this change in the availability of credit for the elite, many of whom were Londoners, reflected in the lesser courts, which traditionally provided small traders, artisans, and peasants with their opportunity to recover money and goods? The courts of Moreton and Shipston, though still quite active in many aspects of their business, did not deal with litigation over debts, and beyond the edge of Heritage's country the borough court of Stratford upon Avon kept up regular meetings every two or three weeks (in 1512–13) to hear pleas of debt and broken contract, and similar business was done in the hundred court of Slaughter, so the idea that a local court could serve the needs of those seeking unpaid debts was not entirely forgotten.[105] The royal Court of Common Pleas offered a last resort, but was only worth the expense and trouble to recover relatively large sums. Despite this lack of written records and courts providing redress for those whose credit arrangements had broken down, sales and loans continued to be made in large numbers, and if they followed the trend indicated by the large debts covered by statute merchant, they were expanding after 1490.

THE TRAJECTORY OF THE BUSINESS

To take a more general view of Heritage's finances, his annual outlay of money (Figs. 4.6 and 4.7, and Appendix 2) amounted to about £300 each year between 1501 and 1509. His peak was reached in 1506 (a long year, see p. 96) when he promised to pay £410 for a total of 58 sacks (761 tods) of wool. In 1510 and 1511 he scaled down his advances to £150, and between 1512 and 1517 was spending

[102] WCRO, CR580, 9/3–30.
[103] H. R. Horowitz, 'Policy and Prosecution in the Reign of Henry VII', *Historical Research*, 82 (2009), 412–58.
[104] Nightingale, 'Gold, Credit and Mortality', 1,083–7.
[105] Centre for Kentish Studies, Maidstone, U269/M75; TNA: PRO, SC2 176/8.

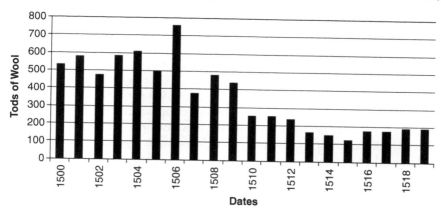

Fig. 4.6. Annual totals of gathered wool.

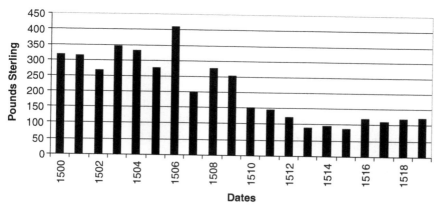

Fig. 4.7. Money paid for gathered wool.

nearer to £100 each year on wool. The corresponding movement in the quantity of wool that passed through his woolhouse followed a similarly downward trend, as in the first nine years the total fluctuated between 28 and 58 sacks each year, and in some years hovered around 40 sacks (520 tods), but in 1510–12 it was reduced down to about 20 sacks (260 tods), and afterwards to around 10–15 sacks. Why did he gradually shrink his business, and apparently give up completely in 1520 or soon after that date?

His profit margin cannot be calculated exactly, but we are given some clues. The average price per tod paid by Heritage in Gloucestershire is easily calculated from hundreds of contracts, but although we are given sums of money that he received in London they are not connected to a precise number of sacks or tods. In the case of his own wool, however, prices are given that apparently derive from sales in London. His wool may have been of a different quality from that bought in the countryside around Moreton, and the wool from Burton Dassett may have been from an inferior breed of sheep. Nonetheless in 1506 wool was being bought around Moreton for an average price of 10.8s per tod, but his own wool was sold in London for £7 13s 4d per sack, which makes the price per tod 11.8s. If the gathered wool in that year was sold for a price similar to his own wool, it would have given him a profit margin of 12d per tod, or 9.3 per cent. The differences in price were not so great in 1503 and 1504, when apparently the wool was sold in London only for 3d per tod more than the purchase price for wool in Gloucester-shire, which suggests a possible profit margin as low as 2 per cent.

Taking the most optimistic profit calculation of 9.3 per cent, and applying it to the wool that Heritage 'gathered' in a normal year in the first decade of the six-teenth century, he could have made from wool bought for £300 a gross profit of £28 from the sale of the best wool, to which should be added £3 profit from the sale of the *remys*. From this speculative total of £31 must be deducted the expenses of sixteen cart journeys to London for £7; the wages of a servant who helped with the business, who must have been paid at least £5 (receiving part of his remuner-ation in kind); Heritage's travelling to London and staying there, cost at least £2; and the maintenance of the woolhouse, the work of winding and packing, with canvas covers for the sarplers (at 4s each), cannot have required less than another £5. No wonder that he charged the cost of winding where possible to the supplier. This would make his net profit about £12. He would have needed to make money on the cartloads of tar and fish being brought back from London to raise his total trading profits above £20. The calculations quoted above that he only gained a return of 2 per cent must be flawed, as he could not have continued in business if the return was no better than £10, which would not have covered his travel and transport costs. The estimate of 9.3 per cent profit is in line with known profit margins in other trades, such as butchery.[106]

An obscure corner of Heritage's business was his sale of wool fells, that is, sheep-skins. They formed an important element in the wool trade, as the skins taken from sheep that were slaughtered or had died before shearing were valued for their wool, and those of sheep which died at any time in the year provided glovers, purse makers, and other artisans with their raw material. Fells were traded within Eng-land and overseas. Heritage's account book recorded his wool purchases and only on one page is there a record of fells, a total of 942, of which 104 were 'my fells'. They were valued at £21, and if this was a regular annual element in Heritage's trade, a few pounds should be added to any estimate of his profits.[107]

At the same time Heritage was himself a grower, and was taking his own wool to London alongside the fleeces that he had gathered from his fellow producers. In his early years at Moreton he was selling his clip for £30 to £40 each year, and later this rose nearer to £50 (Fig. 4.8 and Appendix 2). In 1518, for example, he pro-duced 6 ½ sacks that could be sold for £8 each, producing a gross return of £52.

[106] C. Dyer, *Standards of Living in the Later Middle Ages: Social Change in England c.1200–1520*, 2nd edn. (Cambridge, 1998), 195.

[107] AB, fo.1r.

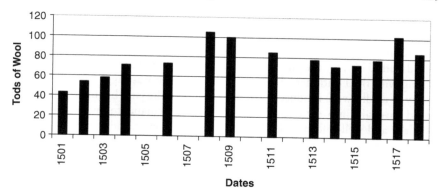

Fig. 4.8. Annual totals of John Heritage's own wool.

To this must be added at least £2 for the sale of his own woolfells (which on other estates generated income between 5 and 10 per cent of the wool sales),[108] and the sale of surplus lambs and the older and weaker animals that could still be fattened by butchers. His cattle and horses that also lived on his pastures brought in an uncertain amount of revenue, but it was not much as they were few in number. The total of livestock sales in the three years of records, 1507, 1509, and 1510, were quite consistent at between £32 and £38.[109] Not all of the pastures were used for his own animals, as he profited by renting out summer and winter pasturage, which could well have yielded an annual £4.[110] His income from these agricultural pursuits in the 1510s could have exceeded £90. His expenses included £30 for the rent of the pastures, wages of shepherds (six full-time employees would not cost more than £18 if they gained much of their remuneration by pasturing their own sheep along with their employer's flock), and the pay of perhaps £3 for part-time hay makers. Fences and buildings would have to be maintained, and new livestock bought occasionally, but his flocks bred their own lambs. Equipment costs would include hurdles, tar, and grease, which together with washing and shearing would amount to £2, judging from the expenditure of Norwich Cathedral Priory in the 1520s. These costs could leave him with a profit near to £30.[111]

Heritage's trading surplus in a good year as a brogger may have been inferior to his profits in pastoral agriculture, on the basis of limited evidence on prices. The big

[108] C. E. Moreton, *The Townshends and their World: Gentry, Law and Land in Norfolk c.1450–1551* (Oxford, 1992), 174 n.70; M. Bailey (ed.), 'The Sheep Accounts of Norwich Cathedral Priory 1484–1534', in *Poverty and Wealth: Sheep, Taxation and Charity in Late Medieval Norfolk*, Norfolk Record Society, 71 (Norwich, 2007), 87–91.

[109] AB, fos.87r, 87v, 91v, 92r, 92v.

[110] Heritage regularly used in barter transactions pasture of sheep and cattle valued at 2s 4d–13s 4d. In 1505 he valued 'wintering of sheep' at 26s 8d, and in 1509 'summering of lambs' was worth 25s. Normally he sold the pasture for cash, and £4 seems a reasonable estimate of the total. AB, fos.23r, 40v.

[111] Bailey, 'Sheep Accounts', 87–8; K. J. Allison, 'Flock Management in the Sixteenth and Seventeenth Centuries', *Ec. HR*, 11 (1958), 98–112, mentions a profit margin of 5d per annum per sheep, which would give Heritage in his later years about £40.

profits in the wool trade were gained by the merchants of the staple on the trade in wool to Calais, and their margins have been estimated at about 20 per cent in the 1470s and 1480s. A brogger was surrounded on all sides by competitors, who could outbid him for the purchase of the wool, and then undercut him when negotiating with the Londoners. Unlike the brogger who was juggling with the uncertainty of credit, wool producers had the stability of the land behind them, and they could diversify into cattle or other products if demand for wool was reduced. Wealthy and well-informed leaders of society were ever ready to take on pastures in Heritage's time, and they must have calculated that rearing large flocks of sheep was a profitable business. Heritage was not alone in his combination of wool dealing and sheep keeping. As well as running busy woolhouses, those who sold wool also produced it on Cotswold pastures: in 1510 Thomas Busshe, the Northleach woolman, leased Withington; around the same time members of the Tame family of Fairford had become lords of Stowell, and among the Stow merchants Thomas Davies leased Upton Wold and William Chadwell held land at Hampen. William Willington has already been encountered at Barcheston and Upton Wold. The synergy seemed to work for them.[112]

Heritage reduced his activity as a brogger at a time when the demand for wool was rising, judging from the price per tod that he felt it necessary to pay, from 10s–12s per tod in his first thirteen years, up to 13s and even 14s in 1514–16, only to fall back to 12s, still a high price by the standards of the first decade of the sixteenth century (see Appendix 2). This would only benefit him if he could maintain his profit margin as he faced competition from such rising stars as William Willington. On the other hand, as a wool producer his expenses remained at much the same level, though Heritage must have been paying more in rent to gain access to larger areas of pasture, and he would be more certain of reaping the benefits of the higher prices. He increased his sheep numbers from between one thousand and two thousand in his early years, to above two thousand by 1510. In the 1510s he was selling between 5 and 6 sacks of his own wool, and presumably maintained his sales of sheep and wool fells (see Fig. 4.8 and Appendix 2).

When after 1513 Heritage reduced the scale of his business as a wool trader to a third of its pre-1510 level, he was probably bringing his profits down from £20 to £7. In 1513–18 his pastoral farming was about a third bigger than it had been in 1501–3, and its profits could have increased from £20 to £30, which suggests that his total income had fallen in his later years, but not drastically.

A new development in his business portfolio appears at the very end of his series of annual accounts. He made a list of nine people, under the heading 'Money lent in 1520', and noted that each owed 6s 8d, 10s, 13s 4d, or 20s, making a total of £6. The names are very familiar from the lists of those supplying wool, such as Bumpas, Mansell, Stevens, and Whete, and they came from the villages where Heritage had focused his business in his later years, Bourton on the Hill, Longborough, Paxford, and other places in Blockley parish. The loans were evidently a develop-

[112] Power, 'Wool Trade', 53–5; Dyer, *Lords and Peasants*, 214–15; *VCH Glos.*, IX, 211, 214; TNA:PROB 11/17, fos. 16–17; WRO, BA2648/8 (i), ref b.716:093, 179.

ment from the advances of earnest money as the first stage of negotiating the purchase of wool. No doubt built into the agreements for the repayment of money the merchant gained some profit. For example, he may have advanced 9*s*, but 10*s* would be repaid, although this is not revealed in writing. While this marks a significant development in Heritage's manipulation of credit, it was not being conducted on a sufficient scale to compensate for the shrinkage of the wool dealing.[113]

If Heritage was not reducing the size of his business as much as the account book's records of wool purchases suggests, there still remains the mystery of his apparent withdrawal from Moreton soon after 1520. He was not very old, having reached his fiftieth year. His trading suggests that he was declining in energy and enterprise, as his circle of suppliers was reduced to a limited range of local people well known to him, and the names of Bumpas, Mansell, Nightingale, Stevens, and Whete are repeated from year to year. On the other hand, Heritage may have been concentrating on managing his sheep. He may have decided to move to London, either in retirement, to have closer contact with his brother and son, or to take on some new apparently undocumented enterprise.

Heritage has left us with documents that tell us a little about him as an individual, but are important sources for the economic mentality of a trader, who kept imperfect but still revealing accounts. By reading between the lines we can reconstruct the brogger's method of working, seeking out suppliers by various strategies, and negotiating with them, which must have been one of the key skills of traders. The woolmen built up a fund of intelligence about their contacts, and used a number of sources of information. We sometimes think of England in 1500–20 as a traditional society, in which business would be determined by ties of kinship, clientage, and personal loyalty. We can see signs of all of these factors, in the role of the Palmers, for example, or the occasional consistent supplier who sold wool to Heritage for successive years. There is also evidence, however, of fierce competition, as canny wool producers switched from Heritage and back again in search of the best possible returns. The account book demonstrates the importance of credit, which operated at every level of trade, and meant that much effort was expended by individuals ensuring that they received their money in good time. Although the lack of customer loyalty reveals pervasive streaks of ruthlessness, the working of the credit system without many written instruments suggests a society based on trust and integrity.

Heritage may seem representative of his age in his business methods, but the decline in his wool dealing was not characteristic. The higher prices, especially in 1514–19, suggest that demand for wool was increasing, and although wool exports were falling, demand from the home market was high, both for satisfying the overseas market for English cloth, but also to cater for the purchase of cloth at home. The rise in records of credit, increased cloth exports, industrial expansion, and technical innovation all suggest that in the years 1495–1520 there were economic opportunities in England as a whole.

---

[113] AB, fo.76r.

5

Pasture, Sheep, Wool, and People

In an earlier chapter Heritage's country was surveyed, and its villages, towns, fields, and pastures were portrayed as the products of long-term evolutions. The rural settlements and fields were formed before the eleventh century, and the towns had been established by 1300. Many peasants had substantial holdings of arable land, and as customary tenants they owed rents and services to manors often belonging to large Church estates. From the mid-fourteenth century the lords had lost authority and they withdrew from direct management of agriculture. Peasants enjoyed more freedom as serfdom receded, and many of them gained greater quantities of land. Agriculture was shifting from arable to pasture, which put some strains on the village communities. Members of families had to adjust to a very mobile society.[1] This chapter and the next are concerned with Heritage's activities in the period 1495 to 1520, and the landscape and society in which he produced and traded. A particular concern will be to explain the part played by him and people like him in connecting the rural population to the trading network, and in identifying the main places and people involved in production and exchange. There is a conventional historical view of this period that the dominant figures were the acquisitive gentry and entrepreneurs, who adopted the roles of engrossers, enclosers, and graziers, and that they rationalized and expanded production of wool at the expense of the peasantry. Can these changes be identified in this period? And how did the period contribute to long-term change?

---

[1] On the general trends in the countryside in the period 1350–1520, M. Bailey, *A Marginal Economy? East Anglian Breckland in the Later Middle Ages* (Cambridge, 1989); I. S. W. Blanchard, 'Population Change, Enclosure and the Early Tudor Economy', *Ec. HR*, 2nd ser., 23 (1970), 427–45; R. H. Britnell, *Britain and Ireland 1050–1530: Economy and Society* (Oxford, 2004); B. Dodds, *Peasants and Production in the Medieval North-East: The Evidence from Tithes 1270–1536* (Woodbridge, 2007); B. Dodds and R. Britnell (eds), *Agriculture and Rural Society after the Black Death: Common Themes and Regional Variations* (Hatfield, 2008); H. S. A. Fox, 'The Chronology of Enclosure and Economic Developments in Medieval Devon', *Ec. HR*, 2nd ser., 28 (1975), 181–202; B. Harvey, *Westminster Abbey and its Estates in the Middle Ages* (Oxford, 1977); P. D. A. Harvey (ed.), *The Peasant Land Market in Medieval England* (Oxford, 1984); J. Hatcher, *Rural Economy and Society in the Duchy of Cornwall, 1300–1500* (Cambridge, 1970); R. H. Hilton, *The Decline of Serfdom* (London, 1969); R. H. Hilton, *The English Peasantry in the Later Middle Ages* (Oxford, 1975); M. E. Mate, *Daughters, Wives and Widows after the Black Death: Women in Sussex, 1350–1535* (Woodbridge, 1998); M. K. McIntosh, *Autonomy and Community in the Royal Manor of Havering, 1200–1500* (Cambridge, 1986); E. Miller (ed.), *The Agrarian History of England and Wales*, III, *1348–1500* (Cambridge, 1991); L. R. Poos, *A Rural Society after the Black Death: Essex 1350–1525* (Cambridge, 1991); J. A. Raftis, *Tenure and Mobility* (Toronto, 1964); R. M. Smith, 'The English Peasantry, 1250–1650', in T. Scott (ed.), *The Peasantries of Europe from the Fourteenth to the Eighteenth Centuries* (Harlow, 1998); J. Whittle, *The Development of Agrarian Capitalism: Land and Labour in Norfolk 1440–1580* (Oxford, 2000); M. Yates, *Town and Countryside in Western Berkshire, c.1327–c.1600: Social and Economic Change* (Woodbridge, 2007).

PEOPLING THE LAND

The fall in population after the early fourteenth century, which accelerated with the arrival of the Black Death in 1348–9 and subsequent epidemics, had particularly severe effects in the Moreton district, and forms an essential backdrop to all of the other changes. Table 5.1 gives a very schematic and impressionistic view of the trends in population numbers based on the tax lists of 1327 and 1524/5. A sample of villages has been selected in order to make a direct comparison between the two lists of taxpayers. The estimate of the population in 1327 depends on the very risky assumption that 50 per cent of the households were exempted because of their poverty, or because they evaded the assessment, and that the average household contained five people, giving us a multiplier of ten. For the early sixteenth century taxes an equally risky estimate is based on a multiplier of seven, because

Table 5.1. Population estimated from tax lists, 1327 and 1524–5: Moreton in Marsh and its hinterland.

Vill	Taxpayers 1327	Population estimate 1327	Taxpayers 1524–5	Population estimate 1524–5
Barton on the Heath	14	140	9	63
Batsford	16	160	6	42
Blockley	16	160	19	133
Blockley vills*	115	1,150	46	322
Bourton on the Hill	15	150	14	98
Broadwell	20	200	19	133
Charingworth	13	130	8	56
Donnington	11	110	4	28
Evenlode	19	190	6	42
Longborough	29	290	26	182
Moreton in Marsh	10	100	28	196
Quinton	29	290	18	126
Tredington	11	110	6	42
Tredington vills*	90	900	35	245
Wolford, Great	27	270	13	91
Wolford, Little	16	160	16	112
Total	451	4,510	273	1,911

*villages and hamlets within the parish

Source: P. Franklin (ed.), *The Taxpayers of Medieval Gloucestershire* (Stroud, 1993); F. J. Eld (ed.), *Lay Subsidy Roll for the County of Worcester*, I, *Edward III*, Worcestershire Historical Society, 6 (1895); W. B. Bickley (ed.), 'Lay Subsidy Roll, Warwickshire 1327', *Transactions of the Midland Record Society*, 6 (1902); G. Wrottesley (ed.), 'The Exchequer Subsidy Roll of AD 1327', *Collections for a History of Staffordshire*, William Salt Archaeological Society, 7 (1886); J. Sheail, *The Regional Distribution of Wealth in England as Indicated in the 1524/5 Lay Subsidy Returns*, II, 'List and Index Society, Special Series, 29 (1998); *B & GLS*; *WT*; TNA:PRO 179 192/122 (Warwickshire Lay Subsidy, 1524).

the amount of exemption was lower in a tax that included some wage-earners.[2] On the basis of these assumptions our sixteen units of taxation over the two centuries lost more than 2,599 people, or 58 per cent of the estimated total. To indicate that such a change is specific to the region, and is not just a product of the methods of taxation or just part of the general national trend, a sample of a dozen units of taxation around the town of Birmingham in 1327 and 1524/5 using the same formulae (Table 5.2) shows an overall increase of 1,279, or 38 per cent. Evidently communities with woodland resources and an involvement in industry were not subject to the same shrinkage found in the champion landscape with a predominantly agrarian economy around Moreton. Similar variations are found in other parts of the country such as Berkshire, where again industrial growth helps to explain why a region was able to avoid the most serious effects of a falling population.[3] The most likely imperfection in these estimates lies in the number of exemptions or evasions in 1327, as this can be shown for individual villages to have been as high as 60 per cent. The decline in population was probably even greater in the sample of villages around Moreton than is shown in Table 5.1, and especially in Moreton itself which is highly unlikely to have supported as few as a hundred people in 1327.[4]

The tax records with all of their imperfections have to stand as a proxy for census records that do not exist. The manorial surveys and rentals are the other indicators of the size of populations, as the tenants that they list correspond approximately to households, though under-recording is a problem because of the exclusion of subtenants. The survey of Blockley in 1299 names 136 tenants, living in the main village and its five subsidiaries, but in 1544 the number had fallen to 67, suggesting that the size of the settlements had been reduced to a half of their thirteenth-century peak.[5] The corresponding figures for the three Westminster Abbey manors

Table 5.2. Population estimated from tax lists, 1327 and 1524–5: Birmingham and its hinterland.

Vill	Taxpayers 1327	Population estimate 1327	Taxpayers 1524–5	Population estimate 1524–5
Total	339	3,390	667	4,669

Source: As in Table 5.1.

---

[2] C. Dyer, *Lords and Peasants in a Changing Society: The Estates of the Bishopric of Worcester 680–1540* (Cambridge, 1980), 109; A. Dyer, '"Urban Decline" in England, 1377–1525', in T. R. Slater (ed.), *Towns in Decline AD 100–1600* (Aldershot, 2000), 266–88, especially 271–2. I have chosen a rather low multiplier for 1327, and a rather high one for 1524–5, to reduce the danger of exaggerating the decline over the two centuries.

[3] R. S. Schofield, 'The Geographical Distribution of Wealth in England, 1334–1669', *Ec. HR*, 18 (1965), 483–510; M. Yates, *Town and Country in Western Berkshire, c.1327–c.1600: Social and Economic Change* (Woodbridge, 2007), 34–54.

[4] Urban tax assessments, compared with those for villages, seem to have recorded a lower proportion of the population.

[5] M. Hollings (ed.), *The Red Book of Worcester*, Worcestershire Historical Society (1934–50), 295–321; WRO, BA 2636, ref.009:1, 18/47765.

of Bourton on the Hill, Todenham, and Sutton under Brailes were 164 tenants around 1300, compared with 68 in *c*.1540, 41 per cent of the earlier total.[6]

The manorial records in the fifteenth century often described a holding with an inhabited house as 'a messuage and a yardland', while using the phrase 'a toft and a yardland' for a holding without buildings, as the toft referred to the plot on which its tenant had once lived. The policy on some estates was evidently to look forward to the day when new houses would be built on the tofts, and lords made efforts to pressurize tenants to repair buildings or to erect new ones. The Quinton rental of 1480 lists thirty-six holdings, of which seven were headed by a toft. Some of the messuages were described as 'built', as if others were not, and one cottage had been recently destroyed by fire.[7] Just as Heritage's childhood and youth was spent in a decaying settlement, so in his adult life he must have taken it for granted that he would ride constantly past the ruins of buildings, or their long abandoned sites, in a depopulated countryside. To him this was unremarkable, but an Italian visitor in *c*.1500 with the fresh eye of someone accustomed to a dense population and labour-intensive agriculture remarked on the thinly inhabited country of England.[8] We can calculate that there was a density below sixty people to each square mile in north-east Gloucestershire in the early sixteenth century, compared with more than a hundred per square mile in parts of eastern England, which would have led a well-travelled visitor to Moreton to have been impressed by the underpopulated state of the district.[9]

Around Moreton, as in other parts of England, the reduction in inhabitants was very uneven, with houses being abandoned in every settlement, either piecemeal, leaving gaps along village streets, as can still be seen in a settlement such as Oddington, or an end of the village was abandoned, as at Admington. Some villages were reduced drastically in size, and must have faced the prospect of total abandonment, not just small out-of-the-way places such as Batsford and Donnington, but potentially rather important villages with large churches and manorial centres, notably Tredington.[10] These villages escaped the fate of depopulation, but others were completely abandoned and their disappearance and replacement by pastures will be discussed below.

Growth in the population of England as a whole came in the first half of the sixteenth century, and there are signs in the Midlands and other regions (though not in the records from the Moreton district) that rent payments had begun to rise after 1470 or in the first decades of the sixteenth century.[11] An extension in the expectation of life was experienced by the well-documented monks of Westminster Abbey, after 1500.[12] In the first twenty years of the sixteenth century epidemics diminished, though manorial court rolls (which record the deaths of tenants) and

---

[6] Harvey, *Westminster Abbey*, 432; WAM, 8383.

[7] Magdalen College, Oxford, 35/B13.

[8] C. A. Sneyd (ed.), *A Relation of the Island of England*, Camden Society, 37 (1847), 31: 'the population does not ... bear any proportion to fertility and riches ...'

[9] J. Sheail, *The Regional Distribution of Wealth in England as Indicated in the 1524/5 Lay Subsidy Returns*, List and Index Society, Special Series, 29 (1998).

[10] *B & GLS*, 353, 414; *WT*, 195.

[11] A. Jones, 'Bedfordshire: Fifteenth Century', in P. D. A. Harvey (ed.), *The Peasant Land Market in Medieval England* (Oxford, 1984), 220.

[12] B. Harvey, *Living and Dying in England, 1100–1540: The Monastic Experience* (Oxford, 1993), 127–9.

wills from the Moreton district show that there was a cluster of deaths in 1512–13, which is recorded as an epidemic year in London.[13] An important influence on levels of population at this period was the age of marriage and fertility within marriage, that is, a tendency for the numbers of births to rise, as well as a modest and temporary reduction in the death rate. The main indication of a new era of population growth in our district comes from the numbers of children mentioned in wills, which we have seen rising above three per testator, and the rising proportion of young people inheriting land, suggesting that would-be tenants, especially men, were not so scarce, and that a rising demand for land made them more interested in acquiring their family's holding (see p. 49–51).

GRAZING THE LAND

Leasows

Low levels of population are often associated with pastoral farming, and between 1350 and 1520 the proportion of land under grass increased. A feature of the countryside in Heritage's day was the 'leasow' (see Fig. 3.8). The word had a general meaning of a pasture field, deriving from lees or leaze, which originally meant untilled ground. Around 1500, legal documents talk of 'meadow, leasow, and pasture', implying that it had a distinct meaning. The term was not confined to the west Midlands, but was much in use in the region. In the Moreton area the name could be applied to a common pasture, for example the 'Beste Leasow' at Barcheston, Ebrington, and Upper Swell, which was a grazing area for the villagers' cattle, from which sheep might be excluded.[14] A much-contested pasture at Maugersbury on the south side of Stow on the Wold provided grazing for the townspeople, hence its name of Portmanslesow.[15]

Many leasows, however, were several pastures, that is, held in separate occupation by a lord or tenant, protected by enclosures, and often of considerable size. Lords could create a leasow by fencing off part of their demesne, if it was held in a block rather than being scattered over the fields and intermingled with the land of tenants. A single piece of demesne arable could be converted to pasture and fenced, as happened at Admington, where the demesne was listed in the early sixteenth century as Frisen Lesow (implying that it was at least partly covered with gorse bushes) and Windsor Lesow.[16] Another type of leasow had been carved out of a large area of common pasture shared by a number of villages for the exclusive use of a single lord, a process that is recorded as early as the twelfth century, though this continued into Heritage's time. Examples include Horneslesow on the high

---

[13] TNA: PRO, SC2 175/77. Deaths recorded in these years: 1504 (1); 1506 (0); 1507 (3); 1508 (0); 1509 (1); 1511 (2); 1512 (7); 1513 (3); 1514 (0); 1516 (1); 1517 (0); 1518 (1). Of 58 wills collected for research for this book, dated 1491–1538, 8 record deaths in 1512 and 1513.

[14] WCRO, CR 580/7; Devon Record Office, 1262M, Glos. Leases E2; TNA: PRO, SC2 175/77.

[15] TNA: PRO, SC2 175/77 (court roll); *VCH Glos.*, VI, 155.

[16] TNA: PRO, SC6 Henry VIII/1240 (accounts).

ground at the east end of Tewkesbury Abbey's manor of Taddington, and Murden-lesow not far away on the same sweep of high ground at the western end of Lower Swell, which belonged to Hailes Abbey.[17] We do not always know whether the land had originally been part of the demesne or a common pasture open to the villagers, though the latter origin is likely for the 'summer leasow' at Barcheston and 'the leasow called the Downs' at Whitchurch.[18] Land previously occupied by a village and its open fields, when converted to pasture, could also be called a leasow. Not all large pastures were known as leasows; for example, the expanse of grassland at the eastern end of Broadway (which was disputed between Broadway and Camp-den) and the pasture called Abbot's Flock on the western end of Bourton on the Hill (see Fig. 3.4) did not have the name applied to them.

DESERTED VILLAGE SITES

Some of the largest leasows or pastures were those occupying the abandoned site and fields of deserted villages. The country where Heritage bought his wool includes one of the most concentrated pockets of abandoned settlements in England – there were about twenty-nine of them. The number is debatable because of uncertainties about the settlements' size and status before desertion, and the extent to which particular villages had been reduced in size in the early sixteenth century (see Appendix 3). The list is confined to places with at least ten households at some time between 1086 and 1400, which functioned as separate villages in the sense that they cultivated and man-aged their own fields, or were recognized as distinct units of government by outside authorities for such purposes as tax assessment. By the early sixteenth century they had either been completely abandoned or were in severe decay, and their former fields were often converted either partly or wholly into pastures. To emphasize the severity of the transformation of parts of Heritage's country we need only dwell on the surroundings of Lark Stoke, in what is now a rather remote valley etched into the scarp of the Cots-wold hills with two isolated houses, but was once a village with a dozen households. Now there are only three villages within a 2-mile (3.2 km) radius of Lark Stoke, but once this was a densely settled landscape with eleven villages and hamlets. In modern times the place name became especially appropriate, as the first element referred to the birds singing in the sky above a countryside largely devoid of people.[19]

The severe decline or abandonment of these settlements can be known from their falling tax payments, or their disappearance from the tax records, as in the case of Norton Subedge. Manorial documents may tell us that the village's holdings had come into the hands of the lord, or had been engrossed by a single tenant (as at Upper Ditchford). They might also report that rents had fallen drastically or were no longer collectable. Tithe accounts can reflect the decline in the cultivation of grain, and church records may reveal that the parish church or chapel was disused or ruined.

[17] GA, P239/1; TNA: PRO, SC6 Henry VIII/1240 (accounts).
[18] WCRO, CR580/1; Shakespeare Birthplace Trust Record Office, DR41/26 (Bloom's transcripts), 54–5.
[19] A. H. Smith, *The Place-Names of Gloucestershire*, I, English Place-Name Society, 38 (1964), 231.

The decline of villages within a few miles of Stratford upon Avon, such as Compton Scorpion, Lark Stoke, and Meon, can be followed by noting the number of inhabitants who joined the fraternity of the Holy Cross in that town, and then observing that recruitment ceased during the fifteenth and early sixteenth centuries.[20]

In most cases there is physical evidence of the village's former existence in the form of earthworks of abandoned streets, boundary banks, property boundaries between individual tofts, and the sites of the houses themselves, as is particularly well displayed at Compton Scorpion and Pinnock (Fig. 5.1; see figs. 5.3 and 5.5). The extent of the earthworks and the number of tofts can suggest the original size of the settlement – for example in Blockley parish, Middle Ditchford, Upper Ditchford, and Upton each had about twenty households at their maximum size in the thirteenth century.[21] The material evidence can tell us about the chronology of the settlement from datable pottery only if the site has been excavated, or if surface scatters have been collected by field walking. Excavation reveals that Upton was occupied from the eleventh century and was abandoned in the fourteenth, while surface collection suggests a similar date for Castlett, but part of Weston juxta Cherington was still inhabited in the seventeenth century.[22]

Good documentary evidence comes from Sezincote, for which there are few material remains. In the course of a dispute in 1509–10 Sir Richard Empson, who was leasing the manor from the Grevilles, excused himself from blame for the ruinous state of the church. It was being used as a shelter for cattle (the word could include sheep at that time) on the initiative of the herdsmen, not with his encouragement. In any case there were no parishioners apart from Empson's servants. In 1535 when the value of the rectory was recorded at £10 3s 4d, most of its revenues came from tithes (presumably on lambs and wool) and from a close worth £1 6s 8d. The 2-yardland glebe was reported to be 'lying unknown in pasture among the lands of John Greville', so the open fields in which the glebe was dispersed as scattered strips had been converted to permanent grazing, and the former boundaries of the selions had been forgotten though the old layout of the fields would have been visible as ridge and furrow, as is still the case. Sezincote had ceased to be a village with arable fields by 1492, when a lease refers to a barn, two meadows, and a pasture, and the tenant was required to repair the 'mounds' – meaning the banks surmounted by hedges or fences that divided the former fields into pasture enclosures.[23]

---

[20] C. Dyer, 'Villages in Crisis: Social Dislocation and Desertion, 1370–1520', in C. Dyer and R. Jones (eds), *Deserted Villages Revisited* (Hatfield, 2010), 28–45, especially 32–7.

[21] This combines the evidence of documents, see Dyer, *Lords and Peasants*, 245, 248–51, and the plans and aerial photographs: R. H. Hilton and P. A. Rahtz, 'Upton, Gloucestershire, 1959–1964', *Transactions of the Bristol and Gloucestershire Archaeological Society*, 85 (1966), 87; M. Beresford and J. K. St Joseph, *Medieval England: An Aerial Survey*, 2nd edn. (Cambridge, 1979), 16 (wrongly called Lower Ditchford); M. Aston and L Vyner, 'The Study of Deserted Villages in Gloucestershire', in A. Saville (ed.), *Archaeology in Gloucestershire* (Cheltenham, 1984), 277–93, especially 285.

[22] Hilton and Rahtz, 'Upton', 123–34; on the two sites mentioned, fieldwork by the author and D. Aldred.

[23] *L and P*, I, 141, 182; J. Caley and J. Hunter (eds.), *Valor Ecclesiasticus temp. Henry VIII, auctoritate regia institutus* (Record Commission, 1810–34), II, 452; Centre for Kentish Studies, U269/T190 (lease in Greville archive in Sackville of Knole).

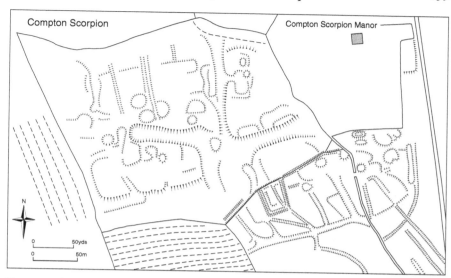

Fig. 5.1. The deserted village of Compton Scorpion in Ilmington parish (see Fig. 5.5 for an interpretation). The earthworks show a cluster plan, in which four village streets marked by holloways meet at a small triangular village green. Building platforms, and the boundaries of the tofts (squarish enclosures) in which houses stood, survive from at least eleven peasant dwellings. To the south-east are earthwork remains of structures that probably relate to the exploitation of the site as a sheep pasture after desertion, notably the sub-rectangular enclosure that could have held livestock. In the same area ditches, again dug after desertion, appear to relate to a scheme for irrigation of meadows. The pasture here was held by the Palmer family in the early sixteenth century, and in 1534 the widow Alice Palmer, John Heritage's sister, was allowed by her husband's will a bequest of sixty ewes 'as they shall run out of the flock'. Source: Plan by author, Bryn Gethin, Ben Morton, David Aldred, and Jenny Dyer.

Often the precise date and circumstances of desertion are not known, and the sources that have been used in the past are not entirely reliable. For example, the list of destroyed villages mostly in Warwickshire made by John Rous of Warwick around 1486 includes six sites in the Moreton district, but they were all named in the context of a polemical diatribe against the greed of those who removed them, which invites suspicion from the modern reader. Sometimes we know that in his condemnatory zeal he exaggerated the extent of the damage, or jumped to the conclusion that a village had once existed when other evidence points to the contrary.[24] Similarly, the 1517 commission into depopulation and enclosure reported the departure of families and the decay of houses in seven of our deserted villages,

---

[24] C. J. Bond, 'Deserted Medieval Villages in Warwickshire and Worcestershire', in T. R. Slater and P. J. Jarvis (eds), *Field and Forest: An Historical Geography of Warwickshire and Worcestershire* (Norwich, 1982), 147–71, especially 150–2.

but usually the numbers given – fewer than six households in all but one case – suggest that the inquiry recorded an episode in a longer history of decline.[25]

Our villages fell into decay in successive phases, beginning with the early fourteenth-century crisis, which seems to have removed Eyford entirely by 1327, while Castlett and Upton, though not recorded as deserted until the 1380s, were probably weakened before the epidemics of the mid-fourteenth century.[26] Eleven of the villages had apparently been abandoned between 1350 and 1490, including two desertions that can be precisely dated to the 1470s and 1480s. Setting aside the four villages which showed signs of troubles in the early sixteenth century but which survived at least in part until the late sixteenth or seventeenth centuries, we are left with eight that were experiencing severe problems in the period 1490–1525. Desertion was a slow process, and did not necessarily happen with a traumatic expulsion of tenants or sudden collapse of a community. A few tenants might remain, struggling to keep their lives together, as will be seen later. But in focusing on the villages that left a legacy of leasows, these large enclosed pastures could be established in part of the village's territory while remaining villagers cultivated their reduced area of fields. At Barcheston 'several leasows...that belong to the manor' were listed before the final stage of desertion. In other cases leasows took over the whole area formerly occupied by fields, as happened at Longdon by 1535, and at Norton Subedge the whole township seems to have been called 'a leasow or pasture' in *c*.1500. At Pinnock in 1542 the pastures were called Woodlesow and Roughlesow. The word 'pasture' was used to describe the land formerly occupied by the village of Upton (in 1513), and at Sezincote. A section of the fields of Clopton was described as the 'pasture called Broad Moor'.[27]

USING PASTURE

The documents give us only hints of the layout and organization of the large leasows. At an early stage they consisted of a single sweep of pasture, well enclosed at the perimeter but without internal divisions beyond the lines of trees and bushes that sometimes grew discontinuously along the internal divisions of the open fields, and which probably remained after the open fields were no longer cultivated. At Eyford, when it was mapped in the eighteenth century, the Great Grounds formed a large expanse of grassland that stretched for a mile and occupied the whole of the northern end of the parish.[28] At Clopton a half of the

---

[25] E. Kerridge, 'The Returns of the Inquisitions of Depopulation', *English Historical Review*, 70 (1955), 212–28, provide a general critique, showing in the case of Clopton that the accusations could not be sustained.

[26] P. Franklin (ed.), *The Taxpayers of Medieval Gloucestershire* (Stroud, 1993), 59; Hilton and Rahtz, 'Upton', 83–5; C. Fenwick (ed.), *The Poll Tax of 1377, 1379 and 1381*, pt. 1, Records of Social and Economic History, new series, 27 (1998), 270.

[27] WCRO, CR 580/1; TNA: PRO, PROB 11/26, fos.26r–26v (will of Richard Freman of Todenham); C1/285/2 (chancery case); GA, D3439/313 (Hockaday Abstracts); WRO, BA 2636, ref.009:1, 37 (iii), 43806, 23r; Centre for Kentish Studies, U269/T190 (lease in Greville archives, Sackville of Knole); GA, D5626, 6/1 (lease).

[28] GA, D802/1.

village's territory consisted of a single piece of land known as Broad Moor. This impression that a village, once deserted, left an empty space within a hedged township or parish boundary is implied by the reports of the enclosure inquisitions of 1517. In the case of seven villages the decay of buildings is mentioned, but enclosure with fences, hedges, and ditches is only specified at Clopton and Hidcote Bartrim.

Carving up the former village fields into a number of separate enclosed fields seems to have developed in stages and was completed some time after conversion to pasture. At Upper Ditchford, which had lost its inhabitants by 1475, the new farmers of 1507 (one of whom was John Heritage) were required by the terms of their leases to make enclosures with ditches, fences made of stakes and brushwood, and planted with bushes and thorns that would eventually grow into live hedges. The map of 1726 shows a series of irregular rectangular closes, some of which could have been the result of that digging and planting activity.[29] Field work there has revealed five field boundaries to the north of the site of the village, which now consist of deep ditches with hedges containing four or five species of bush and tree that could have originated in the Heritage period. The western hedge of a nearby field called Broad Leasow, which was surveyed at 29 acres in 1726, seemed to be of similar character. Other fields at Ditchford were called 'grounds', and in the valley of the Knee Brook lay the 'hams' and the 'meads' that played a crucial role in sheep husbandry as hay meadows for winter feed (Fig. 5.2). A similar pattern of irregular closes had replaced the open fields of Lark Stoke and Weston juxta Cherington, and in the latter case a substantial part of the north-east of the parish, adjoining the village site, was divided according to a map of 1824 between two rectangular fields called Great Leasow and Little Leasow.[30] Most of the new fences and hedges followed the lines of the old furlong boundaries in the former open fields, showing that these features were influencing the decisions of the enclosers. Some of the hedged fields may have been developed when the village was in decline rather than defunct, when parts of the open field were still functioning. Occasionally a new hedge was laid out across the old landscape: at Upper Ditchford, for example, one boundary crosses part of the village site.

The new hedges and fences had a number of purposes. The perimeter hedge around a pasture held in severalty was designed to prevent the farmer's stock from straying, and to keep out the neighbours and their animals: 'rude persons' and 'hurtful cattle' as a later commentator called them. In the case of deserted villages such as Compton Scorpion the hedge had been the parish or township boundary, and had very early origins. The hedges were presumably strengthened when they marked the limits, not of open fields but of a piece of private property. The hedges defining field boundaries within a former village territory may sometimes have been lines of demarcation between the grazier's pastures and land still held by surviving villagers, or may have shown the divisions between land assigned to different lessees

---

[29] Worcester Cathedral Library, MS A6 (2), fos.47, 53v (priory register); GA, D4070/14.
[30] M. Warriner, *A Prospect of Weston in Warwickshire* (Kineton, 1978), xiii.

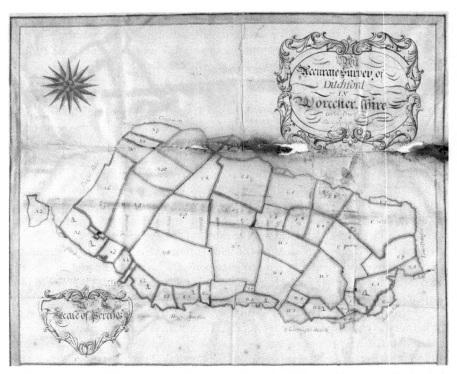

Fig. 5.2. Estate map of Ditchford in 1726. The village of Upper Ditchford had once stood near the house and paddocks in the bottom left of the estate. Some of the hedges shown on the western side of the map may date from the sixteenth century. John Heritage leased part of the pasture and kept a large sheep flock here.

Source: GA, D4070/14.

when (as at Upper Ditchford) the leasehold was divided. Most often their function was simply to manage stock being grazed on a single farm.[31]

Fencing represented the main investment in the pasture, the cost of which has been estimated at £50 for a complete township, though this would have been spread over a number of years. In addition the pasture would have been provided with buildings, sheepcotes, which were substantial structures often 130 feet (40 m) long and large enough to shelter a whole flock in bad weather, and with a loft to serve as a store for fodder. Smaller buildings nearby would have provided accommodation for shepherds and stores for equipment. A well-built sheepcote with a roof of stone slates would have cost £10, and pastures, such as Upper Ditchford, could be provided with two. The accounts compiled by landlords in the period of direct management itemize the expense of

---

[31] N. Blomley, 'Making Private Property: Enclosure, Common Rights and the Work of Hedges', *Rural History*, 18 (2007), 1–21.

building sheepcotes, which were provided with stone foundations, a timber-framed superstructure, and internal fittings such as lofts and feeding racks.[32] The surviving foundations are the most direct indication of their size and substantial structure, and one of the best preserved can be seen overlooking the abandoned village site at Pinnock, from which Heritage received a number of consignments of wool (Fig. 5.3).

Archaeological evidence can also provide insights into the gathering and separation of sheep when they were being treated for disease, or when decisions were being made on which animals to sell and which to keep. A row of pens were being used on a hillside adjoining the buildings at the centre of the Hinchwick pasture, which can still be seen and planned (Fig. 5.4). Once these assets had

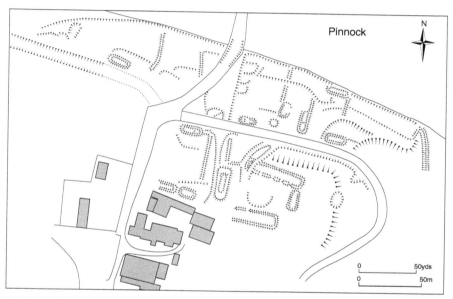

Fig. 5.3. The deserted village of Pinnock in Temple Guiting parish (see Fig 5.5 for an interpretation). The earthworks show a linear plan, in which the houses were arranged along an east-west road, now in use as a farm track. The foundations of buildings with stone walls are visible in squarish tofts on both sides of the road. There were six or seven peasant holdings in the row north of the road, but perhaps only one is visible to the south. The south-east corner of the settlement is occupied by a group of buildings on a larger scale, arranged around a yard. These are either the remnants of a manorial complex or a large farm that emerged at a late stage in the village's history. The long narrow building, the foundations of which suggest two or three entrances in its southern wall, was a sheepcote, capable of holding a flock of three hundred. Heritage bought wool from John Pole and John Wode who lived here, and each kept two to three hundred sheep. Source: Plan by author and David Aldred.

[32] C. Dyer, 'Sheepcotes: Evidence for Medieval Sheepfarming', *Medieval Archaeology*, 39 (1995), 136–64; id., 'Villages and Non-Villages in the Medieval Cotswolds', *Transactions of the Bristol and Gloucestershire Archaeological Society*, 120 (2002), 11–35, especially 20–7.

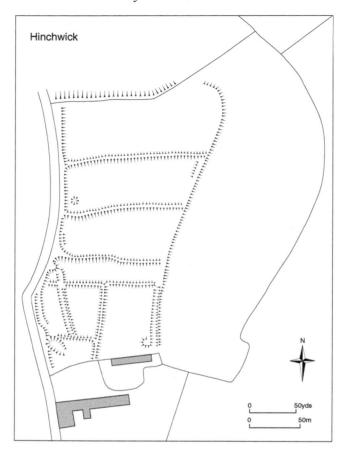

Fig. 5.4. Pens for managing sheep at Hinchwick in Condicote parish. The earthwork banks, which may at some time have been stone walls, originated as a Romano-British field system. They were reused as pens in the Middle Ages in connection with a sheepcote and other buildings at Old Hinchwick, now a farm. The southernmost compartment has been subdivided and altered, probably in the Middle Ages. The pens, each of which contained between ½ acre and 1½ acres, would have been useful for dividing large sheep flocks, e.g. for putting lambs, hogs, ewes, wethers, and rams into separate enclosures, or for selecting those for sale. Hinchwick belonged to Bruern Abbey, which kept five hundred sheep on the pasture each summer, recorded in 1535. Source: Plan by author and David Aldred.

been paid for, upkeep would not have been a major item of expenditure, and much more would need to be spent on acquiring some hundreds of sheep and maintaining their numbers if they did not include ewes that could replenish the flock by breeding (Fig. 5.5).

Some documents suggest that a pasture was a single asset held on lease by one grazier, who was often a merchant, gentleman, yeoman, or butcher. The arrangements look simple and straightforward when John Bradwey, a grazier and wool

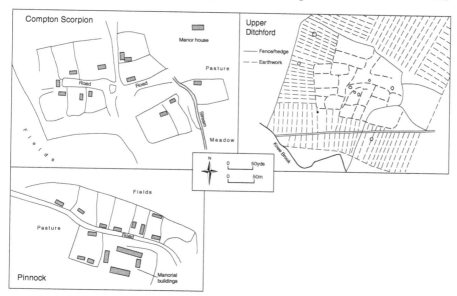

Fig. 5.5. Interpretations of the village plans in Figs. 5.1 and 5.3, with a transcription of the air photograph of Upper Ditchford, where Heritage leased a pasture. The tofts of Upper Ditchford are shown, and the surrounding ridge and furrow. The small circular features dotted over the site are probably mounds for a rabbit warren, of unknown date.

merchant, is seen to be holding the leasow of Norton Subedge on lease in *c.*1500. This valuable asset had been formed out of the fields of the village of Norton that still had peasant tenants cultivating the land in the mid- fifteenth century. When more information is available, complexities of subtenancy are revealed. John Bradwey had sublet the land from Thomas Rous, an esquire who had once farmed nearby Quinton and held the manor of Radbrook in that parish. An agreement was made that Bradwey should pay an annual rent of £33 6s 8d for the pasture to the lord of Norton manor, John Giffard, and £20 to Rous, but the arrangement broke down when the lord of the manor sought to remove Brad-wey.[33] This incidentally indicates the very high profits that an enclosed pasture was expected to yield. A more complex arrangement led the bishopric of Worces-ter to lease the pasture of Upper Ditchford in two parts. Before 1507 there had been four lessees, including Thomas Wilkes, but from that date one half was held by William Greville, the gentleman lord of various nearby manors, and the other half by John Heritage and John Freman. Heritage, however, was keeping sheep there in 1505, perhaps as a subtenant. Less easy to explain was that in 1512 Tho-mas Wilkes of Blockley could bequeath in his will 'my pasture in Ditchford'.[34]

---

[33] TNA: PRO, C/285/2 (Chancery case).
[34] Worcester Cathedral Library, MS A6 (2), fos.47, 53v (priory register); WRO, BA 3590/1, ref.008:7, wills vol II.

The sublettings of Upton Wold cannot easily be unravelled. Following the execution of Richard Empson in 1511, the lease (after he had held it for two years) was granted to John Hornyhold. This was a piece of patronage in favour of an official of the bishopric (he was Receiver) at a low rent of £9 6s 8d, and for a long term of ninety years. As an absentee he must have sublet it, as both Thomas Davies of Stow in 1511 and John Willington of Todenham in 1512 refer to their tenancy of Upton Wold and the sheep that they kept there.[35]

The novelty in the new style of farming lay in the number of enclosed permanent pastures, especially in comparison with the grazing arrangements of the estates managed by the lords and their officials in the fourteenth century. Then the stretches of upland pasture and heath were mostly shared with the peasants, and many animals spent a good part of their lives feeding on the stubbles and fallows of the open fields. The estates of the monasteries of Bordesley, Gloucester, Pershore, Westminster, Winchcombe, and Worcester Priory, the bishopric of Worcester, and the earls of Warwick moved their sheep flocks from one manor to another, and many of the sheep that grazed in the summer on the hills at Blockley, Campden, Bourton on the Hill, Broadway, Cutsdean, and Snowshill were kept in the winter on manors in the rather kinder climate prevailing in the river valleys.[36]

The graziers who kept large flocks and herds in Heritage's time held a number of pastures, but they were often separated from manorial demesnes or village field systems. In acquiring a number of leaseholds the new men of the early sixteenth-century countryside were not bound by the established estate structures that went back before the Norman Conquest. Instead they attempted to bring together a portfolio of assets that were grouped conveniently in a cluster. Heritage's pastures, except for the anomaly of Burton Dassett, lay within 8 miles (13 km) of Moreton, and this was closely paralleled by the Spencers of Althorp with most of their land acquired when they were yeomen graziers rather than gentry within a 10-mile (16-km) radius of their original base of Hodnell. Among the gentry estates, the Lucy pastures between Hunscote and Willicote on the northern edge of Heritage's country similarly were concentrated within 5 miles of Stratford upon Avon. The properties of the Grevilles of Arle included Puckham in Sevenhampton near their Cheltenham base, but Broad Campden, Upper Lemington, Coldicote, and Upper Ditchford all lay near Moreton. Another successful lawyer, Thomas Kebell, in 1500 held a grouping of pastures mostly within 10 miles (16 km) of his home at Humberstone near Leicester.[37] The wealthier and more ambitious gentry were more likely to hold a widely scattered estate that required a bureaucratic administration, such as the Townshends of Norfolk. In Heritage's country we have already

[35] Worcester Cathedral Library, MS A6 (2), fos.65r–65v; WRO, BA 2636, ref.009:1, 37 (iii), 43806, fo.23r; TNA: PRO, PROB 11/17, fos.16v–17r; WRO, BA 3590/2–3, ref.008:1, fos.40v–41v.

[36] Transhumance is discussed in R. H. Hilton, *A Medieval Society: The West Midlands at the End of the Thirteenth Century*, 2nd edn. (Cambridge, 1983), 82–3.

[37] For the Spencer estate see pp. 11, 31; for the Lucy lands, TNA: PRO, SC6 Henry VIII/1109; for Grevilles; TNA: PRO, PROB 11/17, fos.96r–97v; for Kebell, E. W. Ives, *The Common Lawyers of Pre-Reformation England. Thomas Kebell: A Case Study* (Cambridge, 1983), 330–53.

noted that Richard Empson also held land in Northamptonshire, and the Grevilles of Milcote were lords of manors stretching over the Avon valley and the Cotswolds.

The larger and well-funded graziers, like the Spencers and the Lucys, held most of their pastures on lease, but Heritage had formal indentures for only two, Burton and Ditchford, and we do not know precisely on what basis he obtained pasturage at Cutsdean, Little Compton, and other places (Table 5.3). He kept two to three hundred sheep on a regular basis 'on the Heath' to the east of Moreton. This could mean that he had common rights as a tenant, but pasture on the Heath seems not to have been regulated by the Moreton authorities. His short-term arrangements included keeping around four hundred sheep at Little Compton in 1508–10, and about three hundred at Cutsdean in 1510, but occasionally he was pasturing at Wolford, Paxford, and other places. The explanation of his ability to find grazing for sixty-two sheep at Burmington and forty at Tidmington is provided by his occasional references to people: 'With Watkyn Rose, 62' in 1509, and 'Hale of Burmington' in 1507. These must refer to practices that were forbidden in many villages by which individual tenants sold some of their pasture entitlement to outsiders.[38] It had to be done on a small scale because the people acting as hosts, such as Rose and Hale, were probably limited to no more than a hundred sheep by their village's stint and required some of the quota for their own animals. Distributing

Table 5.3. John Heritage's sheep pastures.

Date	Ditchford	'Heath'	Burton	Others*	Total
1504 (29 September)	–	207	705	Wolverton 203	1,115
1505 (11 November)	267	286	818	Farnborough 55	1,426
1506 (20 October)	398	233	396	Rawlens 417; Wolford 66; Paxford 22	1,532
1507 (23 May)	86	272	–	Rawlens 1,206; Farnborough 40; named individuals 304	1,908
1507 (1 June)	479	212	1,038	Campden 207; Burmington 66; Wolford 61; Alice Wilkyns 118	2,181
1507 (10 November)	–	254	839	William Honeybourne 620; Wolford 34; Burmington 62; Tidmington 40; Farnborough 86	1,935
1508 (15 November)	355	215	713	Compton 262; named individuals 93	1,638
1509 (24 April)	390	237	976	Compton 476; named individuals 62	2,141
1509 (22 December)	417	201	829	Wolford 46; Paxford 42	1,535
1510 (25 June)	246	–	1,092	Compton 400; Cutsdean 320	2,058
1510 (14 September)	275	–	1,110	Compton 400; Cutsdean 277	2,062

Source: AB, fos.84r, 90v, 91r, 91v, 93v, 94r.

[38] W. O. Ault, *Open-Field Farming in Medieval England: A Study of Village By-Laws* (London, 1972), 133, 139.

the sheep across the countryside in relatively small numbers was not an efficient method for Heritage to manage his animals, and could have been quite expensive as he would have had to pay for access to the common, and contribute towards the cost of shepherding. The other villagers resented seeing their common pasture taken over by outsiders and their neighbours profiting from the selfish exploitation of collective assets.

Most of the sheep were kept in large flocks in the care of shepherds employed by Heritage, and they were key figures. They received wages in cash (£3 per annum was the rate of pay in Norfolk in the 1520s), but derived considerable independence by owning their own sheep that ran with their employer's animals.[39] The shepherd at Ditchford bought forty-one tithe lambs from Heritage in 1507, and in the following year four ewes and twenty-six lambs. He contributed a lamb to the tithe, suggesting that he was breeding from at least ten ewes. In 1509 he apparently paid for winter pasture, so not all of his grazing was provided by his employer.[40] The fact that he owned some of the animals under his care must have encouraged him to be diligent, and he was being given an incentive to accumulate profit and eventually to found his own enterprise. The work would have been skilled and demanding, as the shepherd had to manage the flock and take decisions on his own because his employer would have been in intermittent contact, especially in the case of the pasture at Burton Dassett. When demesnes were under the direct management of their lords, a shepherd had been expected to look after about 250 animals, and this was the size of the flock on the Heath. The Ditchford flock sometimes rose above 400 (it reached 479 in June 1507) and the shepherd needed at least part-time assistance, while a staff of at least three would have been required to tend the thousand sheep often kept at Burton.

Heritage's sheep (Table 5.4) were managed as a self-contained breeding flock, in which five to six hundred ewes produced enough lambs each year to maintain a good number of hogasters (two-year-olds) and wethers, the adult castrated male sheep that yielded the heaviest fleeces, and to replace the older ewes and rams. In fact five hundred lambs per annum after three or four years would have resulted in an excessive total of older sheep, so surplus younger animals were sold, together with the ewes, rams, and wethers nearing the end of their useful lives. The purchasers included butchers, and the meat trade was more than a mere by-product of the sheep flock's wool production. This self-sufficiency is found in the flocks of other sheepmasters, such as Thomas Kebell and Norwich Priory.[41] Owners of flocks of this type avoided the expense of buying replacement animals, but it was also

---

[39] M. Bailey (ed.), 'The Sheep Accounts of Norwich Cathedral Priory, 1484 to 1534', in *Poverty and Wealth: Sheep, Taxation and Charity in Late Medieval Norfolk*, Norfolk Record Society, 71 (2007), 88–9; the Catesby estates allowed shepherds to graze their own animals: C. Dyer, *Warwickshire Farming 1349–c.1520: Preparations for Agricultural Revolution*, Dugdale Society Occasional Paper, 27 (1981), 21; a gloomy view is taken of shepherds' commitment and productivity in D. Stone, 'The Productivity and Management of Sheep in Late Medieval England', *Ag. HR*, 51 (2003), 1–22, especially 17–20.

[40] AB, fos.87r, 91v, 94r, 95r.

[41] Ives, *Thomas Kebell*, 441–2; Bailey (ed.), 'Sheep Accounts'.

Table 5.4. John Heritage's sheep.

Date	Rams	Ewes	Lambs	Hogs	Wethers	Unknown	Total
1504 (29 September)	0	0	0	293	0	822	1,114 (sic)
1505 (11 November)	0	511	0	574	0	341	1,426
1506 (20 October)	20	594	0	648	6	264	1,532
1507 (23 May)	20	555	691	160	0	482	1,908
1507 (1 June)	8	500	539	286	300	318	2,181
(tithe 1507)			230*				
1507 (10 November)	29	622	0	628	756	0	2,035
1508 (15 November)	15	650	144	253	379	215	1,656
1509 (24 April)	c.10	c.370	540	0	451	772	c.2,143
1509 (22 December)	15	492	280	109	331	308	1,535
1510 (24 or 25 June)	?	553	543	400	0	562	2,058
1510 (14 September)	25	595	548	0	217	677	2,062

*tithes from Blockley and probably Burton Dassett
Source: As in Table 5.3.

possible for them to practise selective breeding. Heritage referred to lambs 'of my own breed' in contrast with those acquired as tithe payments, and his animals might have been of better quality. The weight of his fleeces in 1509, the only year when a calculation can be made, achieved the respectable level of 1.83 pounds, and his ewes seem to have attained quite high rates of lambing, helped by a ratio of rams to ewes that varied between 1:20 and 1:30.[42]

A completely different strategy was pursued by other graziers, who kept a flock of wethers and bought in new animals as required, presumably from breeders such as Heritage, but also from the smaller flock owners, the peasants. Pershore Abbey provided the farmer with four hundred wethers at Broadway, and the Horne family kept five hundred at Sarsden, and such flocks would yield a good weight of wool.[43] These relatively hardy adult animals could be kept through the winter on the hills, while mixed flocks would be best suited to a combination of pastures on upland and lowland, which would enable ewes and lambs to be kept in a sheltered valley in the winter.

This discussion of the use of pasture has inevitably focused on sheep, but many graziers kept cattle in order to take advantage of the ready market for beef, though in Heritage's case we do not know the precise numbers. He sold or bartered a few cows, bullocks, and steers, and once a bull is mentioned, which suggests that he was rearing his own beasts. Perhaps his herd resembled that of Sir Thomas Lucy, who in 1521 kept 106 cattle along with 3,605 sheep. Richard Buller, who held the lease of the pasture that occupied the site of the deserted village of Weston juxta Cherington, left 1,640 sheep, 130 cattle, and 14 horses in his will of 1527.[44]

[42] AB, fos.43v, 91r, 94r, 94v; on lambing rates and ram to ewe ratios, M. Page, 'The Technology of Medieval Sheep Farming: Some Evidence from Crawley, Hampshire, 1208–1349', *Ag. HR*, 51 (2003), 137–54.
[43] WRO, BA 2929, ref.899:154, no.278 (lease of 1490); TNA: PRO PROB 11/22, fos.75r–75v.
[44] TNA: PRO, SC6 Henry VIII/1109 (accounts); E. Rainsberry, *Through the Lych Gate* (Kineton, 1969), 46–7.

Specialist pasture farms, which often contained leasows or even consisted of a single large leasow, must have brought their tenants considerable profits because their lords were able to charge surprisingly high rents. A village with twenty customary tenants would typically yield an annual rental income from holdings totalling about 400 acres of £10, or 6d per acre. Some manorial demesnes such as those at Little Compton, Paxford, Preston on Stour, and Sutton under Brailes, which would consist normally of mixed farms with arable and grassland, could be leased for as little as £4–£6 per annum, which was probably equivalent to 6d per acre or a little less.[45] The demesne close of Admington, however, which was converted to pasture and held as a block of land, yielded an annual total of £26 3s 4d, which was about 12d per acre, and a similarly high valuation must lie behind the Churchill demesne, which was divided into two farms, in which most of the land was enclosed, and together they produced £33 per annum. At some time in the 1490s, however, an extra £20 in rent was added, bringing the total to £53 6s 8d.[46] Other high rents include £33 6s 8d for Norton Subedge leasow, £51 for Sezincote, and £18 10s 0d for Upper Ditchford. Notably lower rents for equally valuable pasture assets can be explained by special circumstances. The £9 6s 8d rent for Upton Wold may have been allowed to fossilize for reasons of patronage, and Barcheston seems to have been leased cheaply in 1505 at £14 6s 8d when the lord was troubled by debt and while the last peasant tenants were occupying part of the land. The lessee who acquired a twenty-year term in Sezincote in 1492 for £13 6s 8d must have felt gratitude for the generous treatment that he was receiving.[47]

DEMESNES AND PASTURE

The main manorial demesnes had been leased out in the period 1380–1420, but often the lords kept some pastures under direct management. These arrangements are still visible in Heritage's day because it was still profitable to retain the pasture. The monastic estates are best documented, and we find that Hailes Abbey grazed six hundred sheep at Lower Swell. Both Winchcombe Abbey and Bruern were managing their pastures in a system of transhumance at Snowshill and Condicote (see p. 74). Some lay lords also retained sheep on their estates, as we have seen in the case of the Horne family at Sarsden.[48]

The separate leasing of the leasows, and the direct management of demesne pasture, still left considerable pastoral resources that were an integral part of the mixed agriculture of the demesnes themselves. The area of the demesne usually lay in the range of 150 to 300 acres, which were used as arable, meadow, pasture, and

---

[45] GA, P329/1 (Compton and Preston); WRO, BA 2636, ref.009:1, 157/no number (Paxford); GA, 1099 M31/80 (Sutton).

[46] TNA: PRO, SC6 Henry VIII/1240; Northamptonshire Record Office, Finch Hatton 362 (court of recognition).

[47] TNA: PRO, C/285/2 (Chancery case); Calendar of Ancient Deeds, I, 109 (A935); Worcester Cathedral Library, MS A6 (2), fos.47, 53r, 65v; WRO, BA 2636, ref.009:1, 37(iii), 43806, fo.23r; WCRO, CR 580/9/15.

[48] J. Caley and J. Hunter (eds), Valor Ecclesiasticus temp. Henry VIII, auctoritate regia institutus, Record Commission, 1810–34, II, 203, 453, 457; see note 47 above.

wood. A lessee rather than the lord practised an integrated husbandry that combined the cultivation of grain with keeping livestock. The animals and especially the sheep contributed their manure to the fertility of the arable, and generated a cash income for the manor. They fed on the 'several pastures' attached to the demesne, on the common with the villagers' animals, on the cornfields after the crop had been carried, and on the arable land left fallow, and they were allowed on to the meadow after the hay harvest. The stored hay provided winter feed, together with a proportion of the crops grown on the arable, such as the peas and beans.

William Skey took on the farm of the demesne of Little Compton in 1508, which gave him the use of the manor house and farm buildings, arable, meadow, and pasture, and was allowed to keep 24 horses, 18 cattle, and 400 sheep. He was not unusual among lessees of mixed demesnes in being entitled to keep flocks of four to five hundred.[49] By a coincidence Heritage was keeping four hundred sheep at Little Compton at this precise time, and it is just possible that Skey, rather than buying his own flock, rented the demesne allocation to the Moreton woolman, but this is mere speculation. The general point to be made is that demesnes taken together grazed formidable numbers of animals, and that in the long run from 1400 onwards these productive resources were being transferred from the monastic, episcopal, and lay estates into the hands of husbandmen like Skey. Of the sixty-nine leases of demesne assets in Heritage's district recorded in the period 1490–1540, fifteen were taken by gentry, and most of the rest were either in the hands of people who are known to have been husbandmen or yeomen, or the lessees cannot be given a social rank, but because of the obscurity of their names they must be assumed to have belonged to the better-off peasantry rather than the gentry. These people would have previously held 2 or 3 yardlands, 60 or 90 acres, and were acquiring a much larger area, in many cases two or three times greater than the area of land that they held on customary or free tenure.

In the 1490s at Quinton the vicar, who had taken up the cause of the villagers, debated the merits of a gentry farmer in comparison with a local villager or villagers. The ambitions of a gentleman 'or a gentleman's man' (meaning a subtenant or employee) were distrusted because such individuals might pursue policies on the demesne that damaged the interests of the village, and the vicar successfully lobbied for the demesne to be leased to a group of villagers instead of Thomas Rous, a farmer recruited from the gentry.[50] This was a special case, and there was no general movement for farmers from below the gentry to take over new leases. Rents do not seem to have increased when the lord had the opportunity to change them when negotiating a new term after the previous lease expired. Occasionally they paid a fine, as when the Adlestrop lease was renewed with new names of future tenants in 1511 for a payment of £5.[51] The

---

[49] GA, P329/1 (Tewkesbury Abbey post-Dissolution accounts).
[50] C. Dyer, *An Age of Transition: Economy and Society in England in the Later Middle Ages* (Oxford, 2005), 81–5.
[51] TNA: PRO, SC2 175/77 (court rolls).

general trend for leaseholds to lengthen was going on through the early sixteenth century, so the farmers could look forward with confidence to a period of twenty, forty, or sixty years in which they and their successors could enjoy profits from the land.

Did they take advantage of this security to invest in their farms and introduce new techniques? Lords did not in general make very many rules about the methods of farming that their lessees should use, but when they did they were presumably reacting against bad practices on their own or other demesnes. Westminster Abbey in 1495 required their farmer at Todenham to apply sheep manure to a specified area of the demesne, as if a predecessor had neglected this basic method of maintaining soil fertility. Farmers were more frequently required to repair buildings and fences, and in the case of William Willington's lease of Barcheston in 1505 it was envisaged that much work was needed, as he was to pay £12 6s 8d for the first fifteen years, and only then would the full rent of £14 6s 8d be required. The indebted lords of the manor had evidently neglected to carry out repairs.[52]

If farmers were changing the agriculture on the demesnes, we would be unable to gain much information about their activities as they have mostly left few archives. They were likely to have joined in the general tendency to use land as pasture rather than arable. The glebe land belonging to the rectory of Little Compton had its lease recorded in 1539, when a quarter of the land, 12 acres from a total of 45 acres, had become leys, meaning that it was grassed over, and as we have seen grass had replaced arable on the much larger demesne of Admington.[53] A precise date for a change in land use could be provided by the enclosure commission, which for example reported that on 4 November 1496 the Abbot of Eynsham at Little Rollright 'converted that land (200 acres) from arable use and converted it into pasture of sheep and other animals'. He presumably did this for the benefit of a tenant, and with his connivance.[54]

In the period immediately after Heritage's active career some farmers were expanding the scale of their operations, already evident from the collections of land made by Greville, Empson, Rous, and others. The documents compiled at the time of the Dissolution of the Monasteries reveals leasing arrangements made in previous years, which show that farmers had taken over a number of adjacent farms that gave them access to hundreds of acres, much of it under grass. At Lower Swell in 1537 Walter and Alice Barston were leasing the farmplace, that is, the main demesne, as well as the park and sheepcote of Bold, and the large several pasture known as Murdenlesow. At adjacent Longborough, John Pinnock and his wife Leticia in 1537 and 1538 acquired the main demesne farm, together with a pasture and sheepcote with a combined rent of £38 15s.[55]

---

52 Westminster Abbey lease book I, fos.75b–76b; WCRO, CR580/9/15 (lease).
53 GA, P329/1; TNA: PRO, SC6 Henry VIII/1240 (accounts).
54 *Dom. Inc.*, I, 328–9.
55 TNA: PRO, SC6 Henry VIII/1240 (accounts).

PEASANTS AND PASTURE

The leasows and large enclosed pastures account for a small proportion of the area of productive land in Heritage's country, no more than 5 per cent of the total. Demesnes and glebes cannot have accounted for more than 20 per cent. The graziers and farmers who occupied these large units of land amounted to no more than 2 per cent of landholders. The rest of the land, three-quarters of it in area, was held and cultivated by numerous peasants, known to contemporaries as yeomen, husbandmen, and labourers, who made up the majority of the rural population. Their small farms, of which most contained between 15 and 90 acres, are to some extent mysterious, as they have left no financial accounts, and few inventories or other detailed descriptions, but they were still of great importance in their combined productive capacity.

We are told about the rules and practices by which villages balanced the needs of arable and pastoral farming, and they show that much land was still devoted to the cultivation of cereals and legumes. The animals contributed to an integrated system, in which the horses and oxen provided the power to haul ploughs, carts, wains, and harrows, and the fertility of the land was maintained by spreading manure by cart from the stalls and yards, or by folding the sheep on the land, which benefited directly from their droppings. The animals were fed on the pasture on the commons and in small separate crofts, and on the meadows after hay making, but as in many villages this type of permanent grassland was limited in area, the livestock depended for part of the year on the grass and weeds that grew between the stalks of the harvested corn in the arable fields after the harvest, and on the section of the land set aside for fallow. Part of the crops, not just the straw but the grain from oats in particular, and the peas and beans often still in their pods, were fed to animals in the winter along with hay and straw, and at other times when they were most active and needed the energy.

Sheep were kept primarily for the profit that derived from selling wool and surplus animals. Payments of tithe can tell us about the cumulative total kept in each parish, and therefore indirectly the numbers owned by the peasants. One lamb in ten, and a tenth of the wool clip, went to the rector, so if we know the quantity that he collected, a simple multiplication will reveal the total production declared for tithe payment. John Heritage bought the Blockley tithe lambs each year between 1504 and 1507, the totals of which lay between 155 and 231. Sometimes these are broken down to give the numbers contributed by individuals or a part of the parish (Table 5.5). Heritage's records in 1507 suggest that the tithe was an accurate reflection of the lambs born, as he contributed 19 tithe lambs, and is known to have kept 189 at Upper Ditchford, so he paid exactly the right figure. We can build on these figures to estimate the total population of sheep starting with the 1,550 and 2,310 lambs that were available for tithe payment each year. To take Heritage's flock as an example, he had 200 ewes to which the 189 lambs had been born (a respectable ewe:lamb ratio of 1:0.95), and in all he was keeping 395 animals at the time of the tithe payment. If the age structure

Table 5.5. Tithe lambs from Blockley parish.

1504	155
1505	231
1506	180 (including 56 from Middle Ditchford)
1507	173 (including 47 from John Palmer; 3 from Richard Freman; 12 from Thomas Wilkes; 19 from John Heritage)

Source: AB, 94r, 94v, 96r.

of the other Blockley sheep flocks resembled Heritage's in 1507, there were about 3,600 sheep in the parish. This would, however, be far too low a figure, because other flocks would contain a proportion of non-breeding animals such as hoggasters and wethers. Richard Freman apparently had relatively few ewes and lambs but many wethers, which meant that the lamb tithe did not reflect accurately the scale of his sheep-keeping. Similarly, the hill pasture of Upton Wold was well suited to wethers, but as a contrast many ewes were being kept in the valley of the Knee Brook at Middle Ditchford, with perhaps as many as six hundred in 1506 when 56 tithe lambs were collected. Blockley as a whole is likely to have had a balanced population of sheep of all ages and both genders, in which case one would expect each generation of lambs to represent about a quarter of the whole flock, so in 1507 when there were 173 tithe lambs, 1,730 had been reared that year, giving a total of about seven thousand sheep. This figure is entirely credible as Blockley was an enormous parish of almost 10,000 acres, including the village of Stretton on Fosse which is now separate. The three largest pastures of the two Ditchfords and Upton together amounted to about a quarter of the total area, and could have pastured three to four thousand sheep, which would leave a similar number in the hands of the peasants of seven villages. There would have been dozens of small-scale producers, like Richard Toll of Blockley who left to his five children six sheep each, but he probably had many more than those thirty animals. The stint is not recorded at Blockley, but judging from the surrounding villages each yardland could have been allowed at least forty sheep, and as there were about ninety tenanted yardlands (not allowing for Stretton), the potential total could have been 3,600.[56] In the real world the animals would have been distributed much more unevenly, with a minority exceeding their stint, even by two or threefold, while others kept none at all.

Revenues from tithes collected in other parishes tend to be expressed in cash rather than numbers of lambs and weights of wool, but rough estimates can be made from these figures. Broadwell was a larger than average parish of 1,800 acres, to which should be added the chapelry of Adlestrop with another 1,300 acres. It had no hill pasture but relatively plentiful meadow. In 1535 its lamb tithe of £2 13*s* 8*d* could be translated into thirty-six tithe lambs, and by using the formula devised for Blockley we arrive at a figure of 1,440 sheep. This excludes the demesne,

---

[56] For Toll: WRO, Worcester wills, no.219, stints are recorded in Table 6.4.

which was exempt from tithes and must have kept hundreds of sheep. Its tithe wool, valued at £4 4s 0d, would imply that 6 tods of wool were collected in tithe, which could represent the fleeces of 988 adult sheep. With lambs the total of peasant flocks would have amounted to well over a thousand, not very different from the figure calculated from the lamb tithe. A smaller lowland parish, Sutton under Brailes, again without its demesne animals, would in 1535 according to its lamb tithe have had 360 sheep, while a calculation based on wool gives a figure of 428.[57] If these figures were regarded as typical of the whole of Heritage's country, taking account of the greater capacity for grazing of the high ground compared with the valleys, we can arrive at a conservative total of eighty thousand sheep. Sheep outnumbered people ten to one. At Blockley the animals may have been divided roughly equally between the substantial flockmasters and the peasants, but in those parishes like Broadwell and Sutton that had no large space for the graziers and their flocks the majority of the animals belonged to peasants. Peasant sheep in the whole Moreton district could have outnumbered those owned by lords, graziers, and farmers, perhaps by as large a margin as two to one.

A PROFILE OF WOOL PRODUCERS

John Heritage's account book contains some occasional and unsystematic records of his own sheep and of the Blockley tithes that we have already used to throw light on both large-scale and peasant pastoral husbandry. The bulk of the book's content, which records wool purchases, provides guidance on the size of flocks, which were directly related to the amounts of wool being traded.

In order to use the figures for the weight of the consignments of wool to calculate the number of sheep, the weight of a fleece must be known. Various statistics have been compiled for mean fleece weights, notably from the huge sample provided by the manors of the bishopric of Winchester's estates that lay mainly in central southern England. The mean for the whole period 1208–1450 was 1.35 pounds, but the figure fluctuated, and in particular had declined in the fifteenth century to little more than 1 pound.[58] North Cotswold fleeces were consistently heavier than those of other regions, and figures are recorded such as 1.69 pounds for the bishop of Worcester's fleeces in 1384, 1.45 pounds in 1434–5 at Bourton on the Hill, and 1.83 pounds for Heritage's own sheep in 1509. The Celys were trading Cotswold fleeces in 1478 that weighed 1.86 pounds after they had suffered some decay.[59] The number of examples is scattered in time and place, and insufficient in number to calculate a scientific mean, so an arbitrary roughly median figure of 1.75 pounds per fleece has been chosen. The weight will have varied with the feeding and breeding of the animals, suggesting that Heritage's sheep would

[57] Caley and Hunter (eds), *Valor Ecclesiasticus*, II, 436.
[58] M. J. Stephenson, 'Wool Yields in the Medieval Economy', *Ec. HR*, 41 (1988), 368–91.
[59] Dyer, *Lords and Peasants*, 145; GA, D1099/M36; AB, fo.91r; A. Hanham, *The Celys and Their World: An English Merchant Family of the Fifteenth Century* (Cambridge, 1985), 112.

have had heavier fleeces than most, and wethers would each have produced more wool than the young animals and the females. The bad weather of 1502, and in other years of which we are less well informed, could have affected fleece weights adversely, and some of the wool came from south Warwickshire pastures, such as Cherington and Stourton, where the Cotswold breed may not have been kept and the weights were consequently lower.[60]

The amount of wool bought by Heritage in a single transaction varied in weight between 4 pounds (2 or 3 fleeces) and 8¾ sacks, which probably contained wool from 1,800 sheep. Two-thirds of his purchases lay between 1 tod and 9 tods (Table 5.6). He was therefore making bargains with people who owned flocks of adult sheep that varied in size between 16 and 144 animals, with a notable clustering around 60 and 90 (4 tods and 6 tods). This would be in accordance with our knowledge of the size of peasant flocks, which were often supposed to be limited by stints declared in the manorial court to 30, 40, or 60 sheep per yardland (though at Moreton the figure was as low as 20, and at Bourton on the Hill as high as 100). As many holdings consisted of 2 or 3 yardlands, flocks of 60, 80, 90, and 100 would have been in accordance with the customary rules, though there were always offenders prepared to exceed the limits. The stint regulations did not just use arbitrary figures, as they were devised by local people who were aware of the capacity of the pastures. They were taking account of the almost universal convention that no one should keep on the common more animals than he or she could feed on their own resources in the winter, and many peasants in the villages such as Bourton and Draycott had crofts at the back of their houses, and often a sheepcote capable of holding thirty during bad winter weather.

Table 5.6. Analysis of the quantity of wool in individual sales in sample years.

Year	Below 1 tod	1t.–4t. 27lb.	5t.–8t. 27 lb.	9t.–12 t. 27lb.	13t.–25t. 27 lb.	26t. and above	Total
1501	7	19	5	6	7	7	51
%	14	37	10	12	14	14	100
1503	7	21	14	4	5	1	52
%	13	40	27	8	10	2	100
1510	1	16	10	6	2	1	36
%	3	44	28	17	6	3	100
1518	6	17	11	3	2	0	39
%	15	44	28	8	5	0	100
1519	5	14	10	4	2	0	35
%	14	40	29	11	6	0	100
Total	26	87	50	23	18	9	213
%	12	41	23	11	8	4	100

Notes: t. = tod(s); lb. = pound(s)
Source: AB 2r–5v; 9r–13r; 45r–48v; 70v–75v.

[60] On the bad weather, W. G. Hoskins, 'Harvest Fluctuations and English Economic History, 1480–1619', *Ag. HR*, 12 (1964), 33 and 44.

A relatively small number of purchases brought Heritage very modest quantities of wool, below 28 pounds, with a cluster around 12 pounds, suggesting that some peasants were keeping about seven adult sheep. These quantities could have come from smallholders who only had enough land for a limited number of animals, or producers who concentrated on other branches of agriculture, such as cattle or pigs, or those who had kept many sheep in their heyday, but had scaled down their operations through old age or incapacity. A few widows were keeping sheep on a small scale, such as Maud Pyper who sold, between 1503 and 1508, 11 pounds in one year and 12 pounds in another. Some of these small producers were men working as shepherds, like John Shepherd who had 10 pounds to sell in 1502, presumably from animals that he was allowed to keep with his employer's flock. Some small amounts came from the son of a larger producer. John Nelme junior, for example, appeared regularly in the account book beside John Nelme senior of Bourton on the Hill. The father produced between 5 and 7 tods, so he kept a hundred sheep, while his son sold quantities such as 20 pounds and 23 pounds, either because he was allowed to pasture a dozen sheep as a member of the family or perhaps he worked as his father's shepherd and was rewarded in kind.

These very small amounts were not making a big contribution to Heritage's business, and took up his time and trouble for no great profit. They mattered, however, a great deal to those who were gaining 5s for seven fleeces, which would have taken them at least a fortnight to earn if they were working for wages. These small-scale suppliers were not very numerous, partly because Heritage may not have encouraged them, or because they found it easier to sell to a neighbour who added their fleeces to his pile (thereby distorting the evidence of the size of flocks estimated from Heritage's purchases). He may have taken some of the small parcels offered to him as an act of kindness, for example to help Maud Pyper and other widows. It is also likely that the poorest sections of village society are not represented in the accounts because they owned no sheep, as they lacked common rights to graze them, but were only allowed to keep a cow (as at Quinton) on the common, or not even a single animal.

At the other end of the spectrum of producers, we have already seen that Heritage could not sustain his initial contacts with gentry graziers, notably William Greville, John Daston, and John Palmer. He negotiated a single, impressively large purchase from each of them, and not again, perhaps because he was unable to afford their requirement that a high proportion of the money should be paid in advance (see pp. 101–2). Some of the other large-scale producers, such as Sir Adrian Fortescue and Winchcombe Abbey, had no dealings with him at all. Lower down the rankings, Heritage did better in his relations with demesne famers, such as Thomas Kyte of Broadwell, William Bayly of Condicote, and Thomas Fletcher of Chastleton, and also with lessees of pastures like John Clotton of Little Rollright, and engrossers of many yardlands, like Piers Barton of Brookend in Chastleton, all of whom had 2 or 3 sacks representing wool from between four and six hundred sheep.

Most of the wool came from those producing on a modest scale, and their prominence in Heritage's records gives us an opportunity to learn more about people who are otherwise hidden from view. The method is prosopography, by which as much information as possible is gathered about individuals until we can understand their position in society, their wealth, and their mentality. Gathering the information, however, meets many obstacles. Starting with the account book, it only rarely gives any more information about each seller of wool other than their name. The woolman did not feel any need to give his supplier's place of residence or his social status. In the royal courts at the time the law required that everyone should be properly identified, but Heritage knew the people and had no need to pigeon-hole them by their social standing ('husbandman') or occupation ('carpenter'). The exceptions were those who attracted his deference, so gentry were called 'master' and parish clergy were described by their title and parish: vicar of Lemington, for example. For him 'Nicholas Spyer' conjured up a face and a personality, but it leaves us in the dark. There are sometimes indications of the place of a supplier's residence from the particular places where the money was paid: Nicholas Rose, for example, once received money at Wolford Wood, and that takes us to the village of Great Wolford where he lived. Another clue can come from the names of intermediaries who took money on behalf of the seller. Otherwise the main sources of information are the manorial documents, wills, deeds, and tax lists. Having combed through these records we cannot be sure that the names that have been found relate to the same person who is mentioned in the account book. One feels confident when the name is an unusual one such as Robert Shelfox, but many of the suppliers' names were found in a number of villages near Moreton, such as Clarke, Coke, Freman, Robyns, and Stevens. Even names that seem unusual to us, such as Bumpas and Perte, occur in a number of places in the area. The ideal sources are the military surveys of 1522, and the subsidy lists of 1524 and 1525, as they allow us to place the seller in a hierarchy of wealth, but while this works well for those appearing in the later years of the accounts, one fears that people who were selling wool in 1501–10 may have changed their circumstances by the early 1520s. It is even possible that the John Benet who supplied wool in 1501 may have been not the John Benet whose wealth was assessed in 1522, but his father.

Taking account of all of these problems, and eliminating as much as possible the doubtful cases, a hierarchy of wool growers can be compiled in terms of social status, landholding, and taxable wealth (Table 5.7). The sample depends on the possibility of identifying the suppliers in documents separate from the account book, which has been possible in fifty-seven cases. At the top are two ranks of wealthy and large-scale producers, lords, farmers, and engrossers, who are over-represented because they are more easy to identify in the records. They are also untypical of the whole period of Heritage's trading as they figure most prominently in the first two years. In all, 96 per cent of those trading with Heritage sold him fewer than 2 sacks of wool, and grazed fewer than four hundred sheep. Also under-represented are the smallholders who are difficult to find in documents, and for reasons already explained would not appear in the account book. But they would not own many sheep in any case.

Three individuals will be sufficient to indicate the information available for examples of suppliers at different levels in the hierarchy. The first is Peter Barton,

Table 5.7. A profile of John Heritage's wool suppliers, 1501–19.

Quantity of wool supplied in each transaction (no. of sheep)*	Number of suppliers	Landholding, status	Tax assessment +		
			Max.	Min.	Median
4 sacks (52 tods) or above (800 + sheep)	5	manorial lord (3), farmer (2)	£4,000	£6 13s 4d	£133 6s 8d
2 sacks (26 tods) – 3 sacks 12 tods (52 tods) (400–800 sheep)	5	demesne farmer (2) farmer of leasow (1) tenant of 8½ yl** tenant of 6 yl	–	–	£20
1 sack (13 tods) – 1 sack 12 tod (25 tods) (200–400)	10	demesne farmer(3) tenant of 2 yl (3)	£80	£5	£16
5 tods–12 tods 27 lbs (80–200)	13	tenant of 3 yl (1) tenant of 2 yl (2)	£30	£6	£12
1 tod–4 tods 27 lb (16–80)	20	tenant of 3 yl (1) tenant of 2 yl (2) tenant of 1½ yl (1)	£30	£2	£4
below 1 tod (15 or less)	4	no evidence	£2	0	£2
Total	57				

*assuming each fleece weighed 1.75 lbs.
** yardland
+ from the military survey of 1522 and the subsidies of 1524 and 1525

known to John Heritage as Piers Barton, and described as 'of Chastleton' in the account book. He was a tenant and resident of Brookend, a decaying village in the north-west of Chastleton parish only two miles from Moreton in Marsh. Barton succeeded his father John in 1488, and presumably inherited the very large holding of a messuage, five tofts, and 8½ yardlands that his father had built up by 1469 by engrossing previously separate holdings.[61] Piers sold wool weighing 27 and 28 tods to Heritage in successive years in 1501 and 1502, which shows that his land was being exploited not as 250 acres of arable, which 8½ yardlands might imply, but largely as pasture for about 450 adult sheep. He let his dwelling deteriorate, and his barn, sheepcote, and shippon had defective thatch in 1499. But he was not poor, as his wool brought him £15 to £16 each year, and he bequeathed a total of £20 to his son and two daughters when he died in 1505.[62] Heritage encouraged him with a large payment of earnest money (more than £10) in 1501, but Barton was probably accustomed to sell his wool to broggers from Chipping Norton, to which town his will suggests an attachment.

William Messenger was the farmer of the manor of Great Wolford, which belonged to the estate of the dukes of Buckingham, from 1497 to 1509.[63] He was

[61] British Library, Harleian Rolls, B12, B13, B14 (court rolls).
[62] Weaver and Beardwood (eds), *Oxfordshire Wills*, 86.
[63] Staffordshire Record Office, D641/1/2/277–279; TNA: PRO, SC6 Henry VII/867 (accounts).

one of Heritage's most consistent suppliers, selling him wool almost continuously between 1503 and 1510. He was unusual as a farmer in that he took on the whole manor, not just the demesne but also the tenants with their rents and dues. As a very efficient tenant, he paid his rent of £14 6s 8d within the year that it was due, which was not the usual practice, as on most manors at least small sums were left unpaid as arrears. He evidently made use of the pastoral potential of the Wolford demesne, as he sold between 8 and 14 tods each year to Heritage, from a flock that numbered between 132 and 224 sheep. The money from the wool, between £4 and £7 each year, made a sizeable contribution to the rent payment. He evidently was assisted by the vicar of Wolford, John Molder, who twice took money from Heritage as part of his payment for wool (Heritage with typical deference called him 'Sir John'). His son was also involved in the same way, and in 1510 was apparently taking over the farm, as William Messenger, described as 'the elder' in the account book, sold much less wool than usual (below 6 tods), and his son apparently sold 2 tods independently. The Messenger family then disappeared from the records. William the elder had, with his wife, joined the Stratford Guild of the Holy Cross in 1501–2, at the same time as a number of people from Shipston on Stour.[64] From a Wolford perspective Shipston would have seemed a convenient place to trade, but perhaps Messenger's loyalty to Heritage derived from a business partnership, as Heritage was keeping a small flock of sheep at Great Wolford in 1506–9, which might have encouraged Messenger to sell him wool rather than going to some Shipston or Stratford woolman (see Table 5.3).

Much more typical of Heritage's suppliers was William Eddon of Paxford. He sold wool to Heritage in 1506–8, increasing from 1½ tods in the first two years to 2 tods 14 pounds in 1508. He may then have been relatively young, and was growing his agricultural activities, as his sheep numbers evidently increased over those two years from about 23 to 40. By the time of the tax assessments of 1524 and 1525 Eddon was modestly prospering, as he paid tax on goods worth £9 in both years.[65] In 1525 he was the fourth wealthiest taxpayer in his village, exceeded by one person with goods worth £16 and two others assessed at £10. In 1529 he was nearing the end of his career, when his son Thomas acquired his holding of two messuages, a toft, and 1½ yardlands (he was an engrosser on a small scale) as a reversion on his death or retirement. Thomas paid a 20s fine, which could mean that the holding was in quite good condition.[66] The 16s to 28s that Heritage gave him for his wool made a large contribution to the economy of the holding. Unlike Piers Barton, who grazed his sheep on the abandoned fields of an almost deserted village, both Messenger and Eddon were farming within settlements that had diminished in size, but still retained their open fields and tradition of mixed farming. Their sheep derived much of their grazing from cornfields after the harvest, rather than large permanent pastures.

[64] *Guild Reg.*, 379.
[65] *WT*, 101, 184.
[66] WRO, BA 2636 ref.009:1, 177/92509.

Most wool producers who had dealings with Heritage were tenants like William Eddon or in the next rank above him in terms of landholding; they made their living from 1, 2, or 3 yardlands, and they kept their sheep on the common fields and common pastures of such villages as Adlestrop, Bourton on the Hill, Little Compton, and Longborough. Some of them leased parcels of land either from the demesne or from former peasant holdings that had been left in the hands of the lord. A few of them, such as John Pole and John Wode, both of Pinnock, or William Colchester at Lark Stoke, could take advantage of a village's decay to extend pastures over former open fields. Some of the wool that Heritage bought and sold came from sheep that were kept on permanent and enclosed pastures, but the majority were grazing for part of their lives on the stubbles and fallows of field systems that had the cultivation of corn as one of their main functions. The husbandmen and yeomen who made up two-thirds of the sample in Table 5.6 mostly held their yardlands on customary tenures in nucleated villages. Their tenancies were regulated in the manorial court, and their farming was subject to the discipline of the village community backed up by the manor court. They marketed a proportion of their produce, in the case of their wool by private treaty, but their surpluses of grain, livestock, and dairy produce were carried to market.

The tax assessments of our sample do not equate exactly with their landholdings, partly because of the fallibility of the tax system, and partly because holdings of land were being exploited at different levels of intensity, depending on the skill, diligence, age, and health of the tenant. Tenants with 1, 2, or 3 yardlands could pay taxes on goods worth as little as £2 or as much as £30. Those goods would often include their sheep, or at least a proportion of them. The eighty sheep of an above-average taxpayer would be worth £8, which could represent a third of the total assessment. A smaller proportion can be calculated for Thomas Palmer of Moreton in Marsh, a close associate of Heritage's, who sheared at least 140 sheep worth £10–£14, but he owned other animals and assets as his taxes were paid on goods valued at £80. The value of the sheep at market interested the tax gatherers and compilers of inventories, but the growers were mainly concerned with the revenue that their wool yielded from year to year. The eighty sheep kept by the tenant of a 2-yardland holding produced enough wool (5 tods) to generate payments from the brogger of £3, which would cover the annual rent of 20s and occasional taxes of 3s–5s, leaving cash to spare to spend on the farm or on personal consumption. Even those with only thirty sheep, like William Eddon, would receive enough money (about 20s) to pay their rent and have cash to spare.

Analysis of the market in wool reveals much about the inequalities of village society, as we can appreciate that a peasant with eighty sheep had a much higher disposable income than one with thirty, and below them were cottagers, labourers, servants, and marginals with no sheep at all, and limited opportunities to spend and even fewer to accumulate wealth. Behind the formal records of landholding, inheritance, and the land market lies a society of constant change of fortunes, dependent on such undocumented factors as family influence, patronage, skill, and talent. One can follow the development of individuals, like Richard Castell of Moreton, who in his early years sold 11 pounds and 14 pounds of wool, but then expanded in 1507 to more than 2 tods, and continued to farm at that level (with about thirty sheep) for the next ten years. A young man would be helped by his father. Such a supportive parent was apparently John Whete of Paxford, who kept a hundred sheep producing 6 tods of wool each year between 1513 and 1519. John Whete junior began with a tod of wool, from about sixteen sheep, but by 1519 he had increased his flock to about fifty. John Whete senior died before 1523, and John Whete junior appears in the 1525 tax assessment as a moderately prosperous husbandman with goods valued at £5. He was living at Aston Magna, the next village to Paxford. At Bourton on the Hill the young William Mansell doubled the size of his flock from fifty to a hundred between 1514 and 1519 but was still operating on a smaller scale than William Mansell the elder who in 1519 had more than 130 sheep, he also having doubled his numbers since 1514. The younger man eventually overtook his father, and by 1522 his assessed wealth reached £30, compared with Mansell senior's £20. Fortune could turn the other way, so that William Nycols of Moreton, never a big player, but loyal in his sales to Heritage, kept enough sheep to sell a tod or two each year between 1503 and 1510, but then suffered some reversal, and could muster only 9½ pounds in 1512 and 18 pounds in 1519.

Women tend to come into view in the records in their widowhood, and we can observe how they coped with the new responsibilities thrust on them by the death of their husbands: they could withdraw from managing the holding, or they could cope, or even flourish. Elizabeth Haklyn of Adlestrop sold 4 tods of wool in 1504, the year of the death of her husband when she received the 2-yardland holding as her freebench, but she sold no more wool as she surrendered the land later in the year. As we have seen, Maud Pyper kept up small-scale sheep-keeping that enabled her to produce wool worth a few shillings for a number of years. Elizabeth Powle, however, of Taddington, took over a substantial holding (probably at least 3 yard-lands) and produced between 1515 and 1519 enough wool (8–12 tods) to show that her flock fluctuated around 160 animals.

CONCLUSION

The Heritage country contained varied resources of specialist pastures (leasows and former village sites) in addition to the common pastures, open-field stubbles, and meadows, providing an environment in which lords, monastic as well as gentry, farmers, engrossers of many holdings, and the middling and upper peasantry could all make money from grazing sheep. The majority of the producers were peasants, but the gentry, graziers, and farmers had larger quantities to sell. Heritage's book is not a perfect source for judging the relative quantities of wool that came from different types of producer. His buying strategy, either because of decisions he made or because of the attitudes of his suppliers, changed after the first few years. In 1502 we can estimate that 76 per cent of his wool came from nine gentry, farmers, and graziers. By 1510 there were at most two producers in those categories, and they accounted for 22 per cent (56 tods) of the wool, and by 1518 the large producers (again two of them) were sending only 26 tods, or 14 per cent of the total. These figures cannot lead to a more general conclusion about the importance of the graziers in comparison with the peasantry. The large-scale sheep-masters are over represented in the early years of Heritage's business, and under-represented towards the end. We can conclude that the advance of the leasows through enclosure and conversion from arable to pasture was an important development, but that the role of the peasants who continued to practise mixed husbandry should not be discounted. John Heritage, by gathering and marketing the relatively small deliveries of wool that came from the peasants, was helping them to maintain their position in agrarian society.[67]

---

[67] The general point that wool broggers handled much peasant wool is in E. Power, *The Wool Trade in English Medieval History* (Oxford, 1941), 47–8.

6

Beyond the Account Book:
Changing the Countryside

The Heritage account book can be read as a depiction of a divided rural society: between enclosed pastures (leasows) and open fields; between entrepreneurial graziers and peasants; and between specialization and mixed farming. Those who created and exploited the leasows represent a spirit of radical change, in which far-sighted innovators could alter the environment for their profit. Peasants meanwhile were farming fields that had existed for at least five centuries, but among them were acquisitive individuals whose interests clashed with those of other villagers. Perhaps these contrasts are not an accurate depiction of a polarized rural world. We ought to explain what had led to this appearance of divergence, by examining the developments in Heritage's period of activity between 1495 and 1520, but also over a longer time span as the structure of landholding and farming methods evolved over many decades.

LORDSHIP

To what extent was the countryside of *c.*1500 controlled and changed by the aristocratic and institutional elite? Traditionally they have been seen as the architects of social and economic life, by wielding discipline and coercion through private jurisdiction and especially by their control over customary tenants. This view of lordly compulsion has some justification, because they did wield power, not just through their own courts but also through their participation in royal government. They also had at their elbows groups of men who could wield influence, for example by 'labouring' (persuading) juries, and they were able in the last resort to threaten their subordinates with force.[1] It is also true that lords had always claimed more authority than they exercised in practice, and were limited in their actions by the laws of the state and the resistance of their inferiors. In particular, after the fall in population in the fourteenth century they lost authority and income, as land was relatively plentiful and tenants, by their scarcity, enjoyed a stronger bargaining power. Serfdom almost disappeared, labour services were no longer demanded, the

---

[1] S. Gunn, 'Henry VII in Context: Problems and Possibilities', *History*, 92 (2007), 301–17, especially 303, 305; C. Carpenter, *The Wars of the Roses: Politics and the Constitution in England, c.1437–1509* (Cambridge, 1997), 233–5.

demesnes were leased out, some tenant holdings lacked occupants, rents tended to decline, and the powers and functions of courts diminished. To all of this the peasants contributed by seeking their own advantage by a reluctance to cooperate, and by occasional resistance. Some lords kept away from their lands and tenants, and their remoteness contributed to a neglect of the vigorous enforcement of lordly rule. The archbishops of York held Oddington near Stow on the Wold and its outlier of Condicote, and were infrequent visitors. Their officials collected a derisory annual rent of 6s 10½d from each yardland. The administration was so slack that in 1508 three smallholdings (called Mondaylands because in earlier centuries their tenants had to work on the demesne every Monday) were reported to have been lost: 'it is unknown at present where the aforesaid Mondaylands lie'.[2] The tenants were required to find the missing land, but as they had presumably divided the holdings among themselves and added the acres to their own yardlands without paying any more rent, it was not in their interests to reveal their whereabouts.

In the period 1495–1520 some dimensions of the power of lords enjoyed a modest revival. One success of lordship had been to maintain the integrity of the yardland holdings, so although they were often held together in groups of two or three, their once separate existence was remembered, and they were not allowed to fragment, which would have threatened the continued collection of their rents and dues. The manor of Little Compton stands as an exception, as the lord of the manor, Tewkesbury Abbey, had allowed the memory of yardlands to lapse, and the holdings were described in a survey by means of an acreage, partly in selions (strips of ploughland in the open fields) and partly in closes.[3] The continued existence of the yardland on most manors was an achievement for conservation, not of an archaic unit of tenure but of the authority of lords.

Most rents were fixed, not just those of freeholds, but those paid by customary land and leasehold were also pegged in practice. Tenants, however, often neglected to pay on the customary days, demonstrating the almost universal practice of delayed payment that we have observed in the wool trade.[4] Estate officials, concerned by the build-up of arrears of rent, devoted energy to ensuring prompt payment, and in this respect attitudes and practices seem to have changed around 1500. Manorial incomes tended to increase, such as those collected from the bishopric of Worcester's manor of Blockley, which produced each year in the dark days of the 1450s and 1460s a median income of £98, but by 1500–20 the bishop gained from it more than £120 per annum.[5] The rise in revenues is partly to be

[2] GA, D621/M8 (reeve's account).

[3] GA, P329/1. On the longevity of virgate tenure, and the relationship between tenure and real landholding, J. Whittle and M. Yates, '"Pays réel or pays légal"? Contrasting Patterns of Land Tenure and Social Structure in Eastern Norfolk and Western Berkshire, 1450–1600', *Ag. HR*, 48 (2000), 1–26.

[4] Arrears, partly caused by delayed rent payments, were especially high on the Duke of Buckingham's estates: C. Rawcliffe, *The Staffords, Earls of Stafford and Dukes of Buckingham 1394–1521* (Cambridge, 1978), 109–15; and they persisted in 1498–1521: B. J. Harris, *Edward Stafford: Third Duke of Buckingham, 1478–1521* (Stanford, CA, 1986), 116–19.

[5] WRO, BA2636, ref.009:1, 168, 174, 175, 176, 177, 178, 191, 192, for receivers' accounts; 157, 170, 174, 177, for manorial accounts.

explained by the reduction in arrears, which accumulated as high as £154 in the depth of the recession around 1450, but in the early sixteenth century they could be as low as £20. Arrears grew when the local manorial official could not collect rents, but after 1500 the tenants tended to pay promptly and in full. Some sources of income showed signs of life, even though they did not rise dramatically. The entry fines that were paid when a tenant took on a new customary holding moved up and down with demand for land, and in response to pressure from the administrators. On the Evesham manors around Stow on the Wold each yardland was expected to pay between 4s and 6s 8d, which were not large sums by the standards of the fourteenth century but stood above the token payments of poultry that are found on some manors around 1450.[6] On the manors near Moreton belonging to other major church lords, fines again were not high, but individual payments as great as 20s are recorded, and 20s was also paid in Shipston on Stour when a 'messuage and a curtilage' (equivalent to a burgage plot in other towns) was inherited. A rising trend at Broadway pushed the fine for a yardland up from a range of 2s to 5s in the 1490s to between 13s 4d and 20s in the years 1509–16.[7]

A bone of contention between lords and tenants arose from the tendency of tenants to neglect buildings, or even to allow them to fall down. This could be a reflection of poverty, and elderly tenants characteristically let their buildings deteriorate. Some tenants, however, were perfectly capable of maintaining the buildings, but chose not to do so. A house or barn might belong to a holding that had been combined with another, and was not therefore useful to the tenant who already had a dwelling and a barn; but the lord wished to maintain the housing stock in the hope that the holding would one day attract a tenant who would pay a decent entry fine and rent. Especially in the century 1380–1480 rather fruitless campaigns for repairs had little effect and caused some ill-will as tenants who allowed their buildings to fall into ruin were expected to pay a few pence in amercements, and were threatened with stiff financial penalties.[8] Towards the end of the fifteenth century and after 1500, lords seem to have accepted that some building plots would remain empty, and even on some manors abandoned the formula of calling a holding without a house 'a toft and a yardland' but instead called it a 'messuage and a yardland' like the other (inhabited) tenements in the village.[9]

Lords took seriously, however, the task of enforcing building repairs on tenants who were living on a holding but had allowed a house or farm building to deteriorate. The warden of New College, Oxford (the academic serving as head of the College) even made a personal inspection of tenants' houses at Kingham, and the manor court required repairs of a very specific kind, naming the part of the buildings that

[6] TNA: PRO, SC2 175/77 (Evesham Abbey court rolls).

[7] Worcester Cathedral Library, E84, E89, E90 (Worcester Priory court rolls); TNA: PRO, SC2 210/32, 33 (Broadway court rolls).

[8] P. Hargreaves, 'Seignorial Reaction and Peasant Responses: Worcester Priory and Its Peasants after the Black Death', *Midland History*, 24 (1999), 53–78, especially 60–71.

[9] For example, on the Evesham Abbey and Worcester Priory estates, using documents cited in notes 6 and 7 above. A similar change has been noted by C. Currie on documents relating to Steventon in Berkshire.

needed attention, and even identifying the timber that needed replacement. For example, in 1515 John Kyrwode was threatened with a penalty of 3*s* 4*d* for 'allowing the wall of his kitchen near the door of the hall at the front to be badly ruinous', and William Pole was required to give attention to 'a jamb of the wall of the chamber, at the end of the chamber, and a jamb of the wall of the barn'.[10] Neither of them were afflicted by poverty, as they were substantial tenants, Kyrwode with a yardland and Pole with a yardland and a half. The College was presumably anxious to keep the holdings in a condition which would ensure that their rents, which together came to 36*s* per annum, would continue. A little before our period Sir William Stonor (himself a wool trader) was pursuing an effective campaign against dilapidations on his manor of Bourton on the Hill and Condicote. In a court held in November 1487 six of the sixteen tenants were ordered to repair defective buildings, and within eight months four of them had complied fully, and a fifth, required to mend walls and the roof, had done the thatching but not the carpentry work.[11] A similar pattern can be observed after 1500 on the manors of Evesham Abbey near Stow, where there were many presentments, suggesting that a substantial minority of tenants needed to carry out repairs. The orders were apparently effective: although some repair orders were repeated, others disappear from the records because, as at Bourton, the work had been completed. Also, as at Kingham and Bourton, tenants with large holdings were reported for neglecting their buildings, and only occasionally are we told that the tenant was impoverished and near the end of his or her active life. Around 1500 the estate authorities were not clashing with their tenants by attempting to impose unrealistic demands for repairs, but rather pushing tenants into doing work that was in their own interests as well as the lord's. The problem was the cost of the work, as carpenters' wages had to be paid and materials purchased. The buildings of a tenant at Bourton, Robert Eddon, were said in 1489 to be in need of repairs costing £3 6*s* 8*d*. He persisted in his failure to carry out the work, which in theory, as a yardlander, he could afford, but his tenancy had ceased five years later, suggesting that his fortunes or capacities were declining.[12]

Estate managers were concerned to keep track of tenants, lest holdings be lost and rents lapse. Subtenancy was a particular concern, and a relatively strict lord such as Worcester Cathedral Priory insisted that tenants at Blackwell should obtain a licence at modest cost. This was not an occasional imposition, as four licences were issued in 1505 alone, with another in 1506 and two in 1507.[13] The Priory also imposed the condition that the subtenant should be well behaved, or the tenant would face eviction. In 1518–19 a number of licences were issued, and it was shown that the rules were not mere formalities, as Richard Rawlyns was evicted for subletting 'against the custom', that is, without permission.[14] Such an unusual step

[10] New College, Oxford, 3797 (court rolls).
[11] TNA: PRO, SC2 175/17. The same record of compliance with repair orders has been noted in the south-east, M. Mate, *Trade and Economic Development, 1450–1550: The Experience of Kent, Surrey and Sussex* (Woodbridge, 2006), 206.
[12] TNA: PRO, SC2 175/17; SC12 7/67 (court roll and rental).
[13] Worcester Cathedral Library, E89, E90 (court rolls).
[14] Worcester Cathedral Library, E95 (court roll).

must have encouraged the other tenants to follow the Priory's wishes. These disciplines were not just imposed by monastic lords, as on the Fortescue manor of Condicote the farmer was deprived of his tenancy for subletting.[15]

In spite of these assertions of the rules, lords had lost authority, well demonstrated by the almost complete ending of the once common practice of pursuing litigation through the manor courts on such matters as debt and trespass. There were some survivals and revivals of seigneurial power. At its manor of Blackwell, for example, the Priory of Worcester kept up an old method for enforcing the court's control by requiring in 1510 and 1512 that two pledges be appointed to ensure that widows observed their obligations as tenants when they took over their husbands' holdings.[16] The long-established lordly monopoly over the mill was occasionally enforced. When New College, Oxford, discovered that Richard Horley at Kingham had been working for a year 'a little mill called a *querne* for milling malt', 'to the damage of the farmer of the water mill', they ordered him to cease operating his hand mill under threat of paying a penalty of 3*s* 4*d* per month. This draconian charge was designed to convey to the offender the urgency of the matter.[17] Many other hand mills must have been quietly working without being detected in the villages around Moreton. Evesham Abbey was being realistic about the milling monopoly at Maugersbury in 1514. The tenants were ordered to take their grain to the lord's mill 'unless for reasonable cause', and the miller was told to serve the tenants faithfully. In other words, the lord realized that the mill would attract the inhabitants if the miller provided a good service.[18] He was in competition with other mills and hand milling at home, and the lord could cajole but not force the tenants to use the manorial mill. At Shipston the lord's oven was being defended as a monopoly by Worcester Priory and innkeepers were given permission to bake their own bread, providing that they did not sell loaves and compete with the common oven.[19]

Finally, serfdom had receded in importance during the fifteenth century, as the obligations of serfs were reduced, and their numbers dwindled when they moved to manors where their status was soon forgotten. Nonetheless in the early sixteenth century estate officials maintained records of servile families, noting at Blackwell the whereabouts of individuals who had left the manor, and on the bishopric estate serfs and their children were listed.[20] Lords wished to keep memories of the status alive, and presumably stimulated resentment among the few remaining serfs. These reminders of a humiliating legal condition (and a fear that it might be revived) may have prompted one of Heritage's suppliers, John Whete of Aston Magna, to apply to buy his freedom in 1501, and for the Hancocks family of Newbold in Tredington

[15] TNA: PRO, SC2 175/18 (court roll of 1494).

[16] Worcester Cathedral Library, E93a, E94 (court rolls).

[17] New College, Oxford, 3797 (court roll).

[18] TNA: PRO, SC2 175/78; on the end of coercive suit of mills, J. Langdon, *Mills in the Medieval Economy: England 1300–1540* (Oxford, 2004), 286–7.

[19] Worcester Cathedral Library, E95 (court roll).

[20] Worcester Cathedral Library, E89, E93A (court rolls); C. Dyer, *Lords and Peasants in a Changing Society: The Estates of the Bishopric of Worcester, 680–1540* (Cambridge, 1980), 270.

to do the same in 1504.[21] Lords must have expected that serfs would react to the constant reminders of their status, and profited from the payments for manumission.

The power and influence of traditional lordship survived in a diluted form into the early sixteenth century, and some aspects were revived or adapted to current circumstances. A capacity for change is often attributed to the gentry, and in Heritage's country we find a variety of lords in that category, including such old families as Burdet, Lucy, and Rous, together with well-established families with a strong legal background, such as Catesby, Fortescue, and Greville. There are late arrivals of which Richard Empson, a very prominent royal administrator, was the best example, together with the Heritages' patrons, the Belknap family, and the lesser parvenus, Hunkes, Palmer, and Willington. Monastic lords should not be dismissed as impractical and sunk in tradition, as the abbots included able administrators such as Richard Kidderminster of Winchcombe, John Islip of Westminster, and Clement Lichfield of Evesham.[22] All three have left a legacy of buildings to prove their ability to raise money and spend it purposefully, and the Westminster monks in particular employed well-executed administrative devices like the annual summary of the 'state of the manors'.[23] The large monastic estates were provided with professional services and expert advice by stewards, receivers, and council members, all of them recruited from the gentry. These lay administrators must have been especially influential on the policies of the bishopric of Worcester estate, as in the absence of its Italian bishops, practical matters would have been decided by the stewards like Sir Gilbert Talbot and the receivers, of which the longest serving was John Hornyhold.

Important decisions had been taken well before 1500 to lease demesnes, which meant that most of estate income came from rents rather than produce. There had been an intermediate stage when the pastures were still under direct management and the arable demesne was leased, but by our period the pasture was often also put in the hands of a farmer on a number of manors: Bourton on the Hill, Longborough, and Lower Swell, for example. This meant that manors had two pieces of demesne land held on leases, of which one was called a bercary or sheep pasture, named after the *bercaria* or sheepcote that sheltered the flock. At Lower Swell there were three bercaries, which as we have seen were held by the 1530s by the same tenant (see p. 152). Most demesnes were in the hands of one or two farmers, though at Oddington and Paxford the demesne was divided among all the customary tenants, and the Quinton demesne in about 1490 was granted to a consortium of six local lessees. In the circumstances in which parcels of demesne were absorbed into the landholdings of the village, lords could do little to reorganize it, but most

---

[21] Worcester Cathedral Library, MS. A6 (2), fos.18, 33 (register).
[22] P. Cunich, 'Richard Kidderminster (*c.*1461–1533/4), abbot of Winchcombe', *Oxford Dictionary of National Biography* (Oxford, 2004), 31, 534–5; B. F. Harvey and H. Summerson, 'John Islip (1464–1532), abbot of Westminster', *Oxford Dictionary of National Biography* (Oxford, 2004), 29, 436–7; E. A. B. Barnard, 'Clement Lichfield, Last Abbot of Evesham, 1514–1539', *Transactions of the Worcestershire Archaeological Society*, new ser., 5 (1927–8), 38–51.
[23] WAM 6198.

demesnes were held separately from the peasants' tenancies, and when the term of a lease ended, or in midterm if the farmer agreed, radical modifications could be made, of which the most common involved some form of enclosure and large-scale conversion of arable to pasture.

Enclosing the demesne and converting the land to pasture was of course the starting point of the Heritage story at Burton Dassett, and also proved a profitable option in the country around Moreton at Admington and Churchill (see p. 150). It was not easily carried out unless the demesne was already organized in blocs of land, and it could cause great damage to the village if the peasants' livestock normally grazed the demesne after the harvest and on the fallow, but were then excluded. In earlier times the demesne and tenant land had been integrated, and separating them was a revolutionary change. As the vicar of Quinton said, a farmer who ignored the customs on the use of land and common rights was behaving as if the village and the demesne were in different lordships.[24]

The whole issue of the conversion to pasture, enclosure of former open fields, and the displacement of tenants caused heated controversy, and invariably our sources come from partisans who represented enclosure as avarice. This was a matter for the law, as the act of 1489 made depopulating enclosure an offence, and the inquisition of 1517 exposed the guilty men (see Appendix 3). A typical accusation was made against Thomas Rous esquire, who as a gentleman farmer had so offended the people of Quinton that the lord was persuaded in about 1490 that the demesne would no longer be leased to a single tenant. Again as a farmer or lessee Rous was accused of enclosing land in 1498 in the adjoining village of Clopton of which the lord was John Leighton. Rous was said to have converted 120 acres to pasture, resulting in the desolation of two houses, the departure of ten people, and the displacement of two ploughs. Under the law of 1489 Leighton, as lord of the manor where this illegal activity had occurred, was supposed to pay a half of the profit of enclosure to the Crown, but the money was not forthcoming, and the case rumbled on until 1530. Then a group of local people were assembled who disputed the findings of the original inquest, and claimed that the conversion and depopulation had occurred long before 1498, indeed before the statute: the 120 acres had been put down to grass in 1481, and the two houses were in ruins in 1485.[25]

The case made by the defence has plausibility for modern observers because, although there are no documents relating to Clopton in the 1480s, the court rolls of nearby manors report the decay of houses, resulting from migration, as was said to have happened at Clopton. On the other hand Rous had a reputation for disregarding the interests of rural communities and pursuing his own profit, and there is no obvious reason for the events to have been invented, unless the local jurors were finding an excuse to express their hostility towards him. The whole story shows how careful we must be in dealing with these accusations, and it may well

[24] C. Dyer, *An Age of Transition? Economy and Society in England in the Later Middle Ages* (Oxford, 2005), 82.

[25] GA, 5626 1/71; the case figures in E. Kerridge, 'The Returns of the Inquisitions of Depopulation', *Ec. HR*, 70 (1955), 212–28.

be that the decline of Clopton occurred long before Rous and Leighton came on the scene, and the inhabitants left and the fields were turned to grass because of internal problems within the village.[26]

Another legal dispute, at Longborough, belongs to a period after Heritage's period of activity, in 1537, but the episode allows us to see in detail events that were unfolding in obscurity in the Moreton area over a long period beginning well before 1500 and continuing after the 1530s. Here the majority of the customary tenants, twenty in all, many of them better-off peasants holding 2 or 3 yardlands, petitioned the court of Chancery with a complaint that their lord, the abbot of Hailes, had plans to increase his own 'lucre and profit' by following 'his cruel intents' to convert tillage into pasture.[27] All tenants in the village had rights to pasture at a rate of sixty sheep per yardland and had arable land on Longborough Hill. The abbot converted his demesne to pasture, which was held by a farmer, and had increased the number of sheep grazing on the pasture from 240 to 900. Reading between the lines, the abbot had a demesne that consisted of strips intermixed with tenant land, and in order to convert a field that contained his land and his tenants' into pasture he had to require them to grass over their strips: 'he compelled [the tenants] to convert their arable land into pasture'. At the same time they were losing their traditional rights of pasturage on the stubble of that part of the open fields that he had appropriated. The abbot was also accused of using exactions (probably entry fines) to drive them out of their tenancies, as his ultimate aim was to convert the whole manor into pasture. The tenants asked for the extra sheep to be withdrawn, and for the pasture to be converted back to tillage, 'according to the old custom'.

The abbot's reply does not survive, but we can imagine his counter-argument, especially as such documents survive from other similar disputes in other part of the country. He would have said that his changes applied to only part of the field system, and he was not depriving the tenants of their land, but encouraging them to improve their holdings by converting to pasture those strips that lay on Longborough Hill or the Down. He had a right to improve his own land as long as he did not deprive the tenants of pasture. He was also within his rights in raising entry fines, which many lords were doing at that time because of an increase in land values and demand for holdings. He did not intend to impoverish and destroy the tenants, who could afford to pay the fines from their profits, and they would have been well advised in his view to carry out an enclosure by agreement that would make them even more prosperous.

The stereotypes evoked by this conflict can be readily identified. The abbot of Hailes, for example, was being represented as greedy, selfish, and an enemy of peasant communities. He saw himself as enhancing the profits of his estates, while the peasants clung to outmoded customs and resisted all improvements. Lords and peasants could work together, which seems to have happened in the village of

---

[26] C. Dyer, 'Deserted Medieval Villages in the West Midlands', *Ec. HR*, 2nd ser., 35 (1982), 19–34.
[27] TNA: PRO, C1/739/17.

Meon, where the enclosure commission found in 1513 that Sir Edward Greville enclosed 70 acres, but at the same time four tenants enclosed 40 acres, 30 acres, 30 acres, and 32 acres, which suggests that they had been persuaded or pressurized by their lord into joining in an agreed enclosure that covered 4 customary yardlands as well as the lord's demesne. The result, however, was not a happy one for the village, as the commission reported that houses were abandoned as a result, and the village was deserted.[28]

Longborough's survival suggests that the best policy for villagers was to resist and protest if threatened by an ambitious lord. It helped that they were a large community with some wealthy peasants. A number of them, or their immediate predecessors, figure among those selling wool to Heritage, and they presumably continued to produce for the market, which provided money to spend on legal advice necessary to take their complaint to Chancery. The resources that were based on mixed husbandry, including flocks of a hundred sheep and more, gave them standing in society and the confidence to stand up to a wealthy abbot, who incidentally lost his office when his monastery was dissolved within two years of the petition.

The smaller and weaker village of Barcheston was the subject of inquiry by the Commission of 1517, when William Willington, a wool merchant who had recently become lord of the manor, and so established himself as one of the landed gentry, seems to fit into the conventional role of the depopulating encloser. He was said to have allowed five dwellings to decay, and permitted 530 acres to be converted into pasture in 1509. Unusually for one of these inquests, the names by which the holdings were known (for example, 'Lambert's'), and the sizes of the holdings, were recorded. In all there were 10 yardlands in four holdings, showing that there had been a good deal of engrossing, leaving a shrivelled hamlet with a handful of families.[29]

Willington responded in a long petition, which claimed that of the 800 acres of land in the manor, only 160 had been cultivated at the time of the statute in 1489, and the rest of the land had been 'used in pasture and meadow'. He emphasized that he had kept the church in a good state, and had looked after the manor house, a cottage attached to it, and the houses 'parcel of the said manor'. His comments about the tenant holdings were rather obscure, and his claims to have spent money on the church and manor house seem to have been intended to deflect criticisms about the decay of the village houses. He probably did make major changes as the inquest alleged, though the 1517 Commission probably exaggerated the quantity of land that he converted to pasture.[30]

Three other small villages were apparently damaged by farmers and lords in the period 1500–17: Hidcote, Little Rollright, and Weston juxta Cherington. At Hidcote, Robert Hunkes, the farmer, was accused of enclosing 340 acres of arable in

[28] I. Gray, 'A Gloucestershire Postscript to the "Domesday of Inclosures"', *Transactions of the Bristol and Gloucestershire Archaeological Society*, 97 (1979), 79–80.

[29] *Dom. Inc.*, II, 416–17; C. Dyer, 'Villages in Crisis: Social Dislocation and Desertion, 1370–1520', in C. Dyer and R. Jones (eds), *Deserted Villages Revisited* (Hatfield, 2010), 40–2.

[30] M. W. Beresford, *The Lost Villages of England*, revised edn. (Stroud, 1998), 126–7.

1509–10 and depriving Evesham Abbey of its pasture, though the main losers would have been the three tenants of large customary holdings, totalling 242 acres that had apparently been incorporated into the demesne by 1542. Another farmer, Robert Lewsham, was said to have allowed buildings to be devastated and land to be converted to pasture at Little Rollright in 1505, amounting to three messuages and 200 acres, which had especially bad effects on the village because the lord, the abbot of Eynsham, had in 1496 been responsible for the decay of two messuages and the conversion of 100 acres. In 1509 a newly installed lord of the manor of Weston, a London grocer called Henry Kebell, allowed eight dwellings to decay and 200 acres to be converted.[31] In none of these cases do we know precisely how these radical changes to the villages and their fields were implemented, but rather than direct eviction of tenants one suspects that enclosure of the demesne and disruption of the common fields so damaged the peasant economy that the inhabitants had to leave. The inquests tend to use phrases in describing the removal of houses that they 'allowed' or 'permitted' to decay, which avoid the accusation that buildings were directly destroyed, though they make it plain that the departures of inhabitants were traumatic and unwilling – the inhabitants of Little Rollright in 1496 left 'tearfully' and were forced into idleness.

The farmers of the demesnes are sometimes seen to have played a prominent role. Lessees such as Rous, Hunkes, and Lewsham are sometimes named in the inquests, but when they are not they are likely to have been collaborating with the lord or even urging changes in the demesne. Farmers are mentioned in the Longborough dispute, and among the gentry named in the 1517 inquests some may well have been accused of offences committed by their tenants. At Weston juxta Cherington, for example, the lord, Henry Kebell, is likely to have been absent in London, and the demesne was farmed by Richard Buller, who had a strong bias towards pastoralism judging from the impressive list of livestock in his will.[32] Evesham Abbey, the lord of Hidcote, may have complained about the loss of pasture, but the monastery is likely at some stage to have been complicit in the activities of their farmer Hunkes. Willington at Barcheston was lord when the tenants had left, but previous to his purchase of the manor he had leased it, and no doubt began to make changes at that time. Some lords leased the whole manor, including the tenant holdings, which saved the lord administrative costs, but put powers into the hands of the farmer. Eynsham Abbey leased not just the manor but also the rectory of Mickleton to a single farmer in 1517, but we do not know whether this had great consequences for the inhabitants.[33] Smaller manors that were leased in this way included Alscote in Preston on Stour, Lower Lemington, Sezincote, and Tidmington in Tredington, all of which villages were deserted or severely reduced in size by Heritage's day, but we do not know whether a lease of the whole manor was regarded as appropriate because there were few tenants, or whether the farmer took

---

[31] TNA: PRO, E159/298 m.xi (Memoranda Roll); GA 3439/281 (Hockaday abstracts, survey after Dissolution); *Dom. Inc.*, I, 328, 372; II, 415–16.
[32] E. J. Rainsberry, *Through the Lych Gate* (Kineton, 1969), 46–7.
[33] H. E. Salter, *Eynsham Cartulary*, Oxford Historical Society, 51 (1908), II, 252.

over the lease of a manor with a functioning village and undermined the inhabitants and their farming methods.[34] A clue is sometimes given in the lease that a change has already taken place, such as the requirement at Alscote in 1534 that the people of the nearby village of Loxley should be able to use their customary road to the mill at Preston on Stour, which suggests that some dramatic changes had been made to the landscape of Alscote that threatened to put hedges and fences across public roads.[35]

The partnership between lords and farmers worked in relation to investment as well as in more general policies towards the use of land. The formal written indenture often made the tenant responsible for the upkeep of buildings and fences, but lords would be committed to provide materials such as timber, and in practice, if the farmer applied for help, the lord might pay for repairs. We have seen that together, sometimes with the lord in the lead, sometimes on the initiative of the farmer, they could in a minority of manors in our district make radical changes that increased the productive capacity of the land, and generated more profit for both those paying the leasehold rents and those receiving them.

Lords were able to innovate in their agriculture, but they often did so with the help of their farmers. They met with obstacles from their own tenants as well as from the king's courts and the enclosure commission. Many lords were content to maintain well-established routines of traditional lordship, though they were adept at ensuring that they obtained the rent money on time, and prevented the accumulation of arrears.

PEASANTRY

Peasants are often represented as lacking power and being inherently conservative. They were attached to their customs, and adapted to changes rather than initiating them. This misrepresents them, and we will see that they made differences to their own way of life, but also to society as a whole. Our starting point must be the demonstration in Heritage's account book that they were playing an important role in wool production, and probably marketing at least as much wool as the large-scale sheepmasters. It was already known that most of the wool exports at their peak in the first decade of the fourteenth century came from peasant sheep, so that this is just confirming that the balance between small and large producers continued. Peasant sheep flocks, however, increased in size between 1300 and 1500. The fallible tax assessments of the early fourteenth century, making allowance for under-counting, suggest that the median peasant flock in the Midlands was no larger than thirty animals. Among Heritage's suppliers of wool the median for an individual grower was just under 5 tods, or fleeces from about seventy-five

---

[34] GA, P329/1; J. Caley and J. Hunter (eds), *Valor Ecclesiasticus temp. Henry VIII auctoritate regia institutus*, Record Commission, 1810–34, II, 203 (for Sezincote); TNA: PRO, SC6 Henry VIII/4047 (Tidmington).

[35] GA, P329/1 (Tewkesbury Abbey post-Dissolution account).

sheep, so a much reduced number of peasants were keeping many more sheep per head. In the following discussion of peasant agriculture we will consider seven ways in which they were adapting and innovating. This capacity to keep a greater number of sheep represents just one dimension of the growth in the size of peasant holdings, which must be the first of the changes on which we should focus here. Before the Black Death tenants with a yardland formed a privileged minority. In Heritage's period more than 40 per cent of the tenants in rentals and court rolls were living on 2 and 3 yardlands (see Table 3.1), and it was these tenants who contributed much of the wool bought by the brogger (see Tables 5.5 and 5.6). The rise in the size of holdings was a long-term process, but was it still continuing in the period 1495–1520? Wills (mostly made by the wealthy) show that fathers were concerned to leave something for each child, but they avoided fragmenting land excessively by bequeathing houses, goods, money, or small parcels of land to younger sons and daughters. They could observe the old practice of leaving property that they had acquired in their own lifetime to the lesser heirs and heiresses, in order to preserve the main inheritance. Succession to customary holdings in the manorial court rolls shows that on death multiple holdings of 2 or 3 yardlands, or 1 yardland and a cottage, tended to be inherited intact by the next generation. This does not take account of transfers, often by reversion, of holdings to younger sons during the tenant's lifetime, but the central thread of the land market and inheritance is that accumulations of land tended to be kept together. In other words there was no great change in the distribution of land, and if a trend can be detected it favoured a modest increase in the size of holdings. Individuals can be seen collecting large amounts of land, like John Heritage's well-heeled son-in-law Richard Fretherne. He acquired a yardland at Adlestrop in 1516, and the reversion of two others, and in the same year he gained the prospect of succeeding his father in a messuage and two closes when he became a joint-tenant with his father.[36] At Quinton there were four holdings in excess of 60 acres in 1480, and seven in 1517–18; in addition the second rental omitted the parcels of demesne that since 1490 raised the size of holdings of the wealthiest tenants above 100 acres each.[37] Some of the reports to the enclosure commissions throughout the country of houses falling into decay and of families leaving the land are recording a process by which ambitious tenants were attaching holdings to their existing acreage in the period 1489–1517. All of this reflects the official record of landholding maintained by lords' officials. The procedures of the manor court allowed various manipulations of the inheritance custom and the land market, such as the granting of reversions already noted. The most mysterious of these devices was subletting, which appears to have been prevalent when a vigilant lord such as Worcester Cathedral Priory insisted that licences be obtained, but this rarely led to the naming of the subtenant. The presence of a subtenancy can be deduced from the inability of the tenant to live on or near the holding, such as John Fretherne of Worcester who cannot have occupied the yardland that he held at Coldicote in Moreton, and no one else could have

---

[36] TNA: PRO, SC2 175/77, 78 (court rolls).
[37] Magdalen College, Oxford, 35/13; 35/7.

lived there as it was provided with two tofts rather than a messuage.[38] Some sublets could have been to provide smallholders with cottages, as the whole district seems to have been chronically short of wage labour, but others, like the Coldicote yardland, no doubt added yet more acres to the holding of some relatively wealthy tenant.[39]

The various shifts in the size of holdings was not a 'natural' consequence of the level of population or the state of the market. Social trends were the results of deliberate decisions made by large numbers of people who thought alike in pursuing inheritance strategies and taking advantage of opportunities to acquire land, both in the official land market and the hidden transfers of land through subtenancy.

The second characteristic of peasant society was the tendency for people to move. We have already seen that migration was a feature of rural society throughout the fifteenth century, which continued into Heritage's time. For contemporary observers this tendency was socially dangerous, because they associated it with vagabondage, unemployment, and a culture of begging. The enclosure commissions sometimes reported that the people who left a village were reduced to idleness because they had lost their agricultural livelihood. Historians used to see migration as a sign of rural poverty, and assumed that those who moved contributed to the growth of towns. Towns did not grow very much at this time, however, and most of those who departed were exercising a choice to find a new living in a village that offered them better conditions. Initially young people obtained work as servants; they also found marriage partners in nearby villages, or sometimes took over a vacant holding. A negative dimension of migration is apparent in villages where emigrants outnumbered the newcomers, and this unequal flow of people rather than the damage inflicted by lords and farmers often lay behind the desertion of villages. At Brookend in Chastleton, for example, there is no evidence that the lord of the manor, Eynsham Abbey, did anything to harm the village. With sixteen tenants before the Black Death, it survived that catastrophe with thirteen tenants in 1363, but for much of the fifteenth century it was reduced to only four tenanted holdings.[40]

Two of these holdings changed hands regularly, with five different families holding each of them in the last forty years before 1499. One holding was continuously in the hands of the difficult James family who persistently quarrelled with their neighbours and seem not to have prospered, though their problems in paying rent and repairing buildings may have been caused by their refusal to accept authority or observe social conventions. Agnes James was especially prone to anti-social behaviour and lashed her neighbours with her tongue. The other holding, containing near to half of the land in the village, 8½ yardlands or 272 acres, was managed successfully by the Bartons, of whom Peter Barton has featured

---

[38] WAM, 8365.

[39] On the practice of adding cottages to holdings so that they could be rented to labourers, H. S. A. Fox, 'Servants, Cottagers and Tied Cottages during the Later Middle Ages: Towards a Regional Dimension', *Rural History*, 6 (1995), 125–54.

[40] Dyer, 'Villages in Crisis', 38–40.

among those selling wool to John Heritage, and thereby revealing that he had 450 sheep (p. 159). The problems of Brookend are epitomized by Thomas Harvey who took a 2-yardland holding in April 1490, and surrendered it in 1491.[41] He went rapidly perhaps because he experienced the village's problems and could not cope with them. Its territory was invaded by livestock from Moreton in the west (Heritage's father-in-law, Richard Palmer, was a trespasser on a large scale), and there were encroachments from the south from Chastleton. Difficulties within the village prevented a tenant like Harvey from cultivating land when so much of the open field was occupied by the sheep belonging to the Barton family, and there was the lack of labour within the village, which meant that workers would have to be hired from Little Compton or Moreton. Harvey would also face verbal abuse from Agnes James.

Brookend's problems were rather extreme, but other villages were losing inhabitants because they had little to offer their inhabitants. Some of them resembled Brookend because they were quite small, with twenty households or less, and were in out-of-the-way places with few facilities – they often had a small chapel, but were not distinguished from their neighbours in any other way. Tenants can be shown migrating from Lark Stoke and Barcheston, both of which were eventually abandoned. At Barcheston, the families who had been living there in 1487, Coly, Gilbert, Glover, Gryme, Harrys, Ingyll, Jones, Pye, and Turche, had all gone by 1503. In that year Thomas Castell, Thomas Gardener, and Thomas Lambard, who seem to have been the three remaining tenants, had all arrived since 1487, and all were to go by 1509.[42] A rather transient tenant population is also found in weak villages that managed to survive, such as Quinton. The positive point is surely the success of the more attractive villages in retaining their populations. No village actually grew in size in Moreton's hinterland, but some remained quite large communities and clearly offered benefits to their inhabitants, or to newcomers seeking a relatively rewarding place in which to live: they included Bourton on the Hill, Broadwell, and Longborough (see Table 5.1). They were sited on or very near to main roads, with varied populations of wealthy people and cottagers; each had at least one manor house, a parish church, alehouses, and retail traders. They all had their problems, but seemed to manage their fields and farming.

Peasants did not have complete freedom to move from village to village, but the decision to move was normally made by the individual within some constraints. Restrictions on the movement of serfs had virtually disappeared, and families could attempt to influence young people but not control them. If they applied to take over a vacant holding of land, their new lord could in theory refuse them if he felt that they were inadequate in some way, such as being 'badly governed', but candidates were not very plentiful so lords had little choice.

The assertion of tenant rights is the third active contribution that peasants could make to changing rural society in our period. The interests of lords and tenants inevitably differed, and that conflict found a variety of expressions.

---

[41] British Library, Harleian Roll B13 (court roll).
[42] WCRO, CR580/7, 8 (court roll).

The people of Barcheston expressed hostility towards their lord, William Durant and his family, in unusually forceful ways. In 1503 a servant of the demesne farmer assaulted Agnes Durant, William's daughter, and in a separate incident his sons, Henry and Nicholas, were attacked in the fields of Barcheston by two servants from nearby Shipston on Stour. Going back to 1473, the Durant family, including the lord himself, had been assaulted and verbally insulted on a number of occasions, which resulted in surprisingly weak responses from the lord's own manorial court, in the form of amercements (fines) that could be as low as a shilling or two.[43] The reasons for the strong antagonism and its violent expression may lie in the low status of the Durants, who were very minor gentry, scarcely qualifying for public office, who received a low income and became seriously indebted. Their family quarrels, such as the dispute between William and his son Henry, must have been known in the village. Henry reveals in a candid account of his dealings with his father that in the 1490s William entered into a contract with the farmer of nearby Chelmscote to provide grazing for four hundred sheep at Barcheston, and that he was negotiating for another grazier, either John Bradwey or Robert Hunkes, to become lessees of the demesne.[44] The tenants, with good cause, may have feared for the consequences of bringing these notorious figures into their village. In the event William Willington (another profit-seeking outsider) took on the lease, and the agreement included a statement that Durant would not intervene in the manor court, suggesting that he had a reputation for difficult behaviour. In short, Durant did not inspire respect and the villagers treated him forcefully and with little concern for the conventions of the social hierarchy. This series of episodes at Barcheston may have been the result of peculiar and special circumstances, but it has more general implications because in the light of the Barcheston experience it would be difficult to argue for a universal and automatic deferential regard among the lower orders of society for the aristocracy.

The people of Shipston, adjoining Barcheston, would have no cause to admire their lords, Worcester Cathedral Priory, because their long memory would have preserved the tradition from the early years of the fifteenth century that a radical agitation against the Priory was answered with the imprisonment of the leading townspeople, and the abolition of any reference to the town's status as a borough – whereas almost every town in the Midlands was composed of burgage plots held by privileged burgesses, the tenants of Shipston each held 'a messuage and a curtilage'.[45]

The daily routine in most manors of villages did not involve bloodshed or restrictive oppressions of the kind experienced at Barcheston or Shipston, but a constant dialogue was taking place between lords and their subjects. Lords claimed that grain should be taken to their mill for grinding, but tenants went to the mill of another lord, to save travel, or to spend less time in a queue, or to pay a lower toll. Alternatively, hand mills were used at home, especially for

---

[43] WCRO, CR580/6, 7, 8 (court roll).   [44] WCRO, CR580/11.
[45] C. Dyer, 'Small-Town Conflict in the Later Middle Ages: Events at Shipston-on-Stour', *Urban History*, 19 (1992), 183–210.

milling malt (see p. 168). Another restriction came from lords who forbade sub-letting land without licence, but nonetheless a holding or part of a holding would be granted to a neighbour in return for rent, and the tenant and subtenant hoped that no one would notice. In pursuit of profit for the lord, his officials collected tolls at markets and fairs, which encouraged traders to make deals in their houses or inns, or claimed exemption, by invoking the custom, for example, that purchases of foodstuffs for domestic consumption should not pay toll.[46] Similarly, a lord would collect a rent that was peculiarly meaningless and gave those paying it no reciprocal benefit, so they would refuse to pay. The rent col-lector at Todenham in 1497 owed the lord a large sum of money because a col-lective annual customary rent of 6s 8d due from the village of Whatcote had not been paid for fifty-five years.[47] Often the failure to comply with the manorial rules should have been noticed by an official and reported to the manorial court or the lord, but the bailiffs, tithing men, jurors, and others were themselves ten-ants who would quietly overlook the lapses and illicit actions of their neigh-bours. William Hale, reeve of Oddington, presented his annual account that contained much potentially controversial material: for example in 1508, he said that he had received 5s 8½d for 'tak' or pannage of pigs, paid at the rate of 1d for each pig feeding in the lord's wood, but it must be doubted whether everyone with a pig had made their contribution. Hale may not have been able or willing to enforce this payment.[48]

The everyday avoidance of payments and quiet neglect of duty in themselves involved no declarations of principle or major confrontations, but gradually eroded the power and income of lords. These actions had often been discussed by the peasants in advance, and were sometimes informed by the belief that lords were not entitled to levy certain dues. Evidence that principles lay behind these actions comes from occasional disputes, such as the minor revolt at Sutton under Brailes in 1509, when the village collectively was amerced 6s 8d for 'contradict-ing copies at this court'.[49] As the next entry in the court roll recorded that the bailiff had been ordered by the court to seize three messuages and 2 yardlands which had formerly been held by William Eddon, the villagers must have felt that there was some doubts about a copy of court roll relating to this land. The controversy was probably provoked by a reversion of land arranged by the prom-inent Eddon family, which had been agreed some years before, and was being implemented in 1509.

In former times the manor court was the last resort for customary tenants who had some grievance, and as the court was the lord's, with the lord's steward acting as judge, tenants would be unlikely to prevail if the lord's interest was in question. In Heritage's day, however, courts of equity, Chancery and Requests, could be

---

[46] J. Masschaele, *Peasants, Merchants and Markets: Inland Trade in Medieval England, 1150–1350* (New York, 1997), 67. On the general issue of lord-tenant relationships, P. R. Schofield, *Peasant and Community in Medieval England, 1200–1500* (Basingstoke, 2003), 159–69, and on the importance of small-scale acts of resistance in a wider context, J. C. Scott, *The Weapons of the Weak: Everyday Forms of Peasant Resistance* (New Haven, CT, 1985).
[47] GA, D1099/M30/64.   [48] GA, D621/M8.   [49] WAM, 8364.

petitioned, and we have seen that Chancery received the complaint of the Longborough tenants about their exclusion from part of the open field, though we do not know with what result. They were able, no doubt encouraged by their lawyers, to use extravagant language in which the abbot of Hailes could be accused of cruelty, pursuit of lucre, and aiming at the ultimate removal of the tenants. Behind the document lay a great deal of organization and expense, as the tenants would have raised money to pay their lawyers, and have spent many hours in meetings deciding on their tactics and the precise terms of their petition.[50] Such collective efforts, also evident in the Sutton dispute and the refusal of the Whatcote rent, show that the village community was still a potent force in peasant society, and lords had to take note of the strong resistance that they could provoke if they asserted their authority carelessly.

The fourth way in which peasants were altering their circumstances was by changing their use of fields. As most of their land lay under common management, they needed to engage the cooperation of the community, or be prepared to resist the opposition of their neighbours.

In the same fashion as everyone else, the peasants aimed to adjust the balance between arable and pasture, but this was difficult for them as they were committed to cultivating strips in fields originally designed to grow the maximum quantity of grain. Two hundred years before Heritage's day the arable land stretched from one edge of a parish to the other. Corn was being grown on hill slopes and near streams, and some village territories were so extensively ploughed that very little permanent pasture or meadow was left.[51] The village community had played a part in the expansion of the common arable, and the agreement of the same body was required to reverse the process. An important device for achieving this result was to introduce leys into the common fields, as happened at Quinton by 1517, when part of the cornfield on Meon Hill had been put down to leys.[52] The leys were groups of former arable strips on which grass had grown, either for a period of years or semi-permanently. This had been done comprehensively at Little Compton by 1540, where 16 per cent of the arable was described as uncultivated, but the amount of land converted to pasture may have been greater than this because 295 acres, described as 'on the hill', are likely also to have been under grass (Table 6.1).

Table 6.1. Tenant land at Little Compton, 1540.

Types of land	Pasture	Arable	Uncultivated Arable	Meadow
Acres	18	803.75	132	29

Source: GA, P329/1.

[50] On peasants' use of lawyers at this period, M. Tompkins, '"Let's Kill All the Lawyers": Did Fifteenth-Century Peasants Employ Lawyers When they Conveyed Customary Land?', in L. Clark (ed.), *The Fifteenth Century*, 6 (2006), 73–87.

[51] This is based on field observation and work on aerial photographs.

[52] Magdalen College, Oxford, ECB4 (court roll).

Communities changed the rotation of crops in the arable fields in order to use the reduced area under cultivation more intensively, and to gain more fodder crops. In earlier centuries the two-field system provided that a half of the land was planted each year, and the other half was fallowed. This gave the livestock an opportunity to feed on a large area, allowed the land to rest, and the soil acquired manure, in preparation for the following year's crops. The two fields were now divided into four quarters, of which only one was fallowed each year. This had emerged at Quinton by 1495, and was recorded at a number of Oxfordshire villages, Churchill, Cornwell, and Kingham in later centuries, with no known date for its introduction.[53] The moment of the beginning of the new arrangements was described at Adlestrop in 1498. The village had evidently experimented before that date with a system (found elsewhere in our region, at Chipping Norton and Temple Guiting) by which part of the two fields was designated as the 'hitching' and cultivated every year. Now in 1498 the hitching was abandoned and put together with most of the two fields into four divisions, which were to be rotated in the order of wheat, fallow, barley, and pulse (peas and beans).[54] A complication, which was partly made necessary by the problem of feeding sheep in the early summer, was to keep a field outside the new arrangements at Ferndich hedge, which would be cultivated on a two-course rotation, and the part of that field left fallow would be reserved for the farmer's sheep between May and August. This new field system is known to have been implemented, because when the demesne was leased in 1511 the farmer was allowed as seed corn roughly equal amounts of wheat, drage (a barley-oats mixture), and fodder corn (oats and pulse). The great advantage of the new four-field system lay in the large acreage of peas and beans, which could be fed to sheep. A lowland township without much permanent pasture could produce more effectively both corn and wool.

An Adlestrop tenant with 2 yardlands, Elizabeth Haklyn, was able to sell to Heritage in 1504 the fleeces of sixty-six sheep, which had doubtless in the winter received supplementary feed of the peas and beans grown under the new system.[55] Such supplies of fodder for sheep were especially important because of the limited amount of hay from meadows. At Adlestrop 2 cotlands were added to the village meadow in the early sixteenth century, but usually the area of meadow was finite, as it was limited by nature to the land lying alongside rivers and streams.[56] The introduction of water meadows is now acknowledged to have been a feature of late medieval agriculture, based on the catchwork system by which channels were dug to irrigate the meadow in the winter, to stimulate the early growth of grass in the spring. A small area of meadow was treated in this way further down the valley of the Evenlode in the vicinity of Bruern Abbey, where 2 acres of 'water mede' were valued in 1535 at 20*d* per

[53] Magdalen College, Oxford, 75/14, which refers to the tenants having common pasture after the harvest in every fourth year; H. L. Gray, *English Field Systems* (Harvard, MA, 1915), 126–7, 136, 493.
[54] TNA: PRO, SC2 175/77 (court roll).   [55] AB, fo.16v.
[56] TNA: PRO, SC2 175/77 (court roll).

acre – a high figure.[57] In the Heritage country channels dug across meadows, such as a striking example at Compton Scorpion (see Fig. 5.1), probably formed part of such a system of 'floated' meadows, but the evidence is not precisely datable, and the work may have been carried out after the villagers had departed.

What were the consequences of the changes in rotation for arable productivity? The adoption of hitchings concentrated production on a smaller area, whereas the four-course rotation meant that three-quarters of the land designated for cultivation was ploughed and planted each year, but as at Adlestrop the area under cultivation did not cover the whole area previously managed in two fields. One of the four quarters was planted with peas and beans, which should have fixed nitrogen in the soil and benefited the grain sown on the same land in the following year. Yields per acre cannot be assumed to have increased generally, however, as the shortage of labour would have made extra ploughing, weeding, and the careful application of manure difficult to accomplish.

A more individualistic approach to changing the use of land was to enclose at least small parcels of the open field. At Little Compton each holding included a close containing an acre or so near the village, probably at the backs of the houses, and at both Adlestrop and Maugersbury tenants were told to keep in repair the hedges round their closes, though some of the Maugersbury ones were walled.[58] Modern maps that reflect the earlier layout of villages, such as those for Broadway in 1771 and Long Compton in 1812, depict small enclosures attached to house plots, or occupying the ground between house plots. At Broadway the rectangular crofts behind the houses on the south side of the main street are presumably those mentioned in conveyances that describe holdings as containing both yardlands and crofts.[59] This land was kept under grass, and it accommodated animals in the colder months that at other times would graze on the common pastures, following the rule that tenants should put no more livestock on the common than they could keep on their own holdings in the winter.

The extent to which arable was converted to grazing land in general, which included fields managed by villages rather than by lords, lessees, and specialist graziers, is shown by the estimates of land use made in inquisitions post-mortem and feet of fine (Table 6.2a). These documents were compiled by local people as required by the institutions of the central government, to indicate the nature of the land being inherited after the death of a tenant in chief, or being conveyed between free tenants. They supplied round figures, but not fanciful or incredible ones. Their chief deficiency is that they exclude common pasture, as access to grazing could not be expressed as an acreage, and therefore the quantity of pasture was underestimated. They show that grain cultivation retained its importance in the lowlands, where arable accounted for 49 per cent of the recorded land, though pasture was

---

[57] Caley and Hunter (eds), *Valor Ecclesiasticus*, II, 203; on the general picture of late medieval 'floated' meadows, H. Cook, K. Stearne, and T. Williamson, 'The Origins of Water Meadows in England', *Ag. HR*, 51 (2003), 155–62.
[58] GA, P329/1 (Tewkesbury Abbey post-Dissolution accounts); SC2 175/77 (court roll).
[59] WRO, BA 368, ref. r 264.72; TNA: PRO SC2 210/32, 33; WCRO, Z695 (L)/1 (Long Compton map).

assessed at 41 per cent. In the uplands pasture predominated with two-thirds of the area assessed, and arable accounted for only a quarter. In both types of land meadow was restricted by the topography of narrow valleys and minor streams, and woods were unevenly distributed and small in size. Similar documents from the early fourteenth century show an overwhelming predominance of arable even on the uplands. In a sample based on the same types of sources in the period 1300–20, making no distinction between the upland and lowland, the percentage of arable recorded, 79 per cent, reflects the high levels of cultivation when demand for arable crops was at its height (Table 6.2b).

A further confirmation of the changed balance between arable and pasture comes from tithe records, which were made fifteen years after Heritage's time but are likely to reflect circumstances earlier in the sixteenth century (Table 6.3). In these mostly lowland parishes, the corn tithe was valued at about a half of the total, and the lambs, wool, calves, and other pastoral products provided between 30 per cent and 46 per cent of the total. The highest pastoral proportion came from Lower Swell, which included much land on the hills, though most of this was in the hands of big farmers rather than peasants. Tithes as historical evidence have the virtue that all types of producers were included, and peasant land cumulatively exceeded that of the larger landowners, so they provide an insight into the produce

Table 6.2a. Statistics of land use in Heritage's country from feet of fines and inquisitions post-mortem, 1493–1507.

	Arable	Meadow	Pasture	Wood	Heath/Moor	Total
Lowland						
Total	2,340	362	1,970	30	100	4,802
%	49	8	41	1	2	100
Upland						
Total	1,400	276	3,530	90		5,296
%	26	5	67	2	0	100

Table 6.2b. Statistics of land use in Heritage's country, both lowland and upland, from feet of fines and inquisitions post-mortem, 1300–1320.

	Arable	Meadow	Pasture	Wood	Heath/Moor	Total
Total	1,645	171	228	50	0	2094
%	79	8	11	2	0	100

Sources: 1493–1507: *Calendar of Inquisitions Post Mortem, Henry VII*, 3 vols. (London, 1898–1955); L. Drucker (ed.), *Warwickshire Feet of Fines*, 3, *1345–1509*, Dugdale Society, 18 (1943); C. R. Elrington (ed.), *Abstract of Feet of Fines Relating to Gloucestershire, 1360–1508*, forthcoming; 1300–20: E. A. Fry (ed.), *Abstracts of the Inquisitiones Post Mortem for Gloucestershire, 1302–1358*, British Record Society, 40 (1910); J. W. Willis Bund (ed.), *The Inquisitions Post Mortem for the County of Worcester*, part 2, Worcestershire Historical Society (1909); C. R. Elrington (ed.), *Abstract of the Feet of Fines Relating to Gloucestershire 1300–1359*, Gloucestershire Record Series, 20 (2006); F. T. S. Houghton, E. Stokes, and L. Drucker (eds), *Warwickshire Feet of Fines*, 2, *1284–1345*, Dugdale Society, 15 (1939).

Table 6.3. Tithe payments of 1535 from parishes in the vicinity of Moreton in Marsh.

Parish	Corn	Hay	Lambs	Wool	Other livestock	Other	Total
Broadwell	£15 6s 6d	£24s 10d	£2 13s 8d	£4 4s	£1 7s 4d	£1 16s 8d*	£27 13s
%	55	8	10	15	5	7	100
Broadway	£19 16s 0d	...	£1 6s 8d	£6 0s		£5 18s 4d	£33 1s
%	60	...	4	18		18	100
Sutton under Brailes	£4 13s 8d	17s 4d	13s 4d	£1 16s 6d	£1 6s*	£1 1s 7¼d	£10 8s 5d
%	45	8	6	18	13	10	100
Lower Swell	£1 13s 4d	13s 4d	17s 0d	£2. 8s 0d	9s 9d	11s 6d	£6 12s 11d
%	25	10	13	36	7	9	100
Upper Swell	£2 15s 4d	6s 8d	9s 1d	£1 16s	6s 10d	7s 3d	£6 1s 2d
%	46	5	7	30	6	6	100

*includes flax and hemp
Source: Caley and Hunter (eds.), *Valor Ecclesiasticus*, II, 436 (Broadwell and Sutton); 437 (Lower and Upper Swell); III, 259, 261 (Broadway).

of the small units of landholding.[60] Tithes reflect production, not profit, and while much of the grain was consumed in the household or on the farm, most of the pastoral products were sold. It is useful to see that Heritage's principal commodity of wool represented between 15 per cent and 36 per cent by value of the total produce of agriculture in the district in which he conducted his business.

The importance of cultivation should not, however, be overlooked. The reduction in the area under the plough still left grain and pulses as very important outputs from the land. Large quantities of grain were being harvested, in spite of all of the changes of the late fourteenth and fifteenth centuries. One of Heritage's many sidelines was to farm the tithe of the barley crop from the small village of Dorn to the north of Moreton. In 1517, after the threshing and winnowing of the sheaves collected from the fields, he received 28 quarters of grain, worth about £3, and in another year (which his notes do not identify) the tithe amounted to 26 quarters.[61] This small village territory was therefore planting (along with wheat and legumes) about 200 acres of barley. By chance we know how much money came from the leasing of the Dorn tithes, along with others in Blockley parish, for a period of just over 140 years, from 1384 to 1526.[62] These leasehold rents tended to move slowly or even to fossilize, so they are not a sensitive barometer of the harvest, but they were connected to the real world. In the whole period the value of the tithe declined from £43 to £25. This reflected the area under crop more than changes in corn prices, which were remarkably steady. There were dramatic changes during that period in the tithe corn of Middle

[60] B. Dodds, 'Demesne and Tithe: Peasant Agriculture in the Late Middle Ages', *Ag. HR*, 56 (2008), 123–41.
[61] AB, fo.88v.   [62] Dyer, *Lords and Peasants*, 250.

and Upper Ditchford, which towards the end of the fifteenth century ceased grain production completely. As this consequence of conversion of cornfields to pasture accounted for much of the fall in the value of tithes, other villages in the parish did not reduce their cultivation drastically. The value of tithes halved in Dorn and Paxford, but those of Draycott and Northwick remained much the same. They did not change at all in Heritage's time, between 1506 and 1526. This should not surprise us, as some grain and pulse was fed to animals, but above all people, even the rich, lived on a diet containing a high proportion of bread, ale, and pottage based on cereals. Heritage himself demonstrates the point that much grain was consumed within a subsistence economy. Why, we might ask, should a grazier and merchant with a turnover of £200 per annum bother with the farm of the tithes of the barley crop in a small village? The answer was that Dorn lay a mile from Heritage's home, and that 26–28 quarters of barley per annum could be brewed into 6 gallons of ale per day, just enough for a household of six or seven people.

A fifth strategy available to the peasant community lay in the careful management of the village's resources by taking advantage of the manorial court as a forum for deciding policies and as an organization that, in spite of its dwindling authority, could still take steps to enforce the rules. An important regulation was to impose a stint, which limited the number of animals that tenants of standard holdings could keep on the common (Table 6.4). The number of sheep allowed to a yardland varied between twenty (at Moreton in Marsh) and one hundred (at Bourton on the Hill), but the numbers most often stipulated were forty and sixty. Cattle and horses were also stinted, with 'rother beasts' or cattle varying in number from three to six, and horses from three to seven. The rules discriminated against smallholders, who were usually not mentioned at all, but cottagers at Maugersbury were each allowed a cow, and at Broadway in 1503 cottagers' pigs were limited to two each, defined more closely in 1511 as two pigs or a sow. The stints were clearly devised by the tenants of larger holdings, who had the largest voice in the courts and tended to occupy such offices as jurors and affeerers (who fixed penalties). In deciding a number they were using their detailed knowledge of the village and its pastoral resources, and there must be a good explanation for the variations between villages. Moreton, for example, had a very low stint, yet John Heritage kept more than two hundred sheep on the Heath adjoining Moreton, and his father-in-law Richard Palmer in 1490 had as many as 240, but perhaps the Heath was administered by some undocumented authority with representatives of all the adjoining villages. Just as the stint varied from place to place, it could be changed over time; we know that the allowance of sheep at Maugersbury was reduced from sixty to forty in the sixteenth century, doubtless because of fears of overgrazing, and the same tendency may have been felt in other villages. The declaration of a stint was usually a reminder of the established customary limits, not a new rule, and it was aimed at a minority of selfish and acquisitive individuals like John Spyre of Maugersbury who in 1512 exceeded his entitlement by 120 sheep, and Richard Wynsmor at the same time who broke his quota by 100 animals.[63]

---

[63] *VCH Glos.*, VI, 155; TNA: PRO, SC2 175/77; on fifteenth-century by-laws, W. O. Ault, 'Village By-Laws by Common Consent', *Speculum*, 29 (1954), 378–94.

Table 6.4. Stints declared in manorial courts (numbers of animals that could be kept by a yardland), 1490–1530.

Village	Sheep	Cattle	Horses
Barcheston	40	4	–
Bourton on the Hill	100	9	–
Broadway	60	3	2
Cherington	40	3 (summer) 4 (winter)	
Little Compton	50	4	3
Churchill	24	4	
Ebrington	60	3	
Maugersbury	60	6	
Moreton in Marsh	20		
Oddington	40	4	3
Shipston on Stour	40		
Stanton	80	10	4
Stanway	40	4	3
Sutton under Brailes	60		7
Upper Swell	60		
Todenham	40	5	4

Sources: WCRO, CR580/9/31 (Barcheston); *VCH Glos.*, 6, 92, 202, 228, 245 (Oddington, Bourton on the Hill, Stanway, Moreton in Marsh); TNA: PRO, SC2 210/32 (Broadway); SC2 207/16 (Cherington); SC2 175/77 (Maugersbury, Upper Swell); GA, P239/1 (Little Compton); D3439/349 (Stanton); D1099 3/M30 (Todenham); Northamptonshire Record Office, FH 365 (Churchill); Devon Record Office, Fortescue papers, 1262M/E12 (Ebrington); Worcester Cathedral Library, E94 (Shipston); WAM 8383 (Sutton).

The other customary law that was universal, and known to every villager, forbade the sale of pasture rights to outsiders. Churchill tenants were not to receive sheep for 'agistment', which meant that they were forbidden to sell to people in another village access to common grazing. At Todenham in 1514 beasts of strangers were prohibited from the common pastures. Such was the strength of feeling against the practice at Broadway that the manor court in 1510 threatened offenders with a penalty of 40s, and ordered that the animals be impounded.[64] The by-laws required repetition because they were broken. There was clearly a connection between receiving outsiders' sheep and transhumance by which flocks were moved on to the hills in the summer, and we have seen that there was a trade in winter and summer pasture between Stanway and Temple Guiting, and among the inhabitants of different parts of Stanway (see p. 86). Those keeping sheep at Stanway had the advantage that the parish's territory straddled both high and low ground, but a peasant at Broadwell or Great Wolford could only gain access to hill grazing by

[64] Northamptonshire County Record Office, FH365 (court roll); WAM 8365 (court roll); TNA: PRO, SC2/210/33.

taking his flock to another village. The emphasis on outsiders must have meant that stints could be bought and sold within the village, so that individuals could legitimately exceed the stint of their own holding if they had come to an arrangement with a neighbour who did not keep all of the animals to which he or she was entitled. Heritage was apparently breaking the rules when he put sheep to graze at Burmington and Tidmington – he was the type of 'stranger' denounced in the by-laws.

The by-laws were concerned to maintain balance between different animals that had their own feeding habits. Sheep should not enter the beast pasture, because they grazed so closely that the cattle would be left without grass, and pigs and geese had to be controlled because they rooted (pigs), and fouled the grazing (geese). Sheep owners had to be restrained from seeking the benefit for their animals and endangering their neighbours' crops of hay and corn. They could not enter the meadows until 1 August (Lammas), and it was ordered that all animals should be kept out of the stubble of the cornfields until the harvest was completed, or until 29 September (Michaelmas).

These rules about the routine patterns of grazing were very old by Heritage's day, but their repetition in his time suggests that they were still not universally observed. A new development in the early sixteenth century seems to have been a special concern for the role of the common herdsman. The 'herd' or 'common servant' serving all of those owning animals in the village was not new, and the duty of everyone with livestock to pay him in food and cash was so well established a routine that in the fourteenth and much of the fifteenth century there was no need to spell out the obvious in by-laws. In the early sixteenth century, however, reminders to pay the herd, and to put animals in his care, suggests a problem more profound than mere forgetfulness. Some difficulty may have arisen because tenants with large numbers of animals preferred to employ their own herd, no doubt believing that their livestock would receive better care. A sense of a clash between the values of the community and the interests of the individual can be read in the Cherington by-law of 1518, which says that tenants' cattle ought to be kept 'before the common keeper', 'unless it is on their own soil'.[65] A new development in the employment of the common herd was the collective effort to provide him with a house. In 1518 all of the tenants of Churchill were ordered to repair the holding in which the common herd lived, and at Broadwell in 1538 the lord of the manor, Evesham Abbey, granted to all the tenants a parcel of land on the lord's waste 24 feet by 13 feet (7 by 4 m) with the intention that they would rebuild a house for the common servant, for which they would pay a collective rent of 4*d* per annum for thirty years.[66] In both cases problems are exposed because the building was in disrepair, but those are the special circumstances in which the existence of such a building would be revealed – as commonplace parts of the village scene, if they were well maintained they escaped mention in the written sources. The significance of these

[65] TNA: PRO, SC2/207/16 (court roll); other examples of these provisions are to be found in W. O. Ault, *Open-Field Farming in Medieval England* (London, 1972), 143.
[66] Northamptonshire Record Office, FH363 (court roll); TNA: PRO SC2/175/21 (court roll).

dwellings is that in order to attract a herd, the village had to offer him more than a wage and a corner of a villager's house. Perhaps herds were being recruited from an older age group than in previous generations, and the job was becoming more onerous and responsible as the number of animals increased and their owners became more demanding.

Finally, a feature of the management of a village's resources, which incidentally fell in the first place on the common herd, was the defence of the territory from incursions from outside. Flocks and herds from neighbouring villages were allowed, sometimes encouraged in the view of the irate victims of these invasions, to cross the boundary and feed on vegetation to which they had no claim. The people of Maugersbury felt particularly beleaguered, primarily because the townspeople of Stow on the Wold, which lay to the north of their village, had rights in a common pasture more than a mile to the south, and consequently drove their animals through the fields of Maugersbury, causing damage as they did so. Other trespassers came from Oddington, Wick Rissington, Upper and Lower Slaughter, and Icomb.[67] Every village was threatened by encroachments from at least one neighbouring settlement. The best countermeasures included maintaining the merestones that marked the boundary clearly, and keeping in good order hedges and fences on the edge of the parish. Trespass within the village had once found a remedy in litigation in which the injured party sought compensatory payments and damages for the crops trampled and eaten by straying animals. With the disappearance of such legal responses to trespass, the villager whose beans or cabbages had suffered had recourse to informal action by which animals found in the wrong place were driven to the village pound, which put their owner to the trouble of reclaiming them, perhaps for a payment, though this is not recorded. At Brookend this was one of the methods that neighbours attempted to use against the antisocial Agnes James, but she broke the pound and recovered the animals.[68]

The community's management of the village's agriculture was partly a matter of defending common interests, but their conservation policy did not prevent innovations. The communities that attempted to hold the line on stints and the sale of agistment were also capable of reorganizing their fields, as happened at Adlestrop. The sixth of the developments in peasant farming concerns the quality of their husbandry, and their ability to make improvements in production. What animals did they own? The stints record official limits on livestock, but in the real world some broke the law and kept more, and others lacked the wealth or the ability to own so many. Evidence for animal ownership, though unfortunately only as a glimpse at unrepresentative samples, comes from the heriots (death duties) paid by tenants when they died or surrendered a holding, and strays that were reported to the courts to give the owner an opportunity to claim them (Table 6.5).

Sheep were, and are, notoriously prone to squeeze through hedges, which explains why they appear often as strays. They were not very valuable at 2s or less,

---

[67] TNA: PRO, SC2 175/77, 78 (court roll).
[68] British Library, Harleian roll B13 (court roll).

Table 6.5. Animals taken as heriots and proclaimed as strays, 1490–1530.

	Horses	Cattle	Sheep	Pigs	Total
Heriots	62	65	3	0	130
%	48	50	2	0	100
Strays	26	30	93	5	154
%	17	20	60	3	100

Sources: Manorial court rolls of manors of Evesham Abbey, Pershore Abbey, Westminster Abbey, Worcester bishopric, and Worcester Priory.
Note: for Broadway (Pershore) both heriots and mortuaries have been included.

so they were rarely chosen as the best beast that was taken as a heriot. Pigs were also not as valuable as cattle, and as they were often kept in sties and pens, and most households kept only one or two of them, they were not prominent among the strays. The figures support the generalization that sheep were numerous, but we depend on other sources of information, such as the constantly repeated by-laws that pigs should have rings inserted in their noses to discourage rooting, or that they should not go 'at large', to suggest that pig ownership was widespread. For Oddington, a list of pigs feeding in the lord's wood was compiled in 1529 in order to collect pannage, and this reveals some pig rearing that extended beyond supplying the peasant household with bacon. From the nineteen tenants who fed a total of fifty-nine pigs, two owned five animals, some of which were being reared for sale.[69] As would be expected, cattle and horses, which were valued at 8*s*–10*s*, were usually taken as the 'best beast' for heriot.

The striking feature of the list of heriots, combined with the stints on larger animals (see Table 6.4), is that there were almost as many horses as there were cattle. As the cattle included cows and young beef animals, this means that as draught animals horses could have been more numerous than oxen. The ownership of oxen was widespread, and they were used for ploughing and for hauling wains, which were robust vehicles suitable for heavy loads. Horses were so numerous that some may have been used for ploughing, and most haulage depended on horse-drawn carts or pack horses. The increased employment of the horse was a long-term development that in the Moreton area probably extended over centuries, but could have been continuing in Heritage's day.[70] The horses were not just more numerous, but also rising in quality, judging from their price, as in the fifteenth century they could be valued at a few shillings, but in Heritage's day horses taken as heriots were sometimes said to be worth 12*s* and 13*s* 4*d*, that is, more than a cow or an ox. Plentiful strong horses should have made a contribution to the effectiveness of peasant farming, by enabling the strips in the field to be ploughed in preparation for sowing more than once to kill weeds, and the ploughed land could be harrowed efficiently to break clods and create a good seedbed. In a rainy summer, crops could

---

[69] GA, D621/M3 (court roll).
[70] J. Langdon, *Horses, Oxen and Technological Innovation: The Use of Draught Animals in English Farming from 1066–1500* (Cambridge, 1986), 204–12.

have been carried promptly to shelter. Riding would have been commonplace, so that Heritage's suppliers could easily reach him, or travel to market towns. His business depended on the ready availability of horse-powered transport, both for himself and his merchandise, and for transporting wool to London he would have hired carting services either from specialists in the market towns or from the local peasants who, at the right time of year, would have been able to gain extra income from such commissions.

Peasants had the ability to breed animals selectively, at least in order to maintain their output of heavy and high-quality fleeces associated with the Cotswold sheep. Heritage was able to introduce peasant tithe lambs into his flock at Ditchford, which might suggest that the peasant animals were not greatly inferior in quality. They may even have been 'Cotswold lions', so named from the manes of wool growing on their heads and shoulders. The cattle owned by lords and peasants alike were described as 'red', which suggests a distinctive local or regional breed.[71]

Buildings made a contribution to the quality of husbandry. It does not matter that most of our evidence relates to barns, stables, and other structures in want of maintenance and reconstruction, as the records of the attempts by lords to pressurize their tenants into carrying out repairs informs us of the normal state of buildings, and reveals the variety of special functions that buildings were intended to perform. Buildings in poor condition were not uncommon, but their decayed state was regarded as unacceptable by the lord, and the orders to carry out repairs were often obeyed. Perhaps the tenants, while grumbling at the demands of the courts, accepted that the work was necessary, just as they would have grudgingly complied with the by-laws regulating their farming.

Agricultural buildings were mentioned in the documents more than dwellings, partly because they were more likely to be neglected, but mainly because they were relatively numerous. (Table 6.6 gives statistics from three series of court rolls, but the generalizations that follow are based on all of the records from the area.) Holdings were often provided with a cluster of buildings. At Brookend one tenant in 1499 had a dwelling, a cart-house, a barn, a sheepcote, and a shippen. Another holding at Sutton under Brailes in 1507 consisted of a dwelling house, barn, stable, sheepcote, and dovecot.[72] Almost every holding was equipped with a barn, which served primarily as a store for crops in sheaf and hay, but had other general uses. The most frequently named housing for animals were sheepcotes, followed closely by stables and byres. Pigsties were not often mentioned, perhaps because they were not substantial enough for their repair to be required. Some buildings were constructed in line, such as 'a barn and stable under one roof', but such a description

---

[71] The 'Lions of Cotswold' were ironically mentioned in proverbial phrases, as in 'Ye are wont to be as bold as it were a lyon of cottyswold', of *c.*1500; B. J. Whiting and H. W. Whiting, *Proverbs, Sentences and Proverbial Phrases from English Writings Mainly Before 1500* (Cambridge, MA, 1968), L331. This resemblance to lions did not mean that Cotswold sheep were very large, as bone evidence indicates a relatively small breed in the region. Somerset and Gloucestershire cattle were red in colour in the sixteenth and seventeenth centuries: J. Thirsk, 'Farming Techniques', in J. Thirsk (ed.), *The Agrarian History of England and Wales, IV, 1500–1640* (Cambridge, 1967), 186.

[72] British Library, Harleian rolls B14; WAM 8362 (court rolls).

Table 6.6. Buildings subjected to orders for repair, 1497–1525.

	Hall	Chamber	Kitchen/ Bakehouse	Barn/ Granary	Byre	Stable	Sheepcote	Pigsty	Dovecot	Cart house	Hay house	Total
Broadway												
	2	4	3	15	2	2	17	1	0	1	0	47
%	4	9	6	32	4	4	36	2	0	2	0	100
Evesham Abbey manors: Adlestrop, Maugersbury, Upper Swell												
	25	10	4	31	7	8	19	3	1	1	0	109
%	23	9	4	28	7	7	17	3	1	1	0	100
Kingham												
	15	4	9	19	6	6	3	1	0	0	1	64
%	23	6	14	30	9	9	5	2	0	0	2	100

Source: TNA: PRO, SC2 210/32,33; SC2 175/77,78; New College, Oxford, 3797.

shows how carefully the functions were separated, even if contained within a single structure. Repair orders give details of materials and size, showing that farm buildings, like dwellings, were founded on stone foundations, or even were constructed with walls up to the eaves. Most were timber framed, with major timbers such as 'couples' (crucks), first pieces (long horizontal timbers at the apex of the roof), and jambs (around doors). The buildings were usually thatched, though it is likely that some of them were roofed with the locally produced stone slates. Buildings with these characteristics were produced by specialist craftsmen, and costs – we have already noticed repairs, not rebuilding, priced at more than £3 – reflected the wages of the artisans and the purchase of materials, especially the timber that in most villages was not locally available in a wood to which the inhabitants had common rights.

Barns and animal houses were often of two or three bays, similar to the size of houses. A sheepcote of three bays, that is, 15 by 45 feet (5 by 15m), would be able to shelter seventy sheep, and perhaps like those built by lords had lofts for storing hay and the peas and beans which we know that peasants grew, at Adlestrop for example. So peasant sheep could be treated in a similar fashion to those on demesnes and leasows in terms of shelter and supplementary feed, though unlike some of those in larger flocks, they were less likely to experience transhumance. Heritage apparently regarded most peasant wool as of the same quality as that from the large-scale producers, because he paid the same price.

On the arable side a three-bay barn could have stored 44 quarters of wheat in sheaf (applying a formula devised for those auditing accounts in the thirteenth century).[73] A 2-yardland holding that was being managed on an orthodox two-field system with 30 acres sown would produce 44 quarters of corn of the various kinds if each sown acre yielded about 12 bushels. In Heritage's time, however, a proportion of the acreage of each yardland would have been converted to leys or some other form of temporary or permanent grass, reducing the sown acreage of each yardland to 10 acres or an even lower figure, so the barn of three bays was probably big enough to store the crops of 3 yardlands.

Our conclusion of this review of peasant farming techniques must be uncertain, as we do not have figures for yields or profits. We can appreciate that peasants were not following mindless routines, but actively managed the fields and pastures for the common good, sheltered crops and animals, and were capable of innovation, as for example in reforming field systems and extending their employment of horses.

The seventh and final part of this review of peasant activities must be to emphasize their variety, and their ability to take advantage of small-scale sources of profit. They kept poultry and geese, and a few even had a dovecot; their beehives are recorded because tithe was levied on the wax and honey, and they grew crops outside the main fields, such as flax, and garden produce. Cows were widely kept and

---

[73] On the capacity of sheepcotes, C. Dyer, 'Sheepcotes: Evidence for Medieval Sheepfarming', *Medieval Archaeology*, 39 (1995), 136–64; on barns, D. Oschinsky (ed.), *Walter of Henley and other Treatises on Estate Management and Accounting* (Oxford, 1971), 475.

butter and cheese would have been made and sold. Osiers (used for basket making) were grown in the Stour valley, and a few tenants took on the management of rabbit warrens.[74] They did not engage much in crafts, though they played a part in quarrying, and were employed as carters. Many trees grew in the hedgerows around the houses and the small crofts and closes attached to them, which must have given a village from a distance the appearance of a piece of woodland. The timber and fuel belonged to the lord of the manor, and this was not just a theoretical possession as lords would go to the trouble of valuing them, but nonetheless tenants, assertive and seeking to avoid restrictions, would fell trees and put them to their own use or sell the timber.

LABOUR

The problem of the shortage of workers has been repeated at regular intervals throughout this book. The social history of servants with particular concern for their employment by the woolman and his circle has already been discussed (pp. 41–4). The subject deserved fuller attention in the context of village society, and the long-term and short-term changes affecting the countryside.

In all villages a good proportion of households were cultivating enough land to need extra workers if sons were not available, and relatively few tenants had the smallholdings that required a supplementary income from wages. Considering the villages together, two-fifths of the tenants held 60 acres or more, and only a fifth were smallholders. Scattered through the district of Moreton were dozens of demesne farmers each anxious to recruit four, five, or six workers to cope with two or three hundred acres. The traditional sources of labour were not without problems. Family labour was not always abundant, as the number of children, though increasing, was limited. Even those fortunate enough to have two or three sons would often find that they would leave home to seek employment and independence elsewhere. Young servants could be engaged, but their supply depended on other families having children to spare.

The labour problem caused general anxiety, as is apparent from the statute of 1495, which attempted to regulate rates of pay and working hours, but in particular to combat the idleness of vagrants, and to deal with the problem of time wasted in playing games. The villagers surely shared in these sentiments, but the legislation did not help them because it was so difficult to enforce.[75]

One practical response to the problem lay in the reduction in the amount of work, which was one of the motives for transferring arable land to pasture, as one shepherd could be employed to keep a flock of sheep on land that would need hundreds of days of hard labour to plough, harrow, weed, and harvest.

[74] Caley and Hunter (eds), *Valor Ecclesiasticus*, II, 436–9; GA, P329/1 (post-Dissolution accounts for Tewkesbury Abbey).
[75] P. Cavill, 'The Problem of Labour and the Parliament of 1495', in L. Clark (ed.), *The Fifteenth Century*, 5 (2005), 143–55.

The available labour in the household could be retained if parents could keep a son at home by offering him the reversion of the holding when they died or surrendered the land. In fifteenth-century Devon it is thought that tenants with large holdings acquired cottages as part of their multiple holding in order to sublet them to labourers, with the expectation that the subtenants would be obliged to work for the tenant.[76] The clearest case of similar arrangements in our area may be the grant by Evesham Abbey, the lord of Broadwell, of three cottages to the customary tenants collectively.[77] The village already had a common herdsman or common servant who lived in a cottage built by the village community, so the work that these three cottagers would be expected to do is not clear. Perhaps they were employed by the wealthier villagers in rotation. Individual cottage holdings that may have been sublet to labourers included three held in conjunction with three messuages and a yardland by John Wollington of Todenham in 1514; and at Blackwell a cottage, cotland, three messuages, and 3 yardlands were surrendered by Thomas Mannder to his son William in 1518.[78] The new tenant in the second example received permission from the lord to sublet, but we do not know whether this was intended to be applied to the cottage or some other part of the holding. Examples are not numerous enough to suggest that tied cottages were a regular feature of the villages around Moreton in Marsh, but the arrangements may have been so informal as to be invisible in the documents. It was an accident that a complaint survives against a demesne under-farmer at Quinton in the late fifteenth century, which revealed that by an informal arrangement cottagers were allowed to cultivate parcels of the demesne (suggestive of the allotments assigned to labourers in the nineteenth century), as if this was a way of encouraging them to remain in the village.[79]

Servants seem to have provided the main solution to the problem of labour supply in Heritage's period. We have seen the anecdotal evidence for them in wills and court records, but the wills are telling us partly about domestic servants in the richest households. By a fortunate accident those collecting the 1525 instalment of the lay subsidy in some villages in north-east Gloucestershire listed 'servants' or 'servants and labourers' separately (Table 6.7). These were paying 4*d* each on wages assessed at 20*s*, whereas everyone else had their tax assessed on goods valued at 40*s* or more. In 12 villages with 172 taxpayers, 59 were described and taxed as servants, all of them male, making this type of wage earner 34 per cent of the total of inhabitants. The phrase 'servant and labourer' in tax lists of the two towns of Moreton in Marsh and Chipping Campden suggests a different pattern of employment, and a much higher proportion of wage earners appears in these towns – 54 per cent and 67 per cent respectively – which is characteristic of urban society in general. We have to presume that servants differed from labourers, because they had no household of their own, but lived with their

[76] Fox, 'Tied Cottages'.
[77] TNA: PRO, SC6 Henry VIII/4047 (post-Dissolution accounts of Evesham Abbey).
[78] WAM 8365; Worcester Cathedral Library, E95 (court rolls).
[79] Magdalen College, Oxford, Quinton 56.

Table 6.7. Servants and wage-earners recorded in 1522 and 1525.

Village (1525, Glos.)	No. of taxpayers	No. of servants	% of servants**
Admington and Lark Stoke	16	4	25
Berrington*	10	8	80
Bourton on the Hill	14	5	36
Condicote	8	3	38
Ebrington and Hidcote	26	9	35
Mickleton	29	8	28
Quinton	18	4	22
Saintbury	20	8	40
Westington*	11	2	18
Weston Subedge	20	8	40
Total	172	59	34

Town (1525, Glos.)	No. of taxpayers	'Servants and labourers'	%
Chipping Campden	75	50	67
Moreton in Marsh	28	15	54
Total	103	65	63

Village (1522, Warwicks.)	No. of taxpayers	Servants	Labourers	%
Long Compton		8	13	
	71	21		30

*rural part of Chipping Campden
Source: *B & GLS; L & P*, III, no. 3685.
**Note: or servants and labourers if figures are given for both

employers. In a rural context the 1522 military survey for Long Compton names the labourers and servants separately, showing that contemporaries could make the distinction. Eight of the fifty-nine servants in the 1525 sample had the same surnames as taxpayers assessed on goods in the same village, and one also recognizes unusual names which suggest that at least a minority of servants came from a nearby village, so these may be young people taken into the households of employers known to their parents. The number of servants and labourers must have been greater than these figures imply, as only those with relatively high earnings would be taxed, so there must have been a good number of servants who were exempt, including younger employees, and especially women, who are not formally documented. We should also allow that some of those taxed on goods worth 40s, the lowest category, would have needed to earn wages part time. These two categories would surely push the total in the twelve villages gaining all or most of their living from wage work well above eighty, which, together with all-important family members, gave the better-off peasants and farmers much of the labour that they needed.

There would still have been problems at the harvest time, and then temporary migrants would have filled the gap, though our evidence for Welsh harvest workers comes from the late fourteenth century, and Welsh lodgers caused alarm at More-ton in the early fifteenth. Judging from the names of Thomas Jones at Stow, John Williams at Blockley, and Geoffrey ap Rice at Wood Stanway, all recorded in 1525, some of these transients settled in the area.[80]

CONCLUSION

The pattern of wool sales recorded in Heritage's account book reflects the farming community in which he lived and worked. The lords still had influence, and some of them produced from their demesnes, but their presence is scarcely depicted among the woolman's purchases because they preferred to sell their products else-where. He did buy from demesne farmers, and from some of those who were mak-ing radical changes in order to specialize in pastoralism. Most of his suppliers were peasants who were active in defending their position, but also themselves intro-duced new methods of cultivation and land management.

POSTSCRIPT: SIGNS OF GROWTH

The period was one of relative material comfort for a wide range of people. A labourer at Blockley in the mid-1520s was paid 4*d* per day, as would have been the case in Heritage's period of activity between 1495 and 1520.[81] Skilled workers such as carpenters and masons received about 6*d* per day. Such wages, if they could have been obtained for most of the year, would have provided a family with a more than adequate supply of food, and with cash to spare for clothing, housing, and other necessities. Many households were in receipt of more than one wage or source of income, because of the earnings of women and children, and because many artisans had access to some land. Table 6.8 indicates the balance between types of food and drink served when manorial officials (reeves and rent collectors) attended the audit of Westminster Abbey's estate in the region, held at Bourton on the Hill in 1508. The Abbey was treating its officials generously, which meant that meals better than everyday fare were served, but it was not a feast of the kind that some estates once provided, and occasionally still provide, as 'an audit dinner'.

Table 6.8. Expenditure on food and drink (in shillings) at Bourton on the Hill, 1508.

	Bread	Ale	Dairy	Fish	Meat	Other	Total
	1.25	2.25	0.5	2.6	1.9	0.5	9.0
%	14	25	6	29	21	6	100

Sources: TNA: PRO, SC6 Henry VIII/7237.

[80] *B & GLS*, 353, 44; *WT*, 183. On the importance of servants in this period, L. Poos, *A Rural Society after the Black Death: Essex 1350–1525* (Cambridge, 1991), 183–206.
[81] WRO, BA 2636, ref.009:1, 157/92010; on prevalent rates of pay, see p. 7 above.

The food was prepared not for a single meal but for two days. Ale was plentiful, accounting for a quarter of the cost, but the most striking feature was that fish and meat accounted for half of the value of the food and drink. Such high proportions can sometimes be found in the meals given to building artisans around this time. Comparison with diets recorded before 1350, for example for another relatively privileged group of workers, those bringing in the harvest, makes us aware of a transformation in diet after the Black Death, with a drop in the proportion of cereal-based foods, especially bread, a decline in dairy produce, especially cheese, and a great growth in the proportion of fish and meat.[82] The prominence around 1500 of butchers and their shambles at Shipston and Stow, and also the presence of a butcher at Blockley to whom Heritage sold animals, and also at Bourton on the Hill and Broadway, are readily explained by this rise in demand.[83]

Having satisfied their food needs, consumers bought textiles and leather goods, and spent money on housing. When Joan Heritage drafted her will she had two white coverlets for beds, a length of tawny cloth for making gowns, a sanguine (red) kirtle, and some black silk. Some of these items, especially the silk, was probably bought by John on one of his visits to London.[84] Other will makers also owned a range of clothing, some of it made from cloth bought from drapers in the local market towns. Joan Heritage, again like many of her well-off contemporaries, owned pewter vessels. Expenditure on ordinary domestic buildings is known from documented repairs on tenant buildings, and the surviving houses built with cruck frames, such as that in Sutton under Brailes, though its precise date is not known.[85]

This was a period of many additions and refurbishments of parish churches, reflecting occasionally the wealth of rich gentry like William Greville and merchants like William Bradwey, but also demonstrating a general surplus wealth that ordinary parishioners could be persuaded to give or bequeath. Striking examples of parish churches with extensive work of this period include Bourton on the Hill with its windows, clerestory, parapets, roof, and gargoyles. There is some truth in the proposal that the church reflects the wealth of the community that it served, but this is not always the case when the church of a decayed settlement like Barcheston was funded by the lord of the manor almost to serve as a private chapel. But even in this case local wealth was being displayed.

This then was a period in the Moreton region, as in many other parts of England, in which consumers ate well and could afford to buy goods for their households. Collectively they put a great deal of wealth into churches. They paid for these things from the profits of agriculture, but was there also an industrial ingredient in the local economy? Stone quarries were scattered over the hills, and a specialist

---

[82] For a local example, harvest workers at Mickleton in 1338 were given bread (38 per cent of expenditure), ale (38 per cent), dairy produce (11 per cent), fish (7 per cent), and meat (6 per cent): BL, Harleian Roll E27.

[83] For country butchers, AB, fo.91v; WRO, BA 2636, ref.009:1, 177/92509 (hundred court roll); WAM 8346 (court roll); TNA: PRO, SC2 210/32, 33.

[84] AB, fo.87v.

[85] N. W. Alcock (ed.), *Cruck Construction: An Introduction and Catalogue*, Council for British Archaeology Research Report, 42 (1981), 157.

craft at Snowshill and Guiting prepared the stone slates that attracted buyers over many miles, but this was not a major source of employment, any more than the cutting of osiers in the valley of the river Stour.[86]

Clothmaking was the industry that could be expected to have developed in the area, but the evidence is elusive. There were major textile centres within 20 or 30 miles, at Worcester and in nearby towns to the north-west, in Coventry to the north-east, and in the south not just the very busy industry of the Stroud area, but also in Burford and Witney in west Oxfordshire.[87] Heritage was selling wool of a quality appropriate for a local industry to traders in Batsford and Preston on Stour.

There were five fulling mills near to Moreton, at Blockley, Broadway, Donnington, Shipston, and Stanway. A mill at Sutton under Brailes, which was provided with a tenter ground for stretching and drying fulled cloth, had ceased to function by the 1490s.[88] Other villages, such as those on the Stour above Shipston, seem to have been provided with more mills than was needed for grinding corn, and perhaps some of these were used for fulling. The presence of such machinery, and even of mills that were not attached to manors, is notoriously hard to find in documents. If a mill could deal with 150 cloths each year, five mills might have been processing as many as 750, but we do not know whether they were working to full capacity.[89] At Chipping Campden, William Bradwey's inventory of 1488 reveals that he owned twenty white (undyed) cloths and two others, each of about 24 yards in length, which would have been sold for about 1s 8d per yard, a relatively low price.[90] They would bring in more money if they had been through the expensive dyeing process and dyestuffs were being traded, at Shipston for example. Cloth was also being made in Chipping Norton or nearby, as two whole cloths were bequeathed by William Paxford in 1501, and Richard Smyth left a white cloth in 1503, to his brother in London, which could have been part of a regular trade with the capital and perhaps abroad.[91] Weavers were working in Heritage's country, but their numbers are not known.

This fragmentary evidence is too circumstantial to make a fully convincing story, and the case for an industry of some size would be strengthened if there was a larger potential labour force of cottagers and smallholders revealed in manorial surveys and rentals. In any case this is not strictly relevant to the question of growth in Heritage's time, as the clothmaking may have developed much earlier in the fifteenth century and was merely continuing in the 1495–1520 period.

---

[86] These Cotswold quarries were a source of slates for buildings at Stratford upon Avon. [W. J. Hardy] (ed.), *Stratford-on-Avon Corporation Records: The Guild Accounts* (Stratford upon Avon, 1880), 35. For osiers GA, P329/1 (post-Dissolution account of Tewkesbury Abbey). On the quarry of Guiting Power, GA, D3439/222 (Hockaday abstracts); also F. B. Andrews, 'The Compotus Rolls of the Monastery of Pershore', *Transactions of the Birmingham Archaeological Society*, 57 (1933), 33.

[87] E. Kerridge, *Textile Manufactures in Early Modern England* (Manchester, 1985), 14–21.

[88] WAM 26012.

[89] J. H. Munro, 'Textile Technology in the Middle Ages', in *idem*, *Textiles, Towns and Trade* (Aldershot, 1994), 19, suggests that a cloth took 9–20 hours to full.

[90] TNA: PRO, PROB 2/21.

[91] J. R. H. Weaver and A. Beardwood (eds), *Some Oxfordshire Wills*, Oxfordshire Record Society, 39 (1958), 69–70, 80–1.

Table 6.9. Profits of fairs at Blockley

Accounting Year	Profits of Fairs
1453-4	46s 8d
1456-7	53s 8d
1458-9	26s 8d
1463-4	50s 0d
1464-5	50s 0d
1467-8	53s 4d
1469-70	40s 0d
1500-1	43s 4d
1501-2	40s 8d
1502-3	40s 8d
1503-4	43s 4d
1504-5	35s 4d
1505-6	40s 6d
1506-7	39s 8d
1509-10	36s 2d
1510-11	35s 0d
1514-15	35s 0d
1516-17	30s 0d
1522-3	8s 3d
1523-4	12s 11d
1524-5	15s 4d
1525-6	16s 4d

To pursue this line of inquiry there is little evidence for either urban growth or decline. The two rural markets established in the fourteenth century at Long Compton and Guiting Power had both apparently ceased to function, which was the normal pattern throughout the country. Among the market towns, Shipston, the best documented, had very few vacant tenements, and most properties that became available were quickly taken by tenants prepared to pay sizeable fines, such as 20s for a plot with a building in 1506. The town had made a good recovery from the fire of 1478, indicated by its lively victualling trade (see pp. 209–10), tannery, and forge, and it attracted traders from towns as far afield as Gloucester, who were prepared to pay an annual rent of 5s for a shop.[92] At Moreton two burgage plots were sold for £12, and Stow seemed well established with its four inns, butchers' shops, and well-heeled merchants.[93] The fair at Blockley, for which we have a series of records of toll payments, was valued at 80s to 120s around 1300, and in the mid-fifteenth-century depression had declined to around 50s (Table 6.9). It was still yielding a respectable 40s in 1500–7, declined in the teens, and suffered a seri-

[92] C. Dyer, 'The Great Fire of Shipston-on-Stour', *Warwickshire History*, 8 (1992–3), 179–94.
[93] TNA: PRO, C1/294/67.

ous loss of business around 1520. Do the tolls accurately depict the volume of trade at this event, or do the figures partly reflect evasion and administrative slackness?

All of this suggests that the industrial, urban, and commercial economies of Heritage's country were at best modestly successful, and show some signs of decline. In the countryside there are stronger tendencies for growth. In the west Midland region beyond Heritage's country, both to the north (north-west Warwickshire) and the south (the Stroud valley), rural metal and cloth industries were flourishing. Prices of agricultural produce were low by the standards of the fourteenth century, but grain prices (assuming that they followed national trends) were rising just before 1520, and the price of wool that Heritage paid increased after 1513. Rents were not increasing, except for pastures that had been newly formed from previously cultivated land and enclosed, which could yield some very high returns. Entry fines did not increase dramatically, but were clearly moving upwards at Broadway. The fall in arrears indicates that rents were being paid on time. A modest tendency for more holdings to be inherited suggests that young people could detect a rising demand for land. Buildings were being repaired, and the number, variety, and quality of farm buildings signal investment and higher standards of husbandry. More horses were being put to work on the land. Fields were being managed in new ways, and peasants adjusted the balance between arable and pasture. The long-term importance of these changes was probably not a great increase in output and profits in the period 1495–1520 but the preparation of land and its organization, which enabled advantage to be taken of the upswing when it came after 1520.

7

Individuals and Communities

This chapter looks at John Heritage and his contemporaries in their social environment. It will be concerned with the tensions and conflicts between individuals and collective organizations in social, economic, religious, and cultural life. It will examine the nature of communities, and consider whether they had a strong influence on the individuals, even to the detriment of their economic success. This book began with an anatomy of the patriarchal family at Burton Dassett, in which John Heritage and his brothers and sisters were socialized, supported, and ruled, and this chapter will continue to examine how individuals made their way in a disciplined collective social environment.

Late medieval society was composed of associations of many kinds: households, kin groups, peer groups, communities based on towns, villages, and parishes, people residing in hamlets and neighbourhoods, guilds, fraternities, companies, work gangs, religious orders, monastic communities, inmates of hospitals and almshouses, orders of chivalry, pupils in schools: the list could be extended further, but it encompasses all ranks of society, occupations, and ages, and some could include women as well as men, or even women without men. Although people might belong to a number of these communities, some of them more formal and exclusive than others, each person also functioned as an individual or as a member of a nuclear family. It has been suggested that the strength of private property and market orientation, combined with the weakness of extended families and village government, made even the English rural cultivator of the thirteenth century individualistic.[1] A more traditional view has argued that as the economy became more commercial, and profit-seeking depended on decisions about investment, credit, and market opportunities, individualism developed in the later medieval and early modern periods.[2] The entrepreneur of this period seemed to be locked in conflict with the communitarian values of the village and the urban guild, and was offending against the moral precepts advocated by that most powerful of coordinated communities, the Church.[3]

---

[1] A. MacFarlane, *The Origins of English Individualism* (Oxford, 1978).

[2] R. H. Tawney, *The Agrarian Problem in the Sixteenth Century* (London, 1912); W. G. Hoskins, *The Age of Plunder: The England of Henry VIII 1500–1547* (London, 1976).

[3] Merchants were much criticized in sermons for avarice and other sins: D. H. Sacks, 'The Greed of Judas: Avarice, Monopoly and the Moral Economy, ca.1350–ca.1600', *Journal of Medieval and Early Modern Studies*, 28 (1998), 263–307. A moralistic tradition valued the merchant also: L. Farber, *An Anatomy of Trade in Medieval Writing: Value, Consent and Community* (Ithaca, NY, 2006).

In the early sixteenth century the problems of reconciling the interests of the individual and the wider community were being conceived anew by the writers who advocated the idea of commonwealth. Thomas More, writing his *Utopia* in 1515, put into the mouth of one of the intellectuals involved in a debate the view that he presumably shared: 'wherever you have private property, and money is the measure of all things, it is hardly possible for a commonwealth to be governed justly or happily'.[4] He was concerned to address the current problems of crime and poverty, and in particular was touched by the sufferings of the south-western rebels of 1497 and of the large numbers of criminals every year who faced execution. More had been influenced by his experiences as under-sheriff of London since 1510.[5] He conjured up a picture of an ideal state composed of large households grouped in cities, in which people lived a disciplined life under the rule of the male heads of household. They worked to a moderate extent, and lived comfortably without ostentation or waste. This of course was not a naive picture of an ideal world, but was designed to dislocate the thinking of his sophisticated readers (he told them, for example, that the Utopians made their chamber pots from gold), and its intention was partly to satirize, not just the conventional society of the early sixteenth century but also humanist attitudes towards it.[6]

Turning to his own country, Thomas More believed that the concord, justice, and equality that should be characteristic of a commonwealth were threatened by the selfish actions of the rich, who broke the rules in order to pursue their own profit. He identified specific social ills and famously referred to the sheep that ate men, because wealthy landowners enclosed fields, converted the land to pasture, and removed the inhabitants to make way for profitable flocks. A series of social problems including high prices, crime, poverty, and begging resulted from the greed of the rich.[7]

In the world as depicted by official documents it was much more difficult to identify the villains who were responsible for these attacks on communities, and to reverse their actions. Enclosers were brought before the courts after the legislation of 1489, and they were systematically pursued by Wolsey's commissions in 1517–18.[8] The commissioners and jurors came from the same landed class as those who enclosed and depopulated, which inevitably blunted the attempts to enforce the law. As they were revealed in the reports of the juries, the offences were not clear cut – often the houses that had been destroyed were said to have been 'permitted'

---

[4] G. M. Logan and R. M. Adams (eds), *Thomas More: Utopia* (Cambridge, 1989), 38.

[5] S. Rees Jones, 'Thomas More's "Utopia" and Medieval London', in R. Horrox and S. Rees Jones (eds), *Pragmatic Utopias: Ideals and Communities, 1200–1630* (Cambridge, 2001), 117–35.

[6] J. Guy, *Thomas More* (London, 2000), 84–105.

[7] Logan and Adams (eds), *Utopia*, 18–21.

[8] The earlier prosecutions are found in TNA: PRO, E159, and they can be traced in IND1/7041, 7042. The inquisitions for some counties are printed in *Dom. Inc.*, and in I. S. Leadam (ed.), 'The Inquisition of 1517: Inclosures and Evictions, part 1', *Transactions of the Royal Historical Society*, new ser., 6 (1892), 167–314; *idem* (ed.), 'The Inquisition of 1517: Inclosures and Evictions, part 2', *Transactions of the Royal Historical Society*, new ser., 7 (1893), 127–292; *idem* (ed.), 'The Inquisition of 1517: Inclosures and Evictions, part 3', *Transactions of the Royal Historical Society*, new ser., 8 (1894), 251–331; I. Gray, 'A Gloucestershire Postscript to the "Domesday of Inclosures"', *Transactions of the Bristol and Gloucestershire Archaeological Society*, 97 (1979), 75–80.

to fall into ruin, rather than being deliberately demolished. The accused had many plausible explanations for depopulation, blaming earlier generations and the general economic climate well before 1489. They claimed themselves to be acting in the interests of the commonwealth, by planting hedgerow timber in a countryside lacking in trees, and refurbishing the parish churches, many of which were not turned into sheepcotes as Thomas More had complained.[9]

The same ambiguities are found when examining the village community's by-laws, which were promulgated and enforced in the manor court. The interests of the community were represented by the influential people who devised the rules, persuaded the lord's officials to use the authority of the court to enforce them, and reported the lawbreakers to the court. As jurors and affeerers they decided whether the offenders had been truly presented, and deliberated on the amercement that they should pay. Those who failed to comply belonged to the same rank, that is, of better-off peasants, who were likely to have offended by exceeding the numbers of animals permitted by the stint, or driving their flocks on to the common pasture ahead of the time fixed by law. Sometimes the guilty men were also jurors and seem to have accepted that they should pay the amercement of a few pence, which they could well afford.[10] In many manor courts positions of responsibility were occupied by perhaps a dozen leading villagers, so the common good depended on the opinions and decisions of a relatively small number of middle-aged men endowed with above-average holdings. At the national level the commonwealth advocated by the intellectuals did not in their imagination include everyone, but was composed of the sober householders who had such a dominant role in More's *Utopia*.

JOHN HERITAGE THE INDIVIDUAL

John Heritage seems to epitomize the individualistic spirit of his age. In his mid-twenties he was compelled by his father Roger's death to take on responsibility as sole executor of his will, as his principal heir, and as farmer of land at Burton Dassett. He made his own way in the world when he changed his career and moved to Moreton, and pursued the rather isolated life as woolman and grazier, for neither of which occupations was there an association or collective group. He pursued his business by a series of bilateral agreements and contracts – with his landlord Edward Belknap when the landscape of Burton Dassett was transformed, with his

[9] E. Kerridge, 'The Returns of the Inquisitions of Depopulation', *English Historical Review*, 70 (1955), 212–28; M. W. Beresford, *Lost Villages of England* (London, 1954), 125–8; H. Thorpe, 'The Lord and the Landscape, Illustrated Through the Changing Fortunes of a Warwickshire Parish, Wormleighton', *Transactions of the Birmingham Archaeological Society*, 80 (1962), 38–77, especially 62–3; N. W. Alcock, 'Enclosure and Depopulation in Burton Dassett: A Sixteenth-Century View', *Warwickshire History*, 3 (1977), 180–4; in the mid-sixteenth century the rhetoric about private greed and the commonwealth can be shown to have a slender basis in the world revealed by administrative documents: M. Yates, 'Between Fact and Fiction: Henry Brinklow's *Complaynt* against Rapacious Landlords', *Ag HR*, 54 (2006), 24–44.

[10] For example, at Todenham in 1507 three of the ten offenders against a by-law relating to the grazing of sheep were members of the jury, namely Nicholas Wollington, William Mannder, and Robert Castell: WAM 8362.

many suppliers when he contracted to buy their wool, and with the London merchants when he sold the proceeds of his 'gathering'. He contracted with individual shepherds to look after his sheep, and had many dealings with neighbours such as Thomas Palmer with whom he settled affairs with a 'reckoning'. He gained his lease of Upper Ditchford accompanied by a single co-farmer, and made more informal agreements with farmers and peasants when he needed extra pasturage in such villages as Little Compton and Great Wolford. Anyone in business has to negotiate deals, but in Heritage's case he was always himself responsible for his own manoeuvres and commitments. In family matters one suspects that he was having to make a series of decisions on his own, in consultation with each sister when he negotiated their marriages, and in helping his eldest son gain a position in London. His brother Thomas doubtless gave John advice, particularly over contacts in the capital, but one has no sense of the family as closely connected by bonds of affection. He was brought up in a household dominated by a strong father, whose will reveals him to have been a disciplinarian, distrustful of his own children. John may have inherited at least a small portion of that approach, which would have equipped him with a spirit of self-reliance and a strong sense of duty. He might have applied these attitudes to his own family and household. His son's account books mention him only once – he was evidently a self-sufficient individual. When Thomas More wrote of the dominant heads of household who ruled in their own families and expected obedience and respect, he could have been thinking of people like the Heritages.

One can use the conventional argument that 'no man is an island' and point to those occasions in Heritage's life that show him associating with others, but it must be said that these collective dimensions are not easily found. The school that he attended may have been that at Warwick, which was a grammar school attached to the group of clergy who officiated in the collegiate church of St Mary. Or he may have been taught in the school at Stratford, which was one of the facilities provided by the successful fraternity of the Holy Cross that brought together the leading traders and artisans and prominent country dwellers in contact with the town. If he went further afield to school, the institution was likely to have belonged either to the Warwick or to the Stratford model, so he experienced life in a group of young people attached to an institution based on common purpose and brotherhood.[11]

Fraternities played an important part in social, religious, and business life, but one cannot know to what extent people were motivated to join because of the benefits to their immortal soul, or whether the principal attraction lay in the feasts and an opportunity to meet potential partners and customers. The answer is that in the mindset of the fraternity members the spiritual, social, and business functions were intertwined and in no way incompatible. John and Joan Heritage joined the Knowle fraternity in 1493, which probably did not commit them to frequent journeys to the guildhall and church 20 miles (32 km) from their then home at Burton Dassett. John's parents and grandparents had both been enrolled in the

---

[11] N. Orme, *English Schools in the Middle Ages* (London, 1973), 205, 317–18.

Knowle fraternity, and the family perhaps felt membership appropriate for young adults. John and Joan did not join the Stratford fraternity until 1504–5, and there is a suspicion that when they decided to enrol they were responding to a certain amount of pressure from the master of the fraternity (see pp. 211–12). They almost certainly belonged to the Moreton and Stow on the Wold fraternities, both of which were presumably essential for anyone trading in those two towns. There are hints of other fraternities or at least groups of people organized around religious objectives in the Moreton district, which may well have attracted Heritage's participation. Six people drawing up their wills in Blockley each made a bequest to the Holy Sepulchre, or the 'service of the Holy Sepulchre', suggesting a rather special liturgical event in the church, which no doubt involved processions and celebrations at Easter attended by the more substantial parishioners.[12] When Heritage moved to London he must have lived near to the guildhall of the fraternity attached to St Giles Cripplegate, and may have joined that organization.[13]

Heritage became an active participant in the government of Moreton, because he was named as one of the twelve jurors in courts held between 1507 and 1515.[14] The courts dealt with the affairs of the group of Westminster Abbey manors, that is, Moreton itself, Bourton on the Hill, Sutton under Brailes, and Todenham, for which places the jurors heard about land transfers, buildings not repaired, failures to observe the assize of ale, petty public-order offences, and other cases. John Heritage once served as one of the affeerors, who discussed with the steward conducting the court the sums of money that would be levied in amercements or threatened as penalties. He could have filled similar positions in the bishop of Worcester's court at Blockley, as his lease of Upper Ditchford made him a major tenant of that manor. Service as juror and in other court offices was a duty of leading townsmen and villagers, but it was not automatic. It was in the lord's interest that court officials should be reliable upholders of law and custom, but it also helped them to perform their role if they were respected by those who attended and whose conduct might be judged. The court business involved conflicts of interest, as Heritage was likely, along with other jurors, to be one of those breaking the rules about the use of common pastures. In 1514, when he was acting as affeeror, his son Richard was amerced 2*d* (a small sum) for making affray.[15] We have noted that his arrangements to put his sheep on commons at places such as Great Wolford were likely to be infringing the villages' rules about the encroachments by the 'beasts of strangers'.

Heritage's involvement in collective organizations extended from membership of fraternities and participation in manorial government to holding office in the parish. In his youth he would have attended church in Burton Dassett, and when

---

[12] TNA: PRO, PROB 11/10, fo.46r; PROB 11/22, fo.247v; WRO, BA 3590/I, ref.009:7, fos.30v, 46v, 104; Worcester wills no. 40.

[13] C. M. Barron, 'The Parish Fraternities of Medieval London', in C. M. Barron and C. Harper-Bill, *The Church in Pre-Reformation Society: Essays in Honour of F. R. H. Du Boulay* (Woodbridge, 1985), 13–37, especially 29.

[14] WAM 8362, 8364, 8365, 8366 (court rolls).   [15] WAM 8365.

he moved to Moreton the chapel in the town would have been his usual place of worship, though for more important services, such as funerals, he and the rest of the people of Moreton would have had to travel to the mother church of Blockley until 1512, when Moreton was granted the right to have its own cemetery. He had dealings with those who managed the benefice of Blockley, both on behalf of the vicar (who received the small tithes, including lambs) and on behalf of the rectory, which received the grain tithes (such as those for Dorn), as Heritage took on the farm of those tithes (p. 185). He was one of the three applicants for the grant of burial rights for Moreton chapel in 1512, when he must have been churchwarden along with Robert Palmer (his brother in law). He had evidently served in this office for some years as in 1508 he paid 2*s* 'to straw for the chapel', which probably refers to the strewing of the floor either with rushes or straw. When in 1509 he paid 2*s* 'to the carver', this again refers to (small-scale) work on the chapel's wooden furnishings or ornaments.[16]

The wills of his contemporaries, particularly members of the Palmer family, showed an allegiance to the Moreton chapel. In 1491 Joan Heritage's brother John Palmer made his commitment clear when he left £5 for the 'great bell' that could be hung in the new tower, and Heritage's father-in-law Richard Palmer in 1496 left money to the 'parish priest of Moreton' but also spread bequests over a number of local churches, including those of Batsford and Bourton on the Hill.[17] The obligation on both men, and the rest of the inhabitants of Moreton, to be buried in the overcrowded churchyard of Blockley, was a legacy from the days of the minster church and did not reflect the social geography and sense of belonging as it had developed by the end of the fifteenth century. The archaic arrangement was perpetuated in the interests of the Blockley clergy, who gained financial benefits from the mortuary payments of those being carried for burial from the outlying villages. John Heritage and Robert Palmer lobbied for burial rights at Moreton in 1512 because they regarded a parish church with a cemetery as necessary for the full expression of the town's identity. A comparable movement, which had its origins in the thirteenth century, won the same result for Shipston on Stour in 1516. Clearly loyalty to a parish was very much alive in Heritage's time, but the parishioners wished to modify and adapt the parish system in order to reflect the secular realities and community loyalties of particular towns, villages, and hamlets.

The lay churchwardens were key figures in coordinating the life of the parish, as it was their responsibility to maintain the material goods and fabric of the parish church, and therefore to devise methods of raising money from the congregation. They represented the interests of the parishioners and villagers to the outside world, and their fund-raising drew them into a range of other work, such as maintaining the roads and relieving poverty. In Heritage's country the loss of the churchwardens' accounts for his period does not allow us to analyse their activities, but that

---

[16] *Calendar of Entries in the Papal Registers Relating to Great Britain and Ireland, 1503–13* (Dublin, 1998), 612, no. 2244; AB, fos.34v, 40v.
[17] TNA: PRO, PROB 11/9, fos.39–40; PROB 11/11, fo.41r.

should not lead to an underrating of their importance. In any case they have left ample evidence of their contribution in the church buildings themselves (see below, pp. 213–18).

INDIVIDUAL AND COLLECTIVE RELIGIOUS PRACTICE

Much of religious life was organized on a collective basis, in the church or chapel congregation, or in the fraternity, or in acts of faith involving groups of people such as the pilgrimage to the shrine at Walsingham on which John Heritage went in 1513.[18] Our impression of a general acceptance of a common set of beliefs is reinforced when we read wills, with their conventional phrases commending the soul to God, Mary, and the holy company of heaven, the money bequeathed to the parish church for tithes forgotten, the small payment to the cathedral church, and much else. The will was bound to be a stereotyped document to some extent because it was following a well-worn formula like any other piece of writing, and the clerk who inscribed it was trained to follow the template.[19] One can pick out some individual choices when testators named the saints whose altars or lights would receive a small bequest. The draft of Joan Heritage's will that survives in the account book mentions St Catherine, St Nicholas, and St Apollonia, a selection of saints that may reflect aspects of Joan's life and personality.[20] St Nicholas was appropriate as the patron saint of merchants, and Apollonia was helpful to those suffering from toothache. Joan's father-in-law Roger Heritage had preferred to remember St John the Baptist and St James, and others who made their wills around Moreton in Heritage's day, although they shared certain favourite cults, such as those of Saints Anthony, Mary, Nicholas, and the Trinity, rarely chose exactly the same combination. These were well-known saints who were honoured throughout Christendom, but one of the attractions of St Apollonia, whose cult in England was not common, was that she was a local saint in the sense she was commemorated with a light in the church of Ilmington.[21]

The religious bequests in wills suggest that testators made individual choices in expressing their piety. These were sometimes predictable reflections of the wealth of the testator, so even among a sample of fifty-eight relatively affluent people, only twelve of them paid for a chantry priest to pray for one or more years (these included Roger Heritage and John Palmer). The same may be true of the possession of private devotional objects, but our knowledge of these depends on the accident of the survival of an inventory, so we know that William

---

[18] AB, fo.56v; on Walsingham's continued popularity, K. Farnhill, 'The Guild of the Annunciation of the Blessed Virgin Mary and the Fraternity of St Mary at Walsingham', in C. Burgess and E. Duffy (eds), *The Parish in Late Medieval England* (Donington, 2006), 129–43.

[19] N. Goose and N. Evans, 'Wills as an Historical Source', in T. Arkell, N. Evans, and N. Goose (eds), *When Death Do Us Part: Understanding and Interpreting the Probate Records of Early Modern England* (Oxford, 2000), 48.

[20] AB, fo.87v.

[21] K. Down and R. A. Cohen, 'Saint Apollonia in Warwickshire', *Warwickshire History*, 7 (1988–9), 97–9.

Bradwey of Chipping Campden owned a St John's head, a container for holy water, and a copy of the Golden Legend – presumably William Caxton's printed version. Others may have owned such artefacts, but we have no means of knowing.[22] Perhaps it was also an indication of greater wealth and status that some testators made bequests to monasteries, which were rarely mentioned in the wills of lesser people, as if these rich and powerful institutions attracted the admiration of those who stood high in the secular world. The will of the most socially elevated of the local testators, William Greville, made bequests to nine religious houses in the region, and two other testators, including Thomas Alen, the merchant of Stow, expressed their attachment to the Cistercian house of Bruern.[23]

Individual preferences that were not directly related to wealth are apparent when will makers left money for charitable purposes, in six cases giving money or clothing to paupers who attended their funerals, and others mentioning individuals such as a 'scholar' in need of patronage. One was rich enough to found an almshouse. It can rightly be said that those who did not specify in their wills that their money be used for charity may have given alms in their lifetime. Also executors may well have interpreted vague instructions about measures for the good of the will maker's soul to mean that charitable distribution was an appropriate use of funds. Individual choice expressed in the will was needed to make sure that a bequest to charity was implemented.

Occasionally an unusual form of words appears in a will that makes it stand out from the normal run of such documents. William Roche, farmer of Hinchwick in Condicote, in a short will written in 1515 left his goods to his wife and young son, but instead of the usual formula about God, Mary, and the saints he expressed his hope that 'with the grace of almighty god and his mercy' it would be possible 'to bring my soul to the joy of heaven'.[24] Perhaps the phraseology was suggested by the clerk composing the will, even by the rector of Condicote, but someone involved in the process of writing the will was breaking away from the routine of convention. A layman with a serious interest in religious matters might seek out a clergyman who could satisfy his spiritual requirements, like Thomas Wilkes of Blockley, well known to John Heritage, who regarded a clergyman from Chipping Campden, John Bonefant, as his 'ghostly father'. Bonefant's unusual religious commitment is suggested by his own will, made in anticipation of the dangers of an overseas pilgrimage, perhaps to Jerusalem.[25] Sometimes laity and clergy fell out with one another. This may explain why William Randall or Bayly of Condicote, who sold wool to Heritage and trusted him to act as his executor, asked to be buried at nearby Longborough rather than in the churchyard of his own parish. A troubled relationship between the vicar and the parishioners at Great Wolford is certainly implied by the will of the priest John Molder (known to Heritage as an

[22] TNA: PRO, PROB 2/21.
[23] TNA: PRO, PROB 11/15, fo.192r; PROB 11/17, fos.96r–97v; PROB 11/22, fo.75.
[24] TNA: PRO, PROB 11/18, fo.57.
[25] WRO, BA 3590, I, ref.008:7, fo.46v; TNA: PRO, PROB 11/19, fo.232.

agent of the demesne farmer), in which he made a bequest to the church, providing that the congregation were loving (which probably means ceased to quarrel) and if they paid the dues that they owed.[26]

Religious life was marked by a constant interaction between the individual and the community, because it is clear that the individual needed the collective structure of parish life, but participation in services and ceremonies in the church, and a strong sense of attachment to the parish church, did not prevent individuals from having their own route to salvation. We can now turn to the town and village communities to see how they contributed to the benefit of those who belonged to them, and to what extent they constrained individual initiative.

TOWN AND VILLAGE COMMUNITIES

Moreton in Marsh and its neighbouring towns were not self-governing in the way that the larger shire towns, and regional capitals such as Coventry and Bristol, were able to elect mayors, run their own finances, and hold their own courts. Although they were ruled by lords, in practice, in the small towns around Moreton the leading townspeople were recruited to serve as bailiffs, jurors, catchpolls, and other officials, and we have seen that John Heritage sat on the jury at Moreton. This allowed the wealthier and influential townspeople (the better and wiser sort, as contemporaries might describe them) to have a considerable say in such matters as the framing of by-laws.[27] Did these small towns suffer from the lack of regulation and management appropriate to their commercial economy? Were individuals affected in any important way by their town's lack of privileges and autonomy?

Lords of the towns occasionally intervened with good intentions to grow their trade, as when Evesham Abbey arranged for the fair dates at Stow to be changed by royal charter. At Shipston the lord, Worcester Priory, built a new row of shops to improve the infrastructure of the market place.[28] In both cases there was probably pressure from the townspeople for the changes to be made, as they would know best what developments might benefit the economy. Of course, we do not know whether similar proposals were made in these or other towns that did not lead to action, and if this happened we can expect that the townspeople grumbled and speculated on how prosperous they would be if they could run their own affairs.

Trade was regulated as it would be in any village, mainly by enforcing the assizes that adjusted the price of ale and the weight of the loaf of bread in line with corn prices. The resulting presentments demonstrated the scale and variety of urban victualling and retailing. At Shipston in 1519 the list of those accused of breaking the regulation included nine tipplers (ale sellers) and seven bakers.[29] The typical village

---

[26] TNA: PRO, PROB 11/14, fo.133v; PROB 11/21, fo.224v.

[27] On the general picture of government in seigneurial boroughs, S. H. Rigby and E. Ewan, 'Government, Power and Authority 1300–1540', in D. M. Palliser (ed.), *The Cambridge Urban History of Britain, I, 600–1540* (Cambridge, 2000), 291–312, especially 293–5.

[28] Worcester Cathedral Library, MS A6 (2), fo.12.

[29] Worcester Cathedral Library, E96 (court roll).

would have no more than two or three of either, and no village would be able to accuse eight butchers, as happened at Shipston, of selling 'putrid and corrupt meat', not because rural butchers sold good meat, but because a village rarely provided a living for more than a single person selling meat of any kind. The Shipston traders were not excessively specialized, as three of the bakers and a butcher sold ale, and a butcher also baked. Brewing was a craft practised by a woman, even when her husband paid the fine for the offence against the assize, which would mean that on occasion two businesses would have been run from the same household. At Moreton there were also two innkeepers who fell foul of the regulations in 1507. None of this was inherently oppressive. Any self-governing town would have enforced these rules, partly to protect consumers, but also to raise revenue. The disadvantage for the seigneurial town was that the profits of the enforcement of the assize went to the lord, not to a municipal fund. Also in a town controlled by a lord there might be restrictive regulations. At Shipston the lord continued, even in the early sixteenth century, to exercise a monopoly over baking, which meant that loaves were supposed to be taken to the common oven, and the baker there paid a rent to the lord for this profitable business. The ostler in charge of the Swan, and another innkeeper, in order to bake bread for their establishments, had to obtain licences in 1518 and 1519 from the lord to bake bread in their own ovens, under the provision of which they were forbidden from selling loaves in the town.[30]

A further disadvantage in some towns was the lack of separation in government between the urban centre and its neighbouring villages. Stow and Chipping Campden were ruled with a clear boundary separating the borough from its rural surroundings. The courts at Moreton, however, dealt with business from the town, the rural population of Old Moreton, and three nearby manors of Westminster Abbey, and Worcester Priory treated Shipston (both New Shipston, the town, and Old Shipston, the village) and rural Blackwell as a single entity. Most of the concerns expressed in the by-laws were purely rural, such as controlling the use of pasture, and very few of them were of direct relevance to the business of the town. At Shipston in the late 1490s people were ordered to remove their pigs and geese from the common street, which was an urban problem, but there were no rules about pollution caused by crafts, or the clearing of the streets for traffic, or the prevention of forestalling, which we would expect to find in towns. Instead the main concern of the Shipston court was the regulation of subtenancy, which was apparently found in both country and town. In a normal town with burgage tenure subtenancy was a healthy sign of an active property market, which encouraged the setting up of new businesses and the accommodation of workers needed in the town's industries. Instead the lord seems to have been driven by a short-sighted concern to discipline his tenants and to ensure that he knew who was responsible for the payment of rents. His insistence that subtenants should be people of good character would, however, have been supported by the townspeople who were always concerned to maintain order.

Townspeople tended towards protectionism, and sometimes expressed a wish to control access to the market by outsiders. A number of the market stalls in Shipston

---

[30] Worcester Cathedral Library, E95 (court roll).

were rented by the Priory to traders from rival towns such as Stratford and Chipping Campden, and these interlopers might not have been welcomed by a mayor and council of Shipston people, but the potential holders of these offices were not able to act on these prejudices because self-government was not allowed.

The townspeople, however, were able to take on some functions of government by developing their fraternities as property-holding organizations (most impressively in the case of the Trinity guild at Stow), which had sufficient funds to provide benefits for the inhabitants, such as building schools and employing schoolmasters. They also organized fraternity feasts and other social occasions that brought the townspeople and country traders into contact, and provided a service for settling quarrels. The almshouses accommodated the infirm or elderly, from which fraternity members often benefited, and the fraternity ensured dignified funerals, and employed chaplains to pray for the souls of departed brothers and sisters.[31] Alongside these collective efforts individual benefactors made their own contributions to the common good: the foundation of the most successful grammar school of the district, at Chipping Campden, was the work of an official of Henry VI; an almshouse at Chipping Norton was provided in 1513 in the will of John Horne, a member of the gentry; and an ostentatious project designed to foster civic pride, the clock and chime at Stow, was an initiative by Heritage's friend Thomas Davies in 1511.[32] Individual gifts were attracted by the presence of a fraternity, as that organization could maintain and develop the buildings and institutions founded by private initiative. A new foundation, such as a school, would be managed by a group of feoffees (who held the endowment of property in trust), appointed from among the town worthies.[33]

Finally, we should not forget the status gained by the elite who could hold office and show off their importance at fraternity occasions. John Salbrygge was known to Heritage, as he was also a farmer and grazier with urban connections. Originally described as a husbandman of Willicote, his career of agricultural management began as a subtenant of William Catesby's leasehold land at Willicote and at Quinton, but he also held land at Alscote in Preston on Stour. By 1496 he was serving (with others) as the agent of George Catesby in conveying landed property, so he was very closely associated with the Catesby family, both before and after their fall from grace in 1485. Having joined the Holy Cross Guild at Stratford in 1472–3, Salbrygge was elevated to be a second master in 1500, and reappears again in the same role in 1504–5 and 1507–8.[34] He seems to have been honoured by the fraternity, which was going through a difficult time, in order to recruit members in an area where he had contacts, judging from the list of names of those joining the

---

[31] G. Rosser, 'Communities of Parish and Guild in the Late Middle Ages', in S. Wright (ed.), *Parish, Church and People* (London, 1988), 29–55.

[32] N. Orme, *English Schools in the Middle Ages* (London, 1973), 203; TNA: PRO, PROB 11/22, fo.75; PROB 11/17, fos.16–17.

[33] Orme, *English Schools*, 206.

[34] TNA: PRO, E159/275 (Memoranda Roll); Magdalen College, Oxford, 35/5, 35/15, 68/12 (rental and court rolls); Oxfordshire Record Office, E24/1/1D/1 (deed, Chastleton House Collection); *Guild Reg.*, 29–30, 299, 375, 458, 460. Mairi Macdonald suggested to me his role as a recruiter.

fraternity in his years in office, from Moreton, Stow on the Wold, and surrounding villages such as Rollright, Donnington, and Cutsdean. Among the names are those of John and Joan Heritage, and a number of people who supplied Heritage with wool. One imagines Salbrygge calling on his associates and acquaintances, recommending the Holy Cross fraternity, and persuading or even pressurizing them to join. Salbrygge, though an example of a rather specialized type of office-holder because of his role as a recruiter, was characteristic of most fraternities in that leading members would be promoted to serve on the governing body for a few years, look after the endowments and finances, earn the respect of their neighbours, and eventually be elected to some office such as master.

Did the urban community, both under the authority of the lord, and sponsored by the fraternity, discourage enterprise and inhibit the activities of individual traders? Perhaps the lack of regulation was an advantage, but on the other hand traders may have suffered from uncontrolled sharp practices. There is little evidence that collective institutions either damaged or advanced the interests of traders. Small towns remained small and their inhabitants did not become immensely rich because of their limited opportunities at the lower end of the commercial hierarchy, not primarily because of their internal constitutions.

We have already seen that the village communities could hope to defend their inhabitants from potential threats from their lords and from neighbouring villages. They managed the common fields and pastures, and were capable of reorganizing them. Their regulations attempted to prevent individuals taking an excessive share of the common grazing. Here the community's contribution will be assessed, and its effects on the actions of individuals considered.

The village community is most visible in the records of the manor court, when the leading villagers are presumed to have had a say in the by-laws that the court endorsed, and their subsequent enforcement. Their content was usually agrarian, most frequently seeking to control the grazing of animals, to ensure that pigs were ringed, and to supervise the employment of the common herd. The obligation to attend the court was reinforced each year by the payment by all of the customary tenants of the common fine, which was a collective payment assessed and levied among themselves. There were many occasions when the community needed to organize itself to maintain common assets, such as the repair of roads and bridges.[35] At Churchill they took steps to prevent the pollution of the common well by the washing of clothes, and at Broadway the protection of the common stream was a major point of contention, as every year or two between 1495 and 1517 orders were issued to forbid ducks from swimming in the water, and to prohibit the dumping of brewers' and butchers' waste. As well as being forbidden to wash clothes, individuals were condemned for allowing sewage to enter the water.[36] More commonly, the court, having heard complaints of roads blocked by flooding, ordered individuals to clean their ditches. The state and lesser authorities could make villages collectively responsible for public works,

---

[35] TNA: PRO, SC2 175/77; WAM 8362 (court rolls).
[36] Northamptonshire Record Office, FH364, TNA:PRO, SC2 210/32,33 (court rolls).

which might include the repair of bridges. But the main intervention of the state required each village to go through a process of levying and collection of the lay subsidy commonly called the 'fifteenth', using a variety of locally accepted methods. Quinton, for example, had been assessed at £5 8s 11d, and had chosen to gather the tax on the basis that each household paid 4d for each of the larger animals (horses and cattle) that it owned. Such a method of assessment ensured that the main weight of taxes fell on the better-off villagers, as cottagers tended not to own large animals. In the same spirit by-laws sometimes show some concern for the welfare of the poorer inhabitants. At Broadway there had been a tradition of allowing the poor to collect peascods from the fields (in June or July when they were green), and gleaning in the cornfields was allowed, once the sheafs had been carried from the field.[37]

Every village had its own character and institutions. Some communities were closely bound together by joint tenancy, as at Oddington and Paxford, where the customary tenants together farmed the lord's demesne. Broadwell, as we have seen, built houses at common expense for wage-earners. At Adlestrop a particular importance was attached to the maintenance of the 'marsh gate', by which the village livestock gained access to the pasture in the valley of the river Evenlode. In a landscape lacking plentiful woodland, the gorse and bushes growing on common land were valued for fuel and fencing. At Adlestrop the furze was owned by individuals, and their rights were protected, while at Churchill thorns were to be taken by the local brewers (for fuel) with the bailiff's permission, which suggests that ordinary households had free access.[38]

For modern observers the striking success of the village community is represented by the still visible work in the majority of parishes on extending, rebuilding, or furnishing parish churches. The most frequent additions and improvements of the late fifteenth and early sixteenth centuries in the parishes around Moreton were to towers and the upper storeys of towers, which were providing suitable structures for hanging peals of bells. Naves were heightened to allow the insertion of clerestories, which, together with the reconstruction of windows in the nave that enlarged the glazed area, introduced more light into the whole building. The windows were also an opportunity to display the elegance of the perpendicular tracery, and to add colourful stained glass. Porches were built and fonts replaced, and moves were made to provide benches (Fig. 7.1).[39]

---

[37] WRO, BA2636, ref.009:1, 177/92509 (hundred court roll, repair of a bridge on the road between Shipston and Blockley); Magdalen College, Oxford, 35/9 (account of 1430–1); R. E. Glasscock (ed.), *The Lay Subsidy of 1334*, British Academy Records of Social and Economic History, new ser., 11 (Oxford, 1975), 94 (the original 1334 assessment was reduced in 1433 and 1446, but the record for Quinton relates to 1430–1); TNA: PRO, SC2 210/32.

[38] TNA: PRO, SC6 Henry VIII/4047 (post-Dissolution accounts of Evesham Abbey) record the Broadwell cottages; for the Adlestrop gate and furze: TNA: PRO, SC2 175/77; thorns at Churchill: Northamptonshire County Record Office, FH364 (court rolls).

[39] These generalizations are based on the architectural descriptions in Pevsner's *Buildings of England*, visits to the churches, and (when available) the *VCH*. There are forty-three churches in Heritage's country with substantial surviving structures of the period before 1540, of which the following numbers had changes made in the fifteenth and early sixteenth centuries to these features: towers (18), clerestories and windows (25), porches (6), fonts (16), and benches (6). In many churches benches were replaced in recent times, so 6 represents a high number.

Fig. 7.1. The parish church of Bourton on the Hill, from the north. The main fabric of the church dates from the twelfth century, and the tower was built in the fourteenth. The square-headed windows of the nave and clerestory, the roof, gargoyles, and porch all were built in the fifteenth century, mostly in its later decades. These extensive alterations were typical of those made to many of the parish churches in Heritage country in or near to his time (author's photograph).

Church building is sometimes assumed to have been funded by the lord of the manor, but most lords in the Moreton district were absentees with many churches on their estates. Evesham Abbey for example, which was heavily committed to a building programme on the abbey itself in the early sixteenth century, would have been very unlikely to have made more than a modest donation for work at Adlestrop or Stow, and Westminster is an improbable major benefactor for funding extensive improvements to Bourton on the Hill or Moreton in Marsh. William Greville provides a special case of a lord paying to modify a church substantially, when he added a south aisle at Todenham as a burial place for himself and his family.[40] The other explanation commonly offered for church building in the Cotswolds at this time is summed up by the phrase 'wool church'. This might be an appropriate attribution for Chipping Campden (Fig. 7.2), where woolmen are known to have made large donations

---

[40] TNA: PRO, PROB 11/17, fos.96–7.

Fig. 7.2. Chipping Campden church tower and nave of the the the late fifteenth century. The parishioners, including the Campden woolmen, supported the building programme, and looked to the parish church as one of the defining institutions of their town (photograph by Arthur Cunynghame of Loose Chippings Books).

for the fabric, notably £67 from William Bradwey in 1488, but often the gifts of those who had prospered in the wool trade were helpful but not decisive, like the Davies clock at Stow for which he donated £3. For Heritage, with his chronic short-age of cash, gifts to the church need not have been a drain on his capital. His wife's draft will does not necessarily indicate his own resources and sense of obligation, but it is worth recording that she was proposing to bequeath to three churches (Blockley, Bourton, and Moreton) a very modest total of 5s 4d. Major building projects at Thame in Oxfordshire in the fifteenth century were financed by special collections, to which dozens of parishioners contributed an average of 1s 8d each.[41]

The funds for church building, whenever we have detailed evidence, were gath-ered in relatively small contributions from the majority of the parishioners. In the absence of churchwardens' accounts from the Moreton district, some insights can be gained into the likely activities in the parishes, from the records of Badsey to the west of Moreton and Spelsbury to the east, both covering years in the 1520s and early 1530s.[42] The Badsey accounts show money coming from bequests, with small

[41] AB, fo.87v; J. Carnwarth, 'The Churchwardens' Account of Thame, Oxfordshire, c.1443–1524', in D. J. Clayton, R. G. Davies, and P. McNiven (eds), *Trade, Devotion and Governance: Papers in Late Medieval History* (Stroud, 1994), 177–97, especially 193.

[42] E. A. B. Barnard, *Churchwardens' Accounts of the Parish of Badsey with Aldington* (Hampstead, 1913), 9–22; F. W. Weaver and G. N. Clark (eds.), *Churchwardens' Account of Marston, Spelsbury, Pyrton*, Oxfordshire Record Society, 6 (1925), 35–50.

amounts from a church ale, though the most effective sources of money were the 'young men' who in 1528–9 collected 2*s* 2*d*, the 'maids' who had 'gathered' 4*s* 1*d*, and the 'little maids' who contributed 8½*d*. The females would have held dancing events and probably sold ale. Another sum arose from another community event, as 21*d* was raised as 'cock money', which probably refers to the ritual of throwing sticks at a tethered cockerel at Shrovetide.[43] At Spelsbury a church ale yielded 30*s* in one year and 50*s* in another, but a similar amount came from rents of church property and from the renting out of sheep. We know that churches often kept small flocks that had been given or bequeathed by parishioners, as Heritage would buy the wool, paying 11*s* 8*d* for the church wool of Bourton on the Hill in 1505, and 10*s* 8*d* for Lemington's wool in 1509.[44] The quantities suggest that each parish was keeping a flock of about fifteen sheep.

Churchwardens, who were anxious to bring in a good income from church ales, would also organize the building of premises where these events could be held, and 'church houses' that were substantial halls with brewhouses attached are recorded at Ebrington in 1473 and Preston on Stour in 1539–40. The building at Ebrington, or its successor, can be observed tucked into the northern edge of the churchyard, and another is depicted on a seventeenth-century map of Todenham (Fig. 7.3).[45] A building still stands on the same site, now converted into a public house and therefore continuing the ale-selling tradition. Finally, it should be noted that for all of their success in fund-raising, the churchwardens also spent money with care. They could organize work to be done by parishioners without monetary cost. At Broadway the custom recorded in 1532 for the repair of the churchyard wall assigned 6 yards to each of forty tenants.[46] Although the churchwardens made many changes to the church fabric, they often retained the existing foundations and walls, and inserted new features such as windows that created the semblance of a new building. Evidently these church officials applied to their public role experience gained from managing their private finances. John Heritage, to cite the obvious example, served as a churchwarden.

The church-renewal campaigns of our period were inspired by specific religious objectives, as the choice of furnishings and fittings suggests that the nave was being seen as the setting for sermons, to be heard by a seated congregation. The nave was made lighter and more spacious by the addition of larger and more numerous windows, especially high up in the clerestory, in a move away from the dark and mysterious atmosphere of some Romanesque churches. The churchwardens wished to draw attention to certain sacraments such as baptism by installing new fonts, and they designed churches as backdrops to occasions such as funerals, with bells

---

[43] On these female associations, and a general survey of parochial fund-raising, see K. French, *The People of the Parish: Community Life in a Late Medieval Diocese* (Philadelphia, PA, 2001), 127. Revenue raising and its wider meaning is discussed in B. Kümin, *The Shaping of a Community: The Rise and Reformation of the English Parish c.1400–1560* (Aldershot, 1996).

[44] AB, fos.20r, 40v.

[45] Devon Record Office, 1262M/Gloucestershire leases, E47; GA P329/1; GA, D1099/P2. On church houses in general, E. H. D. Williams, 'Church Houses in Somerset', *Vernacular Architecture*, 23 (1992), 15–23.

[46] Society of Antiquaries of London, Prattinton Collection, 5, 100.

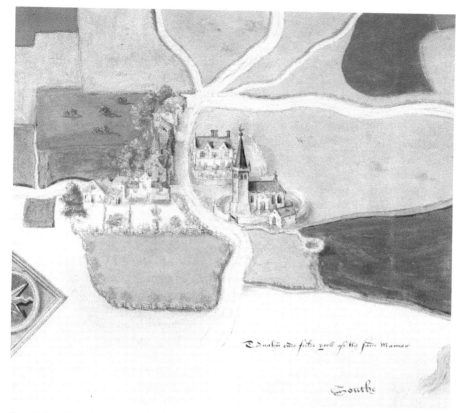

Fig. 7.3. Church house at Todenham. This striking estate map of the early seventeenth century contains a bird's-eye view of the village, church, and manor house, with the church house encroaching on the churchyard. Ale was sold at the house for church funds, organized by the churchwardens. The map's foreground illustrates an enclosure surrounded by a hedge typical of the period, with an irregular line of bushes and trees, and with gaps filled by fencing.
Source: GA, D1099/P2.

hung in high towers. Tredington church was equipped with a veil for the ritual of re-enacting the scene in the Temple in Jerusalem on the first Good Friday, and banners and streamers at Long Compton must suggest elaborate processions out of the church. Brass censers in every church imply that the atmosphere within them on occasion was heavy with incense. Just as churchwardens aimed to keep abreast of the new architectural styles, they followed developments in the liturgy. Further evidence of the scale of investment in the material goods of a church, and of the desire of churchwardens for services to be dignified and impressive, comes from the 'church goods' listed in 1552, but recording items acquired over many years, including our period. A small and remote church, Cutsdean, was provided with a chalice of silver gilt, a pyx (for communion bread), a cope, and vestments. The cope was of linen, but the vestments had been made from green silk. Larger and more opulent parishes, such as Broadway, Ilmington, Long Compton, and Tredington, had a number of chalices and pattens of silver or silver gilt, even a pyx of ivory (at Tredington), and copes and vestments of silk cloth, including velvet, satin, and damask. These textiles were expensive, and had been imported. Bells were included in the inventories; the larger churches often had four each, and the lesser churches made do with two or three. Replacing a bell at Tredington, it was estimated, would cost £5.[47] Some of these items had been given to the church by wealthy patrons, as is recorded in wills, but some had been bought or at least maintained from the income gathered by the churchwardens.

Churches also had a secular role in the community, stimulating local pride in their architecture, providing useful services such as the distribution of alms to the poor (recorded at Batsford and Bourton), and also at Bourton the bells were said to have a utilitarian function to warn of fire and flood.[48] Churches were meeting places and landmarks, and at Stow the tower that overlooked the marketplace indicated the times of trading with its chiming clock.

Historians have to remember their critical faculties when approaching the village community, as it is presented to us in the sources as a model of amity and cohesion: phrases such 'with the consent of all tenants and inhabitants' often preface the announcement of a by-law, for example. The villagers' attachment to neighbourliness, and the good intentions expressed in the by-laws, might encourage us to be nostalgic about a lost idyll. No one can resist approving of fund-raising efforts by maids and 'little maids' holding dances, and we tend to react positively when we imagine the large amounts of ale drunk (no doubt accompanied by cakes) for the same purpose. The end-product of these efforts, such as the intricate perpendicular tracery of the new windows, the accomplished wood carving of the rood screens, the stained glass, and wall paintings, all speak of the well-informed choices of the churchwardens and excellent standards of craftsmanship of the artisans employed by them. On a less high-minded aspect of community life the field at Broadway should be mentioned, which was called 'play-hey' where games, probably including football, were enjoyed. Archery combined a civic duty with a sport, and the manor court at Broadway in 1513 ordered that the targets be maintained, perhaps prompted by a recent statute.[49] All of this conjures up such positive emotions that we may be seduced into creating an unrealistic image of a misleadingly idealized world.

---

[47] A. D. Brown, *Popular Piety in Late Medieval England: The Diocese of Salisbury 1250–1550* (Oxford, 1995), 124–9; J. A. F. Thomson, *The Early Tudor Church and Society 1485–1529* (Harlow, 1993), 309–18; H. B. Walters (ed.), 'Inventories of Worcestershire Church Goods, 1552', *Transactions of the Worcestershire Archaeological Society*, 30 (1953), 62–4; 31 (1954), 32; 32 (1955), 43–4; J. Fetherston (ed.), 'Inventory of Church Goods, in the County of Warwick, temp. of Edward the Sixth', *Warwickshire Antiquarian Magazine* (1859–77), 272, 273, 275, 279.

[48] J. Caley and J. Hunter (eds), *Valor Ecclesiasticus temp. Henry VIII auctoritate regie institutus* (Record Commission, 1810–34), II, 452; J. Maclean, 'Chantry Certificates, Gloucestershire', *Transactions of the Bristol and Gloucestershire Archaeological Society*, 8 (1883–4), 297.

[49] *VCH Worcs*, IV, 38. On archery practice as civic duty, see S. Gunn, 'Archery Practice in Early Tudor England', *Past and Present*, 209 (2010), 53–81.

The village community did not always succeed. The deserted and shrunken villages such as Brookend and Barcheston (pp. 176 and 178) broke down into discordance. Disputes reached such a pitch at Sutton under Brailes in 1510 that the dominant Eddon family fell into a disagreement with the twelve jurors 'in the matter of Steven Cheryngton and Thomas Stowte', and this was only one of a number of quarrels suggesting that the Eddons were the focus of trouble and resentment.[50]

The community that we can observe was seriously biased towards the interests of the upper rank of villagers. Some villagers felt the need to discipline a lower class who might be feckless and idle, like young Walter Carpenter of Todenham, who was reproved for playing cards (that is, gambling) in 1509. The poor at Broadway could gather peascods and glean in the fields not as a right but by concession, and on condition that they did not collect stray ears until the harvested corn had been carried. The by-law was motivated by the suspicion that gleaners stole sheaves. In the same village it was ruled that cottagers could not cut furze on the common until the other tenants had taken their needs. An alternative source of fuel might have been the dead wood in hedgerows, but in 1502 the poor women of Broadway who were tempted to raid their neighbours' hedges were threatened with both a financial penalty and imprisonment.[51] The village community was essentially an association of the more substantial tenants, and even that group could not always agree among themselves. While some parishes were rebuilding their church in perpendicular style, others, notably Lower and Upper Swell, retained their Romanesque naves and did no more than add a few new windows. Chapels belonging to smaller settlements fell into disuse and ruin.[52]

Any realistic assessment of communities must conclude that they were often not able to restrain individuals who behaved selfishly and ignored the interests of their neighbours. The courts were not completely lacking in authority, as we have seen that they succeeded in pressurizing tenants to repair their buildings. That was partly because the lord's interest was directly engaged, and as the demand for land was just beginning to revive, tenants felt the pressure on them to obey orders. The rules governing the operation of the open fields were mainly of interest to the tenants, and the absence of many specific presentments of offenders suggests that by-laws were made but not rigorously enforced. The by-laws set the normal standards of behaviour, but their observance depended on informal neighbourly pressure. Occasionally we can observe individuals who were brought before the courts for flagrantly breaking the rules, of which an impressive example was Richard Strayne of Broadway, who had the largest holding recorded in the manor, containing 8 yardlands (perhaps in excess of 200 acres). He had relatives in the village, and this gave him considerable influence, as in 1506 he was serving on the jury along with two other members of the

[50] WAM 8383; 26012; 8364.

[51] WAM 8364; TNA:PRO, SC2 210/32; on the general development of social regulation, M. K. McIntosh, *Controlling Misbehavior in England, 1370–1600* (Cambridge, 1998).

[52] For example, in 1564 a deed refers to the 'piece of ground in Hidcote' (Boyce) where the 'chapel sometime stood': Devon Record Office, 1262M/Gloucestershire leases E49. A number of others have now disappeared and presumably decayed around this time: Admington, Alscote, Talton, and Lark Stoke, for example.

Strayne family. When he was innkeeper in 1501–3, another Strayne was miller. Buildings on one of his messuages burnt down, but he did not replace them because he had plenty on his other holdings. He neglected to scour his ditches, control his pigs, or answer a lawsuit about a debt. His most anti-social act, however, was to sell his pasture rights to outsiders, allowing large numbers of alien sheep to graze on the Broadway common, for which he was supposed to pay a penalty of 40*s*.[53]

The history of the village was not just a struggle between the community and wealthy and acquisitive individuals. Those who wished to change their farming system could do so to some degree within the framework of the open fields, or they were able to persuade their neighbours, as at Adlestrop, to make radical modifications. Those who wished to embark on some entirely different course, by acquiring a leasow with its enclosures and specialized pastoral economy, had to do so outside the traditional field system. Heritage characteristically followed both strategies – he found ways of intruding his sheep onto the common pasture of open field villages at Great Wolford, Cherington, and other places to the north-east of Moreton, and also enjoyed the benefits of separate leasows at Ditchford and Burton Dassett. He is representative of the individuals who were influenced by communities, but not controlled by them.

To move to another dimension of social responsibility, Heritage the wool brogger and his contemporary traders were well aware that the Church had adopted specific positions on such matters as usury and the just price that might threaten the merchants' way of life. All of our evidence indicates that the economic morality advocated by the Church did not hold back normal business activities. When Heritage bought and sold wool, the price was determined by the prevailing market, which was in line with the Church's teaching. It would have been a different matter if he had agreed with the other woolmen to buy below the prevalent purchase price, and to attempt to push up the selling price, but all of our indications are that those buying wool were competing with one another, and their suppliers changed from one to another accordingly. Heritage was guilty of the practice of buying wool before shearing, which at one time was made illegal, but others did the same and their competition prevented him from creating a monopoly. Heritage gave credit, and towards the end of his time lent money, but he would avoid problems with his own conscience and the Church courts if he charged reasonable interest rates, in practice below 10 per cent.[54]

In general Heritage's thinking remains elusive. There is, however, good reason to believe him to have conformed to the ideas of his time, and behaved according to the conventions of economic morality. A clue comes from a random item in the account book, which bears a small resemblance on occasion to the commonplace books kept by London merchants and provincial men of affairs like Richard Hill and Robert Reynes of Acle.[55] The passage occupies about half a page, and states

[53]   TNA: PRO, SC2 210/32, 33.
[54]   D. Wood, *Medieval Economic Thought* (Cambridge, 2002), 117–20, 133–44, 159–205.
[55]   Balliol College, Oxford, MS 354; C. Louis (ed.), *The Commonplace Book of Robert Reynes of Acle: An Edition of Tanner MS.407* (New York, 1980).

that: 'Thes ben seven thyngs that man desyryth ynterley whych he shall not perfectly obtayne yn thys present lyve. The first is conyng without ignorance as not knowing all thyngs', and Heritage went on to list another six sentiments: health without infirmity, life without death, joy without pain, peace without trouble, liberty without bondage, riches without poverty.[56]

This was not an original piece of literature, but was one of many similar compilations of popular philosophy that circulated orally and were periodically committed to writing. Heritage could have quoted a list of 'evils of the time' or 'abuses of the age' which might have revealed that old men were witless, young men reckless, and women shameless, or which commented on the degeneration of virtues: 'Richness into robbery, Might is turned into right', and so on.[57] Instead Heritage preferred to note down these bland statements of the obvious. One should not think of Heritage as unusually lacking in originality, but simply as one of many who derived comfort and satisfaction from conventional wisdom.

CONCLUSION

To concentrate on the debate between public and private at the national and local level, the assumption of the triumphant advance of individualism at the expense of communities is not always supported by the evidence.

Government was accepting the idea that it had a duty to support the common-wealth, and turned its attention to problems of poverty, from the legislation to control beggars before 1500 to the poor laws that were emerging later in the sixteenth century. Efforts were being made to wrestle with the problem of 'the putting down of towns'. Village and town communities expressed their disapproval of anti-social behaviour, and demonstrated (over a longer period than 1495–1520, but definitely including those years) the effectiveness of their collective efforts in the clerestories, towers, and porches that are found in a good proportion of the churches of the district. Church houses, labourers' cottages managed by the village, and remodelled field systems all point to the enterprise of the village leaders, and the same material evidence for civic pride in towns is apparent in new almshouses, clocks, and guildhalls. In many ways communities were more vigorous in this period than had been the case fifty or a hundred years earlier.

The state, the Church, urban authorities, and village communities all sought to limit the selfish excesses of those who pursued their profits too vigorously: depopulators, usurers, profiteers in the food and drink trades, and those who overburdened the commons were all condemned. These prohibitions often did not succeed, and innovators who did not always fall into these extreme categories were able to pursue their interests while belonging to active communities.

---

[56] AB, fo.88v. In modern English, 'These are seven things that man desires utterly which he shall not perfectly obtain in this present life. The first is cunning without ignorance or not knowing all things'.

[57] C. Lewis, 'Proverbs, Precepts and Monitory Pieces', in A. Harting (ed.), *A Manual of the Writings in Middle English 1050–1500*, 9 (New Haven, CT, 1993), 2,957–3,048; S. Wenzel, *Preachers, Poets, and the Early English Lyric* (Princeton, NJ, 1986), 174–208.

Conclusion

This book is not a biography, but an exploration of the insights that an individual life can throw on the structures and trends of a particular period. When little evidence is available, historians tend to fit the people they study into a conventional category. When John Heritage first appeared on the scene at Burton Dassett, it seemed appropriate to place him in the box labelled 'ambitious capitalist' as his actions in 1497 resembled those of a ruthless, profit-hungry, restless young man. He cooperated with an acquisitive lord, and may even have prompted him. Together they damaged the lives of John's less wealthy and influential neighbours by pushing them off the land in the interests of extending an efficiently organized pasture. Rejecting any sentiment towards his family home, he sold it to his lord in order to tidy up the otherwise complicated landscape of his village.

As more evidence is produced, Heritage emerges as a more interesting and complex person, enmeshed in difficult circumstances. At the time of his life-changing decisions of 1497 he had been for two years in his mid-twenties acting as executor of his father's will, serving as the head of a large family of brothers and sisters, while at the same time having to cope with the consequences of his father-in-law's death. We can only guess at the pressures, such as conflicting demands from the two families to which he was committed, which led him to settle his affairs at Burton and move to Moreton. He embarked on a new life as a merchant, advancing money that he did not have, and plunging into a dangerous sea of credit and promises. He was not the master of his destiny, and while he coped with the wool trade for a decade, he failed to win the custom of the really big producers, and wound down the business in the period 1510–20. He resourcefully expanded his role as a grazier, but had use of only two or three really large pastures where his tenure was secure, and he was assembling in a rather haphazard fashion access to common pastures in defiance of the local by-laws. He lacked capital, which made the funding of his trade precarious, and deprived him of a strong property base for his pastoral farming. He gained a more than adequate income and would have been accounted one of the wealthiest men in Moreton in Marsh (a dubious distinction), but he was frustrated if he aspired to better things, for example if he hoped to buy a substantial amount of freehold property.

Judging from his account book John Heritage was a very fallible business man, who was incapable of making a full record of all of his dealings. He must have been regarded well by some of those who entrusted their wool to him, or he would not have survived in trade for twenty years, but he must have infuriated some of his suppliers with his promises to pay that were fulfilled slowly and with much irregularity. We do not know how his competitors conducted their affairs, and perhaps all of them also existed from hand to mouth. We can be sure that anyone who lived in England in his time was very aware of duty and morality, but obligations to family and the community were not always compatible with the codes of conduct advocated by the Church and State. In any case, values and rules tended to be inconsistent. So Heritage was a pillar of his local community, while breaking the rules about pasturage in a number of local communities.

But it is not our aim to make moral judgements, or to guess at flaws of character on the basis of evidence that even in Heritage's case is very incomplete. Instead a more important line of inquiry is to ask how his life fitted into the circumstances of his time and place, and to ask whether he, or people like him, made some change to the world in which they worked.

One line of approach would be to represent him as the peasants' friend, because he provided the small producers with the means of selling wool at a good price. They were unlikely to be cheated over price, as the market was so competitive, and to prove this, few producers stayed loyal to the same dealer over many years. As peasants stood at the productive base of the rest of society, a point that poets and commentators rehearsed constantly to their readers, the wool money funded every part of the commonwealth. The cash paid rents to lords, taxes to the state, and funds for the clergy and the parish, and peasants were able to buy goods at markets and fairs that benefited industry and commerce.

To gain a decent income from wool sales, the better-off peasants needed only to manage their existing assets within the structure of the open fields. If he observed the stint fixed by the community, a yardlander could keep sixty sheep, but many of Heritage's suppliers had nearer to a hundred because tenants had accumulated two yardlands. They could therefore expect an annual income of £2 or £3. This potential income stimulated adaptations of the traditional management of village agriculture, within the framework of the open fields, which helps to explain the modifications to the rotation, whether by means of inhoks, leys, four-course rotation, and increases in legume cultivation. Piecemeal enclosure, usually of parts of the fields, would also enable an increase in the size of peasant flocks.

The importance of peasant flocks is not a new discovery, and was not confined to the period before 1520 or to the country around Moreton. The sheep censuses of 1547 and 1549 throw light on the balance between the peasants' smaller flocks and the larger numbers kept on large pastures and former villages.[1] The earlier survey suggests that in western Northamptonshire large flocks on enclosed pastures had greater significance, but the 1549 lists show that almost half of the recorded flocks consisted of 140 animals or fewer.

The activities of woolmongers cannot, however, always be regarded as having such positive outcomes. We have already seen that Heritage was a beneficiary of the depopulation of Burton Dassett, and probably played an active role in undermining the community there. He bought wool from other graziers who were using former village fields as pastures, such as William Colchester of Lark Stoke, and the tenant of a very large engrossed holding at Brookend, Peter Barton. In managing his own sheep flocks Heritage encroached onto common pastures by paying a tenant for

---

[1] M. W. Beresford, 'The Poll Tax and Census of Sheep, 1549', *Ag. HR*, 1 (1953), 9–15; J. Martin, 'Sheep and Enclosure in Sixteenth-Century Northamptonshire', *Ag. HR*, 36 (1988), 39–54.

agistment, thus depriving the other villagers of grazing. He did this at Burmington, for example, which was not a healthy village, judging from its small population in the sixteenth century. It should be said, however, that he did not repeat in later life the story of Burton Dassett. At Upper Ditchford the former village fields on which he kept a considerable flock had ceased to be cultivated a quarter of a century before his time, and no peasant was deprived of pasture by his lease of that land. The merchants of the staple who exported wool were sometimes distrustful of the middlemen who supplied them. We have seen, for example, that they were so concerned about dishonest packers that they went to inspect the process of 'winding' (as Heritage called it) in the woolhouse of such a well-known woolman as William Midwinter of Northleach. In general they accepted the service that the woolmen provided, which greatly reduced their workload in scouring the countryside remote from London.

Heritage was too small a fish to be able to make waves in the economy of his day. He facilitated an existing channel of commerce, and much was traditional in the way that wool was produced and marketed. The most dynamic force of the period, the growth of industry and especially clothmaking, had a small impact on Heritage's country. He was involved in supplying wool for manufacture in England, but significantly his largest single sale went to an Essex clothier.

A move towards expansion in Heritage's country, which may have been encouraged by the rising price of wool so well recorded in the account book, was the increased demand for land. One symptom is apparent in the relatively high proportion of sons succeeding to their father's landholding, and another is provided by occasional modest rises in entry fines, together with a more general tendency for tenants to pay their annual rents in good time. The relatively high demand for wool and meat encouraged further episodes in the long-term tendency to make more radical changes to fields to create large enclosed pastures or leasows, leading to the 'putting down of towns'. This was apparently happening in the first two decades of the sixteenth century at Barcheston and Meon. Upper Ditchford may not have been the only existing pasture to be provided with internal hedged subdivisions at this time.

With the benefit of hindsight we can say that the enclosed pasture pointed the way forward in farming, but that was not apparent at the time, and these new ventures accounted for only a small proportion of the countryside. Villages with their relatively large number of 2- and 3-yardland holdings (accounting for two-thirds of the tenanted land) prospered modestly with the help of the money from wool sales. In moments of stress they (or the intellectuals who claimed to defend their interests) sometimes claimed that they feared imminent destruction, but most of them were not under immediate threat.

Again in the light of later developments it can be appreciated that England was well organized for trade, with secure government, stable currency, network of markets and fairs, and informal but effective credit arrangements. We can be critical of Heritage's rudimentary accounting system, with its haphazard recording of transactions and lack of sophistication such as double-entry bookkeeping. He had no need of such methods, or of the paraphernalia of bills, recognizances, bonds, and letters. He relied on a good memory and a fund of trust and goodwill. He was continuing a trading system that was established in the thirteenth century, and that worked with reasonable efficiency. The whole of society had been drawn into the commercial network, so that Heritage's integration into the peasant economy was not a new development.

The pages of the account book, for all of their poor handwriting and unsystematic jottings, still reflect the economic reality of Heritage's time. The great lords are not there, but that absence only exaggerates and does not misrepresent the withdrawal of the monasteries, bishops, earls, and barons from agricultural production. The estates and manors of the lords are included, in the form of the farmers of the lords' demesnes, people in much the same position as Heritage himself. The many deliveries of wool by the upper ranks of the peasants are also signalling the upheaval in the countryside, which had created a class of superior peasants. They were not just relatively well provided with land and sheep, but they were also self-confident and ambitious – one only has to see the way that the peasant community of Longborough resisted the attempts by the abbot of Hailes to undermine their farming. An insight into the new social world has emerged from the research for this book, because a reading of every document relating to fifty contiguous villages in a short period throws up the same names over again. They were merchants, farmers, and graziers who knew each other well and often did business together. They operated mostly below the level of the gentry, but may have been a more effective network with, one suspects, political influence as well as considerable wealth. The names will be very familiar to anyone who has read this book closely: Bradwey, Colchester, Davies, Freman, Fretherne, Gibbes, Hunkes, Palmer, Salbrygge, Willington. The sources, reflecting as they do the decisions made by the most active, set our sights at that social level, and we still know very little about the lower to middling peasants, the half-yardlanders and yardlanders, who did not produce much wool, and the servants and labourers, who have received some attention in this study, are still a very poorly understood category. Everyone we have studied was a servant in his or her youth, including Heritage, but what of those who remained at the bottom of the social heap?

Two more points need to be made. Firstly, the living that these people made from the land and the market was not an easy one. These were hard times for everyone involved in production, because prices, especially of corn, hardly covered the cost of growing the crop, and labour was very scarce and expensive. It was, however, out of that experience that many of the economic changes came. Every decision had to be made carefully, every change that would cut costs and add a sliver of profit had to be made. The many modest wool producers who appear on the pages of the account book – Bumpas, Perte, Pole, Stevens, and the others – had graduated in the hard school of economic adversity.

Secondly, this was an intensively competitive scene. This refers not just to the cut-throat world of the rival broggers, outbidding one another to secure the wool, and doubtless making unrealistic promises about the speed of payment, but also the producers themselves. Throughout, the contrast has been noted between the farmers of the leasows and the peasants in the open fields. It was once thought that the history of the period consisted of the graziers (or rather their landlords) swallowing up the peasants, but the account book shows how important the peasants were, and the contemporary manorial records demonstrate their adaptability and flexibility. They had to make these changes, because they were competing with the men with the leasows. And they did not lose that contest.

APPENDIX 1

Sample pages from the account book

Anno xv [c] v (= 1505)
Furst resevyed off Thomas Bumpas 9 tod 22lb
prec' the tod 11s and put owth the remys.*   Tot £5 7s 7d
Payd yn ernys 46s 8d. Payd at delyveryng 20s.
Payd to the Wynddur 5d. Payd at mychelmas 20s.

Thomas Cokrell 12 tod 23 lb prec' the tod 11s.   Tot £7 0s 11d
Payd yn ernys £4 13s 4d. Payd at delyveryng   [£6 17s 6d]
13s 4d. Payd at mychelmas 34s 3d.

Thomas Kyte 42 tod prec' the tod 11s and to geve 2   Tot £23 2s 0d
flesys yn. Payd yn ernys 40s. Payd at delyveryng 40s.
Payd on Mychelmas evyn £6. Payd yn Blokley £3. Payd
yn Crystmas Halydays 40s. Payd on Goodtyde Tewysday
[40s] 42s. Payd be hys servand the 28 day of April £4.
Payd yn Stowe 20s.

Alysannder Hante' 28 tod 12 lb prec' the tod 11s and to   Tot £15 12s 5d
rebate 14 lb for that ys geve yn. And soo restyth with 27
tod 26 lb. Payd yn ernys 40s. Payd at delyveryng [40s]
£3. Payd be (Alys)annder More 40s. Payd be Haukys 40s. Payd
the 12 day of February £4 9s 0d.

Thomas Peryn 8 tod 3 lb prec' the tod 11s and to geve a   Tot £4 8s 8d
flese yn. Payd yn ernys 20s. Payd the 10 day of November
29s 2d. Payd yn Stowe 20s.

Tot 7 sacks [9 tod 21 lb] 10 tod 2 lb
Tot £55 [8s 7d] [11s] 11s 7d

*Note: *put owth the remys* interlined.
[] struck through

Source: WAM 12258 fo.18v.

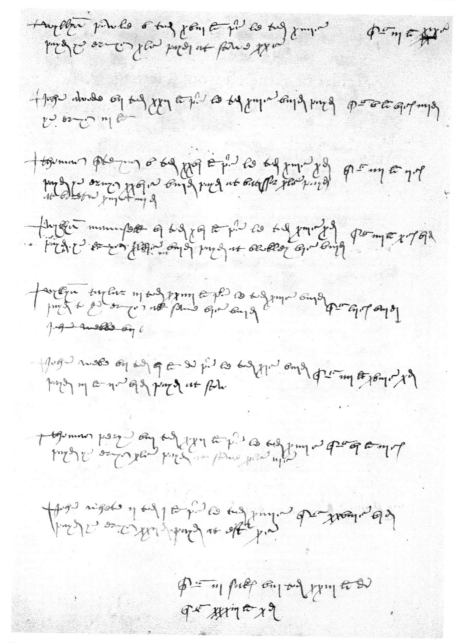

Fig. Appendix 1.1. Page from the account book WAM 12258 fo. 63v, 1515. (Copyright Dean and Chapter of Westminster)

APPENDIX 2

Tables of gathered wool, Heritage's own wool, and wool prices

Table a. Gathered wool.

Date	Quantity of wool acquired			Money paid		
	sacks	tods	lbs	£	s	d
1500	*40*	*10*	*17*	*315*	*16*	*5**
1501	44	6	25	313	7	3
1502	36	6	13	267	4	6
1503	45	0	12.5	347	8	5
1504	46	10	18	331	9	2
1505	38	8	1	274	12	11
1506	58	7	7	409	19	5
1507	28	11	23	201	8	4
1508	36	11	19	276	6	2
1509	33	9	21	254	9	6
1510	19	6	27	150	4	6
1511	19	7	4	144	6	10
1512	18	2	14	121	19	3
1513	12	9	4	91	0	1
1514	11	3	2.5	96	8	3
1515	9	8	17.5	86	8	10
1516	13	7	4.5	120	1	6
1517	13	6	13	108	17	6
1518	14	5	7	118	6	5
1519	14	10	9	121	10	9

Note: * for 1500 the total alone is known, on the first folio of the account book.
Source: AB.

Table b. Annual totals of John Heritage's own wool.

Date	Quantity of wool sold			Money gained		
	sacks	tods	lbs	£	s	d
1501	3	4	0			
1502	4	2	0	32	10	8
1503	4	6	0	35	13	4
1504	5	5	14	40	19	4
1505	-					
1506	5	8	4	38	6	8
1507	-					
1508	8	0	14			
1509	7	8	14			
1510	-					
1511	6	6	14			
1512	-					
1513	6	0	2			
1514	5	6	0			
1515	5	8	0			
1516	5	12	20*			
1517	7	10	20*			
1518	6	6	16			

Note: *estimated totals.
Source: AB.

Table c. Prices for gathered wool (in shillings per tod of 28lbs).

Date	Mean price (shillings)
1501	10.8
1502	11.3
1503	11.9
1504	10.9
1505	10.9
1506	10.8
1507	10.7
1508	11.5
1509	11.6
1510	11.8
1511	11.4
1512	10.3
1513	11.0
1514	13.2
1515	13.8
1516	13.6
1517	12.4
1518	12.6
1519	12.6

Source: AB

APPENDIX 3

Deserted villages

A list of villages (settlements with at least ten household) that existed before 1500, and were abandoned or severely shrunken by 1700.

Village name	Parish	Size before desertion	Evidence for decay/desertion
Barcheston	Barcheston	c.15 (c.1300)	6 'inhabitants' (meaning households) 1428 5 houses abandoned 1509 4 houses in 1670
Brookend	Chastleton	16 (1279)	4 houses inhabited 1479
Castlett	Guiting Power	5 (1327)	1 household in 1381 Pasture 1504
Clopton	Quinton	10 (1327) 12 (1381)	No guild members after 1480 2 abandoned houses, enclosure 1481–5
Compton Scorpion	Ilmington	10 (1279)	No guild members after 1440 In Rous's list 1486 200 ac. pasture 1495 3 houses 1670
Daylesford	Daylesford	9 (1327)	6 taxpayers 1525
Ditchford Frary	Stretton on Fosse	9 (1327)	In Rous's list 1486
Ditchford, Middle	Blockley	13 (1327)	In Rous's list 1486 Arable ceased 1482–97
Ditchford, Upper	Blockley	20 (1299)	In Rous's list 1486 Arable ceased by 1482 Leased as pasture 1475
Dorn	Blockley	16 (1327)	5 taxpayers and cultivation 1525
Eyford	Upper Slaughter	13 (+ 8 slaves) (1086) 1 (1327)	
Foxcote	Ilmington	13 (1327)	No guild members after 1470 In Rous's list 1486 5 houses in 1670
Hidcote Bartrim	Mickleton	7 (1327) 14 (1381)	180 ac. enclosed 1509–10
Lark Stoke	Ilmington	6 (1327) 10 (1381)	No guild members after 1510 In Rous's list 1486 4 assessed 1522
Lemington, Lower	Lemington	14 (1327)	10 assessed 1522
Lemington, Upper	Todenham		Low assessment 1524

Village name	Parish	Size before desertion	Evidence for decay/desertion
Longdon	Tredington	8 (1327)	No guild members after 1480 1 taxpayer 1525 Pasture by 1535
Meon	Quinton	16 (1327) 14 (1381)	No guild members after 1480 4 houses abandoned and enclosure, 1513
Northwick	Blockley	10 (1327)	14 taxpayers,1525
Norton Subedge	Weston Subedge	17 (1327) 17–21 (1381)	11 tenants 1447 No guild members after 1440
Pinnock	Temple Guiting	–	7 taxpayers in 1524 and 1525
Rollright, Little	Great Rollright	23 (1279)	5 houses abandoned 1496–1517
Sezincote	Sezincote	14 (+ 20 slaves) (1086) 2 (1327) 4–10 (1381)	Enclosed pasture 1492 Church ruined 1509
Taddington	Stanway	10 (1327)	7 assessed 1522
Talton	Tredington	6 (1327)	No guild members after 1490
Tidmington	Tredington	15 (1327)	8 taxpayers 1525
Upton (Wold)	Blockley	16 (1299)	Tax paid by lord 1383 Used as pasture 1383
Weston juxta Cherington	Long Compton	24 (1279) 25 (*c.*1300)	8 houses abandoned 1509
Whitchurch		23 (1327)	Enclosed by 1534

Note: the entries for 1279, 1299, and *c.*1300 give numbers of tenants; the entries for 1327 give numbers of taxpayers, which are likely to represent at least twice as many households; the entries for 1381 estimate the number of households from the numbers of individual taxpayers.

Sources: A. Farley (ed.), *Domesday Book* (London, 1783); P. Franklin (ed.), *The Taxpayers of Medieval Gloucestershire* (Stroud, 1993); F. J. Eld (ed.), *Lay Subsidy Roll for the County of Worcester*, I, *Edward III*, Worcestershire Historical Society, 6 (1895); W. B. Bickley (ed.), 'Lay Subsidy Roll, Warwickshire 1327', *Transactions of the Midland Record Society*, 6 (1902); J. Sheail, *The Regional Distribution of Wealth in England as Indicated in the 1524/5 Lay Subsidy Returns*, II, 'List and Index Society, Special Series, 29 (1998); *B & GLS*; *WT*; *MSG*; TNA: PRO 179 192/122 (Warwickshire Lay Subsidy, 1524); *Guild Reg*; T. Hearne (ed.), *Joannis Rossi Historia Regum Angliae* (Oxford, 1745); T Arkell and N. Alcock (eds), *Warwickshire Hearth Tax Returns*, Dugdale Society, 43 (2010); *Dom Inc*; C. Dyer, *Lords and Peasants in a Changing Society: The Estates of the Bishopric of Worcester 680–1540* (Cambridge, 1980); T. John (ed.), *The Warwickshire Hundred Rolls of 1279–80*, Records of Social and Economic History, new series, 19 (1992); K. J. Allison, M. W. Beresford, J. G. Hurst, *The Deserted Villages of Oxfordshire*, Leicester, Department of English Local History Occasional Papers, no. 17, 1966; *Valor Ecclesiasticus*; *Feudal Aids*; Dorset Record Office, D/WLC/M/233.

Bibliography

UNPRINTED PRIMARY SOURCES

Birmingham Archives and Heritage
Norton Collection
Zachary Lloyd

Cambridge, King's College
College Estate Archives

Cumbria County Record Office
Bishopric of Carlisle
Pennington Family Archives

Devon Record Office
Fortescue Papers

Dorset Record Office
Weld of Lulworth Castle

Gloucestershire Archives
Hockaday Abstracts
Petre Collection

Centre for Kentish Studies, Maidstone
Sackville of Knole

Leicester, Leicestershire and Rutland Record Office
Noel, Lords Campden

London, British Library
Add. Charters, Add. MSS (West), Add. Rolls
Harleian Rolls

London, Guildhall Library
Livery Company Records

London Metropolitan Archives
Court of Hustings
Courts of Aldermen

London, National Archives: Public Record office
Chancery C1
Common Pleas CP40
Court of Requests REQ
Exchequer E159; E179
Probate
Special Collections SC2, SC6, SC11, SC12
Star Chamber STAC

London, Society of Antiquaries
Prattinton Collection

London, Westminster Abbey
Muniments (WAM)
Registers

Northamptonshire Record Office
Finch Hatton
Temple of Stow

Nottingham University Library
Willoughby of Wollaton

Oxford, Bodleian Library
Kingham lease

Oxford, Corpus Christi College
Temple Guiting

Oxford, Magdalen College
Chipping Norton
Letters
Quinton

Oxford, Merton College
Great Wolford

Oxford, New College
Kingham

Oxfordshire Record Office
Chastleton House Collection

Staffordshire Record Office
Stafford Papers

Stratford upon Avon, Shakespeare Birthplace Record Office
Bloom Collection
Leigh Collection

Warwickshire County Record Office
Gist of Barcheston

Worcester Cathedral Library
Court Rolls (E series)
Registers
Rentals and Accounts (C series)

Worcestershire Record Office
Church Commissioners
Diocese
Wills

York Minster Library
Archbishopric of York Lease Registers

PRINTED PRIMARY SOURCES

Alcock, N. W. (ed.), *Warwickshire Grazier and London Skinner 1532–1555*, British Academy Records of Social and Economic History, new ser., 4 (Oxford, 1981).

Andrews, F. B., 'The Compotus Rolls of the Monastery of Pershore', *Transactions of the Birmingham Archaeological Society*, 57 (1933).

Bailey, M. (ed.), 'The Sheep Accounts of Norwich Cathedral Priory 1484–1534', in *Poverty and Wealth: Sheep, Taxation and Charity in Late Medieval Norfolk*, Norfolk Record Society, 71 (Norwich, 2007).

Barnard, E. A. B., *Churchwardens' Accounts of the Parish of Badsey with Aldington* (Hampstead, 1913).

Bickley, W. B. (ed.), *Register of the Guild of Knowle* (Walsall, 1894).

—— 'Lay Subsidy Roll, Warwickshire 1327', *Transactions of the Midland Record Society*, 6 (1902).

Blanchard, I. S. W. (ed.), *The Duchy of Lancaster's Estates in Derbyshire 1485–1540*, Derbyshire Archaeological Society Record Series, 3 (1971).

Brewer, J. S., Gairdner, J., and Brodie, R. H. (eds), *Letters and Paper, Foreign and Domestic, of the Reign of Henry VIII* (London, 1864–1920).

Brodie, D. M. (ed.), *The Tree of Commonwealth: A Treatise Written by Edmund Dudley* (Cambridge, 1948).

Calendar of Inquisitions Post Mortem, Henry VII, 3 vols. (London, 1898–1955).

Calendar of Patent Rolls, Henry VII.

Caley, J. and Hunter, J. (eds), *Valor Ecclesiasticus temp. Henry VIII auctoritate regia institutus*, Record Commission (1810–34), 6 vols.

Corrie, G. E. (ed.), *Sermons by Hugh Latimer*, Parker Society (1844).

Drucker, L. (ed.), *Warwickshire Feet of Fines, 3, 1345–1509*, Dugdale Society, 18 (1943).

Dyer, A. and Palliser, D. M. (eds), *The Diocesan Population Returns for 1563 and 1603*, Records of Social and Economic History, new ser., 31 (Oxford, 2005).

Eld, F. J. (ed.), *Lay Subsidy Roll for the County of Worcester*, I, *Edward III*, Worcestershire Historical Society, 6 (1895).

Elrington, C. R. (ed.), *Gloucestershire Feet of Fines 1360–1509*, Gloucestershire Record Series, forthcoming.

Faraday, M. (ed.), *Worcestershire Taxes in the 1520s: The Military Survey and Forced Loans of 1522–3 and the Lay Subsidy of 1524–7*, Worcestershire Historical Society, new ser., 19 (2003).

—— (ed.), *The Bristol and Gloucestershire Lay Subsidy of 1523–1527*, Gloucestershire Record Series, 23 (2009).

Fegan, E. S. (ed.), *Journal of Prior William More*, Worcestershire Historical Society (1914).

Fenwick, C. (ed.), *The Poll Tax of 1377, 1379 and 1381, Pt 1*, Records of Social and Economic History, new ser., 27 (1998).

Fetherston, J. (ed.), 'Inventory of Church Goods, in the County of Warwick, temp. of Edward the Sixth', *Warwickshire Antiquarian Magazine* (1859–77).

Franklin, P. (ed.), *The Taxpayers of Medieval Gloucestershire* (Stroud, 1993).

Glasscock, R. E. (ed.), *The Lay Subsidy of 1334*, British Academy Records of Social and Economic History, new ser., 11 (Oxford, 1975).

Gray, I., 'A Gloucestershire Postscript to the "Domesday of Inclosures"', *Transactions of the Bristol and Gloucestershire Archaeological Society*, 97 (1979).

Grundy, G. B., *Saxon Charters and Field Names of Gloucestershire*, Bristol and Gloucestershire Archaeological Society (Gloucester, 1935), 2 parts.

Hanham, A. (ed.), *The Cely Letters 1472–1488*, Early English Text Society (Oxford, 1975).

[Hardy, W. J.] (ed.), *Stratford-on-Avon Corporation Records: The Guild Accounts* (Stratford-upon-Avon, 1880).

Hollings, M. (ed.), *The Red Book of Worcester*, Worcestershire Historical Society (1934–50).

Houghton, F. T. S., Stokes, E., and Drucker, L. (eds.), *Warwickshire Feet of Fines, 2, 1284–1345*, Dugdale Society, 15 (1939).

Hoyle, R. (ed.), *The Military Survey of Gloucestershire, 1522*, Gloucestershire Record Series, 6 (1993).

John, T. (ed.), *The Warwickshire Hundred Rolls of 1279–80: Stoneleigh and Kineton Hundreds*, British Academy Records of Social and Economic History, 19 (1992).

Keene, D. and Harding, V., *A Survey of Documentary Sources for Property Holding in London before the Great Fire*, London Record Society, 22 (1985).

Lambert, J. J., *Records of the Skinners of London, Edward I to James I* (London, 1933).

Leadam, I. S. (ed.), 'The Inquisition of 1517: Inclosures and Evictions, part 1', *Transactions of the Royal Historical Society*, new ser., 6 (1892).

——(ed.), 'The Inquisition of 1517: Inclosures and Evictions, part 3', *Transactions of the Royal Historical Society*, new ser., 8 (1894).

——(ed.), *The Domesday of Inclosures 1517–1518*, 2 vols., Royal Historical Society (London, 1897).

Logan, G. M. and Adams, R. M. (eds), *Thomas More: Utopia* (Cambridge, 1989).

Louis. C. (ed.), *The Commonplace Book of Robert Reynes of Acle: An Edition of Tanner MS.407* (New York, 1980).

Macdonald, M. (ed.), *The Register of the Guild of the Holy Cross, St Mary and St John the Baptist, Stratford-upon-Avon*, Dugdale Society, 42 (2007).

Maclean, J., 'Chantry Certificates, Gloucestershire', *Transactions of the Bristol and Gloucestershire Archaeological Society*, 8 (1883–4).

McSheffrey, S. and Tanner, N. (eds), *Lollards of Coventry 1486–1522*, Camden Society, 5th ser., 23 (London, 2003).

Neuss, P. (ed.), *John Skelton, Magnificence* (Manchester, 1980).

Oschinsky, D. (ed.), *Walter of Henley and other Treatises on Estate Management and Accounting* (Oxford, 1971).

Pugh, T. B. (ed.), *The Marcher Lordships of South Wales, 1415–1536: Select Documents* (Cardiff, 1963).

Rhodes, J. (ed.), *A Calendar of the Registers of the Priory of Llantony by Gloucester*, Gloucestershire Record Series, 15 (2002).

Salter, H. E., *Eynsham Cartulary*, Oxford Historical Society, 51 (1908), 2 vols.

Sneyd, C. A. (ed.), *A Relation of the Island of England*, Camden Society, 37 (1847).

Statutes of the Realm, 11 vols., Record Commission (1810–28).

Sutton, A. F. and Visser-Fuchs, L. (eds), *The Book of Privileges of the Merchant Adventurers of England 1296–1483*, British Academy Records of Social and Economic History, new ser., 42 (Oxford, 2009).

Toulmin Smith, L. (ed.), *Leland's Itinerary in England and Wales* (London, 1909).

Vanes, J. (ed.), *The Ledger of John Smythe 1538–50*, Bristol Record Society, 28 (1974).

Walters, H. B. (ed.), 'Inventories of Worcestershire Church Goods, 1552', *Transactions of the Worcestershire Archaeological Society*, 30 (1953); 31 (1954); 32 (1955).

Weaver, J. R. H. and Beardwood, A. (eds), *Some Oxfordshire Wills*, Oxfordshire Record Society, 39 (1958).

Weaver, F. W. and Clark, G. N. (eds), *Churchwardens' Accounts of Marston, Spelsbury, Pyrton*, Oxfordshire Record Society, 6 (1925).

SECONDARY WORKS (SELECTED ITEMS)

Acheson, E., *A Gentry Community: Leicestershire in the Fifteenth Century c.1422–c.1485* (Cambridge, 1992).

Alcock, N. W., 'Enclosure and Depopulation in Burton Dassett: A Sixteenth-Century View', *Warwickshire History*, 3 (1977).

——(ed.), *Cruck Construction: An Introduction and Catalogue*, Council for British Archaeology Research Report, 42 (1981).

Allen, M., 'The Volume of the English Currency, 1158–1470', *Ec. HR*, 54 (2001).

——'English Coin Hoards, 1158–1544', *British Numismatic Journal*, 27 (2002).

——'Silver Production and the Money Supply in England and Wales, 1086–c.1500', *Ec. HR*, 64 (2011).

Allison, K. J., 'Flock Management in the Sixteenth and Seventeenth Centuries', *Ec. HR*, 11 (1958).

Almond, R. and Pollard, A. J., 'The Yeomanry of Robin Hood and Social Terminology in Fifteenth-Century England', *Past and Present*, 170 (2001).

Amor, N. R., 'Merchant Adventurer or Jack of All Trades? The Suffolk Clothier in the 1460s', *Proceedings of the Suffolk Institute of Archaeology and History*, 40 (2004).

Andrews, D. D. and Milne, G. (eds), *Wharram: A Study of Settlement on the Yorkshire Wolds, I, Domestic Settlement, Areas 10 and 6*, Society for Medieval Archaeology, Monograph Series, 8 (London, 1979).

Aston, M. and Bond, C. J., *The Landscape of Towns* (London, 1976).

—— and Vyner, L., 'The Study of Deserted Villages in Gloucestershire', in Saville, A. (ed.), *Archaeology in Gloucestershire* (Cheltenham, 1984).

Aston, T. H. and Philpin, C. H. E. (eds), *The Brenner Debate: Agrarian Class Structure and Economic Development in Pre-Industrial Europe* (Cambridge, 1985).

Ault, W. O., 'Village By-Laws by Common Consent', *Speculum*, 29 (1954).

—— *Open-Field Farming in Medieval England: A Study of Village By-Laws* (London, 1972).

Bailey, M., *A Marginal Economy? East Anglian Breckland in the Later Middle Ages* (Cambridge, 1989).

—— *Medieval Suffolk: An Economic and Social History 1200–1500* (Woodbridge, 2007).

Baker, J. H., *The Oxford History of the Laws of England, VI, 1483–1558* (Oxford, 2003).

Barnard, E. A. B., 'Clement Lichfield, Last Abbot of Evesham, 1514–1539', *Transactions of the Worcestershire Archaeological Society*, new ser., 5 (1927–8).

Barron, C. M., 'The Parish Fraternities of Medieval London', in C. M. Barron and C. Harper-Bill, *The Church in Pre-Reformation Society: Essays in Honour of F. R. H. Du Boulay* (Woodbridge, 1985).

—— 'Introduction: The Widow's World', in C. M. Barron and A. F. Sutton (eds.), *Medieval London Widows 1300–1500* (London, 1994).

—— *London in the Later Middle Ages: Government and People 1200–1500* (Oxford, 2004).

Bassett, S., 'The Administrative Landscape of the Diocese of Worcester in the Tenth Century', in N. Brooks and C. Cubitt (eds), *St Oswald of Worcester: Life and Influence* (Leicester, 1996).

Bean, J. M. W., *The Estates of the Percy Family 1416–1537* (Oxford, 1958).

Bell, A., Brooks, C., and Dryburgh, P., *The English Wool Market c.1230–1327* (Cambridge, 2007).

Beresford, M. W., 'The Poll Tax and Census of Sheep, 1549', *Ag. HR*, 1 (1953).

—— *The Lost Villages of England* (London, 1954).

—— *New Towns of the Middle Ages* (London, 1967).

—— and St Joseph, J. K., *Medieval England: An Aerial Survey*, 2nd edn. (Cambridge, 1979).

Blanchard, I. S. W., 'Population Change, Enclosure and the Early Tudor Economy', *Ec. HR*, 2nd ser., 23 (1970).

Bliss, M. and Sharpe, F., *Church Bells of Gloucestershire* (Gloucester, 1986).

Blomley, N., 'Making Private Property: Enclosure, Common Rights and the Work of Hedges', *Rural History*, 18 (2007).

Bond, C. J., 'Deserted Medieval Villages in Warwickshire and Worcestershire', in T. R. Slater and P. J. Jarvis (eds), *Field and Forest: An Historical Geography of Warwickshire and Worcestershire* (Norwich, 1982).

Bowden, P. J., *The Wool Trade in Tudor and Stuart England* (London, 1962).

—— 'Agricultural Prices, Farm Profits, and Rents', in J. Thirsk (ed.), *The Agrarian History of England and Wales*, IV, *1500–1640* (Cambridge, 1967).

Brenner, R., 'Agrarian Class Structure and Economic Development in Pre-Industrial Europe', *Past and Present*, 70 (1976).

Brett, C., 'Thomas Kytson and Wiltshire Clothmen 1529–1534', *Wiltshire Archaeological and Natural History Magazine*, 97 (2004).

Britnell, R. H., *Growth and Decline in Colchester, 1300–1525* (Cambridge, 1986).

—— *The Commercialisation of English Society 1000–1500* (Cambridge, 1993).

—— 'Price-Setting in English Borough Markets, 1349–1500', *Canadian Journal of History*, 31 (1996).

—— *The Closing of the Middle Ages? England, 1471–1529* (Oxford, 1997).

—— *Britain and Ireland 1050–1530: Economy and Society* (Oxford, 2004).

Brown, A. D., *Popular Piety in Late Medieval England: The Diocese of Salisbury 1250–1550* (Oxford, 1995).

Campbell, B. M. S. and Overton, M., 'A New Perspective on Medieval and Early Modern Agriculture: Six Centuries of Norfolk Farming, c.1250–c.1850', *Past and Present*, 141 (1993).

Campbell, M., 'The Table and Feasting', in R. Marks and P. Williamson (eds.), *Gothic: Art for England 1400–1547* (London, 2003).

Carpenter, C., *Locality and Polity: A Study of Warwickshire Landed Society, 1401–1499* (Cambridge, 1992).

—— *The Wars of the Roses: Politics and the Constitution in England, c.1437–1509* (Cambridge, 1997).

Carter, H., *An Introduction to Urban Historical Geography* (London, 1983).

Carus-Wilson, E. M., 'Evidences of Industrial Growth on some Fifteenth-Century Manors', in *idem* (ed.), *Essays in Economic History*, II (London, 1962).

Carus-Wilson, E. M. and Coleman, O., *England's Export Trade 1275–1547* (Oxford, 1963).

Catchpole, A., Clark, D., and Peberdy, R., *Burford: Buildings and People in a Cotswold Town* (Chichester, 2008).

Cavill, P. R., 'The Problem of Labour and the Parliament of 1495', in L. Clark (ed.), *The Fifteenth Century*, 5 (2005).

Challis, C., *The Tudor Coinage* (Manchester, 1978).

Clark, G., *A Farewell to Alms: A Brief Economic History of the World* (Princeton, NJ, 2007).

Cleere, H. and Crossley, D., *The Iron Industry of the Weald*, 2nd edn. (Cardiff, 1995).

Coleman, D. C., *The British Paper Industry 1495–1860* (Oxford, 1958).

Colvin, H. M. (ed.), *The History of the King's Works*, 6 vols. (London, 1963–82).

Cook, H., Stearne, K., and Williamson, T., 'The Origins of Water Meadows in England', *Ag. HR*, 51 (2003).

Creighton, C., *A History of Epidemics in Britain*, 2nd edn. (London, 1965).

Crosby, A. W., *The Measure of Reality: Quantification and Western Society, 1250–1600* (Cambridge, 1997).

Cunich, P., 'Richard Kidderminster (*c*.1461–1533/4), abbot of Winchcombe', *Oxford Dictionary of National Biography*, 31 (2004).

Davis, J., *Medieval Market Morality: Life, Law and Ethics in the English Marketplace, 1200–1500* (Cambridge, 2012).

Day, J., 'The Great Bullion Famine of the Fifteenth Century', in *idem*, *The Medieval Market Economy* (Oxford, 1987).

Dodds, B., *Peasants and Production in the Medieval North-East: The Evidence of Tithes, 1270–1536* (Woodbridge, 2007).

—— 'Demesne and Tithe: Peasant Agriculture in the Late Middle Ages', *Ag. HR*, 56 (2008).

—— and Britnell, R. (eds), *Agriculture and Rural Society after the Black Death, Common Themes and Regional Variations* (Hatfield, 2008).

Down, K., 'The Administration of the Diocese of Worcester under the Italian Bishops, 1497–1535', *Midland History*, 20 (1995).

Draper, G. M., 'Writing English, French and Latin in the Fifteenth Century: A Regional Perspective', in L. Clark (ed.), *The Fifteenth Century*, 7 (Woodbridge, 2007).

Dyer, A., *Decline and Growth in English Towns, 1400–1640* (Basingstoke, 1991).

—— '"Urban Decline" in England, 1377–1525', in T. R. Slater (ed.), *Towns in Decline AD 100–1600* (Aldershot, 2000).

Dyer, C., *Lords and Peasants in a Changing Society: The Estates of the Bishopric of Worcester, 680–1540* (Cambridge, 1980).

—— *Warwickshire Farming 1349–c.1520: Preparations for Agricultural Revolution*, Dugdale Society Occasional Paper, 27 (1981).

—— 'Deserted Medieval Villages in the West Midlands', *Ec. HR*, 2nd ser., 35 (1982).

—— 'Small Town Conflict in the Later Middle Ages: Implications of Events at Shipston-on-Stour', *Urban History*, 19 (1992).

—— 'The Great Fire of Shipston-on-Stour', *Warwickshire History*, 8 (1992–3).

—— 'The Hidden Trade of the Middle Ages: Evidence from the West Midlands', in *idem*, *Everyday Life in Medieval England* (London, 1994).

—— 'Were There Any Capitalists in Fifteenth-Century England?', in *idem*, *Everyday Life in Medieval England* (London, 1994).

—— 'Sheepcotes: Evidence for Medieval Sheep Farming', *Medieval Archaeology*, 34 (1995).

—— *Standards of Living in the Later Middle Ages: Social Change in England c.1200–1520*, 2nd edn. (Cambridge, 1998).

—— *Making a Living in the Middle Ages: The People of Britain, 850–1520* (New Haven, CT, 2002).

—— 'Small Places with Large Consequences: The Importance of Small Towns in England, 1000–1540', *Historical Research*, 75 (2002).

—— 'Villages and Non-Villages in the Medieval Cotswolds', *Transactions of the Bristol and Gloucestershire Archaeological Society*, 120 (2002).

—— *An Age of Transition? Economy and Society in England in the Later Middle Ages* (Oxford, 2005).

—— 'A Suffolk Farmer in the Fifteenth Century', *Ag. HR*, 55 (2007).

—— 'Villages in Crisis: Social Dislocation and Desertion, 1370–1520', in C. Dyer and R. Jones (eds), *Deserted Villages Revisited* (Hatfield, 2010).

Edwards, J., 'The Mural and the Morality Play: A Suggested Source for a Wall-Painting at Oddington', *Transactions of the Bristol and Gloucestershire Archaeological Society*, 104 (1986).

Emden, A. B., *A Biographical Register of the University of Oxford to 1500*, 2 (Oxford, 1958).

Epstein, S. R., *An Island for Itself: Economic Development and Social Change in Late Medieval Sicily* (Cambridge, 1992).

—— *Freedom and Growth: The Rise of States and Markets in Europe, 1300–1750* (London, 2000).

Everitt, A., 'The Marketing of Agricultural Produce', in J. Thirsk (ed), *The Agrarian History of England and Wales*, IV, *1500–1640* (Cambridge, 1967).

—— 'River and Wold: Reflections on the Historical Origins of Regions and *Pays*', *Journal of Historical Geography*, 3 (1977).

Farber, L., *An Anatomy of Trade in Medieval Writing: Value, Consent and Community* (Ithaca, NY, 2006).

Farnhill, K., 'The Guild of the Annunciation of the Blessed Virgin Mary and the Fraternity of St Mary at Walsingham', in C. Burgess and E. Duffy (eds), *The Parish in Late Medieval England* (Donington, 2006).

Finberg, H. P. R., 'The Genesis of the Gloucestershire Towns', in H. P. R. Finberg (ed.), *Gloucestershire Studies* (Leicester, 1957).

Fox, H. S. A., 'The Chronology of Enclosure and Economic Developments in Medieval Devon', *Ec. HR*, 2nd ser., 28 (1975).

—— 'Servants, Cottagers and Tied Cottages during the Later Middle Ages: Towards a Regional Dimension', *Rural History*, 6 (1995).

French, H. R., and Hoyle, R. W., *The Character of an English Rural Society: Earls Colne, 1550–1750* (Manchester, 2007).

French, K., *The People of the Parish: Community Life in a Late Medieval Diocese* (Philadelphia, PA, 2001).

Gay, E. F., and Leadam, I. S., 'The Inquisitions of Depopulation in 1517 and the "Domesday of Inclosures"', *Transactions of the Royal Historical Society*, new ser., 14 (1900).

Glennie, P., 'In Search of Agrarian Capitalism: Manorial Land Markets and the Acquisition of Land in the Lea Valley *c.*1450–*c.*1560', *Continuity and Change*, 3 (1988).

Goheen, R. B., 'Peasant Politics? Village Community and the Crown in Fifteenth-Century England', *American Historical Review*, 96 (1991).

Goldberg, P. J. P., *Women, Work and Life Cycle in a Medieval Economy: Women in York and Yorkshire c.1300–1520* (Oxford, 1992).

Goose, N. and Evans, N., 'Wills as an Historical Source', in T. Arkell, N. Evans, and N. Goose (eds), *When Death Do Us Part: Understanding and Interpreting the Probate Records of Early Modern England* (Oxford, 2000).

Grassby, R., *The Idea of Capitalism before the Industrial Revolution* (Lanham, MD, 1999).

—— *Kinship and Capitalism* (Cambridge, 2001).

Gray, C. M., *Copyhold, Equity and the Common Law* (Cambridge, MA, 1963).

Gray, H. L., *English Field Systems* (Harvard, MA, 1915).

Grierson, P., *The Coins of Medieval Europe* (London, 1991).

Gunn, S., 'Henry VII in Context: Problems and Possibilities', *History*, 92 (2007).

—— 'Archery Practice in Early Tudor England', *Past and Present*, 209 (2010).

Guy, J. A., *The Public Career of Sir Thomas More* (New Haven, CT, 1980).

—— *Thomas More* (London, 2000).

Gwyn, P., *The King's Cardinal: The Rise and Fall of Thomas Wolsey* (London, 1990).

Haines, R. M., *The Administration of the Diocese of Worcester in the First Half of the Fourteenth Century* (London, 1965).

Hanham, A., *The Celys and their World: An English Merchant Family in the Fifteenth Century* (Cambridge, 1985).

Harris, B., *Edward Stafford, Third Duke of Buckingham, 1478–1521* (Stanford, CA, 1986).

Hartman, M. S., *The Household and the Making of History: A Subversive View of the Western Past* (Cambridge, 2004).

Harvey, B. F., *Westminster Abbey and its Estates in the Middle Ages* (Oxford, 1977).

—— *Living and Dying in England, 1100–1540: The Monastic Experience* (Oxford, 1993).

—— and Summerson, H., 'John Islip (1464–1532), abbot of Westminster', *Oxford Dictionary of National Biography* (Oxford, 2004).

Harvey, P. D. A. (ed.), *The Peasant Land Market in Medieval England* (Oxford, 1984).

—— *Manorial Records*, British Records Association, Archives and the User, 5, revised edn. (London, 1999).

Hatcher, J., *Rural Economy and Society in the Duchy of Cornwall, 1300–1500* (Cambridge, 1970).

—— *English Tin Production and Trade before 1550* (Oxford, 1973).

—— 'Mortality in the Fifteenth Century: Some New Evidence', *Ec. HR*, 2nd ser., 39 (1986).

—— *The History of the British Coal Industry, I, Before 1700: Towards the Age of Coal* (Oxford, 1993).

—— and Barker, T. C., *A History of British Pewter* (London, 1974).

—— Piper, A., and Stone, D., 'Monastic Mortality: Durham Priory, 1395–1529', *Ec. HR*, 59 (2006).

Hayward, M., *Rich Apparel: Clothing and the Law in Henry VIII's England* (Farnham, 2009).

Hilton, R. H., 'Winchcombe Abbey and the Manor of Sherborne', in H. P. R. Finberg (ed.), *Gloucestershire Studies* (Leicester, 1957).

—— *The Decline of Serfdom* (London, 1969).

—— *The English Peasantry in the Later Middle Ages* (Oxford, 1975).

—— *A Medieval Society: The West Midlands at the End of the Thirteenth Century*, 2nd edn. (Cambridge, 1983).

—— (ed.), *The Transition from Feudalism to Capitalism* (London, 1976).

Hilton, R. H. and Rahtz, P. A., 'Upton, Gloucestershire, 1959–1964', *Transactions of the Bristol and Gloucestershire Archaeological Society*, 85 (1966).

Holton, R. J., *The Transition from Feudalism to Capitalism* (London, 1985).

Hoppenbrouwers, P. and Luiten van Zanden, J. (eds), *Peasants into Farmers? The Transformation of Rural Economy and Society in the Low Countries (Middle Ages–19th Century) in Light of the Brenner Debate* (Turnhout, 2001).

Horowitz, H. R., 'Policy and Prosecution in the Reign of Henry VII', *Historical Research*, 82 (2009).

Hoskins, W. G., 'Harvest Fluctuations and English Economic History 1480–1619', *Ag. HR*, 12 (1964).

—— *The Age of Plunder: The England of Henry VIII 1500–1547* (London, 1976).

Hoyle, R. W., 'Tenure and the Land Market in Early Modern England: Or a Late Contribution to the Brenner Debate', *Ec. HR*, 2nd ser., 43 (1990).

—— 'Resistance and Manipulation in Early Tudor Taxation: Some Evidence from the North', *Archives*, 20 (1993).

—— 'The Land-Family Bond in England', *Past and Present*, 146 (1995).

Hughes, P. L., and Larkin, J. F., *Tudor Royal Proclamations, I, The Early Tudors* (New Haven, CT, 1964).

Ives, E. W., *The Common Lawyers of Pre-Reformation England. Thomas Kebell: A Case Study* (Cambridge, 1983).

James, M. K., *Studies in the Medieval Wine Trade* (Oxford, 1971).

Jones, A. C., 'Bedfordshire: Fifteenth Century', in P. D. A. Harvey (ed.), *The Peasant Land Market in Medieval England* (Oxford, 1984).

Kermode, J., *Medieval Merchants: York, Beverley and Hull in the Later Middle Ages* (Cambridge, 1998).

Kerridge, E., 'The Returns of the Inquisitions of Depopulation', *English Historical Review*, 70 (1955).

—— *Textile Manufactures in Early Modern England* (Manchester, 1985).

Kowaleski, M., *Local Markets and Regional Trade in Medieval Exeter* (Cambridge, 1995).

Kümin, B., *The Shaping of a Community: The Rise and Reformation of the English Parish c.1400–1560* (Aldershot, 1996).

Langdon, J., *Horses, Oxen and Technological Innovation: The Use of Draught Animals in English Farming from 1066–1500* (Cambridge, 1986).

—— *Mills in the Medieval Economy: England 1300–1540* (Oxford, 2004).

Laughton, J., Jones, E., and Dyer, C., 'The Urban Hierarchy in the Later Middle Ages: A Study of the East Midlands', *Urban History*, 28 (2001).

Lee, J. S., *Cambridge and its Economic Region, 1450–1560* (Hatfield, 2005).

—— 'Urban Policy and Urban Political Culture: Henry VII and his Towns', *Historical Research*, 82 (2009).

Leech, R., *Historic Towns in Gloucestershire*, Committee for Rescue Archaeology in Avon, Gloucestershire and Somerset, Survey no. 3 (1981).

Letters, S., *Gazetteer of Markets and Fairs in England and Wales to 1516*, 2 vols., List and Index Society, Special Series, 32 and 33 (2003).

Lindenbaum, S., 'Ceremony and Oligarchy: The London Midsummer Watch', in B. A. Hanawalt and K. L. Reyerson (eds), *City and Spectacle in Medieval Europe* (Minneapolis, MN, 1994).

Litzenberger, C., *The English Reformation and the Laity: Gloucestershire, 1540–1580* (Cambridge, 1997).

Lloyd, T. H., *The Movement of Wool Prices in Medieval England*, Economic History Review Supplement, no. 6 (1973).

—— *The English Wool Trade in the Middle Ages* (Cambridge, 1977).

Martin, J., 'Sheep and Enclosure in Sixteenth-Century Northamptonshire', *Ag. HR*, 36 (1988).

Masschaele, J., *Peasants, Merchants and Markets: Inland Trade in Medieval England, 1150–1350* (New York, 1997).

Mate, M. E., 'The East Sussex Land Market and Agrarian Class Structure in the Late Middle Ages', *Past and Present*, 139 (1993).

—— *Daughters, Wives and Widows after the Black Death: Women in Sussex, 1350–1535* (Woodbridge, 1998).

—— *Trade and Economic Developments, 1450–1550: The Experience of Kent, Surrey and Sussex* (Woodbridge, 2006).

Mayhew, N., 'Population, Money Supply and the Velocity of Circulation in England, 1300–1700', *Ec. HR*, 48 (1995).

McIntosh, M. K., *Autonomy and Community in the Royal Manor of Havering, 1200–1500* (Cambridge, 1986).

—— *Controlling Misbehavior in England, 1370–1600* (Cambridge, 1998).

—— 'Women, Credit and Family Relations', *Journal of Family History*, 30 (2005).

—— *Working Women in English Society 1300–1620* (Cambridge, 2005).

Miller, E. (ed.), *The Agrarian History of England and Wales, III, 1348–1500* (Cambridge, 1991).

Mitterauer, M. and Sieder, R., *The European Family: Patriarchy to Partnership from the Middle Ages to the Present* (Oxford, 1982).

Moreton, C. E., *The Townshends and their World: Gentry, Law and Land in Norfolk c.1450–1551* (Oxford, 1992).

Muldrew, C., *The Economy of Obligation: The Culture of Credit and Social Relations in Early Modern England* (Basingstoke, 1998).

Munro, J. H., 'Textile Technology in the Middle Ages', in *idem, Textiles, Towns and Trade* (Aldershot, 1994).

—— 'Spanish Merino Wool and the Nouvelles Draperies: An Industrial Transformation in the Late Medieval Low Countries', *Ec. HR*, 58 (2005).

Newman, C. M., *Late Medieval Northallerton: A Small Market Town and its Hinterland c.1470–1540* (Stamford, 1999).

Nightingale, P., *A Medieval Mercantile Community: The Grocers' Company and the Politics and Trade of London, 1000–1485* (New Haven, CT, 1995).

—— 'Some New Evidence of Crises and Trends of Mortality in Late Medieval England', *Past and Present*, 187 (2005).

—— 'Gold, Credit and Mortality: Distinguishing Deflationary Pressure in the Late Medieval English Economy', *Ec. HR*, 60 (2010).

Noble, E., *The World of the Stonors: A Gentry Society* (Woodbridge, 2009).

Norris, M., *Monumental Brasses: The Memorials*, I (London, 1977).

North, J. J., *English Hammered Coinage, II, 1272–1662* (London, 1960).

Oldland, J., 'The Allocation of Merchant Capital in Early Tudor London', *Ec. HR*, 63 (2010).

Orme, N., *English Schools in the Middle Ages* (London, 1973).

—— *Education in Early Tudor England: Magdalen College Oxford and its School* (Oxford, 1998).

—— *Medieval Children* (New Haven, CT, 2001).

—— 'The Other Parish Church: Chapels in Late Medieval England', in C. Burgess and E. Duffy (eds), *The Parish in Late Medieval England* (Donington, 2006).

Ormrod, W., 'England in the Middle Ages', in R. Bonney (ed.), *The Rise of the Fiscal State in Europe, c.1200–1815* (Oxford, 1999).

Page, M., 'The Technology of Medieval Sheep Farming: Some Evidence from Crawley, Hampshire, 1208–1349', *Ag. HR*, 51 (2003).

—— and Jones, R., 'Stability and Instability in Medieval Village Plans: Case Studies in Whittlewood', in M. Gardiner and S. Rippon (eds), *Medieval Landscapes: Landscape History after Hoskins*, 2 (Macclesfield, 2007).

Pearson, S., 'The Chronological Distribution of Tree-Ring Dates, 1980–2001: An Update', *Vernacular Architecture*, 32 (2001).

Phelps Brown, E. H. and Hopkins, S. V., *A Perspective of Wages* (London, 1981).

Phythian-Adams, C., *Desolation of a City: Coventry and the Urban Crisis of the Late Middle Ages* (Cambridge, 1979).

Poos, L. R., *A Rural Society after the Black Death, Essex 1350–1525* (Cambridge, 1991).

Postan, M., *The Medieval Economy and Society: An Economic History of Britain 1100–1500* (London, 1972).

Power, E., *The Paycockes of Coggeshall* (London, 1920).

—— 'The Wool Trade in the Fifteenth Century', in E. Power and M. Postan (eds), *Studies in English Trade in the Fifteenth Century* (London, 1933).

—— *The Wool Trade in English Medieval History* (Oxford, 1941).

Quattrone, P., 'Books to be Practiced: Memory, the Power of the Visual, and the Success of Accounting', *Accounting, Organizations and Society*, 34 (2009).

Quiney, A., *Town Houses in Medieval Britain* (New Haven, CT, 2003).

Raftis, J. A., *Tenure and Mobility* (Toronto, 1964).

Ragg, J. M. et al., *Soils and Their Use in Midland and Western England*, Soil Survey of England and Wales, Bulletin no. 12 (1984).

Ramsay, G. D., *The Wiltshire Woollen Industry in the Sixteenth and Seventeenth Centuries* (Oxford, 1943).

Ramsey, P., 'Some Tudor Merchants' Accounts', in A. C. Littleton and B. S. Yamey (eds), *Studies in the History of Accounting* (London, 1956).

Rawcliffe, C., *The Staffords, Earls of Stafford and Dukes of Buckingham 1394–1521* (Cambridge, 1978).

Razi, Z., 'The Myth of the Immutable English Family', *Past and Present*, 140 (1993).

Rees Jones, S., 'Thomas More's "Utopia" and Medieval London', in R. Horrox and S. Rees Jones (eds.), *Pragmatic Utopias: Ideals and Communities, 1200–1630* (Cambridge, 2001).

Richards, G. C. and Shadwell, C. L., *The Provosts and Fellows of Oriel College, Oxford* (Oxford, 1922).

Rigby, S. H., 'Urban Population in Late Medieval England: The Evidence of the Lay Subsidies', *Ec. HR*, 63 (2010).

Rigby, S. H. and Ewan, E., 'Government, Power and Authority 1300–1540', in D. M. Palliser (ed.), *The Cambridge Urban History of Britain, I, 600–1540* (Cambridge, 2000).

Roberts, B. K. and Wrathmell, S., *An Atlas of Rural Settlement in England* (London, 2000).

Rodwell, K. (ed.), *Historic Towns in Oxfordshire: A Survey of the New County* (Oxford, 1975).

Rosser, G., 'Communities of Parish and Guild in the Late Middle Ages', in S. Wright (ed.), *Parish, Church and People* (London, 1988).

—— 'Going to the Fraternity Feast: Commensality and Social Relations in Late Medieval England', *Journal of British Studies*, 33 (1994).

Sacks, D. H., 'The Greed of Judas: Avarice, Monopoly and the Moral Economy, ca.1350–ca.1600', *Journal of Medieval and Early Modern Studies*, 28 (1998).

Saul, N., 'The Wool Merchants and their Brasses', *Transactions of the Monumental Brass Society*, 17 (2008).

Schofield, P., *Peasant and Community in Medieval England, 1200–1500* (Basingstoke, 2003).

Schofield, R. S., 'The Geographical Distribution of Wealth in England, 1334–1669', *Ec. HR*, 18 (1965).

Scott, J. C., *The Weapons of the Weak: Everyday Forms of Peasant Resistance* (New Haven, CT, 1985).

Shagan, E. H. (ed.), 'Rumours and Popular Politics in the Reign of Henry VIII', in T. Harris (ed.), *The Politics of the Excluded, c.1500–1850* (Basingstoke, 2001).

Sheail, J, *The Regional Distribution of Wealth in England as Indicated in the 1524/5 Lay Subsidy Returns*, 2 vols., List and Index Society, Special Series, 28 and 29 (1998).

Simons, E., Phimester, J., Webley, L., and Smith, A., 'A Late Medieval Inn at the White Hart Hotel, Chipping Norton, Oxfordshire', *Oxoniensia*, 70 (2005).

Slack, P., *From Reformation to Improvement: Public Welfare in Early Modern England* (Oxford, 1999).

Slater, T. R., 'The Analysis of Burgages in Medieval Towns: Three Case Studies from the West Midlands', *West Midlands Archaeology*, 23 (1980).

Smith, A. H., *The Place-Names of Gloucestershire*, I, English Place-Name Society, 38 (1964).

Smith, R. M., 'The English Peasantry, 1250–1650', in T. Scott (ed.), *The Peasantries of Europe from the Fourteenth to the Eighteenth Centuries* (Harlow, 1998).

—— 'Plagues and Peoples: The Long Demographic Cycle, 1250–1670', in P. Slack and R. Ward (eds), *The Peopling of Britain: The Shaping of a Human Landscape* (Oxford, 2002).

Spufford, M., 'Peasant Inheritance Customs and Land Distribution in Cambridgeshire from the Sixteenth to the Eighteenth Centuries', in J. Goody, J. Thirsk, and E. P. Thompson, *Family and Inheritance: Rural Society in Western Europe 1200–1800* (Cambridge, 1976).

Spufford, P., *Money and its Use in Medieval Europe* (Cambridge, 1988).

Stephenson, M. J., 'Wool Yields in the Medieval Economy', *Ec. HR*, 41 (1988).

Stone, D., 'The Productivity and Management of Sheep in Late Medieval England', *Ag. HR*, 51 (2003).

Stretton, T., 'Marriage, Separation and the Common Law in England, 1540–1660', in H. Berry and E. Foyster (eds), *The Family in Early Modern England* (Cambridge, 2007).

Stride, K. B., 'Engrossing in Sheep-Corn-Chalk Areas: Evidence in Norfolk, 1530/1–1633', *Norfolk Archaeology*, 40 (1989).

Sutton, A., *A Merchant Family of Coventry, London and Calais: The Tates, c. 1450–1575* (London, 1998).

—— *The Mercery of London: Trade, Goods and People, 1130–1578* (Aldershot, 2005).

Swanson, R. N., *Church and Society in Late Medieval England* (Oxford, 1989).

—— 'Parochialism and Particularism: The Dispute over the Status of Ditchford Frary, Warwickshire, in the Early Fifteenth Century', in M. J. Franklin and C. Harper-Bill (eds), *Medieval Ecclesiastical Studies in Honour of Dorothy M. Owen* (Woodbridge, 1995).

Tawney, R. H., *The Agrarian Problem in the Sixteenth Century* (London, 1912).

Thirsk, J., 'Farming Techniques', in J. Thirsk (ed.), *The Agrarian History of England and Wales, IV, 1500–1640* (Cambridge, 1967).

—— (ed.), *The English Rural Landscape* (Oxford, 2000).

Thomson, J. A. F., *The Early Tudor Church and Society 1485–1529* (Harlow, 1993).

Thorpe, H., 'The Lord and the Landscape, Illustrated through the Changing Fortunes of a Warwickshire Parish, Wormleighton', *Transactions of the Birmingham Archaeological Society*, 80 (1962).

Tiller, K. and Darkes, G. (eds), *An Historical Atlas of Oxfordshire*, Oxfordshire Record Society, 67 (2010).

Tinti, F., *Sustaining Belief: The Church of Worcester from c.870 to c.1100* (Farnham, 2010).

Tompkins, M., '"Let's Kill All the Lawyers": Did Fifteenth-Century Peasants Employ Lawyers When they Conveyed Customary Land?', in L. Clark (ed.), *The Fifteenth Century*, 6 (2006).

Veale, E. M., *The English Fur Trade in the Later Middle Ages* (Oxford, 1966).

Victoria County History, Gloucestershire, Warwickshire, Worcestershire.

Wager, S., *Woods, Wolds and Groves: The Woodland of Medieval Warwickshire*, British Archaeological Reports, British Series, 269 (1998).

Warriner, M., *A Prospect of Weston in Warwickshire* (Kineton, 1978).

Watkins, A., 'Maxstoke Priory in the Fifteenth Century: The Development of an Estate Economy in the Forest of Arden', *Warwickshire History*, 10 (1996).

Webb, J. G., *Great Tooley of Ipswich: Portrait of an Early Tudor Merchant* (Ipswich, 1962).

Welsford, A. E., *John Greenway, 1460–1529: Merchant of Tiverton and London. A Devon Worthy* (Tiverton, 1984).

Wenzel, S., *Preachers, Poets, and the Early English Lyric* (Princeton, NJ, 1986).

Whiting, B. J. and Whiting, H. W., *Proverbs, Sentences and Proverbial Phrases from English Writings Mainly Before 1500* (Cambridge, MA, 1968).

Whiting, R., *Local Responses to the English Reformation* (Basingstoke, 1998).

Whittle, J., 'Individualism and the Land-Family Bond: A Reassessment of the Land Transfer Patterns among the English Peasantry, c.1270–1580', *Past and Present*, 160 (1998).

—— *The Development of Agrarian Capitalism: Land and Labour in Norfolk, 1440–1580* (Oxford, 2000).

——and Yates, M., '"Pays réel or pays légal"? Contrasting Patterns of Land Tenure and Social Structure in Eastern Norfolk and Western Berkshire, 1450–1600', *Ag. HR*, 48 (2000).

Whybra, J., *A Lost English County: Winchcombeshire in the Tenth and Eleventh Centuries* (Woodbridge, 1990).

Wood, D., *Medieval Economic Thought* (Cambridge, 2002).

Woodward, D., *Men at Work: Labourers and Building Craftsmen in the Towns of Northern England, 1450–1750* (Cambridge, 1995).

Wrightson, K., 'Sorts of People in Tudor and Stuart England', in J. Berry and C. Brooks (eds.), *The Middling Sort of People: Culture, Society and Politics in England, 1550–1800* (Basingstoke, 1994).

—— *Earthly Necessities: Economic Lives in Early Modern Britain* (New Haven, CT, 2000).

Wrigley, E. A. and Schofield, R. S., *The Population History of England, 1541–1871: A Reconstruction*, 2nd edn. (Cambridge, 1989).

—— *English Population History from Family Reconstitution* (Cambridge, 1997).

Yates, M., 'Between Fact and Fiction: Henry Brinklow's *Complaynt* against Rapacious Landlords', *Ag. HR*, 54 (2006).

—— *Town and Countryside in Western Berkshire, c.1327–c.1600: Social and Economic Change* (Woodbridge, 2007).

Youngs, D., *Humphrey Newton (1466–1536): An Early Tudor Gentleman* (Woodbridge, 2008).

Zanden, J. L. van, *The Long Road to the Industrial Revolution: The European Economy in a Global Perspective, 1000–1500* (Leiden, 2009).

Zell, M., 'Fifteenth- and Sixteenth-Century Wills as Historical Sources', *Archives*, 14 (1979).

—— *Industry in the Countryside: Wealden Society in the Sixteenth Century* (Cambridge, 1994).

Index

9 780198 715986